Praise for
Library Lin's Curated Collection of Superlative Nonfiction

66As a die-hard nonfiction book lover, I am excited about this curated collection of books. It has a variety of titles that weren't previously on my radar and will keep my reading list full for a long time to come. Any fellow reader of nonfiction will definitely enjoy this fun book. Highly recommended!"

—Stephanie Chandler, CEO, Nonfiction Authors Association

66Picking a book to read is always a difficult decision because there are so many to choose from. Linda Maxie has done readers a great service by culling through numerous reputable sources to provide a wonderful roadmap to some of the best books available. Although her list is not definitive, and many outstanding books don't make the cut, her carefully curated list is an excellent companion for any book lover."

—Eric Jay Dolin, author of *Rebels at Sea: Privateering in the American Revolution*

66Stupendous! Amazing! Fantabulous! Linda Maxie's *Library Lin's Curated Collection of Superlative Nonfiction* is everything it claims to be. It's a book to dip into, drink from its information stream, and be inspired to storm the ramparts of knowledge for the books she profiles. Not only does it provide hundreds of suggestions for great reading, but the thumbnail descriptions themselves offer hours of good, clean fun."

—Thomas C. Foster author of *How to Read Nonfiction Like a Professor: A Smart, Irreverent Guide to Biography, History, Journalism, Blogs, and Everything in Between*

66For lovers of the written word, this book is like an enticing menu in a fine restaurant. Each dish sounds more tasty than the last. But this is a menu long enough to provide delicious intellectual meals for decades to come."

—Adam Hochschild author of *Rebel Cinderella: From Rags to Riches to Radical, the Epic Journey of Rose Pastor Stokes*

66*Library Lin's Curated Collection* is a pirate's treasure chest of nudges and discoveries, a lifetime list of wonderful reading. Dig in!"

—Richard Rhodes, Pulitzer Prize–winning author of *The Making of the Atomic Bomb*

Library Lin's Curated Collection of Superlative Nonfiction

Library Lin's Curated Collection *of Superlative* Nonfiction

Linda Maxie

Spoon Creek Press • Patrick Springs, Virginia • 2022

Library Lin's Curated Collection of Superlative Nonfiction
© 2022 Linda Maxie. All rights reserved.

Published by Spoon Creek Press
An imprint of Spoon Creek Books, LLC
PO box 492
Patrick Springs, Virginia 24133
spooncreekpress.com
publisher@spooncreekpress.com

Contact the author through librarylin.com.

Name: Maxie, Linda, author
Title: Library Lin's curated collection of superlative nonfiction
Description: Patrick Springs, VA: Spoon Creek Press
Identifiers: LCCN 2022904425 | ISBN 9798985923407 (trade paperback) |
9798985923414 (ebook)
Subjects: Best books | Books and reading—United States
Classification: LCC Z1035.9 | DDC 028.9

Library of Congress Control Number: 2022904425

ISBN: 979-8-9859234-0-7 trade paperback
       979-8-9859234-1-4 electronic book

Dewey and the DDC are registered trademarks of OCLC.

OCLC is the registered copyright holder of the Dewey Decimal Classification
system.

Design and composition: Dick Margulis, dmargulis.com

First printing

MANUFACTURED IN THE UNITED STATES OF AMERICA

To all those who love to read and learn

Contents

Acknowledgments

PUTTING THIS BOOK TOGETHER WAS a three-year labor of love that would not have happened without a lot of help. Writing is a solitary process, and the perspectives of others brings fresh ideas, making it much more coherent and engaging.

First, I'd like to thank my husband, Roger Maxie, for his patience, suggestions, and support. Without him, this book would not exist. I'd also like to thank my sons, Ben Maxie and Jack Maxie, as well as Ellen Boggs and Taylor Maxie for cheering me on, listening to my complaints, and offering feedback. Your support and belief in me means more than you will ever know.

My mother, Fay Fisher, helped look up call numbers and gave me ideas for the types of books people would be most inclined to read. Barry Fisher and Michael North provided excellent feedback on book structure that was much appreciated.

I'm grateful to Linda Carr and Margaret Fey who gave suggestions for the book's formatting and introduction.

While the book was still an idea rattling around in my head, I got wonderful suggestions on the structure from Lyndee Breeding, Katherine Britton, James Fey, Stephen Henderson, and Jennifer Turner.

I had a team of beta readers who read over sections of the book and helped me consider issues with the book I would never have thought of on my own. They are listed here followed by the DDC sections they helped with: Emma Babbitt (literature), Ellen Boggs (introduction), Linda Carr (languages and literature), Greg Carter (natural science, especially the earth science and paleontology sections), Kim Carter (applied sciences, especially the health and medicine section), Margaret Fey (natural sciences), Steve Friedman (philosophy and psychology, geography, biography, and history), Maggie Gigandet (general knowledge, social sciences, natural sciences, and literature), Stephen Henderson (arts and recreation and literature), Ellena Leavitt (religion and literature), Trenda Leavitt (natural sciences and geography, biography, and history), Craig McCroskey (languages and applied science), Mei-Ling Marshall (general knowledge and computer science, religion, languages, and literature), Julia Moore (arts and recreation and literature), Sherry Rogers (philosophy and psychology and social sciences) Hallie Louise Sianni (languages and arts and recreation), and Debra Simpson (natural and applied sciences).

Three introverted writer friends and I got together every two weeks throughout 2021 to discuss our writing projects and provide support and feedback for one another. We laughed and shared good times and bad. The support and feedback of these supportive and creative souls has been crucial for the book's completion: Steven Friedman, the author of *The Corporate Introvert*, Sherry Rogers, and Jody Townshend.

Former librarian turned author and book coach Roger Leslie provided feedback on my ideas. With his past experience, he understood what I was trying to do and provided valuable insights into turning the book into a reality. He also had great suggestions for getting the word out once it's published.

Two friends have been listening to me talk about this book since well before I started working on it. Nancy Carlson and Liz Wallace have served as sounding boards and emotional support. They are strong, smart women who put starch in my drooping spirits when I need them to.

Dick Margulis, my editor, designer, and project manager has been a life-saver. He helped me shape my exceedingly rough manuscript into something I could proudly offer the world. His professionalism, design sense, and publishing knowledge have saved my sanity and made the book the best it could be. The book's proofreader, Janet Werner, caught hundreds of errors large and small and made many valuable suggestions. A book of this scope cannot be perfect, but the team certainly did its best.

Finally, I'd like to thank all the librarians—those I've studied with, worked with, and patronized over the years, and all the ones I've never met. You have been my inspiration. Your unselfish dedication to promoting reading and getting information out to your patrons is always inspiring and sometimes amazing. It's an often thankless job, and to me, you are true heroes.

Library Lin's
Curated
Collection
of Superlative
Nonfiction

Introduction

LISTED BETWEEN THESE COVERS IS a tiny sampling of the books you might find in any public library in the U.S. I scoured lists of best books and award winners dating back a century to find them. My mission is to get you to read something new. If you need no prodding and you're eager to start browsing the titles, skip this introduction. Seriously. It explains how I picked and arranged the titles. You can come back to it later if you'd like. Feel free to dive in anywhere. You can begin with chapter 2 or chapter 10. The chapters don't build on one another, so feel free to skip around. Put the book aside to read anything that catches your attention. Come back when you're ready.

You may wonder why I compiled this collection. For as long as I can remember, I've been obsessed with books. After becoming a librarian with an undergraduate degree in library science and educational media, I worked in a Virginia K–7 public school. Then, after earning a master of library science degree, I worked in public libraries for several years. But I ultimately returned to school libraries because there I had the freedom to run an entire library myself.

I finished out my career in a high school library. Collection development was my favorite task, because I actually enjoyed reading tons of book reviews and trying to figure out which titles would best meet my library's needs.

Reader's advisor was my second favorite job. The grade 8–12 school I served had a coterie of avid readers. And while I purchased the fiction my students requested, I also tried to make the nonfiction section as appealing as possible. I tried all sorts of tactics, sneaky and brazen, to get them to try nonfiction. Sometimes I succeeded, and some students were surprised to find they actually enjoyed reading outside their comfort zones.

I appreciate nonfiction because I love to learn. Reading is a conversation between the author and me. Sometimes there are hiccups because my knowledge on the topic is spotty. But the effort itself enriches my mind.

Whatever the topic, I require three things of a nonfiction book. First, it must teach me something new. Second, it must change the way I look at life in some small way. And finally, it needs to keep the pages turning with a clear, engaging writing style. For me, searching out books that meet those criteria and then recommending them to others gives me joy.

Intended Audience

If you are a curious person, then you should enjoy this book. Book lovers, autodidacts, writers, and librarians should find it useful.

Book lovers and autodidacts are often interchangeable. Autodidacts are those who seek to educate themselves, and many book lovers are consciously or unconsciously seeking education about something. If you belong in either category, you'll find many titles of interest here.

Writers may find topics to spark ideas for future projects. And sprinkled throughout are reference books that may make valuable additions to your book collection.

Librarians might use this book as a collection development aid. While these books will one day be outdated, the lists I used to find them are in the appendix, on page 363. They can be checked every so often for more recent titles.

Library Selection

Since I selected and arranged the titles in this book using my library training, I'll highlight some relevant points about it. My library education was pre-Internet, and I'm still an old-school librarian in some ways. I obtained my master's degree in 1992. Our professors stressed using the Library Bill of Rights, available on the American Library Association (ALA) website, ala.org/advocacy/intfreedom/librarybill/. The core idea is that libraries are for *everyone*. How I feel about your beliefs and interests has nothing to do with how I serve you. I'm obligated to take your suggestions seriously and do my best, within budget constraints, to get quality information on topics you want. At the same time, I keep in mind that I also must do the same for people who are very different from you. Everyone matters.

It's possible to have books that argue there is no God along with books that insist one must believe in a specific deity. As long as both books are making sincere arguments by authors using reputable sources to back their assertions, they are reasonable purchases. After all, people can disagree on anything. As the reader, it's up to you to ensure the information you read is accurate before basing significant decisions (like surgery) on something you find in any book. While reading books is no substitute for thinking critically for yourself, it's an excellent supplement.

Selections in This Collection

With the above in mind, my selection policy for this portable library is pretty simple. First, the books included needed to be well researched and well written. And the writing should be understandable to the average person.

To increase the odds these books meet those requirements, I used 65 lists of books that you can find in the appendix on page 363. All these books come from one of these categories:

- Traditional award winners or award nominees
- Contest winners in which author or publisher nominates books
- Publisher best books lists from national newspapers, magazines, journals, online publishers, and so on
- Book reviewer best books lists
- Association best books lists

Since I couldn't read all these books, I trusted the people responsible for choosing them to meet their standards. They all strive to ensure quality in their choices.

In addition to quality, I tried to have a balance of views on each topic. For instance, some political science titles are liberal, while some are conservative. But for some subdivisions, this wasn't possible for one of two reasons. First, there weren't enough, or any, titles expressing a particular point of view. And second, I was unaware of any debate. Being human, I don't know everything. If you're searching for other titles because you find these inadequate, you can use the subject headings as preliminary keywords to find other options in libraries, book stores, or online.

The editions cited are those that appeared on one of the lists I used. For example, a dictionary may have been singled out for an award in 1968 by the American Library Association but then never listed again. If, since then, the dictionary has been revised and republished three times, I used the 1968 publishing information in the citation, but indicate whether there are updates in the edition and title in the summary. Please use updated copies as you see fit.

On Libraries

This book is structured as a portable public library, so let's briefly discuss public libraries in the U.S. and how they arrange their books. But first, please allow me to indulge in a short love note to these institutions.

Libraries are wondrous. They provide books, magazines, movies, and many other helpful materials for free. I once dreamed I had gone to heaven. It was a vast library.

When you browse through shelves in a library, serendipitous, happy surprises happen frequently. Many times I have walked into a library looking for something specific. But in wandering around, reading the titles on the shelves, I've found better books nearby. Or I've spotted something on an entirely different topic that opened up a whole new interest.

Ideas are like plants in that they need cross-pollination to grow. Libraries are gardens of thought, not dark, dusty, lifeless spaces.

A Brief History of Libraries

Libraries have been around since antiquity. *Libraries: An Unquiet History*, by Matthew Battles, covers the topic well. In earlier days, the codex, our familiar book format with two covers, a spine, and pages that turn, didn't exist. The earliest books were collections of inscribed wax or clay tablets bound together, and later, scrolls of papyrus, parchment, or paper. While some libraries in antiquity were quite large, by the Middle Ages, bookmakers commonly used the codex. Examples of beautiful handmade books from those times still exist. But because producing a book by hand was so labor-intensive, books cost a fortune, and libraries contained few of them.

All that changed with Johannes Gutenberg's perfection of the printing process in 1440. Suddenly books were much less costly to produce. The numbers exploded. Now libraries had a problem: what was the best way to arrange all those books? Before, with smaller collections, librarians organized books on shelves in the order they received them. Or, they placed them together by size. But once the average library contained thousands of volumes, finding any specific title or book on a particular subject became a challenge.

Enter Dewey

Melvil Dewey was the father of modern library services. He began his career as a library assistant at Amherst College in Amherst, Massachusetts, in the mid-1800s. Dewey combined two previously developed knowledge classification schemes to create what is known as the Dewey Decimal Classification (DDC) system. He borrowed the first from the British Museum, which assigned a specific spot for each book. The second came from a peer, the American philosopher and educator William Torrey Harris. Harris had classified humanity's accumulated knowledge by borrowing from a still earlier system developed by Sir Francis Bacon and Natale Battezzati.

The DDC was a breakthrough for rapidly growing libraries, because now books were shelved together by subject while remaining fixed by assigned call numbers. The system's flexibility allowed adding books around the existing volumes as needed. And the system could morph to hold any book on any topic—even topics as yet undiscovered.

Today, critics rightly fault Melvil Dewey for his sexist and anti-Semitic sentiments, which were common in his time. His views shaped his classification system in ways that offend some users. I briefly discuss some of these at the beginning of the relevant chapters. But his profound influence on modern libraries is indisputable.

Dewey was only 21 when he published the first edition of the classification system in 1876. He helped establish the ALA the same year, and it's still going strong today. In addition, he cofounded the well-respected, scholarly *Library Journal* and founded the first library school, at Columbia University, in 1887.

The DDC Today

Now that Dewey is gone, the Library of Congress (LOC) and the Online Cataloging and Library Cataloging Service (OCLC) share the task of keeping up with newly published materials. They guide libraries on classifying books with tricky topics. For example, a book on decorative blacksmithing might belong in the 600s with blacksmithing books or the 700s in decorative arts. If the book focuses on blacksmithing to make something useful, like knives, it would belong in the 600s. If it's about making ornaments, it would most likely belong in the 700s. The LOC and OCLC also decide where new topics, such as mass spectrometry, should go.

For most of the 20th century, Forest Press organized, edited, maintained, and published the DDC manual. In 1988, OCLC purchased the press and took over most of its functions, including appointing the editor-in-chief. The LOC helps keep the system up to date. Full-time LOC staff members examine newly published books for topic shifts that might call for changes to the DDC system.

OCLC publishes the changes to the classification system on WebDewey, which is available to libraries by subscription. Their blog, *025.341: The Dewey Blog*, is accessible online for everyone and makes for entertaining reading on the DDC system's issues and changes. If you're interested or if you want more information about the system as a whole, check it out at https://ddc.typepad.com/.

Libraries are bastions of freedom and enrichment for their communities. They deserve accolades for the outstanding services and materials they provide with ever-dwindling support. Please support them where you can.

Portable Library Arrangement

I used the DDC to arrange this book with the kind permission of OCLC, which owns rights to DDC®. The table of contents lists the ten major DDC divisions, each of which has ten subdivisions. For example, in the 500s (the natural sciences), the second subdivision, the 510s, is for mathematics. Within the mathematics section, there are ten subdivisions of math topics. For example, geometry, algebra, and probability have specific numbers.

Most of the divisions have quirks that may confuse or irritate some people. It's beyond this book's scope to cover them in detail. But at the head of every chapter, I briefly discuss that section and its peculiar issues.

Every entry is listed under the first three numbers of the DDC call number for that book as assigned by either the LOC or the OCLC Experimental Classification site. You can access both these collections online. Many titles are multidisciplinary, meaning they cover many topics. While catalogers work to place them in the most suitable spot, people sometimes disagree with the choice. Individual libraries aren't bound to the call numbers assigned by the LOC and may place a book in a different division. In this book, however, I used the LOC or OCLC numbers because these books aren't arranged for a particular library clientele.

As you read through this book, you'll find missing subdivisions. If there are no titles under a particular number, no books met my criteria for inclusion, so it was omitted. If you want to learn more about the missing numbers, OCLC has all 1,000 categories of the DDC listed for free on its website.

Some categories are labeled *unassigned* or *optional*. The *unassigned* designation means either the previous subject area is obsolete and therefore no longer used or is it was left open to make room for new categories as needed. Computer science, for example, was not a subdivision in the early system. The *optional* designation is for local libraries to use as they see fit.

Miscellaneous Notes

On the Summaries
While I wish I could read all these titles, I can't. So I used information from publisher book blurbs and book reviews to write the summaries.

Index
If you are disappointed to find one of your favorite authors or titles omitted, please check the author and title index to see whether it's in a different category. Some of your favorites were inevitably left out, as were some of mine. Make notes of books you want to remember and check other places for additional books to read.

Further reading blog: Space constraints limited this collection. Thousands of books meeting my criteria were trimmed because I wanted to keep the size manageable. Please see my blog at librarylin.com to find many of these omitted books. I add more once or twice per week.

Disconcerting Matters

Biography

Biographies sometimes confuse. Traditionally, libraries group biographies in the 920s section. And some libraries shelve them in a separate area under "B" or "Bio." But many libraries now place biographies into the subject category. For example, a book about Frank Lloyd Wright will most likely be in the 720s (architecture) section. In this book, some biographies, mostly older ones, are in the 920s because that is where the LOC has them classified.

When a topic is a person, William Shakespeare, for example, there may be books listed under the topic while others are listed under biography. Here's the difference: if a book is primarily about the work a person accomplished, it is not a biography, even if it contains biographical material. Conversely, if the book focuses mainly on the events of their life, it *is* a biography, even if it talks about their inventions, works, or whatever they have accomplished. Book placement is a matter of the overarching emphasis in the book's discussion.

Biographies and memoirs are both books about people. Biographies are a person's entire life story presented with fairly balanced attention across the lifespan. If someone else writes the book, it's biography; if the subject writes it about themselves, it's autobiography. An individual may also write a memoir. The stress in memoirs is on problems, life-changing events, or a specific time frame, like childhood, and not on the facts about the entire lifespan.

Fiction vs. Nonfiction

The differences between fiction and nonfiction can also be perplexing. For example, mythology books aren't true, fact-based accounts. Instead, they are stories from historical times, but they are shelved in the 200s (religion) section, not in fiction. Likewise, folktales and fairytales (which are not fact-based) are shelved in the 300s (the social sciences) because they reveal important information about a people's social history.

Some people find the 800s (literature) division, chapter 9, incredibly confusing. Works like novels, short stories, essays, and poetry *can* be in the literature section. Still, most public libraries shelve novels and short stories in separate areas to avoid confusion and keep the 800s from becoming overcrowded.

For a book to be considered literature, it generally needs to be of high intellectual and aesthetic quality. I used to tell my students that literature is "art made from words." So Charles Dickens's novels may or may not be shelved in the fiction section, but books that *discuss* his novels do belong in the literature section. Books *about* Dickens go there because he was famous for his contributions to literature. New novels that are written for entertainment are almost always shelved in fiction, not in literature.

Call Number 741

And finally, one call number causes consternation for many people. The call number 741 is where libraries place comic books and drawing books. Sometimes fiction is published in "comic book format" (called *graphic novels*), and shelved in 741. Occasionally, publishers use this format for nonfiction books; and those, too, may be classified in 741. The reason you find the *March* series by John Lewis in 741 is for the form, not to disparage Lewis, his service, or his book.

Final Advice

Reading a particular book may not go well for you for a variety of reasons. You may not be ready to receive the writer's content because you lack the needed background knowledge to understand the material. If that's the case, consider finding a book for young adults or adult beginners on the topic to read first. Or watch a few videos on the topic to gain an overview. You can also simply move on to something else that looks more promising.

You may find that books published decades ago don't follow the modern conventions used today. For example, when I was in graduate school, we were expected to refer to humans of unspecified gender as "he." Always "he." That was the convention of the time. My inclusion of these older books is not meant to offend anyone. I included them if they've had a lasting influence in their field or if more recent titles are unavailable.

Occasionally, you may dislike the author's voice. I once picked up a book so condescending toward librarians that I couldn't finish it. Not liking the author's attitude is an acceptable reason to put the book down and find another. But these issues are personal. I've included books that are unappealing to me because they may be perfect for you.

You have my permission to follow the two-chapter rule. Here's how it works. Read the first two chapters. Then stop and evaluate. Do you want to keep going or not? If not, no matter why, it's okay to stop. Find a different book on the topic or choose something completely different. No one has time to waste. If you dislike it, it's not a good fit for you, at least, not at present.

If you purchased a print copy of this book, please write in the margins! Jot down similar books you discover. Highlight the ones you want to read. Check them off when done. Put big X marks on the ones you didn't like. Look at this as your learning and exploration journal.

For more books to explore, please check out librarylin.com. There you'll find excellent books that were omitted only for lack of space.

I hope you find books here that pique your curiosity and compel you to read them. We've been participating in great conversations with one another since we learned to talk and write. Books are an essential part of them. I urge you to enter discussions yourself. You never know where you may wind up. I wish you many happy adventures!

Library Lin

Sources Consulted

American Library Association; "Library Bill of Rights." Updated January 29, 2019. ala.org/advocacy/intfreedom/librarybill/.

Battles, Matthew. *Library: An Unquiet History.* New York: W. W. Norton, 2003.

Houston, Keith. *The Book: A Cover-to-Cover Exploration of the Most Powerful Object of Our Time.* New York: W. W. Norton, 2016.

Kyrios, Alex. *025.431: The Dewey blog.* ddc.typepad.com.

Library of Congress. "The Dewey Program at the Library of Congress." loc.gov /aba/dewey/.

Library of Congress. "About the Dewey Program." loc.gov/aba/dewey/about.html.

Library of Congress. "About the Dewey Program: Frequently Asked Questions." loc.gov/aba/dewey/faq.html.

OCLC. "Resources." oclc.org/en/dewey/resources.html.

CHAPTER 1

000-099

General Knowledge & Computer Science

THE BOOKS IN THIS SECTION focus on meta-knowledge—our knowledge about knowledge. The world has changed since Dewey created his system. Many of the subcategories in this division are empty. Some are no longer in use, and others were never assigned. When Dewey developed his classification system, computers as we know them today were nonexistent. In this chapter, you can find general books on computers and software, while those on hardware are in chapter 6.

000 General Knowledge

001 Knowledge

Nancy Duarte, *DataStory: Explain Data and Inspire Action Through Story*, 2019.
Studies have proven that stories help people understand information that may be incomprehensible without them. Silicon Valley CEO Nancy Duarte helps companies use their data to craft stories for their customers.

Carl Sagan, *The Demon-Haunted World: Science as a Candle in the Dark*, 1995.
Carl Sagan wrote his last work to point out bad consequences of mass belief in popular pseudoscience and occultism. He wanted to help readers understand the importance of testing and challenging ideas through the scientific method.

Kristen Sosulski, *Data Visualization Made Simple: Insights Into Becoming Visual*, 2018.
Information, operations, and management sciences expert Kristen Sosulski, introduces data graphics—helping make data understandable to everyone. With this guide, businesses and individuals can make their information more engaging.

**Will Storr, *The Unpersuadables:
Adventures with the Enemies of Science*, 2014.**
> Investigative journalist Will Storr examined why people believe things that
> are provably false. He discovered that intelligence, education, and logic have
> nothing to do with susceptibility. Instead, our brain's structure is to blame.

**Ronald D. Story and J. Richard Greenwell, editors,
The Encyclopedia of UFOs, 1980.**
> Though the 1980 version is out of date, this book was updated and released
> in 2012 as *The Mammoth Encyclopedia of Extraterrestrial Encounters*,
> edited by Ronald D. Story, which earned high marks for objectivity
> and completeness.

002 The Book

**Nicholas Basbanes, *A Gentle Madness: Bibliophiles,
Bibliomanes, and the Eternal Passion for Books*, 1995.**
> This highly recommended history of books and the people who love them
> focuses on Great Britain and North America. Despite the copyright date, seri-
> ous book collectors will still find it helpful.

**Aaron Lansky, *Outwitting History: The Amazing Adventures
of a Man Who Rescued a Million Yiddish Books*, 2006.**
> Aaron Lansky, the founder of the Yiddish Book Center, relates how a small
> group of people saved millions of books from the basements and libraries of
> Yiddish-speaking immigrants.

003 Systems

**James Gleick, *Chaos:
The Making of a New Science*, 1987.**
> *Chaos* is the first book to bring chaos theory to the general reader. James
> Gleick explains how the theory attempts to find order in randomness. The
> implications apply to all branches of science and philosophy.

004 Data Processing; Computer Science

**George Dyson, *Turing's Cathedral:
The Origins of the Digital Universe*, 2012.**
> George Dyson explains that the individual characteristics and quirks of
> the 20th-century computer science pioneers influenced the industry we
> have today.

**Walter Isaacson, *The Innovators: How a Group of Hackers,
Geniuses, and Geeks Created the Digital Revolution*, 2014.**
> Walter Isaacson examines the individuals and groups of people who brought

us the digital revolution. By analyzing their interactions with one another, he isolates traits that innovators tend to share.

Nancy Jo Sales, *American Girls:*
Social Media and the Secret Lives of Teenagers, 2016.

Nancy Jo Sales interviewed more than 200 girls ages 13–19 for this shocking book. She demonstrates how rampant sexism in apps and on the Internet affects our young women. She also discusses the devastating impacts of cyberbullying.

005 Computer Programming, Programs, Data

Amy M. Bucher, *Engaged:*
Designing for Behavior Change, 2020.

Behavior change design is a relatively new field that Amy M. Bucher introduces for design professionals. While this book is primarily used for marketing, it can also help people learn and achieve their goals.

Vikram Chandra, *Geek Sublime:*
The Beauty of Code, the Code of Beauty, 2014.

Computer programmer and novelist Vikram Chandra writes about the history of coding and its relationship to writing.

Cathy O'Neil, *Weapons of Math Destruction:*
How Big Data Increases Inequality
and Threatens Democracy, 2016.

Cathy O'Neil's book explores the dark side of big data. While it's unregulated, the algorithms that run it have all sorts of built-in biases that can affect you. How much you pay for insurance is just one example.

006 Special Computer Methods (AI, Computer Pattern Recognition, Computer Sound Synthesis, Computer Graphics)

Robert Kyncl, *Streampunks:*
YouTube and the Rebels Remaking Media, 2018.

Robert Kyncl, who has worked at YouTube, Netflix, and HBO, gives the backstory for all three corporations, but he concentrates on YouTube. After sharing its history and the stories of famous YouTubers, he provides advice on starting your own YouTube channel.

Jill Lepore, *If Then:*
How the Simulmatics Corporation Invented the Future, 2020.

While going through MIT's archives, historian Jill Lepore came across a forgotten American corporation called Simulmatics, a business that pioneered the methods and overreaches of today's Silicon Valley. Beginning in the Cold War and run by social scientists, Simulmatics attempted to influence everything from purchases to U.S. elections. By its closing in 1970, the corporation had been accused of war crimes. Lepore reveals the company's involvement in the dystopian factors we accept as a part of life today.

Amy Webb, *The Big Nine: How the Tech Titans and Their Thinking Machines Could Warp Humanity*, 2019.

Artificial intelligence is here. Unfortunately, its designers didn't have our best interests at heart. Amy Webb, a quantitative futurist, uncovers how nine largely unregulated tech giants—Amazon, Google, Facebook, Tencent, Baidu, Alibaba, Microsoft, IBM, and Apple—have designed these systems for their benefit, not for ours. She spells out the past and future consequences of those decisions.

David Weinberger, *Everyday Chaos: Technology, Complexity, and How We're Thriving in a New World of Possibility*, 2019.

Philosopher and technologist David Weinberger provides an optimistic look at the future of artificial intelligence. He shows how AI can be used to prepare for the future and to manage our world. While he acknowledges that it can be dangerous, Weinberger asserts we can use AI creatively to produce as many capabilities for the future as possible.

010 Bibliography

016 Of Works on Specific Subjects

Catherine Blakemore, *Mixed Heritage: Your Source for Books for Children and Teens about Persons and Families of Mixed Racial, Ethnic, and/or Religious Heritage*, 2012.

Parents, teachers, and librarians will find the annotated lists of fiction and nonfiction titles organized by specific heritage useful in finding reading materials for specific children. In addition, the author gives age level, bibliographic information, and the subject matter for each entry.

P. William Filby, *A Bibliography of American County Histories*, 1985.

Scholar P. William Filby compiled state-by-state lists of all significant county histories published up to 1984. He obtained his information from the LOC, the New York Public Library, and state archives.

020 Library & Information Science

James Gleick, *The Information: A History, A Theory, A Flood*, 2011.

James Gleick traces the history of information transmission across physical distances, from drum communications to digital devices. Along the way, he delves into the math, physics, and logic that made these methods possible.

025 Library Operations

Mary W. George, *The Elements of Library Research: What Every Student Needs to Know*, 2008.

In this guide for college students in the early days of the Internet, Mary W. George instructs students on everything from turning a topic into a research question to methods and timelines for completing research.

Joshua Hammer, *The Bad-Ass Librarians of Timbuktu: And Their Race to Save the World's Most Precious Manuscripts*, 2016.

Joshua Hammer relates the true, nail-biting history of the priceless, ancient manuscripts collected in Timbuktu, Mali. When jihadists took over the country in 2012, the endangered manuscripts were smuggled out of the city, under al-Qaeda's nose, by a brave group of librarians.

Safiya Umoja Noble, *Algorithms of Oppression: How Search Engines Reinforce Racism*, 2018.

When scholar Safiya Umoja Noble analyzed textual and media searches on search engines, she found radically different results when querying "White women" and "Black women." Specifically, sexually explicit terms are much more likely to result from searches for "Black women." Noble explores the social consequences of these differences.

027 General Libraries

Susan Orlean, *The Library Book*, 2018.

In 1986, a mysterious fire broke out in Los Angeles's downtown library branch. While the case is still unsolved, Susan Orlean uncovers intriguing information about the tragedy that destroyed 400,000 books and kept the library closed for seven years.

028 Reading & Use of Other Media

H. J. Jackson, *Marginalia: Readers Writing in Books*, 2001.

H. J. Jackson studied thousands of books with marginalia, the notes that people make in the margins of books while reading them, and he found examples by both the famous and the obscure. The result is an amusing look at conversations between readers and authors, other readers, and future generations, involving over 300 years of reading.

Peter Mendelsund, *What We See When We Read*, 2015.

Have you ever read a book you loved, gone to see the movie, and been shocked by how the characters and the scenery looked so different from what you pictured? Peter Mendelsund explores what affects what we see with our mind's eye while we read.

James Mustich, *1,000 Books to Read Before You Die: A Life-Changing List*, 2019.

I can attest that this book about books is a complete joy. James Mustich, a former bookseller who cofounded the book catalog *A Common Reader: Books for Readers with Imagination*, gathers eclectic lists of fiction, nonfiction, and children's books with marvelous annotations.

James J. Owens, ed., *The World is Just a Book Away*, 2017.

This anthology provides stories from 60 famous people about the books that influenced them. The featured individuals include world leaders, scientists, entertainers, and humanitarians.

030 General Encyclopedic Works

031 American

Steven Anzovin and Janet Podell, *Famous First Facts*, 3rd ed., 1964.

First compiled by Joseph Nathan Kane, this reference is a staple in most U.S. libraries. Most of the facts share American firsts, such as inventions, discoveries, and events. New, updated editions are released periodically, and the most recent print edition is the 7th, published in 2015.

Charles Panati, *Panati's Extraordinary Origins of Everyday Things*, 1989.

This book provides background stories on American holidays, customs, superstitions, food items, toys, and other everyday items in 500 entries.

032 In English

REFERENCE

Before the *Encyclopedia Britannica* went out of print in 2012, most libraries shelved it in the reference section under the call number 032. It is the oldest well-regarded general encyclopedia in the English language. The print version was best suited for public and college or university libraries as it is a scholarly ency-clopedia unsuitable for elementary school aged children. You can find it online in both free and subscription editions. Check your local library for access to the paid version.

040 Unassigned

Occasionally numbers are unassigned when a category is removed or intention-ally kept blank for new types of information.

050 General Serials and Their Indexes

This category had no titles that met the criteria for inclusion.

060 General Organizations & Museology

061 In North America

Jane Clapp, *Professional Ethics and Insignia*, 1975.
While Jane Clapp's book is dated, it is one of the few places you can track down the codes and ethics of many professional organizations in the U.S. This book includes professional organizations for engineers, physicians, financial analysts, academics, and authors, as well as many others.

069 Museology (Museum Science)

**Nancy Moses, *Lost in the Museum:*
Buried Treasures and the Stories They Tell, 2008.**
Nancy Moses explores selected artifacts stored away from the public in the world's museums. The objects and the reasons they are kept hidden are surprising, and they give you a peek at factors that influence museum decision-making.

Lawrence Weschler,
Mr. Wilson's Cabinet of Wonder:
Pronged Ants, Horned Humans, Mice on Toast,
***and Other Marvels of Jurassic Technology*, 1995.**
The first half of Lawrence Weschler's book introduces a small museum in Los Angeles where most of the displays are bogus: the Museum of Jurassic Technology. In the second half, Weschler muses on 16th-century "wonder cabinets," which were the origins of modern museums.

070 News Media, Journalism, Publishing

Joel Friedlander and Betty Kelly Sargent,
The Self-Publisher's Ultimate Resource Guide:
Every Indie Author's Essential Directory to Help You Prepare,
Publish, and Promote Professional Looking Books, **2017.**
 Friedlander and Sargent's guide reports on what leaders in the self-publishing
 industry recommend.

Vivian Gornick, *Unfinished Business:*
Notes of a Chronic Re-reader, **2020.**
 In nine essays, book critic Vivian Gornick celebrates excellent books and the
 benefits of re-reading them throughout a lifetime. In this combination of
 criticism, memoir, and biographical work, Gornick approaches books through
 different lenses, such as which character she can most relate to at various
 times of life.

Josh Karp, *A Futile and Stupid Gesture: How Doug Kenney*
and National Lampoon Changed Comedy Forever, **2005.**
 Douglas Kenney, the co-founder of *National Lampoon,* died in a mysterious fall at age 33. Karp interviews over 130 famous and obscure people
 that Kenney worked with during his brief life to shed light on his character
 and influence.

Paul David Pope, *The Deeds of My Fathers:*
How My Grandfather and Father Built New York
and Created the Tabloid World of Today, **2010.**
 Paul David Pope inherited the tabloid *National Enquirer* from his father. He
 provides a history of New York's Italian American community (and some
 of its most famous residents). Equally entertaining are the stories of his
 family's tabloid.

BIOGRAPHY

A. Scott Berg, *Max Perkins:*
Editor of Genius, **1978.**
 Max Perkins was one of America's most influential editors. A. Scott Berg
 shares how, while working with 20th-century literary stars like Hemingway,
 Fitzgerald, and Wolfe, Perkins did whatever was needed to bring their works
 to print, and how, in the process, he became intimately involved with many of
 his writers' lives.

Katharine Graham, *Personal History,* **1998.**
 Katharine Graham's autobiography intertwines with the history of the
 Washington Post, which was owned and run by her father and her husband,

and then by Graham herself. Her position placed her at the vanguard of the women's movement. In retelling her colorful life, Graham shares the scoop on presidential elections, Watergate, and the pressmen's strike of the mid-1970s.

Seymour M. Hersh, *Reporter: A Memoir*, 2018.

Seymour Hersh, an investigative journalist, known for his My Lai and Abu Ghraib coverage, writes his memoir, which should be of interest to current and aspiring journalists.

David Nasaw, *The Chief: The Life of William Randolph Hearst*, 2000.

David Nasaw details the life of William Randolph Hearst, the media mogul of the early- to mid-20th century, who owned 28 newspapers, a movie studio, radio stations, and 13 magazines.

Mark Ribowsky, *Howard Cosell: The Man, the Myth, and the Transformation of American Sports*, 2011.

In the latter half of the 20th century, Howard Cosell was the most famous sportscaster on the air. His loud style inspired love and hate. Mark Ribowsky's appreciative book outlines Cosell's rise to prominence, his influence, and his fall in the early 1980s for excessive bragging and drinking on the job.

Ann M. Sperber, *Murrow: His Life and Times*, 1986.

One of modern journalism's most influential figures, Edward R. Murrow became synonymous with honest, courageous reporting for his efforts during the McCarthy era. Ann M. Sperber traces Murrow's story from its beginnings in World War II, when he aired his war reports from London rooftops during the blitzkrieg.

Barbara Walters, *Audition: A Memoir*, 2008.

For years, on ABC's *20/20*, Barbara Walters interviewed the most famous people in the world. In her memoir, she recounts how she reached the top of her field and the lessons she learned along the way.

071 In North America

Tom Fenton, *Junk News: The Failure of the Media in the 21st Century*, 2009.

Emmy-winning journalist Tom Fenton argues that corporate takeovers are ruining newspapers and broadcast media. Cuts in funding for in-depth journalism and an entertainment-style format, designed to maximize profits and save corporate money, hobble reliable reporting. Fenton says these developments have led to the polarization that has devastated civil discourse and society.

**John McMillian, *Smoking Typewriters:
The Sixties Underground Press and the Rise
of Alternative Media in America*, 2011.**
> Mimeograph technology made publishing cheap and accessible in the 1960s.
> John McMillian reveals how the resulting underground presses, run mainly
> by leftist young people, helped launch massive protests and social change.

**Ed Madison and Ben DeJarnette, *Reimagining Journalism
in a Post-Truth World: How Late-Night Comedians, Internet
Trolls, and Savvy Reporters Are Transforming News*, 2018.**
> While Madison and DeJarnette's discussion revolves around the 2016 U.S.
> presidential election, their focus is on problems in modern journalism,
> not politics. They find concentration on polls to the neglect of issues is a
> major pitfall.

**Susan E. Tifft and Alex S. Jones, *The Trust:
The Private and Powerful Family Behind* The New York
Times, 1999.**
> It's hard to overestimate the political and historical influence of the Ochses
> and Sulzbergers, the families who have owned the *New York Times* for over
> a century. For much of the paper's history only family members were at
> the helm. The spousal team of professor Susan E. Tifft and Pulitzer Prize–
> winning journalist Alex S. Jones deliver the story.

072 In British Isles: In England

**Nick Davies, *Hack Attack:
The Inside Story of How the Truth Caught Up with Rupert
Murdoch*, 2015.**
> Unchecked capitalism can cause harm in unexpected ways, especially in
> the news media. A former *Guardian* reporter, Nick Davies tells how Rupert
> Murdoch's tactics to increase U.K. *News of the World* sales ruined lives.
> During the resulting trial, Murdoch's empire was called a criminal conspiracy.
> Still, Davies asserts that consumers of Murdoch's style of journalism are as
> guilty of damaging society as Murdoch himself.

080 General Collections

**Mortimer Jerome Adler and Charles Lincoln Van Doren,
eds., *Great Treasury of Western Thought: A Compendium
of Important Statements and Comments on Man and His
Institutions by the Great Thinkers in Western History*, 1977.**
> Both Adler and Van Doren were well-respected scholars and authors in the

20th century. This book contains passages from traditionally honored works in the West that continue to have a tremendous influence on both our history and culture.

081 American

Albert Einstein, *Ideas and Opinions*, 1954.
Albert Einstein chose these popular essays on relativity, nuclear weapons, religion, science, human rights, economics, and government. Reading them helps us understand Einstein himself.

Anita King, ed., *Quotations in Black*, 1981.
Anita King's reference contains quotations from Black politicians, writers, activists, theologians, and other influential figures throughout history. In addition, King includes over 400 anonymous proverbs particular to Black culture. King updated her work in 1997 with *Contemporary Quotations in Black*.

Laurence Urdang and Frederick G. Ruffner Jr., eds., *Allusions—Cultural, Literary, Biblical, and Historical: A Thematic Dictionary*, 1982.
This dictionary has almost 13,000 allusions arranged by 730 themes, followed by a list of definitions, origins, and sources. It also contains a bibliography and index. Renamed as *Ruffner's Allusions*, it was revised and released in its 3rd edition in 2009.

George F. Will, *The Pursuit of Happiness, and Other Sobering Thoughts*, 1978.
Influential conservative commentator George Will has been well respected in part for his relatable and accessible writing. Nevertheless, he has managed to anger readers on the left with opinions on climate change (which he came to deny), and on the right with views on Donald Trump (whom he left the GOP over). But Will's honesty is a rare trait in today's political and media environment.

090 Manuscripts & Rare Books

This category had no titles that met the criteria for inclusion.

CHAPTER 2

100–199

Philosophy & Psychology

O F THE TEN SUBDIVISIONS IN the Philosophy and Psychology division, only one (150–159) is reserved for psychology. When Dewey created the system, psychology was a relatively new science. In contrast, philosophy had been a well-respected field for thousands of years, so it garnered most of the available call numbers. But because the system still allows for psychology books to be shelved with a great deal of specificity, having fewer numbers doesn't present an insurmountable problem for libraries.

100 Philosophy, Parapsychology & Occultism, Psychology

Margreet de Heer, *Philosophy: A Discovery in Comics*, 2012.
While Margreet de Heer discusses axiomatic (self-evident) reasoning from Socrates to Nietzsche, in this book she mainly introduces philosophical thought for the uninitiated.

Justin E. H. Smith, *The Philosopher: A History in Six Types*, 2016.
Justin E. H. Smith sums up philosophical thought in six job descriptions, such as natural philosopher and courtier. Then, in explaining the roles they've played throughout history, he clarifies why philosophy matters today.

103 Dictionaries & Encyclopedias

Barbara Cassin, ed., et al., *Dictionary of Untranslatables: A Philosophical Lexicon*, 2015.
This book contains over 400 entries by 150 scholars. They cover philosophical, literary, and political terms and concepts that make complex ideas easy to understand.

107 Education, Research & Related Topics

Peter Worley, *The Philosophy Shop:*
Ideas, Activities, and Questions to Get People,
***Young and Old, Thinking Philosophically,* 2012.**
   Written by Peter Worley with contributions by other professional philosophers, this book contains ideas, thought experiments, activities, short stories,
   pictures, and questions to stimulate thought. Use it as a teaching tool for
   yourself or others. It can also help you enliven your party conversations.

109 Historical & Collected Biography

Dean Chavooshian, *The Pursuit of Wisdom:*
A Chronological Inquiry of the World's Most Influential
Seekers of Wisdom in the Fields of Theology,
***Philosophy, and Science,* 2015.**
   Dean Chavooshian examines the big questions, like "Is the soul immortal?"
   and "Did man evolve or was he created?" He provides the answers using
   comparisons of what theologians, philosophers, and scientists have said about
   these topics through the ages.

Bertrand Russell, *A History of Western Philosophy,* 1945.
   Welsh philosopher, historian, logician, mathematician, and rationalist
   Bertrand Russell explores the West's traditionally regarded great thinkers
   and ideas.

110 Metaphysics

Scott Adams, *God's Debris:*
***A Thought Experiment,* 2001.**
   Dilbert cartoonist Scott Adams conducts a thought experiment in which he
   leads you to consider big topics, from free will to God.

111 Ontology

William Barrett, *What is Existentialism?,* 1963.
   William Barrett, a philosophy professor, clearly and accessibly probes existentialism through the works of Martin Heidegger.

Alexander Nehamas, *Only a Promise of Happiness:*
***The Place of Beauty in a World of Art,* 2007.**
   Scholar Alexander Nehamas laments the lack of appreciation for beauty in our
   world today. He wants to make the concept honored again because it contrib-
   utes to our happiness.

113 Cosmology (Philosophy of Nature)

Jim Holt, *Why Does the World Exist?* *An Existential Detective Story*, 2012.

Jim Holt, when he was a child, was not happy with the standard explanation that God created everything. So, as an adult, he asks, "Why does the world exist?" to some of the world's top thinkers. Here are their answers.

Theodore Richards, *Cosmosophia:* *Cosmology, Mysticism, and the Birth of a New Myth*, 2011.

Theodore Richards explores why so many people believe life is meaningless, and he shares ideas to help us find meaning. Throughout, he argues we need to integrate science with myth in ways that will connect us to the world and each other.

115 Time

David Allen Park, *The Image of Eternity:* *Roots of Time in the Physical World*, 1980.

David Allen Park explores ideas on time in philosophical and scientific thought. Warning: math is involved. Nevertheless, the concepts should be accessible to the average person.

120 Epistemology, Causation, Humankind

121 Epistemology (Theory of Knowledge)

Berislav Marušić, *Evidence and Agency:* *Norms of Belief for Promising and Resolving*, 2015.

Promises aren't always easy to keep. Berislav Marušić explores why we make promises we can't or won't keep.

Kathryn Schulz, *Being Wrong:* *Adventures in the Margin of Error*, 2010.

Kathryn Schulz's treatise on the value of making and embracing mistakes also explores why we believe in demonstrably untrue things.

122 Causation

John Grant, *Debunk It! Fake News Edition:* *How to Stay Sane in a World of Misinformation*, 2019.

How do you know whether you're consuming fake news? John Grant pulls examples from recent headlines to explain how to spot faulty arguments. He demonstrates how people mislead with rhetorical techniques. Learning to spot unreliable sources can help you stay in control of your decisions and your life.

L. A. Paul and Ned Hall, *Causation: A User's Guide*, 2013.

L. A. Paul and Ned Hall's college-level textbook uses causation to explain how to pursue a philosophical discussion on a particular topic.

123 Determinism & Indeterminism

Nassim Nicholas Taleb, *Fooled by Randomness: The Hidden Role of Chance in Life and in the Markets*, 2001.

Nassim Nicholas Taleb, a former quantitative trader and researcher in probability, provides expert discussion of chance that may change your views of the topic.

David Foster Wallace, *Fate, Time, and Language: An Essay on Free Will*, 2010.

David Foster Wallace refutes philosopher Richard Taylor's assertions that free will does not exist.

126 The Self

Raymond Martin and John Barresi, *The Rise and Fall of Soul and Self: An Intellectual History of Personal Identity*, 2006.

Martin and Barresi examine theories of the soul and the self from ancient Greece to the present. Changing ideas have radically transformed the way we view ourselves and our place in the world.

128 Humankind

Ted Chu, *Human Purpose and Transhuman Potential: A Cosmic Vision for Our Future Evolution*, 2014.

Ted Chu asserts that humans are still evolving. However, he believes we are on the cusp of an evolutionary leap with recent technological breakthroughs and that we are at a point where we can radically change what we are and become entirely new forms of life.

Mark Gober, *An End to Upside Down Thinking: Dispelling the Myth That the Brain Produces Consciousness, and the Implications for Everyday Life*, 2018.

While philosopher and cognitive scientist Daniel Dennett argued that we are biological machines dependent on our bodies for awareness, Mark Gober argues the opposite. He provides scientific support for his belief that consciousness is located outside our bodies and not in our brains.

Lynne McTaggart, *The Bond:*
***Connecting through the Space Between Us*, 2012.**
Lynne McTaggart examines scientific evidence that we are connected. She asserts that by focusing on cooperation and collaboration, we can overcome our divisions.

Lewis Mumford, *The Conduct of Life*, 1951.
An influential thinker, American historian, and philosopher, Lewis Mumford discussed and provided solutions for religious and ethical issues that confronted humanity midway through the 20th century. The book is available for free online through archive.org.

Marjorie Hines Woollacott, *Infinite Awareness:*
***The Awakening of a Scientific Mind*, 2016.**
Before she began meditating, Marjorie Hines Woollacott was a materialist who believed chemistry and electricity in our brains determine our experience. Now she investigates the meaning and location of consciousness.

129 Origin & Destiny of Individual Souls

Julia Assante, *The Last Frontier:*
Exploring the Afterlife and Transforming Our Fear of
***Death*, 2012.**
Julia Assante explores research into consciousness from physics, parapsychology, and quantum biology. In addition, she examines communication with the dead, studies of near-death experiences, and the medical records of near-death patients.

Leslie Kean, *Surviving Death:*
***A Journalist Investigates Evidence for an Afterlife*, 2017.**
Investigative journalist Leslie Kean provides case studies involving children with verified memories of past lives. She also looks at scientific evidence on mediumship and near-death experiences.

130 Parapsychology & Occultism

Etzel Cardeña, et al., eds., *Parapsychology:*
***A Handbook for the 21st Century*, 2015.**
Well-respected scientists have researched phenomena such as telepathy, precognition, and psychokinesis, concluding that some of these phenomena are real. This book explores the recent research.

131 Parapsychological & Occult Methods

Susan Shumsky, *Color Your Chakras: An Interactive Way to Understand the Energy Centers of the Body*, 2016.
> This adult coloring book explains the chakra system in terms of color and function.

133 Specific Topics in Parapsychology & Occultism

Etzel Cardeña, et al., *Varieties of Anomalous Experience: Examining the Scientific Evidence*, 2nd ed., 2014.
> Expert analysis of experiences like synesthesia, out-of-body experiences, and alien abductions are provided in this publication of the American Psychological Association.

Melissa Cynova, *Kitchen Table Tarot: Pull Up a Chair, Shuffle the Cards, and Let's Talk Tarot*, 2017.
> Melissa Cynova's beginner-friendly explanation and instruction present tarot card reading as a form of storytelling. Various meanings of the cards and the practice of interpretation are discussed, along with the ethics involved in reading tarot for others.

Michael Goddart, *In Search of Lost Lives: Desire, Sanskaras, and the Evolution of a Mind and Soul*, 2017.
> Michael Goddart writes of reincarnation based on his knowledge of his own past incarnations on Earth and other planets. He discusses karma and how it affects individual lives and collective experiences.

Peter Manseau, *The Apparitionists: A Tale of Phantoms, Fraud, Photography, and the Man Who Captured Lincoln's Ghost*, 2017.
> Peter Manseau narrates the tale of William Mumler (1832–1884), who claimed to capture images of the dead with photographic equipment. Before Mumler stood trial for fakery, even Mary Todd Lincoln was one of his devotees. While many have tried to replicate his photos, no one has discovered his methods.

Richard Rowe, *Imagining the Unimaginable: A System Engineer's Journey into the Afterlife*, 2019.
> When Richard Rowe, a scientist with over 120 patents, recovered from a near-death experience, he began his research into the scientific evidence on NDEs. He reveals what he discovered, his experiments with past-life regression hypnosis, and his interviews with fellow survivors.

Richard Webster, *Spirit Guides & Angel Guardians: Contact Your Invisible Helpers*, 1998.
  Richard Webster says we all have invisible beings who watch over us and help us when we ask. He teaches you how to communicate with them to enhance your spiritual and personal growth.

135 Dreams & Mysteries

Laurin Bellg, *Near Death in the ICU: Stories from Patients Near Death and Why We Should Listen to Them*, 2015.
  As an intensive care unit critical care physician, Laurin Bellg writes of her observations and her patients' experiences involving near-death phenomena. She maintains these experiences are not imaginary and medical staff must use sensitivity when handling them.

Christina Donnell, *Transcendent Dreaming: Stepping Into Our Human Potential*, 2008.
  Christina Donnell encourages people to examine their dreams. She shares how hers have shown her that through them, we can connect with all creation.

Erich Fromm, *The Forgotten Language: An Introduction to the Understanding of Dreams, Fairytales, and Myths*, 1951.
  Twentieth-century psychoanalyst Erich Fromm was one of the first psychiatric thinkers to encourage people to analyze their dreams. Dreams contain universal symbols from myths, art, and literature, and he believed they connect us to our inner wisdom.

136 [Unassigned]

H. A. Overstreet, *The Mature Mind*, 1949.
  In the aftermath of the Second World War, H. A. Overstreet proclaimed that children must be systematically socialized. He said children must be taught how to behave and consider others; otherwise, they wreak havoc when grown. With proper social training, the world might be saved from future horrors.

140 Specific Philosophical Schools

142 Critical Philosophy

Sarah Bakewell, *At the Existentialist Café: Freedom, Being, and Apricot Cocktails with Jean-Paul Sartre, Simone de Beauvoir, Albert Camus, Martin Heidegger, Maurice Merleau-Ponty and Others*, 2016.
  Existentialism reached its pinnacle of influence in Paris in the mid-20th

century. Many of its philosophers, artists, and writers were acquainted with one another. Sarah Bakewell imagines a conversation among a small group of them together in a French cafe.

144 Humanism & Related Systems

Philip F. Gura, *American Transcendentalism: A History*, 2007.
America's first intellectual movement was transcendentalism. Philip F. Gura discusses its proponents—Emerson, Thoreau, and Henry James. Because of transcendentalism's early split into radical individualism versus social activism, some facets of the current culture wars trace back to this movement.

146 Naturalism & Related Systems

Daniel C. Dennett, *Darwin's Dangerous Idea: Evolution and the Meanings of Life*, 1995.
In this book, philosopher Daniel Dennett seeks to convince influential thinkers that evolutionary theory matters. While critics have faulted the book's writing style and unsuccessful argument, Dennett, an evangelical atheist, has greatly influenced the general conversation in this arena for decades.

149 Other Philosophical Systems & Doctrines

Joshua Foa Dienstag, *Pessimism: Philosophy, Ethic, Spirit*, 2006.
While many people frown on negativity, Joshua Foa Dienstag argues that pessimism, a philosophical system whose proponents include Rousseau, Freud, and Foucault, is a counterbalance to the unrealistically optimistic ideas that dominate discussion today.

Evelyn Underhill, *Mysticism: A Study of the Nature and Development of Man's Spiritual Consciousness*, 1911.
In this classic and influential early-20th-century study of spiritual thought, Evelyn Underhill examines the relationship between mysticism and the science of psychology. She also outlines stages of mystical consciousness.

150 Psychology

Shirzad Chamine, *Positive Intelligence: Why Only 20% of Teams and Individuals Achieve Their True Potential and How You Can Achieve Yours*, 2012.
Shirzad Chamine identifies ten character traits that can harm you and those

you work with. He helps you identify yours and offers steps to help you overcome them.

Carl G. Jung, *The Undiscovered Self*, 1958.

These two essays, written late in Carl G. Jung's life, share his predictions for society in the wake of World War II. The first essay urges people to become more self-reflective and avoid becoming absorbed by consumer culture. The second discusses dreams and how they help us understand our unconscious needs.

Rollo May, *Man's Search for Himself*, 1953.

American existential psychologist Rollo May addressed his patients' complaints of anxiety and emptiness and explained why people experienced these problems and how they could work with them.

Alexandra Rutherford, *Beyond the Box: B. F. Skinner's Technology of Behavior from Laboratory to Life, 1950s–1970s*, 2009.

Behaviorist B. F. Skinner had an outsized influence on all areas of life in the mid- to late-20th century, especially in the self-help industry. Alexandra Rutherford examines how his studies were peddled to American society, altering the entire social and psychic environment.

Erel Shalit, *The Cycle of Life: Themes and Tales of the Journey*, 2011.

Jungian psychoanalyst Erel Shalit asserts that life has two phases of growth. The first requires us to form a stable identity, separate from our parents, to create an independent, productive life for ourselves. The second phase requires we find our way back home. Shalit shows how dreams can help with this task.

BIOGRAPHY

Howard M. Feinstein, *Becoming William James*, 1984.

Howard M. Feinstein examines William James's preoccupation with meaningful work: finding it and performing it. He looks at James's complex family dynamic and mental illnesses in light of more recent psychological thought.

Peter Gay, *Freud: A Life for Our Time*, 1988.

Biographer Peter Gay discusses Sigmund Freud, the father of modern psychiatry, and focuses on Freud's view that humans are animals victimized by civilization's restraints. He also examines Freud's astute observations on education.

152 Sensory Perception, Movement, Emotions & Drives

Paul Bloom, *How Pleasure Works: The New Science of Why We Like What We Like*, 2011.

Paul Bloom says pleasure begins in our minds with expectation. And so, he says, the objective qualities of any experience matter less to our experience than we think.

Heather Havrilesky, *What If This Were Enough?*, 2018.

These essays by Heather Havrilesky consider the impacts social and digital media have on us as individuals and as a society. She considers what we can do to mitigate the negative messages we absorb from the media.

Karla McLaren, *The Language of Emotions: What Your Feelings Are Trying to Tell You*, 2010.

Karla McLaren shows why we should value all our emotions—the pleasant and the unpleasant—because they all have something to teach us. She outlines five skills to help us process difficult emotions and heal old traumas.

Samara O'Shea, *Loves Me . . . Not: How to Survive (and Thrive!) in the Face of Unrequited Love*, 2014.

Unskillful reactions to unrequited love can damage lives and reputations. Samara O'Shea offers advice from famous historical figures and today's celebrities on how to survive rejection.

Jon Ronson, *So You've Been Publicly Shamed*, 2015.

The Internet and social media give the average person an amplified voice. As a result, lives have been ruined by as little as a thoughtless tweet. Jon Ronson looks at this phenomenon and urges us to consider the damage done to the victim of public outrage. But he also looks at the damage done to those who distribute the punishment.

Friedemann Schaub, *The Fear and Anxiety Solution: A Breakthrough Process for Healing and Empowerment in Your Subconscious Mind*, 2012.

Fear and anxiety affect both health and performance. Friedemann Schaub provides principles and exercises to help you work with them.

153 Conscious Mental Processes & Intelligence

Dan Ariely, *Predictably Irrational: The Hidden Forces That Shape Our Decisions*, 2008.

Dan Ariely's research has shown that people's economic decisions often make little sense. Ariely argues that since people don't act in their own best interests, like saving for retirement, the government should step in and force them to. He shows that if left alone, poor decisions will ultimately cost society more than curbing them would.

Robert B. Cialdini, *Influence:*
The Psychology of Persuasion, 1984.
In the 1994 revised edition of this classic work, Robert B. Cialdini identifies six forms of influence that impact people's decisions and teaches how to use them to influence others.

David Epstein, *Range:*
Why Generalists Triumph in a Specialized World, 2019.
We're all familiar with the adage, "Quitters never win." But when David Epstein investigated the most successful people in the world, he found, paradoxically, that those who have varied interests, quit pursuits frequently, and embrace failure are the ones who thrive.

Nir Eyal, *Indistractable:*
How to Control Your Attention and Choose Your Life, 2019.
With our phones pinging and co-workers chatting, we all understand distraction. Researcher Nir Eyal reveals the price we pay for our distraction, and he provides a four-step research-based model to help us pay attention to what matters whenever we need to.

Daniel Kahneman, *Thinking Fast and Slow*, 2011.
Daniel Kahneman says we have two thinking systems—a fast, effortless one, our intuition, and a slow and logical one that requires more effort. He focuses on how to use this slow thinking system to our advantage.

Dominic Streatfeild, *Brainwash:*
The Secret History of Mind Control, 2006.
Brainwashing is an attempt to wipe a person's mind clean and reconstruct it with new thoughts and attitudes. Dominic Streatfeild explains how the practice has been used since the Cold War to extract information, among other objectives.

154 Subconscious & Altered States

David Luke, *Otherworlds:*
Psychedelics and Exceptional Human Experience, 2018.
Using neuroscience, psychology, parapsychology, anthropology, and transpersonal studies, David Luke explores extraordinary experiences that people have had while under the influence of psychedelics. These paranormal events include entity encounters, mediumship, and trips to other dimensions.

Robert Waggoner and Caroline McCready,
Lucid Dreaming, Plain and Simple: Tips and Techniques for
Insight, Creativity, and Personal Growth, 2020.
> Waggoner and McCready share insights into lucid dreaming gained from
> cognitive psychology research and give pointers on how to experience it for
> yourself and use it for understanding and growth.

155 Differential & Developmental Psychology

Ashton Applewhite, *This Chair Rocks:*
A Manifesto against Ageism, 2016.
> Why do people believe that older people are inferior to younger people?
> Ashton Applewhite researches the history of ageism and its damage to both
> society and individuals.

Joanne Cacciatore, *Bearing the Unbearable:*
Love, Loss, and the Heartbreaking Path of Grief, 2018.
> Joanne Cacciatore is a bereavement educator, researcher, Zen priest, and
> counselor. Using stories, she helps you process grief. Her book is useful for
> clergy, social workers, educators, and anyone who helps others cope with loss.

Susan Cain, *Quiet: The Power of Introverts*
in a World That Can't Stop Talking, 2012.
> Introvert Susan Cain argues that, far from being misanthropic loners, intro-
> verts have a great deal to offer the world when their talents and unique means
> of expression are recognized.

Joseph Bharat Cornell, *The Sky and Earth Touched Me:*
Sharing Nature Wellness Exercises, 2013.
> Joseph Bharat Cornell was a nature educator who wrote about children and
> nature in the 1970s. This book invites you to head outside and perform exer-
> cises designed to increase your awareness of the natural world.

Philip Zimbardo, *The Lucifer Effect:*
Understanding How Good People Turn Evil, 2007.
> Philip Zimbardo is a social psychologist and creator of the Stanford prison
> experiment. He examines what his research reveals about how good people
> are convinced to do bad things. He then reflects on what this says about the
> nature of good and evil.

156 Comparative Psychology

Roger Fouts and Stephen Tukel Mills, *Next of Kin:*
My Conversations with Chimpanzees, 1997.
> Chimpanzees share more than 98 percent of human DNA, making them our

closest biological relatives. Roger Fouts spent decades learning to communicate with them through sign language. His relationships with these animals compelled him to risk his career to speak out against their use in biomedical labs.

158 Applied Psychology

Hiro Boga, *To Be Soul, Do Soul: Adventures in Creative Consciousness*, 2017.

Hiro Boga is a teacher and business strategist who provides mini-experiments to help you become aware of and develop your creative potential.

Richard Boyatzis, Melvin Smith, and Ellen Van Oosten, *Helping People Change: Coaching with Compassion for Lifelong Learning and Growth*, 2019.

If you've tried to help someone else change their life, you understand how complicated the process can be. Even changing ourselves is challenging. But emotional intelligence expert Boyatzis and colleagues Smith and Van Oosten assert that it's possible to change if the desire is connected with a positive vision or goal.

Laurie Buchanan, *Note to Self: A Seven-Step Path to Growth and Gratitude*, 2016.

Laurie Buchanan says we all have seven selves within, and each has characteristics, both visible and hidden. She helps you find which characteristics may be holding you back and presents tips and exercises to help you release them.

Oliver Burkeman, *The Antidote: Happiness for People Who Can't Stand Positive Thinking*, 2012.

We all want to avoid pain and unhappiness. Oliver Burkeman gives an alternative to the self-help movement's relentless focus on keeping things positive. Instead, he argues that embracing and dealing with problems and failures is the key to happiness.

Andreas Elpidorou, *Propelled: How Boredom, Frustration, and Anticipation Lead Us to the Good Life*, 2020

Andreas Elpidorou argues that we need boredom and other negative psychological states for achievement. He says instant gratification and overemphasis on pleasure actually make us feel worse.

Ryan Holiday, *Ego Is the Enemy*, 2016.

In our culture of self-promotion and image-consciousness, Ryan Holiday argues that our focus on ourselves holds us back from living a meaningful life. By examining literature, philosophy, and history, he helps us see that our problem is us, and he offers a way out of self-absorption.

Jon Kabat-Zinn, *Mindfulness for Beginners:*
Reclaiming the Present Moment—and Your Life, **2006.**
A meditation practice can improve our lives in many ways. Jon Kabat-Zinn is
a scientist who helped bring the method to the international mainstream. He
outlines how meditation helps you and tells you how to begin a practice.

160 Philosophical Logic

Stuart Chase, *Guides to Straight Thinking,* **1957.**
Sadly, most of us were never formally taught logical thinking. Stuart Chase
produced a straightforward introduction to logic that still provides practical
benefits to those who learn it.

Michael Shenefelt and Heidi White, *If A, then B:*
How the World Discovered Logic, **2013.**
This book does not teach logic. Instead, it provides a history of logic from
ancient times to today. Shenefelt and White discuss political, economic, technological, and geographic features that spurred advances among thinkers like
Aristotle, George Boole, and Alan Turing and consider reason in the context
of society.

169 Analogy

Douglas Hofstadter and Emmanuel Sander, *Surfaces and*
Essences: Analogy as the Fuel and Fire of Thinking, **2014.**
How is it possible to listen to a complex story and get the gist of it in a split
second? Douglas Hofstadter and Emmanuel Sander say it's by analogies—
those bits of information that link to other, similar bits. They explain how this
happens with engaging examples that make the complex understandable.

170 Ethics (Moral Philosophy)

Kwame Anthony Appiah, *Ethics of Identity,* **2005.**
African Studies scholar Kwame Anthony Appiah examines the complicated
relationship between our sense of ourselves as individuals and our cultural
identities as a collective. Humans generally identify themselves in the context
of group memberships, whether by race, religion, gender, or others. His analysis makes it hard to narrow our views down to merely "us and them."

Larissa MacFarquhar, *Strangers Drowning:*
Grappling with Impossible Idealism, Drastic Choices,
and the Urge to Help, **2015.**
Most of us admire people who live lives of self-sacrifice. What causes someone to give up all their possessions to serve the poor or risk their life to save a

drowning victim? Larissa MacFarquhar offers a deep discussion of what these ethical actions mean.

Jonathan Sacks, *Morality: Restoring the Common Good in Divided Times*, 2020.

How did we get to the place where civil discourse is rare and democracy is endangered? Faith leader and intellectual Jonathan Sacks says a lack of shared character is the key and traces the concepts of right and wrong from ancient Greece to today. He says we have given our moral code over to the market and crass self-interest. Only through resurrecting a shared morality does he see a way we can have true freedom.

Desmond Tutu and Mpho Tutu, *Made for Goodness: And Why This Makes All the Difference*, 2011.

Nobel Peace Prize winner Archbishop Desmond Tutu argued that humans were created to be good. Because that is our essential nature, he saw goodness winning out in the end for us and the planet. He wanted this book to be a light in dark times.

171 Ethical Systems

Philip Kitcher, *The Ethical Project*, 2011.

When searching for ethics in the natural sciences, social sciences, and philosophy, Philip Kitcher sees principles like right and wrong as evolving systems. We build upon the insights and errors of our forebears to come up with values that fit our times. Ethical systems are something that we all create to a greater or lesser degree.

172 Political Ethics

Patricia S. Churchland, *Conscience: The Origins of Moral Intuition*, 2019.

How do we develop a sense of conscience? What does science tell us about those, like psychopaths, who have none? Philosopher Patricia S. Churchland explores why societies form differing ethical standards and pass them on to children and what past philosophers have had to say about cultures and their respective moral standards.

Paul Collier, *The Bottom Billion: Why the Poorest Countries Are Failing and What Can Be Done About It*, 2008.

Economics professor Paul Collier uses his personal experience fighting poverty to write about 50 failed states that most of us know little about. While there are many causes for their lack of achievement, corruption is one of the most prominent. The solution he lays out will require global leadership and cooperation.

174 Occupational Ethics

Jacob Appel, *Who Says You're Dead? Medical and Ethical Dilemmas for the Curious and Concerned*, 2019.

Using his two decades of teaching in top medical schools, Jacob Appel looks at medical headlines and case studies presenting complex ethical dilemmas. He challenges you to grapple with these messy situations in light of what philosophers, courts, political commentators, and medical professionals say about them.

Alice Dreger, *Galileo's Middle Finger: Heretics, Activists, and One Scholar's Search for Justice*, 2015.

While researching intersex people and their treatment, medical historian Alice Dreger was so shocked and outraged at the abuses she uncovered that she became an activist for patient's rights. When her work came under attack from fellow progressives, she decided to turn her investigative skills to unearthing the truth about global controversies between these activists and the scientists determined to share uncomfortable facts.

Mary C. Gentile, *Giving Voice to Values: How to Speak Your Mind When You Know What's Right*, 2011.

Mary C. Gentile says the problem with modern business ethics isn't a failure to determine what's right. Instead, it's a matter of knowing how to do the right thing while under pressure to do wrong from bosses, customers, or shareholders. Her suggestions help you stand up for your beliefs in the face of pressure.

Marianne M. Jennings, *The Seven Signs of Ethical Collapse: How to Spot Moral Meltdowns in Organizations*, 2008.

Marianne M. Jennings offers seven warning signs to look for before taking a job or investing resources. These begin with pressure to maintain numbers and ends with the belief that doing good in some areas excuses misbehavior in others. This book will help you understand why these things happen and how to avoid being a victim of ethical failure.

James H. Jones, *Bad Blood: The Tuskegee Syphilis Experiment*, New and Expanded Edition, 1981.

Many of us know about the experiments conducted at the Tuskegee Institute between 1932 and 1972 on over 400 Black male sharecroppers who had syphilis. Tragically, the researcher denied these men healthcare and never told them they had the disease. Jones tells the story of this travesty and how it helped create the widespread mistrust of the medical establishment held by Black Americans even today.

Rachel M. McCleary and Robert J. Barro,
The Wealth of Religions:
The Political Economy of Believing and Belonging, **2019.**
McCleary and Barro's study of how religion and economics affect one another
looks at factors such as belief in heaven and hell in the marketplace and
industry. The authors examine specific faiths throughout history, such as
Tibetan Buddhism and Protestant vs. Catholic Christianity, to see what sorts
of economic impacts each engenders.

Michael J. Sandel, *What Money Can't Buy:*
The Moral Limits of Markets, **2013.**
Political philosopher Michael J. Sandel encourages us to look at the effects the
"everything is for sale" ethos has on our society. He says it has affected every
area, cheapening medicine, law, sports, and our relationships. Finally, Sandel
asks us to consider how we can protect our lives from the market's harm.

176 Ethics of Sex & Reproduction

Jane Maienschein, *Whose View of Life?*
Embryos, Cloning, and Stem Cells, **2003.**
Jane Maienschein examines the ethics involved in human embryo research.
While her perspective is multidisciplinary, she strives to take a midline
approach that avoids the extremes of both sides.

177 Ethics of Social Relations

Donna Cameron, *A Year of Living Kindly:*
Choices That Will Change Your Life
and the World Around You, **2018.**
The world can be a heartless place, but Donna Cameron has an antidote.
She relates her experiences during a 365-day commitment to practicing
kindness. Suggestions for turning kindness into a lifestyle make it easy for us
to do the same.

179 Other Ethical Norms

Angeles Arrien, *Living in Gratitude:*
A Journey That Will Change Your Life, **2011.**
Angeles Arrien presents a 12-month plan to increase your capacity for gratitude. Along the way, she shares research, stories, prayers, and practices on
thankfulness from cultures worldwide.

William H. Colby, *Unplugged:*
Reclaiming Our Right to Die in America, **2007.**
William H. Colby discusses the right-to-die debate in America. He points out

that we must examine the issue in light of our technological ability to prolong life almost indefinitely.

Kathleen Dean Moore and Michael P. Nelson, *Moral Ground: Ethical Action for a Planet in Peril*, 2010.

Over 80 visionaries contribute to this anthology of writings on the destruction of our planet. They combine a scientific perspective with moral considerations to formulate a new vision for our policies and lifestyle choices, offering practical advice for individual action.

Sunaura Taylor, *Beasts of Burden: Animal and Disability Liberation*, 2018.

Sunaura Taylor offers her perspective on the relationship of animals to humans as a disabled person, disability activist, and animal advocate.

180 Ancient, Medieval, Eastern Philosophy

181 Eastern Philosophy

James W. Heisig, et al., eds., *Japanese Philosophy: A Sourcebook*, 2011.

These essays give you an overview of Japanese philosophy and the debates within it. Top scholars discuss writings from all eras and schools of thought. In addition, they cover the religious ideas of Japanese Buddhism, Confucianism, and Shinto.

Leonard Perlmutter, *The Heart and Science of Yoga: The American Meditation Institute's Empowering Self-Care Program for a Happy, Healthy, Joyful Life*, 2017.

Leonard Perlmutter, the founder of the American Meditation Institute, provides a valuable reference on yoga science. In covering meditations, prayers, breathing practices, Ayurvedic health principles, and other techniques, Perlmutter gives a comprehensive view of the discipline and its benefits.

Benjamin I. Schwartz, *The World of Thought in Ancient China*, 1989.

Benjamin I. Schwartz provides a scholarly look at the formation of Chinese culture with information on early Confucianism, Taoism, and the "five classics."

Alan Watts, *Alan Watts—In the Academy: Essays and Lectures*, 2017.

Alan Watts was a serious scholar and philosopher with a master's degree in theology and a doctorate in divinity. These essays and lectures reveal the depth and breadth of his thinking on psychedelics, religion, mysticism, and other topics.

182 Pre-Socratic Greek Philosophies

A. H. Coxon, *The Fragments of Parmenides: A Critical Text With Introduction and Translation, the Ancient Testimonia and a Commentary*, 2009.
A. H. Coxon's scholarly work isn't light reading. The 2009 edition revised and expanded the original book and covers the surviving work of Parmenides of Elea, who was a philosopher from the fifth century BCE.

183 Sophistic, Socratic, Related Greek Philosophies

Emily Wilson, *The Death of Socrates*, 2007.
Classical studies scholar Emily Wilson analyses the death of one of Western civilization's most influential figures, Socrates. First, she looks at the accounts of his death from its time, and then she moves forward, examining how literature, philosophy, and art have portrayed the event ever since.

184 Platonic Philosophy

J. Angelo Corlett, *Interpreting Plato's Dialogues*, 2007.
Interpretations of Plato's dialogues have varied across the ages. J. Angelo Corlett provides a new approach to interpretation by examining the discussions through the lens of Plato's relationship to, and respect for, his teacher Socrates.

Rebecca Newberger Goldstein, *Plato at the Googleplex: Why Philosophy Won't Go Away*, 2014.
Novelist Rebecca Goldstein imagines what would happen if Plato found himself in the 21st century. What would he have to say to us? She explores the possibilities in an imaginary speaking tour.

190 Modern Western Philosophy

Peter Gay, *The Enlightenment: The Rise of Modern Paganism*, 1967.
Award-winning historian Peter Gay examines the 18th-century Enlightenment era by looking at the philosophies and ideas of the period from a 20th-century perspective.

Kris M. McDaniel, *The Fragmentation of Being*, 2017.
Kris M. McDaniel asks rarely considered questions about being. For example,

"There are many kinds of beings, but are there also many kinds of being?"
While most modern philosophers would answer no to these questions,
McDaniel speculates on why the answer would be yes.

191 Philosophy of United States & Canada

David D. Karnos and Robert G. Shoemaker, *Falling in Love with Wisdom: American Philosophers Talk About Their Calling*, 1994.

Philosophy has fallen in prominence. Modern philosophers are tucked away in
academia and have little contact with popular culture. The editors present the
stories of 64 philosophers and delve into why they chose this particular career.

Ken Wilber, *The Integral Vision: A Very Short Introduction to the Revolutionary Integral Approach to Life, God, the Universe, and Everything*, 2007.

In this sweeping exploration of everything, Ken Wilber, the founder of
Integral Theory, shares his findings from decades of study on human potential for growth. Here, he combines what he's learned into a vision that can
improve every area of the lives of individuals.

BIOGRAPHY

Jeffrey C. Stewart, *The New Negro: The Life of Alain Locke*, 2018.

Alain Locke was raised in Philadelphia and became the first African American
Rhodes Scholar, with a doctorate in philosophy from Harvard. In his teaching career, Locke immersed himself in cultures from around the world and
became the father of the Harlem Renaissance. In addition, he encouraged
Black artists, musicians, and writers and was one of the most influential
figures of Black culture in Jazz Age America. Jefferey C. Stewart tells Locke's
personal and professional story.

192 Philosophy of British Isles

Isaiah Berlin, *The Proper Study of Mankind: An Anthology of Essays*, 1998.

Isaiah Berlin was one of Britain's leading 20th-century liberal thinkers. This
book contains his most famous essays, including his studies of Machiavelli
and Pasternak.

Philip Pettit, *Made with Words: Hobbes on Language, Mind, and Politics*, 2008.

According to Philip Pettit, Thomas Hobbes originated the language thesis,
which argues that language leads us to achieve greater heights and connection
in groups. But it is, unfortunately, also the genesis of despair because through

it we can contemplate the future. In this work, Pettit examines Hobbes's thinking on this and other areas of philosophical discourse.

BIOGRAPHY

Catherine Drinker Bowen, *Francis Bacon: The Temper of a Man*, 1963.

Catherine Drinker Bowen's portrayal of Elizabethan philosopher Francis Bacon seeks to balance contradictions in his life and work.

193 Philosophy of Germany & Austria

BIOGRAPHY

Maria Rosa Antognazza, *Liebniz: An Intellectual Biography*, 2008.

Gottfried Wilhelm Leibniz (1646–1716) was a giant intellect credited with ushering in modern philosophy. Maria Rosa Antognazza relates the events of his life and describes his philosophical teachings as grounded in the Holy Roman Empire in which he lived.

Julian Young, *Friedrich Nietzsche: A Philosophical Biography*, 2011.

Friedrich Nietzsche proved to be an extremely influential, if controversial, thinker. Yet his life was a mass of contradictions and puzzles. Julian Young's biography traces Nietzsche's life and clarifies his philosophy.

194 Philosophy of France

BIOGRAPHY

James Miller, *The Passion of Michel Foucault*, 1993.

Political scholar James Miller presents a new interpretation of Michel Foucault's work and life by tracing Foucault's life (1926–1984) from the earliest events to his late-life preoccupation with sexuality and personal identity.

199 Philosophy in Other Geographic Areas

BIOGRAPHY

Steven Nadler, *Spinoza: A Life*, 1999.

Steven Nadler's biography of 17th-century Dutch philosopher Baruch Spinoza is a well-researched story of one of the most controversial philosophers of all time. Nadler explains why Spinoza's upbringing in Amsterdam's Jewish community and later exile are central to his work.

CHAPTER 3

200–299

Religion

For many, religion is one of the most objectionable Dewey categories because there are far more numbers for Christianity than the assigned numbers of all the other world religions combined. As a late-19th century North American scholar, Dewey catered to attitudes that Christianity is the most important religion in the world. Some libraries are redoing this section to reflect better the sensibilities of their patrons and the greater diversity of beliefs. Because I used the DDC as OCLC officially uses it, there are more books on Christianity. See the Introduction, on page 3, for more information on the system. The unequal distribution of religious coverage in this book is because the books I had to choose from contained more books on Christianity. There were far fewer titles on other religions.

200 Religion

John Bowker, ed., *World Religions:*
***The Great Faiths Explored and Explained*, 2006.**
While covering the major religions of Buddhism, Christianity, Hinduism, Islam, and Judaism, this book also examines ancient religions that are no longer commonly practiced. It delves into the symbolism, iconography, sacred texts, and essential beliefs of each represented faith.

Christopher Hitchens,
***God is Not Great: How Religion Poisons Everything*, 2007.**
In his most famous work, intellectual and anti-theist Christopher Hitchens proclaims, "God did not make us. We made God." He believes religion does more harm than good, so people should base their worldviews on science and reason instead.

Ian Johnson,
***The Souls of China: The Return of Religion After Mao*, 2017.**
Pulitzer Prize–winning writer Ian Johnson lives in Beijing. Since 1984, he has wandered around the country, exploring religious practices. At times, he lived

with underground churches and traveled with Buddhist pilgrims, and in this book he provides an overview of Chinese beliefs and practices.

Whitall N. Perry, *A Treasury of Traditional Wisdom*, 2000.
First published in 1971, this anthology imparts wisdom on faith, suffering, and mercy from the Tao Te Ching, Rumi, Shakespeare, Psalms, and other great writings.

Stephen Prothero, *Religious Literacy: What Every American Needs to Know—and Doesn't*, 2007.
According to religion professor Stephen Prothero, most Americans are uneducated on Christianity and other world religions. Misunderstandings can be tragic, so he argues for a return to religious education, which will help us face our domestic and foreign policy challenges more effectively.

Tomas Prower, *Queer Magic: LGBT+ Spirituality and Culture from Around the World*, 2018.
Tomas Prower presents both historical and current stories of LGBT people's practices and contributions to religions worldwide. In addition, he speaks to spiritual seekers in the queer community to help them find inspiration and fellowship.

201 Religious Mythology & Social Theology

Joseph Campbell, *The Hero with a Thousand Faces*, 1949.
In this introduction to comparative mythology, Joseph Campbell connects modern psychoanalytic thought with global myths.

Daniel Goleman, et al., *Measuring the Immeasurable: The Scientific Case for Spirituality*, 2008.
Until recently, scientists believed that only material factors that could be measured objectively were real. But recent credible scientific studies acknowledge how epigenetics, intention, prayer, and sound waves affect our health. The authors share how practices like meditation, yoga, and energy healing have profound effects on their practitioners.

Susan R. Holman, *Beholden: Religion, Global Health, and Human Rights*, 2016.
Susan Holman, with a background as scholar of both religion and the history of medicine, gives a unique perspective on improving global health. She contrasts the "merciful" approach based on charity with the "aid" approach based on human rights to determine which works best in helping the world's disadvantaged.

Sandra Ingerman and Hank Wesselman,
Awakening to the Spirit World:
The Shamanic Path of Direct Revelation, 2010.
Teachers Ingerman and Wesselman share shamanism's history and advise you on connecting with your spirit guides safely.

Dorling Kindersley Limited (DK), *The Mythology Book*, 2019.
This book, part of Dorling Kindersley's *Big Ideas* series, provides a collection of global myths. There are stories of the well-known gods and goddesses of ancient religions, such as ancient Egypt's Isis and Set, and also lesser-known figures from Oceania and the Caribbean.

Jonathan Sacks, *Not in God's Name:*
Confronting Religious Violence, 2015.
Rabbi Jonathan Sacks examines the history of religion's role in violence within the three Abrahamic faiths of Judaism, Christianity, and Islam. He quotes Abraham from sacred texts of all three to argue against using violence and politics in religious disputes.

202 Doctrines

Tim Crane, *The Meaning of Belief:*
Religion from an Atheist's Point of View, 2017.
Tim Crane explains religious beliefs to atheists to help them better understand believers. He points out that people have an innate sense of the transcendent and that belief serves as glue for social bonding and cohesion.

Patrick J. Hayes, ed.,
Miracles: An Encyclopedia of People, Places,
and Supernatural Events from Antiquity
to the Present, 2016.
This one-volume reference for high school students and general readers explores the occurrence of miraculous events worldwide. Rather than interpreting what happened, this encyclopedia gives the evidence, with respectful consideration of the religious belief involved, and then asks the readers to use critical thinking to draw their conclusions.

Wendell G. Johnson, ed., *End of Days:*
An Encyclopedia of the Apocalypse in World Religions, 2018.
This single-volume reference examines apocalyptic literature from major religions and more minor traditions like Native American belief systems and *The Tibetan Book of the Dead*. It also explores apocalyptic themes in modern literature, art, and film.

Karen Speerstra and Herbert Anderson,
The Divine Art of Dying:
How to Live Well While Dying, 2014.

> Speerstra and Anderson take stories from research on palliative and hospice care, world religions, literature, and movies to examine when the seriously ill make peace with imminent death.

203 Public Worship & Other Practices

Robin Mastro and Michael Mastro,
Altars of Power and Grace:
Create the Life You Desire, 2004.

> If you've ever wanted to create a personal altar, the authors show how to do it using Vastu Shastra, an ancient science from India. They demonstrate that the system enhances your environment and your life.

204 Religious Experience, Life, Practice

Mariana Caplan, *Eyes Wide Open:*
Cultivating Discernment on the Spiritual Path, 2010.

> Spiritual seekers in the West have an infinite number of teachers, paths, and practices to choose from. How do you separate the legitimately helpful from the fraudulent or harmful? Mariana Caplan studied the world's mystical traditions for decades, and she offers sound advice for those on the spiritual path.

Sharon Salzberg, *Real Happiness:*
The Power of Meditation:
A 28-Day Program, 2012.

> Renowned meditation teacher Sharon Salzberg shows you how to begin the practice of meditation to benefit your daily life. Salzberg treats it as a basic routine, like exercising or toothbrushing for the mind.

Sankara Saranam, *God Without Religion:*
Questioning Centuries of Accepted Truths, 2016.

> Sankara Saranam challenges you to find your truth by using sincerity and the ancient method of self-inquiry.

Celeste Yacoboni, ed., *How Do You Pray?*
Inspiring Responses from Religious Leaders,
Spiritual Guides, Healers, Activists,
and Other Lovers of Humanity, 2014.

> Celeste Yacoboni was directed in a vision to ask "How do you pray?" of the world. She then set out to follow the instructions. The responses she received will inspire you to dive into the question yourself.

205 Religious Ethics

Robert D. Lupton, *Toxic Charity: How Churches and Charities Hurt Those They Help (And How to Reverse It)*, 2011.
After revealing how modern charities unintentionally hurt those they mean to help, Robert D. Lupton provides new methods to accomplish real and lasting change.

208 Sources

Brian Arthur Brown, ed., *Three Testaments: Torah, Gospel, and Quran*, 2014.

Brian Arthur Brown, ed., *Four Testaments: Tao Te Ching, Analects, Dhammapada, Bhagavad Gita: Sacred Scriptures of Taoism, Confucianism, Buddhism, and Hinduism*, 2016.
In these two volumes, Brian Arthur Brown presents the sacred texts of the world's largest faiths. Expert commentary accompanies the entire text of each.

209 Sects & Reform Movements

William Wilberforce, *Real Christianity*, 1983.
William Wilberforce wrote "Amazing Grace," which is arguably the most famous Christian hymn of all time. His book, which helped abolish the slave trade in the United Kingdom, was first published in 1797. This version is a modern English paraphrase of the original.

210 Philosophy & Theory of Religion

211 Concepts of God

Reza Aslan, *God: A Human History*, 2017.
Religion scholar Reza Aslan traces the history of religion and our concepts of the divine. He asserts that we cannot help but make our images of God accessible by providing them with human attributes. Doing so helps us feel closer to God and affirms our best impulses. But the consequences can be dire when we also believe God reflects our worst traits. He suggests how we can use our ideas of God to develop a universal spirituality.

212 Existence of God, Knowability & Attributes of God

Karen Armstrong, *The Case for God*, 2009.
Karen Armstrong explores the ways concepts of God and religion have changed from ancient times to today. She looks at why most of us, religious or

not, came to view the idea of God as relatively insignificant. Then she charts how this shift has contributed to our polarization.

Edward Feser, *The Last Superstition: A Refutation of the New Atheism*, 2008.

According to "New Atheism" proponents, the centuries-long conflict between religion and science is over now, and science won. But philosopher Edward Feser refuses to wave a white flag for faith. Instead, he argues there was never a war at all. The disagreement, he says, is one of reason. And he contends that science, not religion, is on the defensive in that arena.

215 Science & Religion

Barbara Bradley Hagerty, *Fingerprints of God: What Science Is Learning About the Brain and Spiritual Experience*, 2009.

Barbara Bradley Hagerty investigates what science says about spiritual concepts such as prayer, meditation, and near-death experiences. She shares how she has come to her current beliefs after being raised as a Christian Scientist.

220 Bible

F. F. Bruce, *The Canon of Scripture*, 1988.

How did the current Protestant Christian Bible come to have the books it contains? Biblical scholar F. F. Bruce answers this and many other questions about the formation of the Protestant Bible.

David Noel Freedman, ed., *Eerdmans Dictionary of the Bible*, 2000.

This dictionary has over 5,000 articles about all aspects of the Christian scriptures written by Bible experts for students and general readers.

Paul Lawrence, *The IVP Atlas of Bible History*, 2006.

Paul Lawrence's atlas provides maps, illustrations, and reconstructions of the entire world of the Bible. While he discusses modern archaeological evidence, his primary aim is to help you see the world as those who lived in it did.

Eugene Peterson, *The Message: The Bible in Contemporary Language*, 2003.

Eugene Peterson, a respected pastor, scholar, and poet, presents the Bible in our modern idiom.

Robert L. Thomas, ed., *New American Standard Exhaustive Concordance of the Bible*, 1981.

This concordance contains Hebrew, Aramaic, and Greek dictionaries.

Mark Vroegop, *Dark Clouds, Deep Mercy:*
***Discovering the Grace of Lament*, 2019.**

Pastor and theologian Mark Vroegop looks at the biblical books of Psalms and Lamentations. He says by using these scriptures, Christians today can stop sweeping problems aside, covering them with a veneer of false and damaging positivity. Instead, they can deal with them honestly by confronting their pain and suffering.

221 Old Testament (Tanakh)

Tikva Frymer-Kensky,
Reading the Women of the Bible:
***A New Interpretation of Their Stories*, 2004.**

Tikva Frymer-Kensky examines the contemporary Jewish perspective on women's experiences in the patriarchy of the Hebrew Bible. From there, she considers the relevance of the Bible itself to modern life.

James L. Kugel, *How to Read the Bible:*
***A Guide to Scripture, Then and Now*, 2007.**

James L. Kugel performs a close reading of the Hebrew Bible, contrasting what it meant to the people who wrote it with modern scholarly interpretations.

222 Historical Books of the Old Testament

Joel Baden, *The Historical David:*
***The Real Life of an Invented Hero*, 2003.**

Many are familiar with the biblical King David, lover of God, composer of Psalms, and avenging warrior. Joel Baden reveals the David of the historical record.

David Hazony, *The Ten Commandments:*
How Our Most Ancient Moral Text Can
***Renew Modern Life*, 2010.**

Most Americans only vaguely understand what the ten commandments are. David Hazony reexamines them one by one, considering what they meant in the past and why they are still needed today.

James L. Kugel, *The Bible as It Was*, 1999.

James Kugel seeks to recover the original meaning of the Hebrew Bible. He contends that an anonymous group of interpreters changed the meaning of the stories included in the Old Testament before the time of Jesus and centuries before the rabbis of the Talmud. By going back to earlier sources, such as the Dead Sea Scrolls, Kugel asserts that these stories didn't initially mean what we now believe them to.

George Robinson, *Essential Torah:*
A Complete Guide to the Five Books of Moses, **2006.**
> George Robinson's reference contains theology and distilled commentary on
> the Torah from ancient times to the present.

223 Poetic Books of the Old Testament

Robert Alter, *The Wisdom Books:*
Job, Proverbs, and Ecclesiastes:
A Translation with Commentary, **2010.**
> This new translation of Job, Proverbs, and Ecclesiastes, by professor of
> Hebrew and comparative literature Robert Alter, is from the original Hebrew.
> He sought to restore the original's beauty and energy to the books.

224 Prophetic Books of Old Testament

Abraham J. Heschel, *The Prophets,* **2001.**
> Rabbi Abraham J. Heschel helps you understand ancient Israel's prophetic
> movement in this classic work, first published in 1962.

225 New Testament

Stephen J. Binz, *Saint Peter:*
Flawed, Forgiven, and Faithful, **2015.**
> Everything we know about the life of Saint Peter, the disciple most known for
> his faults and mistakes, is included in this biography by scholar Stephen J.
> Binz. Though Peter was flawed, he was the disciple upon whom Jesus charged
> the Church to be built.

F. F. Bruce, *Paul:*
Apostle of the Heart Set Free, **1979.**
> While primarily a biography of the apostle Paul, F. F. Bruce's book also dis-
> cusses Paul's letters and the main themes of his thought.

Bart D. Ehrman, *Peter, Paul, and Mary Magdalene:*
The Followers of Jesus in History and Legend, **2006.**
> In the years since the New Testament was written, many legends have sprung
> up about these three prominent followers of Jesus. Bart D. Ehrman examines
> the biblical accounts and compares them to outside sources to find the truth
> about these biblical figures.

Ben Witherington III, *New Testament History:*
A Narrative Account, **2002.**
> Biblical scholar Ben Witherington makes the world of Jesus accessible to
> modern readers.

Ann Wroe, *Pilate:*
***The Diary of an Invented Man*, 1999.**
Ann Wroe examines the historical record, biblical story, and legends that have grown up around the sparsely documented biblical figure of Pontius Pilate.

226 Gospels & Acts

Dietrich Bonhoeffer, *The Cost of Discipleship*, 1937.
Dietrich Bonhoeffer, a German Lutheran pastor and theologian, was put to death by the Nazis in 1945. In this book, he reflects on what being a follower of Christ means in modern times. He concludes that Christianity not only bestows grace but demands sacrifice and duty in return.

Sherri Brown and Francis J. Moloney,
Interpreting the Gospel and Letters of John:
***An Introduction*, 2017.**
This introduction to Johannine literature for beginning bible students begins with a survey of Christianity and how it arose from Judaism. Brown and Moloney also provide maps and further reading lists.

Susan Gubar, *Judas:*
***A Biography*, 2009.**
Susan Gubar's biography of Judas Iscariot provides an unflinching study of Christian anti-Semitism.

Jane Lahr, *Searching for Mary Magdalene:*
***A Journey through Art and Literature*, 2006.**
Jane Lahr begins with the biblical account of Mary Magdalene. Then she examines the Gnostic texts on through the art and literary works that have depicted Mary Magdalene for the past two millennia. This book provides an overview of this mysterious figure throughout time and culture.

Gehard Lohfink, *The Our Father:*
***A New Reading*, 2018.**
In light of current concerns about inclusiveness and plain language, can the Our Father or the Lord's Prayer still be relevant in the 21st century? Gehard Lohfink argues that it's both relevant and crucial. He digs beneath the familiar words to uncover what Jesus meant by them and how they speak to us throughout all time.

227 Epistles

Karl Barth, *The Epistle to the Romans*, 1918.
One of the most important 20th-century theologians, Karl Barth, rejected the liberal Protestantism he was trained in, focusing instead on the meaning of

the scriptures and the paradoxes contained within them. Here he turns his attention to the book of Romans.

Stephen J. Chester, *Reading Paul with the Reformers: Reconciling Old and New Perspectives*, 2017.

Stephen J. Chester applies a scholarly examination to Reformation interpretations of the epistles of Saint Paul, helping us unearth what they had to say. He finds reasons to support arguments made by Luther and Calvin.

228 Revelation (Apocalypse)

Elaine Pagels, *Revelations: Visions, Prophecy, and Politics in the Book of Revelation*, 2012.

Elaine Pagels looks at the historical context of Revelation. She sees the book as an indictment against Rome in light of "the Jewish War" of 66 CE. After this period, Christians discovered and began using the apocalyptic text as a weapon against heresy and infidels.

229 Apocrypha & Pseudepigrapha

Bruce Manning Metzger, *A Concordance to the Apocrypha/Deuterocanonical Books of the Revised Standard Version: Derived from the Bible Data Bank of the Centre Informatique et Bible*, 1983.

Bruce M. Metzger, one of the 20th century's most influential New Testament scholars, compiled this reference.

230 Christianity

Rita Nakashima Brock and Rebecca Ann Parker, *Saving Paradise: How Christianity Traded Love of This World for Crucifixion and Empire*, 2008.

The authors searched the Mediterranean region for early art depicting Jesus either dead or on the cross. They found none. Instead, a thousand years after his death, they found the first images of a dead or dying Christ. They conclude that the original understanding of Jesus was that he was still alive. Next, they trace how he moved from life to death.

Gustavo Gutiérrez, *A Theology of Liberation: History, Politics, and Salvation*, 1971.

Peruvian theologian and Dominican priest Gustavo Gutiérrez published this explosive book to proclaim the gospel of the poor and the marginalized over those who use Christian scripture to perpetuate the status quo. It was a theology of social reform that, while criticized for combining politics with religion, was intended to fulfill the gospel's message.

Roger E. Olson, *The Story of Christian Theology: Twenty Centuries of Tradition Reform*, 2000.

Theologian Roger E. Olson covers the entire history of Christian theology in narrative format, starting with the early days of the Church up through the reforms and splits of 20th-century churches. His work is helpful to anyone who wants to understand the Christian faith and its landscape.

Dorothy L. Sayers, *The Mind of the Maker*, 1941.

British mystery author, translator, and Christian humanist Dorothy L. Sayers explored the fundamental tenets of Christianity and how it related to art. She drew parallels between artistic creativity and the creation of God.

Paul Tillich, *My Search for Absolutes*, 1967.

Top 20th-century theologian Paul Tillich explained how his Christian existentialist philosophy resulted from his earnest search for truth.

BIOGRAPHY

Ursula King, *Spirit of Fire: The Life and Vision of Pierre Teilhard de Chardin*, 1998.

In this biography, Ursula King recounts the life of the influential Jesuit theologian, mystic, and scientist Pierre Teilhard de Chardin. His work in paleontology, suppressed until after his death in 1955, infused his spirituality with an understanding of spiritual evolution.

231 God

Thomas E. Hosinski, *The Image of the Unseen God: Catholicity, Science, and Our Evolving Understanding of God*, 2018.

Thomas E. Hosinski argues that contemporary physics, cosmology, and biology are compatible with a Catholic understanding of Jesus's life and teachings.

Robert Letham, *The Holy Trinity: In Scripture, History, Theology, and Worship*, 2005.

Using the Bible as the basis for his examination of the Trinity, Robert Letham traces the historic understanding of the doctrine and critical issues such as the incarnation of the trinity in humankind through Jesus.

Anne and Jeffrey Rowthorn, *God's Good Earth: Praise and Prayers for Creation*, 2019.

The Rowthorns provide 52 prayer services to help Catholics appreciate and care for the Earth as God's creation.

**Karen Speerstra, *Sophia: The Feminine Face of God:
Nine Paths to Healing and Abundance*, 2011.**
The Divine Feminine has been called the Great Mother and the Holy Spirit.
Karen Speerstra presents its many names, including Sophia, in history, folk-
lore, and fairytales while reflecting on what they have to teach us.

**Edward F. Sylvia, *Proving God: Swedenborg's Remarkable
Quest for the Quantum Fingerprints of Love*, 2010.**
In this book based on the writing of 17th-century scientist and mystic
Emmanuel Swedenborg, Edward F. Sylvia says that scientists and theologians
have the big picture equally wrong. He predicts that humanity is in for a
massive paradigm shift. According to Swedenborg, God is going to make "all
things new."

232 Jesus Christ & His Family

**Edward J. Blum, *The Color of Christ:
The Son of God and the Saga of Race in America*, 2012.**
White supremacists and Native American exploiters have used the image of
Christ to further racist agendas. Edward J. Blum researches the ways Christ
has been misused in America from the earliest days to the present.

BIOGRAPHY

**Reza Aslan, *Zealot:
The Life and Times of Jesus of Nazareth*, 2013.**
Using both the gospels and historical sources, Reza Aslan presents a portrait
of Jesus as a radical preacher seeking political revolution.

233 Humankind

**Peter Enns, *The Evolution of Adam: What the Bible Does and
Doesn't Say About Human Origins*, 2012.**
Biblical studies professor Peter Enns aids Christians who accept evolution but
struggle with reconciling that belief with the biblical account of creation. He
finds no conflict between Christian faith and evolution with a proper understanding of the biblical text.

**Stephen Greenblatt, *The Rise and Fall of Adam and Eve:
The Story That Created Us*, 2017.**
American literary critic Stephen Greenblatt explores the story of Adam and
Eve from the biblical account and to the present to see how the interpretations
of the story have changed in literature and art over the ages.

J. Alasdair Groves and Winston T. Smith,
***Untangling Emotions*, 2019.**

If you feel guilty for your negative emotions, Christian counselors Groves and
Smith offer help. Using the Bible as a guide, they suggest practical ways to
deal with all your feelings while using them to draw nearer to God.

Kelly M. Kapic, *Embodied Hope:*
***A Theological Meditation on Pain and Suffering*, 2018.**

While Kelly M. Kapic's book delves deeply into pain and suffering, his exploration provides a nuanced view that doesn't wholly absolve God.

Tara M. Owens, *Embracing the Body:*
***Finding God in Our Flesh and Bone*, 2015.**

Tara M. Owens asserts that our spirituality and physical bodies are intertwined. Our bodies, she says, are the tools God uses to communicate with us.
She offers exercises for reflection to help you see your body as a temple for
the divine.

234 Salvation & Grace

Max Lucado, *Grace: More than We Deserve,*
***Greater than We Imagine*, 2012.**

Pastor Max Lucado says God's grace is not a tool to be used by us. Instead, it is
a force used by God to bring us into intimate contact with divinity.

Bob Schuchts, *Be Transformed:*
***The Healing Power of the Sacraments*, 2017.**

The seven sacraments are not just rituals used by the Catholic Church to
keep the faithful in line. Instead, therapist Bob Schuchts shows how they
are designed to be a radical connection to Christ that heals our wounds and
makes us whole.

235 Spiritual Beings

Gustave Davidson, *A Dictionary of Angels:*
***Including Fallen Angels*, 1967.**

Gustave Davidson spent 16 years researching sacred texts and other literature
to provide this illustrated reference work.

Susan R. Garrett, *No Ordinary Angel:*
***Celestial Spirits and Christian Claims about Jesus*, 2008.**

New Testament scholar Susan R. Garrett wrote this exploration of angelology
after examining ancient accounts and modern encounters.

James Martin, *My Life with the Saints*, 2006.
James Martin's memoir relates his religious and secular experiences. He reveals how the saints of the Catholic Church kept him company along the way.

236 Eschatology

**Billy Graham, *Approaching Hoofbeats:
The Four Horsemen of the Apocalypse*, 1983.**
America's most famous 20th-century evangelist, Billy Graham, examines the problems of late-20th century society in light of the biblical account of the end times in Revelation.

**Jürgen Moltmann, *The Coming of God:
Christian Eschatology*, 2000.**
Internationally respected theologian Jürgen Moltmann shares his interpretation of Revelation as a blueprint for making all things new.

239 Apologetics & Polemics

**Gregory Koukl, *The Story of Reality:
How the World Began, How It Ends, and Everything
Important That Happens in Between*, 2017.**
Gregory Koukl does not see the Christian religion as one interpretation of reality. Instead, he sees Christianity as truth writ large in every arena.

**Rebecca McLaughlin, *Confronting Christianity:
12 Hard Questions for the World's
Largest Religion*, 2019.**
Rebecca McLaughlin delves into 12 areas that serve as stumbling blocks to belief for non-Christians, like the existence of heaven and hell. Then, using sociology, science, and psychology research, she demonstrates how these biblical principles align with current secular understandings.

240 Christian Moral & Devotional Theology

**Oswald Chambers, *Oswald Chambers—
The Best from All His Books*, 1987.**
Oswald Chambers's writings, including the devotional classic,
My Utmost for His Highest, have inspired Christians for over a century. The two-volume set contains excerpts from his works for inspirational reading. .

241 Christian Ethics

Tomáš Halík, *I Want You to Be: On the God of Love*, 2016.
Czech theologian and Catholic priest Tomáš Halík argues Christians should engage with nonbelievers through service. Their love for God, he says, must be expressed actively.

Anne Lamott, *Hallelujah Anyway:*
Rediscovering Mercy, 2017.
Anne Lamott writes of the mercy that is at the heart of the Christian faith. She points out the ways we've experienced it and why we should pass it on.

C. S. Lewis, *The Four Loves*, 1960.
Beloved Christian apologist C. S. Lewis writes of the four faces of love— affection, friendship, erotic love, and the love of God.

Latasha Morrison, *Be the Bridge:*
Pursuing God's Heart for Racial Reconciliation, 2019.
Racism is still a problem within America's mostly racially divided churches. Latasha Morrison explains why Christians should be leading the way toward racial reconciliation. She provides discussions for believers and actions to help them become catalysts for change.

Joyce Rupp, *Boundless Compassion:*
Creating a Way of Life, 2018.
Joyce Rupp examines compassion from the perspectives of medicine, science, theology, sociology, and psychology. She then offers a six-week program for people to develop and share their empathy.

242 Devotional Literature

Oswald Chambers, *My Utmost for His Highest*, 1926.
Oswald Chambers provides daily devotions in brief scripture readings with his insights into their meaning and message.

Kathy Coffey, *Dancing in the Margins: Meditations for People*
Who Struggle with Their Churches, 1999.
The reasons people become unhappy with their churches vary from theological differences to personality disagreements. Kathy Coffey looks at relevant biblical passages and offers questions to help reflect and find solutions.

Madeleine L'Engle, *Penguins and Golden Calves:*
Icons and Idols in Antarctica and Other Unexpected
Places, 1996.
Best known for young adult novels such as *A Wrinkle in Time*, Madeleine

L'Engle lived an extraordinary life. For example, at age 74, she took a rafting trip to Antarctica. A devout Christian who was greatly influenced by science, L'Engle reflects on her life and how anything can become a window to the divine.

C. S. Lewis, *A Grief Observed*, 1961.
When C. S. Lewis, the author of *The Chronicles of Narnia* and *Mere Christianity,* lost his wife, Joy Davidman, he explored his pain in his writing. While Lewis didn't hide his anger, sorrow, or distress, he kept his faith. His exploration will comfort many grappling with loss.

246 Use of Art in Christianity

Heather Child, *Christian Symbols Ancient and Modern: A Handbook for Students*, 1973.
While exploring early Christian symbols in art, Heather Child considers how theologians have used these symbols through the ages to spread the faith and shape doctrine.

248 Christian Experience, Practice, Life

Gary Caster, *Prayer Everywhere: The Spiritual Life Made Simple*, 2018.
Father Gary Caster clears up confusion Catholics may have about prayer. He stresses that prayer is not as much an activity as a way of life.

Henry Cloud and John Townsend, *Boundaries: When to Say Yes, and When to Say No to Take Control of Your Life*, 1992.
Christians sometimes focus so much on helping others that they ignore their personal limitations and needs. Cloud and Townsend answer questions about when it is okay to set limits with others.

Richard J. Foster, *Celebration of Discipline: The Path to Spiritual Growth*, 1978.
Richard Foster writes about the spiritual practices of the Christian faith. He proclaims that meditation, fasting, prayer, and study are the cornerstones of spiritual growth.

Pope Francis, *Sharing the Wisdom of Time*, 2018.
Pope Francis shares the wisdom and experience of grandparents and elders the world over to offer hope. The stories will inspire you to believe in the power of love and resilience.

David Jeremiah, *My Heart's Desire:*
***Living Every Moment in the Wonder of Worship*, 2003.**
Pastor David Jeremiah explores how to use everyday life as a springboard for continuous worship.

Nabeel Qureshi, *Seeking Allah, Finding Jesus:*
***A Devout Muslim Encounters Christianity*, 2014.**
Nabeel Qureshi shares his story of how he went from a devout Muslim with a loving family to be a Christian, almost against his will. Since converting, he dedicates his life to spreading Christianity.

249 Christian Observances in Family Life

Renee Robinson, *Seeking Christmas:*
***Finding the True Meaning Through Family Traditions*, 2013.**
Renee Robinson aims to help Christian families turn the focus of Christmas from a commercial and social whirlwind to a time of reflection and meaning. She provides devotions and activities to help.

250 Local Christian Church & Religious Orders

251 Preaching (Homiletics)

John R. W. Stott, *Between Two Worlds:*
***The Art of Preaching in the 20th Century*, 1982.**
To John R. W. Stott, a vast gap separates the modern world from the biblical. He explains how they come together through preaching God's word.

252 Texts of Sermons

Martin Luther King Jr., *Strength to Love*, 1963.
Civil rights leader Martin Luther King Jr. tackles the problems of contemporary society in this collection of sermons.

253 Pastoral Work (Pastoral Theology)

Skye Jethani, *Immeasurable: Reflections of the Soul of*
***Ministry in the Age of Church, Inc.*, 2017.**
Ministers and pastors have fallen from the high esteem they once held in American culture. Many now treat their career as a business or as entertainment. Skye Jethani encourages church leaders to examine the roles they play and to consider new measures of success.

Henri J. M. Nouwen, *The Wounded Healer: Ministry in Contemporary Society*, 1979.

Henri J. M. Nouwen, a Catholic priest, believed that the service of ministry requires a dive into suffering. He reminded priests and pastors that they can only help alleviate the sufferings of others through confronting their own.

Harold L. Senkbeil, *The Care of Souls: Cultivating a Pastor's Heart*, 2019.

After more than 50 years' service as a parish pastor, Harold L. Senkbeil provides a collection of encouragement and wisdom for those still working in the field. He reminds them why they began the work, its purpose, and how to serve as an example for their parishioners.

255 Religious Congregations & Orders

Kathleen Norris, *The Cloister Walk*, 1997.

Protestant author Kathleen Norris spent extended time living in Benedictine monasteries in Minnesota. She shares how, rather than becoming alienated or bored with the routine of liturgy and ritual, she found profound meaning and nourishment in them.

259 Pastoral Care of Families & Kinds of Persons

Jerry Aaker, *A Spirituality of Service: Reflections on a Life-Long Journey of Faith and Work Among the World's Poor*, 2012.

Jerry Aaker has spent his life in the service of the world's poor. In this book, he reflects on his experiences and the scriptures that motivated them.

Susan H. Swetnam, *In the Mystery's Shadow: Reflections on Caring for the Elderly and Dying*, 2019.

Many of us find ourselves caring for the elderly or dying at some point in our lives. Susan H. Swetnam has cared for thousands of them throughout her career. She shares stories to help you appreciate the sacredness of this service.

260 Christian Social & Ecclesiastical Theology

261 Social Theology & Interreligious Relations

James Carroll, *Constantine's Sword: The Church and the Jews, A History*, 2001.

James Carroll examines the history of the Church's treatment of Jews since the time of Christ. He says Western culture's failure to deal with these problems is an indictment against the culture.

Michael D'Antonio, *Mortal Sins: Sex, Crime, and the Era of Catholic Scandal*, 2013.

Pulitzer Prize–winning author Michael D'Antonio tells the history of the decades-long scandal of sexually abusive Catholic priests in America. Despite warnings, the Church ignored or covered up thousands of instances of child abuse at the hands of priests. When the story became public, it set off a historic battle that was global in scale and devastating to the Church.

John Fea, *Was America Founded as a Christian Nation?: A Historical Introduction*, 2011.

Historian John Fea presents a balanced view of the debate surrounding the founding fathers' intentions regarding religion in America. He points out the strengths and weaknesses of both sides.

Terry Glaspey, *75 Masterpieces Every Christian Should Know: The Fascinating Stories Behind Great Works of Art, Literature, Music and Film*, 2015.

Terry Glaspey looks at art, music, and literature for outstanding examples of Christian-inspired art. He provides the stories behind each example to help you gain a greater appreciation of them.

Philip Gulley, *If the Church Were Christian: Rediscovering the Values of Jesus*, 2010.

Quaker pastor Philip Gulley offers wisdom to a Church that seems to have lost its way.

Jake Meador, *In Search of the Common Good: Christian Fidelity in a Fractured World*, 2019.

Jake Meador doesn't argue that society seems to be unraveling. Instead, he explores the historical ideologies that led to this point and offers a new viewpoint to help us find our way. He says returning to an older view of social relationships based on our spiritual kinship instead of our economy and politics is critical.

262 Ecclesiology

Walter M. Abbott, ed., *The Documents of Vatican II: With Notes and Index*, 1965.

The Second Vatican Council is crucial to understanding the widespread changes in Catholic practice in its wake. The changes were made to increase the Church's relevance in the modern world. This volume contains all the documents.

Ormond Rush, *The Vision of Vatican II: Its Fundamental Principles*, 2019.

Over 50 years ago, the literature produced by the council of Vatican II contained 16 documents that laid out the new vision for the Catholic Church. Ormond Rush supplies 24 principles to capture its aims.

264 Public Worship

Glenn Byer, *26 Ordinary Ways to Live the Liturgy*, 2018.

Glenn Byer's practical advice for practicing liturgy can lead to deeper faith.

Jonathan A. Stapley, *The Power of Godliness: Mormon Liturgy and Cosmology*, 2018.

Jonathan A. Stapley looks at the rituals and practices of Mormon worship and what they say about the Church of Jesus Christ of Latter-day Saints.

266 Missions

Craig Harline, *Way Below the Angels: The Pretty Clearly Troubled But Not Even Close to Tragic Confessions of a Real Live Mormon Missionary*, 2014.

Mormon youth typically spend two years doing missions work. Craig Harline relates his personal experiences—the good, the bad, and the funny. It's an honest look at the modern missionary experience.

Kathryn Long, *God in the Rainforest: A Tale of Martyrdom and Redemption in Amazonian Ecuador*, 2019.

History professor Kathryn Long tells the story of five evangelical missionaries killed by the Waorani people in the Ecuadorian Amazon. Two women, the widow of one missionary and the sister of another, later established relations with the tribe. These events were used as an example for American evangelical missionaries, while anthropologists decried them throughout the late 20th century. Long examines the story to see what it reveals from all sides.

268 Religious Education

Nick Wagner, *Field Hospital Catechesis: The Core Content for RCIA Formation*, 2019.

Nick Wagner declares the Church is a "field hospital," sent to heal the world's wounded. To accomplish its mission, it must do two things. First, he says, it must proclaim the saving power of Jesus Christ. Next, it must help the injured develop their faith.

269 Spiritual Renewal

Jim Cymbala, *Fresh Wind, Fresh Fire: What Happens When God's Spirit Invades the Heart of His People*, 1997.
For a quarter of a century, pastor Jim Cymbala of The Brooklyn Tabernacle built his church from its humble beginnings to one with a huge active membership. He shares how it happened in this book.

BIOGRAPHY

Billy Graham, *Just As I Am: The Autobiography of Billy Graham*, 1999.
After he turned his ministry over to his son Franklin, evangelist Graham wrote about his life in this autobiography. Graham's influence on evangelical Christianity, and even on world leaders, including U.S. presidents, cannot be overstated.

270 History, Geographic Treatment, Biography

Donald Attwater, *The Penguin Dictionary of Saints*, 1965.
This highly praised dictionary is in its 1995 third revision.

Willie James Jennings, *The Christian Imagination: Theology and the Origins of Race*, 2010.
Racially integrated Christian churches, where the congregants represent the demographics of the broader community, are rare. Willie Jennings explains why by using historical accounts of missed opportunities for unity. He also considers how the Christian faith was used as a tool to take land from, enslave, and marginalize people of differing races and ethnicities.

Diarmaid MacCulloch, *Christianity: The First Three Thousand Years*, 2010.
The son of an Anglican minister, Diarmaid MacCulloch covers the history of Christianity from its Jewish roots to today. He also discusses the effect the religion has had on historical events and intellectual thought.

Christine Schenk, *Crispina and Her Sisters: Women and Authority in Early Christianity*, 2017.
The New Testament speaks of a few influential women, such as Priscilla, but catacomb and tomb art from the earliest Christian communities indicate

there were many others. Christine Schenk presents these neglected women of
Church history.

271 Religious Orders in Church History

Amy L. Koehlinger, *The New Nuns: Racial Justice and Religious Reform in the 1960s*, 2007.
In the 1960s, a shift took place among the American women serving as
Catholic nuns. In particular, they expanded their role to serve non-Catholics,
particularly in African American communities. Koehlinger looks at their
struggles and triumphs and examines how their changing roles affected the
Church regarding race and gender.

Régine Pernoud, *The Templars: Knights of Christ*, 2009.
Medieval historian Régine Pernoud seeks to set the record straight on the
Knights Templar and return them to their rightful place as defenders of the
faith. She says portrayals of them as mercenary and greedy are inaccurate.

BIOGRAPHY

Michael Mott, *The Seven Mountains of Thomas Merton*, 1984.
After studying at Columbia University, one of the most important Catholic
writers of the 20th century, French-born Thomas Merton, became a Trappist
monk in a Kentucky monastery. While there, he wrote 40 books that promoted civil rights and social activism and explored Eastern religions such as
Zen Buddhism. Michael Mott writes Merton's authorized biography.

272 Persecutions in General Church History

Andreas Knapp, *The Last Christians: Stories of Persecution, Flight, and Resilience in the Middle East*, 2018.
Andreas Knapp, a Catholic priest who works with refugees in Germany,
relates the plight of the Christian communities in the Middle East. He tells
stories of people hunted down and persecuted by the Islamic State and
otherwise mistreated for their nationality. Since they are the last surviving
remnants of Christians still speaking the language of Jesus, if they are wiped
out or spread around the globe, their culture and language, our only surviving
link to Christ, will likely be lost.

273 Doctrinal Controversies & Heresies

Elaine Pagels, *The Gnostic Gospels*, 1979.
In 1945, 13 papyrus manuscripts were found that dated to shortly after the
death of Jesus Christ. They offered alternative gospels to the four found
in today's New Testament. Theological scholar Elaine Pagels provides an

accessible exploration of these gospels, what they meant for the people of their time, and what they can tell us today.

275 Christianity in Asia

Liao Yiwu, *God is Red: The Secret Story of How Christianity Survived and Flourished in Communist China*, 2011.

Raised as a communist in China and taught that religion is evil, journalist Liao Yiwu was surprised to discover a community of Christians living in China. He began to document their stories and tells how they survived amid oppression.

277 History of Christianity in North America

James H. Cone, *The Cross and the Lynching Tree*, 2018.

Around 5,000 African Americans were lynched in the years after the Civil War. James H. Cone looks at the cases of lynching and compares them to the image in Acts 10:39, saying that they hung Jesus upon a tree. These two images, the cross and the lynching tree, are potent symbols for Black Americans. He examines them in terms of Christian theology and the Black experience.

Ben Daniel, *Neighbor: Christian Encounters with "Illegal" Immigration*, 2010.

Presbyterian minister Ben Daniel looks at issues of undocumented migration to the U.S. He explores the immigration debate through spiritual, geographical, and legal perspectives and concludes that Christians should meet these migrants as fellow humans and as neighbors.

Frances FitzGerald, *The Evangelicals: The Struggle to Shape America*, 2017.

The evangelical movement began in a period of American history referred to as the Great Awakening. It was a populist rebellion against the mainline churches. Pulitzer Prize-winning author Frances FitzGerald looks at the evangelicals from their beginnings through today and explores how they have shaped the nation's politics.

Robert P. Jones, *White Too Long: The Legacy of White Supremacy in American Christianity*, 2020.

Is it possible to be a racist Christian? On its face, the answer is a simple no. But Robert P. Jones has researched current attitudes and finds that White supremacy is endemic in many, if not most, White Christian churches today. Moreover, in the South, in mainline Protestant churches, in the Midwest, and among Catholics in the Northeast, he finds all have racist attitudes. So, instead of calling for good works to make up for past mistakes, Jones calls for a profound psychological reckoning with the truth.

George M. Marsden,
Fundamentalism and American Culture, 2006.

Jerry Falwell said, "A fundamentalist is an evangelical who is angry about something." The movement itself was born from a protest against the more liberal branches of Protestantism that incorporated scientific discoveries and cultural changes into their beliefs. However, the division ultimately comes down to biblical inerrancy. Here George M. Marsden looks at the rise of Christian fundamentalist political power and its role in our nation's polarization.

Barbara Dianne Savage, *Your Spirits Walk Beside Us:*
The Politics of Black Religion, 2012.

Barbara Dianne Savage examines the diversity in Black church–driven politics in America. She finds that Black religious belief, often assumed to be largely progressive, is much more diverse.

Erin Wathen, *Resist and Persist:*
Faith and the Fight for Equality, 2019.

Have women in today's America achieved equality? Erin Wathen explains why they haven't. Society pressures women to be all and do all, but they are undermined in many ways economically and politically. And religious institutions contribute as well. Patriarchy has never gone away, and Wathen calls for the Church to step up and defend women from unhealthy attitudes and rhetoric.

280 Christian Denominations & Sects

282 Roman Catholic Church

Saad Sirop Hanna, *Abducted in Iraq:*
A Priest in Baghdad, 2018.

In 2006, Bishop Saad Sirop Hanna was abducted by al-Qaeda militants while serving as a visiting lecturer at Babel College, near Baghdad. Here he details the abusive treatment he received. He then looks at the plight of Iraqi Christians, one of the oldest existing Christian communities globally, and reveals how they are currently persecuted.

David I. Kertzer, *The Pope Who Would Be King: The Exile of*
Pius IX and the Emergence of Modern Europe, 2018.

Pope Pius IX led the Church from 1846 to 1878, giving him the longest papal reign in history. While starting as a liberal wishing to keep his citizens happy, he found the changes they demanded were more than he could concede. During his reign, the papacy lost its political rule and modern Europe began.

Timothy Matovina, *Theologies of Guadalupe:*
From the Era of Conquest to Pope Francis, 2018.

In 1531, just outside Mexico City, the Virgin Mary, also known as the Virgin of Guadalupe, appeared four times to Juan Diego. Since then, Our Lady of Guadalupe has been the Patroness of Mexico and has inspired a tradition of worship throughout Latin America. Timothy Matovina traces the history of the tradition from its beginnings through today.

Brandon Vogt, *Why I Am Catholic (and You Should Be Too)*, 2017.

Creator of the website StrangeNotions.com, where atheists and Catholics converse, Brandon Vogt, once an atheist, shares his spiritual journey. In addition, he makes his case for why Catholicism is still relevant today.

BIOGRAPHY

Dorothy Day, *The Long Loneliness: The Autobiography of the Legendary Catholic Social Activist*, 1952.

Social activist Dorothy Day began as a bohemian in 1920s Greenwich Village and went on to found the Catholic Worker Movement. After her conversion to Catholicism, Day became a pacifist and a women's suffrage and worker rights activist.

Joshua J. McElwee and Cindy Wooden, eds., *A Pope Francis Lexicon: Essays by Over 50 Noted Bishops, Theologians & Journalists*, 2019.

Prominent Catholic figures write short essays paying tribute to Pope Francis for his impact on the world. They define his influence under headings from "Joy" to "Tears."

283 Anglican Churches

Barbara Brown Taylor, *An Altar in the World: A Geography of Faith*, 2009.

Barbara Brown Taylor tells how her decision to leave the church where she served as a minister to become a professor led to her encountering God outside the church. She helps us see how we, too, can discover God everywhere and every day of our lives.

284 Protestants of Continental Origin

BIOGRAPHY

Roland H. Bainton, *Here I Stand: A Life of Martin Luther*, 1950.

The Protestant Reformation began when Martin Luther spoke out against corrupt church practices. His actions have remade the entire Western world. Roland H. Bainton's biographical narration of Luther's life is relevant today.

Eric Metaxas, *Bonhoeffer: Pastor, Martyr, Prophet, Spy*, 2011.
German pastor Dietrich Bonhoeffer left America in 1939 to go back to
Germany to fight against Hitler and the Nazis. He went undercover in
Operation 7, working to smuggle Jews into Switzerland. He also participated
in the Valkyrie plot to assassinate Hitler, for which he was caught, sent to a
concentration camp, and later hanged.

285 Presbyterian, Reformed & Congregational

BIOGRAPHY

**Debby Applegate, *The Most Famous Man in America:
The Biography of Henry Ward Beecher*, 2007.**
Henry Ward Beecher, son of a Puritan minister and brother to novelist
Harriet Beecher Stowe, was one of the 19th century's most charismatic
preachers. Instead of his father's emphasis on Old Testament wrath, he
preached of God's love and healing. Everything went well for him until he was
accused of an affair with one of his parishioners. Debby Applegate provides
new evidence to shed light on Beecher's life and the contemporary American
religious and political scene.

George M. Marsden, *Jonathan Edwards: A Life*, 2003.
George Marsden introduces Jonathan Edwards as a brilliant pastor who
worked hard to combine his Puritan upbringing with the new ideas of the
Enlightenment. In many ways, the issues Edwards grappled with are still part
of our public discourse.

286 Baptist, Restoration & Adventist

BIOGRAPHY

Charles Colson, *Life Sentence*, 1979.
Charles "Chuck" Colson, famous for his role as Richard M. Nixon's hatchet
man, went to prison in the Watergate scandal. While there in 1973, he converted to Christianity and began a crusade for prison reform, forming the
Prison Fellowship Ministries after his release in 1976. In this book, Colson
tells how he worked to start his new life after prison.

287 Methodist & Related Churches

**Richard S. Newman, *Freedom's Prophet:
Bishop Richard Allen, the AME Church, and the Black
Founding Fathers*, 2008.**
History professor Richard S. Newman recounts the story of Richard Allen.
Born enslaved in colonial Philadelphia, Allen received his freedom after
the Revolutionary War, becoming a reformer, activist, and minister. He

cofounded the African Methodist Episcopal Church, authored the first pamphlet written by an African American, and convened the first national convention of Black reformers. He was also the first Black American to visit the White House.

289 Other Denominations & Sects

Fred W. Brown and Jeanne McDonald, *The Serpent Handlers: Three Families and Their Faith*, 2000.

They risked their lives to prove their faith, and the snake handlers of Appalachia spoke with Fred W. Brown about their traditions, beliefs, and doctrines.

Miles Harvey, *The King of Confidence: A Tale of Utopian Dreamers, Frontier Schemers, True Believers, False Prophets, and the Murder of an American Monarch*, 2020.

The confidence man is nothing new. Miles Harvey details the largely forgotten story of one of America's most notorious. James Strang was a lawyer and an atheist who disappeared from rural New York in 1843. Turning up among the frontier Latter-day Saints, Strang claimed to be a convert and led hundreds of fellow worshippers to an island in Lake Michigan, where he declared himself a divine king. By the time he was assassinated, he had established a pirate colony where he lived a life of polygamy, theft, and corruption.

Donald B. Kraybill, Steven M. Nolt, and David L. Weaver-Zercher, *Amish Grace: How Forgiveness Transcended Tragedy*, 2007.

On October 2, 2006, Charles Roberts entered a one-room Amish school in Nickel Mines, Pennsylvania, and shot ten girls he held hostage there before killing himself. The families of the slaughtered children quickly offered their forgiveness to the killer. Not only did they forgive, but they also attended Roberts's funeral and supported a fund for his family. This exploration into Amish religious beliefs reveals what allowed such an astounding response.

BIOGRAPHY

Leonard J. Arrington, *Brigham Young: American Moses*, 1985.

Leonard J. Arrington, Church of Latter-day Saints historian, portrays Brigham Young, one of the Church's founders, in this biography.

Dan Vogel, *Joseph Smith: The Making of a Prophet*, 2004.

After 25 years of researching Joseph Smith, Dan Vogel presents a respectful biography covering almost every day in the prophet's life. After a troubled beginning, Smith found comfort in religion.

290 Other Religions

291 [Unassigned]

Joseph Campbell, *The Power of Myth*, 1988.

Joseph Campbell, scholar of comparative mythology, is interviewed by journalist Bill Moyers. Campbell explains that all myths and epics spring from the collective unconscious we all share. Mythology and folk stories embody spiritual, social, and ultimate realities, and they all have common elements that teach us about life.

Stephen L. Carter, *The Culture of Disbelief: How American Law and Politics Trivialize Religious Devotion*, 1993.

Yale Law professor Stephen L. Carter uses liberal arguments to reach a conservative conclusion about religion and politics. First, he outlines our nation's history of religious influence to achieve liberal values such as the antislavery movement and the Vietnam antiwar protests. Without the intervention of the nation's religious groups, these ends would have been harder to achieve. Finally, he reminds us that we do well to nurture and honor our religious communities because they strengthen our democracy.

James George Frazer, *The Golden Bough: a Study in Magic and Religion*, 1925.

First published in 1890, *The Golden Bough* is an international classic on religious studies. James George Frazer, Scottish social anthropologist, was one of the earliest scholars of comparative religion. He gives fascinating insight into the superstitions and practices of early humans. In addition, he viewed humanity's evolution as a progression from primitive magic, through religious belief, to the science that was taking precedence in his own time.

Pierre Grimal, ed., *Larousse World Mythology*, 1965.

This one-volume reference source looks at the essential stories from mythologies worldwide.

William James, *The Varieties of Religious Experience: A Study in Human Nature*, 1901.

American philosopher, psychologist, and physician William James wrote this paradigm-changing view of religious experience at the dawn of the 20th century. Rather than focus on the dogma and tenets of churches and religious faiths, he explored spiritual experiences in people's everyday lives. In this book, James called for respect for individual experience and tolerance of all religions.

Huston Smith, *The Illustrated World's Religions: A Guide to Our Wisdom Traditions*, 1958.

Huston Smith was one of the 20th century's most influential teachers of world religions. This volume revised Smith's earlier classic, *The Religions of Man*, and provides a readable explanation of all the contemporary religious traditions.

292 Classical Religion (Greek & Roman Religion)

Pierre Grimal,
Dictionary of Classical Mythology, 1951.
This dictionary gives concise definitions of allusions to mythological persons, places, and things. In 1992 it was republished as *The Penguin Dictionary of Classical Mythology*.

Edith Hamilton, *Mythology:*
Timeless Tales of Gods and Heroes, 1942.
Educator and historian Edith Hamilton retells the ancient myths of the Greek, Roman, and Norse pantheon. Familiarity with the stories gives students and general readers an understanding of countless allusions in literature and art.

294 Religions of Indic Origin

Adyashanti, *True Meditation:*
Discover the Freedom of Pure Awareness, 2006.
Adyashanti, an American spiritual teacher, guides you through self-inquiry, meditation, and "the Way of Subtraction," in which you ask a spiritual question and discover the essential answer. But he says, ultimately, true mediation is when you drop all techniques to find your true nature.

Deepak Chopra,
The Seven Spiritual Laws of Yoga:
A Practical Guide to Healing Body, Mind,
and Spirit, 2004.
Many people recognize yoga practice as a healthy form of exercise. But as Deepak Chopra points out, it is more than that. If practiced mindfully, yoga can expand your ability to love, increase creativity, and improve your chances of success in all areas of life.

William Dalrymple, *Nine Lives:*
In Search of the Sacred in Modern India, 2010.
William Dalrymple spent 25 years exploring how India's people maintain contact with traditions dating back millennia while also dealing with the changes of modern life.

Dalvir S. Pannu, *The Sikh Heritage:*
Beyond Borders, 2020.
By looking at 84 sites in Pakistan, Dalvir S. Pannu takes the reader through a comprehensive exploration of Sikh history.

Robert Wright, *Why Buddhism is True: The Science and Philosophy of Meditation and Enlightenment*, 2017.

Philosophy and psychology professor Robert Wright explains why Buddhist ideas and meditation can make us see reality more clearly while significantly alleviating our suffering. He uses neuroscience to explain how it works.

John Yates, *The Mind Illuminated: A Complete Guide to Integrating Buddhist Wisdom and Brain Science*, 2015.

John Yates draws on science, Buddhism, and ancient Indian sage Asanga's teachings to present ten stages in the meditative journey. He provides advice and guidance to help the reader through each step.

BIOGRAPHY

Daisaku Ikeda, *The Living Buddha: An Interpretive Biography*, 2012.

The Buddha, known initially as Siddhārtha Gautama, left his life of luxury to search for truth. His story is documented in the Buddhist canon. Buddhist philosopher Daisaku Ikeda relates the story of a regular human being who attained inner peace and founded one of the world's major religions.

Pico Iyer, *The Open Road: The Global Journey of the Fourteenth Dalai Lama*, 2008.

The 14th Dalai Lama, who has spent most of his life in exile from his native Tibet, was a long-time friend of Pico Iyer's father. The Dalai Lama is not only the Tibetan head of state and an incarnation of a Tibetan god, but he is also a philosopher and scientist. His friend Iyer writes a fascinating look at a paradoxical global figure.

296 Judaism

Estelle Frankel, *The Wisdom of Not Knowing: Discovering a Life of Wonder by Embracing Uncertainty*, 2017.

Estelle Frankel, a psychotherapist, draws on teachings from Kabbalah, depth psychology, world religions, and myth to help people access inner resources by tapping into the unknown.

Sarit Kattan Gribetz, *Time and Difference in Rabbinic Judaism*, 2020.

Sarit Kattan Gribetz demonstrates that Jewish rabbis used the concept of time to separate the Jewish faithful from outside cultures such as the Romans and other religious adherents such as Christians. In addition, they used it to create concepts of "man time" and "woman time," which kept gender roles

intact. Gribetz looks at how the idea of God's use of time has impacted the
Jewish conception of reality through the ages.

David Jaffe, *Changing the World from the Inside Out:*
A Jewish Approach to Personal and Social Change*, 2016.
David Jaffe explores social activism through the lens of Jewish wisdom. He
shows the ways you can make the world a better place.

Scott-Martin Kosofsky, *The Book of Customs:*
A Complete Handbook for the Jewish Year*, 2005.
Since the 14th century, *The Book of Customs* has helped Jewish families
practice their faith throughout the year. However, this is the first version
published for English speakers.

Joey Weisenberg, *The Torah of Music*, 2017.
Musician Joey Weisenberg brings together ancient texts of Jewish musical
composition and a bilingual library of songs from the past 3,000 years of
Jewish history. It demonstrates the power of music to connect us to the divine
and each other.

BIOGRAPHY

Edward K. Kaplan, *Spiritual Radical:*
Abraham Joshua Heschel in America, 1940–1972*, 2007.
Edward K. Kaplan chronicles how, after escaping the Nazis and immigrating
to America, Abraham Joshua Heschel became a tremendous influence on
Jewish debate in the postwar years.

297 Islam, Bavism & Bahai Faith

Leila Ahmed, *A Quiet Revolution:*
The Veil's Resurgence from the Middle East to America*, 2013.
Leila Ahmed remembers 1940s Cairo, when most Muslim women wore neither
headscarves nor veils. But in the generations since that time, the trend has
reversed. So Ahmed, an Egyptian American professor of women's studies and
religion, set out to discover why. She expected to find fundamentalist Islamic
oppression a significant factor, but after intensive research, what she found
defied her expectations.

Carla Power, *If the Oceans Were Ink: An Unlikely Friendship*
and a Journey to the Heart of the Quran*, 2015.
This book recounts the year-long exploration of the Quran by two unlikely
friends. Carla Power is a journalist who grew up in the American Midwest,
and her friend is a Madrasa-trained sheikh. They study and debate what they
find in their revealing exploration of the Islamic sacred text.

Yannis Toussulis, *Sufism and the Way of Blame:*
***Hidden Sources of a Sacred Psychology*, 2011.**
Sufi-practitioner Yannis Toussulis looks at a little-known Sufi school called
Malamatiyya, or the Way of Blame. It sought to have its adherents study
themselves for ego and other issues that keep them separate from the divine.
The author looks at this in both Sufism and broader Islam and explores how it
is practiced in Turkey today.

298 (Optional Number)

Tamarack Song, *Whispers of the Ancients:*
***Native Tales of Teaching and Healing in Our Time*, 2010.**
Stories from native peoples the world over are part of this beautifully illustrated volume. Tamarack Song has spent his life apprenticed to the elders and
learning from traditions worldwide. He lived alone for years and temporarily
even lived with a pack of wolves. In this work, Song speaks to people to provide wisdom from ancient stories for dealing with life.

299 Religions Not Provided for Elsewhere

Giulia Bonacci, *Exodus! Heirs and Pioneers, Rastafari Return*
***to Ethiopia*, 2015.**
Giulia Bonacci studies the return of Black settlers to Ethiopia through an
examination of oral histories gathered in Ethiopia, Jamaica, Ghana, and the
U.S. The book was originally published in French.

Don Jose Campos, *The Shaman and Ayahuasca:*
***Journeys to Sacred Realms*, 2011.**
The internationally respected shaman, Don Jose Campos, explains ayahuasca
and its role in the Peruvian shamanic tradition. He describes the history of
the plant's use, then relates how it helps users heal, understand reality, and
live more effectively.

Susan Gregg, *Mastering the Toltec Way:*
***A Daily Guide to Happiness, Freedom, and Joy*, 2003.**
Many readers know Toltec philosophy through the works of Don Miguel Ruiz.
In this book, Susan Gregg explains in detail how to bring the Toltec teachings
into your daily routines to deepen your practice and improve your life.

Nigel Pennick, *The Sacred World of Celts:*
An Illustrated Guide to Celtic Spirituality and
***Mythology*, 1997.**
Nigel Pennick seeks to uncover the original Celtic mythologies and spiritual
practices obscured by Christian and revivalist distortions over the millennia.

Lawrence Wright, *Going Clear:*
Scientology, Hollywood, and the Prison of Belief, **2013.**
Pulitzer Prize–winning author Lawrence Wright looks at L. Ron Hubbard,
creator of Scientology, and David Miscavige, who was tasked with continuing the controversial religion after Hubbard's death. Wright investigates and
reports on the secretiveness, plots of government infiltration, celebrity court-
ing, and violence and abuse allegations.

CHAPTER 4

300–399

Social Sciences

THIS LENGTHY SECTION COVERS TOPICS about society and civilizations. Its books focus on how we work with one another and include diverse topics such as politics, racism, law, education, transportation, and etiquette.

300 Social Sciences

William S. Coperthwaite, *A Handmade Life: In Search of Simplicity*, 2007.

For years, William Coperthwaite lived on Maine's north coast, only buying what he needed and making or growing everything else, including his shelter, food, clothes, and furniture. Here he reflects on beauty, work, education, and design while teaching you how to achieve a similar lifestyle yourself.

Peter Gay, *The Science of Freedom*, vol. 2 of *The Enlightenment*, 1969.

In volume one of this series, Peter Gay delves into the philosophies of the Enlightenment and contrasts the ideas of Classical Greek and Roman authors with Christian beliefs. In this second volume, he looks at the social history of the Enlightenment era.

301 Sociology & Anthropology

Robert Coles, *Children of Crisis, vol. 1 of A Study of Courage and Fear*, 1967.

In the 1950s, medical humanities researcher Robert Coles lived with and interviewed American children from all races, ethnicities, and economic demographics to uncover the problems they faced. Though the book is dated, his findings are still relevant.

Irving Howe, *World of Our Fathers: The Journey of the East European Jews to America and the Life They Found and Made*, 1976.

A steady flow of Eastern European Jews immigrated to America between 1880 and 1920. Irving Howe reflects on how they tried to become American while simultaneously holding on to their Yiddish heritage.

Kate Millett, *Sexual Politics: A Surprising Examination of Society's Most Arbitrary Folly*, 1969.

American feminist Kate Millett explores how patriarchy influenced literature, philosophy, psychology, and politics. Her work caused an upheaval in academia with its recognition that literary classics sometimes degraded women.

Vance Packard, *The Status Seekers: An Exploration of Class Behavior in America and the Hidden Barriers That Affect You, Your Community, Your Future*, 1959.

Vance Packard argued that class determined every aspect of American life in the mid-20th century.

BIOGRAPHY

Piri Thomas, *Down These Mean Streets*, 1967.

Born in 1928 in New York City's Spanish Harlem, Piri Thomas revealed what it was like to be a Puerto Rican-Cuban who relieved his anger with street fighting and drug use. When he shot a police officer at age 22, he was imprisoned in Sing Sing. In this memoir, Thomas wrote of his journey from a troubled young man to a self-confident and and influential advocate for inner-city youth.

302 Social Interaction

Brooke Gladstone, *The Influencing Machine: Brooke Gladstone on the Media*, 2011.

NPR's cohost of *On the Media* discusses the history of newspapers and journalism. She argues that "the media" is not outside our control because we have a crucial part in the conversation. With that in mind, Gladstone explains how to become a more thoughtful information consumer.

Malcolm Gladwell, *The Tipping Point: How Little Things Can Make a Big Difference*, 2000.

How do ideas, fashions, and fads catch on? Malcolm Gladwell explores where the tipping point happens, from build-up to phenomenon.

David Hajdu, *The Ten-Cent Plague: The Great Comic-Book Scare and How It Changed America*, 2008.

David Hajdu says the rise of comic books immediately following World War II marked the true beginning of the youth counterculture in America. After a temporary suppression, comics resurfaced in the 1960s with *Mad* magazine. Hajdu highlights how comics have always been a voice for outsiders and the oppressed.

Carl G. Liungman, *Dictionary of Symbols*, 1938.
Carl G. Liungman's work, republished in 1995, provides graphic symbols with their history, definition, and uses. It's a valuable reference for cultural historians and a tool for designers and artists.

Gretchen McCulloch, *Because Internet:*
***Understanding the New Rules of Language*, 2019.**
Linguist Gretchen McCulloch introduces the ways the Internet is changing our language in real time. She reveals protocols for texting and other online advice and uncovers why memes and emojis go viral.

Charlton D. McIlwain, *Black Software:*
The Internet & Racial Justice, from the Afronet
***to Black Lives Matter*, 2019.**
Charlton D. McIlwain tells the little-known story of the intersection between the computer revolution, the Internet, and civil rights activism. The Internet promotes racial equality while it keeps the status quo intact. But, he says, with suitable systems in place, the Internet could narrow the racial divide in the future.

Edward R. Tufte, *Envisioning Information*, 1990.
This classic of information graphics by statistics, graphic design, and political economy professor Edward Tufte has been explaining how to use a two-dimensional format to communicate complex information for over 30 years.

303 Social Processes

Wade Davis, *The Wayfinders:*
***Why Ancient Wisdom Matters in the Modern World*, 2009.**
Anthropologist Wade Davis helps you appreciate what aboriginal cultures worldwide have to offer us by introducing their surviving members, including the Amazon's peoples of the Anaconda and Borneo's rainforest nomads.

Jennifer L. Eberhardt, *Biased:*
Uncovering the Hidden Prejudice that Shapes
***What We See, Think, and Do*, 2019.**
Psychologist Jennifer L. Eberhardt uses her experiences in police departments, prisons, and courtrooms, along with her lab research, to show how bias is present everywhere. Even if you hate prejudice, you unconsciously harbor some. She reveals ways we can identify and combat it in ourselves.

Hannah Fry, *Hello World:*
***Being Human in the Age of Algorithms*, 2019.**
Researcher Hannah Fry explores the hype surrounding artificial intelligence— both the good and the bad. She examines how we are currently using AI and

the far-ranging effects the algorithms have on everything from transportation to healthcare.

Jaron Lanier, *Who Owns the Future?*, 2013.

Father of virtual reality, Jaron Lanier, exposes how technology threatens us with systems that few of us understand that are designed to concentrate money and power in the hands of digital networks. But he also offers a way to help ordinary people navigate them successfully.

Ian Morris, *War! What Is It Good For?: Conflict and the Progress of Civilization from Primates to Robots*, 2015.

After researching the past 15,000 years of human history, Ian Morris asserts that war, counterintuitively, has often proven itself to be a force for good.

Steven Pinker, *Enlightenment Now: The Case for Reason, Science, Humanism, and Progress*, 2018.

Scholar Steven Pinker urges us to distance ourselves from the news headlines. If we ignore the pundits and examine progress strictly in terms of facts and figures, we are in an excellent position. Maybe, he says, we could reach even greater heights if we stop fighting imaginary dragons.

304 Factors Affecting Social Behavior

Mara Hvistendahl, *Unnatural Selection: Choosing Boys over Girls, and the Consequences of a World Full of Men*, 2011.

In the East, particularly in China, 20th-century parents, given a choice, opted overwhelmingly for male offspring. Mara Hvistendahl found that Asia has 163 million fewer females in the population than they would have through natural reproduction. The West's immigrant communities show the same trend. Studying periods of history in which the numbers of men have been dominant, Hvistendahl predicts a future of instability and violence.

Enric Sala, *The Nature of Nature: Why We Need the Wild*, 2020.

When academic Enric Sala grew tired of writing about the death of the oceans, he became an activist. Using his own research and that of other scientists, he asserts that allowing our natural spaces to revert to wilderness will increase diversity and make the planet more inhabitable for us all.

Rebecca Solnit, *Storming the Gates of Paradise: Landscapes for Politics*, 2007.

Respected activist Rebecca Solnit writes 40 essays in which she explores protests from the past and present.

Luis Alberto Urrea, *The Devil's Highway: A True Story,* **2004**
  Award-winning author Luis Alberto Urrea tells the harrowing story of 26 men
  who attempted to cross the Mexican border into Arizona in 2001. Only 12
  survived the trip.

Isabel Wilkerson, *The Warmth of Other Suns:*
The Epic Story of America's Great Migration, **2010.**
  Between 1915 and 1970, almost six million African Americans moved from
  the American South to the North and West in hopes of improving their lives
  and providing a better future for their children. Isabel Wilkerson focuses on
  three of these people. She affirms how their stories are part of a larger picture
  that altered the course of our history.

305 Groups of People

Katherine Boo, *Behind the Beautiful Forevers:*
Life, Death, and Hope in a Mumbai Undercity, **2012.**
  Katherine Boo tells of a Mumbai slum community, contrasting their heartbreaking poverty with the luxury all around them. Their hopes, dreams, and
  exertions demonstrate the costs of capitalist society.

Carina Chocano, *You Play the Girl: On Playboy Bunnies,*
Stepford Wives, Trainwrecks, & Other Mixed Messages, **2017.**
  From earliest childhood, girls get the message that they are a prop for the
  boys and men in their lives. Carina Chocano enumerates many examples of
  how this happens in popular culture—from *Bugs Bunny* to *Frozen.*

Ta-Nehisi Coates, *Between the World and Me,* **2015.**
  Ta-Nehisi Coates writes to his teenage son about living as a Black person in
  America. He looks at how Blackness is punished by society past and present.
  Finally, he offers a dignified and hopeful way forward.

Lillian Faderman, *The Gay Revolution:*
The Story and the Struggle, **2015.**
  Scholar Lillian Faderman provides a meticulously researched history of the
  struggle for gay, lesbian, and trans civil rights. In the 1950s legal system, gays
  and lesbians were criminals. She recounts their experiences in the years since
  through the AIDS epidemic, the fight to legalize gay marriage, and backlashes
  against the community.

Deepa Iyer, *We Too Sing America:*
South Asian, Arab, Muslim, and Sikh Immigrants Shape Our
Multiracial Future, **2015.**
  Many immigrants have faced increasing violence in the years since 9/11.
  Activist Deepa Iyer discusses specific examples and how politics and religion

play a role in their perpetuation. She also looks at other reform movements, such as Black Lives Matter.

Jenny Nordberg, *The Underground Girls of Kabul: In Search of a Hidden Resistance in Afghanistan*, 2014.

Jenny Nordberg examines the custom in Afghanistan of bacha posh or "dressed up like a boy." These are girls who, in a culture that gives girls no value, are temporarily raised and presented to those outside the family as boys. She follows some of these girls, who, through puberty, are raised to be the favored sex and privileged class, only to have their status stripped away later by forced marriage.

Richard Rothstein, *The Color of the Law: A Forgotten History of How Our Government Segregated America*, 2017.

Through extensive research of Black communities from the 1920s onward, Richard Rothstein demonstrates that our current segregated neighborhoods did not happen accidentally. Instead, zoning laws and urban planning codified them. While the Fair Housing Act of 1968 declared housing discrimination illegal, it did nothing to reverse the damage already done.

BIOGRAPHY

James Baldwin, *Notes of a Native Son*, 1955.

James Baldwin's autobiographical essays shed light on his views on race, civil rights, gay and lesbian issues, and activism. Baldwin's influence on American literature has been immense.

Sujatha Gidla, *Ants Among Elephants: An Untouchable Family and the Making of Modern India*, 2017.

Sujatha Gidla explains what being a dalit is like from firsthand experience. Born in the 1930s and educated by Canadian missionaries, Gidla was raised during political upheaval, activism, and promise in her native India. But these changed little for the dalit.

Margo Jefferson, *Negroland: A Memoir*, 2015.

Margo Jefferson recalls her upbringing in a culture that rejected White and general Black society. As the daughter of a Black elite family—her father was a physician and her mother was a socialite—she looks at a small cultural group and how the civil rights movement affected them.

Paul Monette, *Becoming a Man: Half a Life Story*, 1992.

In this classic coming-out story, Paul Monette recounts his youth as "perfect Paul," who, despite his outward success, is miserable until he discovers why he struggles and comes to see that he's okay.

Kao Kalia Yang, *Somewhere in the Unknown World:*
***A Collective Refugee Memoir*, 2020.**
Hmong American author Kao Kalia Yang tells of her life and her neighbors on
University Avenue in Minneapolis. Once a decaying landscape of boarded win-
dows and drug addiction, it is now a thriving neighborhood for immigrants
from every continent. Yang tells their stories, and her own, in this memoir.

306 Culture & Institutions

Stephen Brill, *Tailspin:*
The People and Forces Behind America's Fifty-Year Fall—
***and Those Fighting to Reverse It*, 2018.**
When we see gaping inequities, the inability of the government to pass
needed legislation, and a lack of justice, we feel uneasy about the state of the
U.S. Stephen Brill looks at events from 1967 to 2017 that show how we got
here and introduces people who are working behind the scenes to repair our
broken systems.

Howard Bryant, *Full Dissidence:*
***Notes from an Uneven Playing Field*, 2020.**
Howard Bryant provides nine essays examining the world of professional
sports from the perspective of players forced to downplay their race and deal
with often hidden inequities. While many believe in the commercial depiction
of a post-racial world, especially in sports, Bryant reveals the true picture.

Tara Y. Coyt, *Real Talk about LGBTQIAP:*
Lesbian, Gay, Bisexual, Transgender, Queer, Intersex,
***Asexual, and Pansexual*, 2019.**
Tara Y. Coyt's reference uses the latest research on the science of sexuality,
gender, and biology. In addition, Coyt discusses the legal, ethical, and reli-
gious issues that surround them.

Jaclyn Friedman and Jessica Valenti, *Yes Means Yes!:*
Visions of Female Sexual Power
***and a World without Rape*, 2014.**
We're all familiar with "no means no," but Jaclyn Friedman and Jessica
Valenti argue that we need a shift in attitudes. They assert that by accepting
female sexuality in all its forms, men will treat women as equals instead of
objects. They say a collaborative attitude will help us raise our children in a
world where rape is mostly a memory.

Ezra Klein, *Why We're Polarized*, 2020.
Journalist and political commentator Ezra Klein explains how identity politics emerged in the U.S. over the last decades of the 20th century. The problem is that voting strictly by identity has become so influential that policies

no longer matter, leading to a breakdown in our government and our society at large.

Andrés Reséndez, *The Other Slavery:*
The Uncovered Story of Indian Enslavement in America, 2016.

While smallpox decimated many Native American populations, Andrés Reséndez argues that illegal Native American slavery was equally destructive. He exposes how this practice continued from the time of the Spanish conquistadors through the 19th century in Mormon and Anglo homes.

BIOGRAPHY

Roxanne Gay, *Hunger*, 2017.

Writer Roxanne Gay looks at a predicament of many women as mirrored in her own experience. Feeling unsafe in a desirable body, they overindulge in food as a means of protecting themselves. But society isn't kind to the overweight. As Gay explores the forces that shape her self-image and body, she uncovers an act of violence that formed them early on.

Jo Invester, *Once a Girl, Always a Boy:*
Family Memoir of a Transgender Journey, 2020.

In sharing his transition story, Jo Invester tells how his politically active family thought they had a daughter. They called Jo a tomboy and indulged his desire for masculine toys and clothing. As a teen, he wondered whether he was a lesbian; at 20, he considered asexuality. Finally, in his mid-twenties, Invester began to transition from biological female to male.

Daniel Mendelsohn, *An Odyssey:*
A Father, A Son, and an Epic, 2017.

Jay Mendelsohn, a retired research scientist, was in his 80s when he signed up for the seminar on *The Odyssey,* taught by his son Daniel, a writer and classicist. Through studying the epic, the two men finally come to understand one another.

Rachel Moran, *Paid For:*
My Journey through Prostitution, 2015.

From the age of 14, when she escaped from her mentally unstable parents, until she was 22, Rachel Moran worked as a prostitute to survive. Later she founded Survivors of Prostitution-Abuse Calling for Enlightenment or SPACE International. Here, she thoughtfully recounts the hardships of life on the streets and in brothels and voices the psychological damage it causes.

Anthony Shadid, *House of Stone:*
A Memoir of Home, Family, and a Lost Middle East, 2012.

Pulitzer Prize–winning journalist Anthony Shadid was raised in Oklahoma City by his Lebanese American parents. But after release from his capture while covering the war in Libya, Shadid goes to his grandfather's broken-down home in Lebanon and begins to rebuild it stone by stone. As he does so, he contemplates the changes that have taken place in the Middle East in just a few generations, and he grapples with what "home" means.

307 Communities

**Anna Badkhen, *Fisherman's Blues:
A West African Community at Sea*, 2018.**
Overfishing and climate change are wreaking havoc on the small fishing villages in West Africa, where the fish that used to be large and plentiful are now scarce. Anna Badkhen tells of a culture once steeped in wonder that is facing ecological disaster.

Ross Chapin, *Pocket Neighborhoods: Creating Small-Scale Community in a Large-Scale World*, 2011.
A sense of community is now scarce in American landscapes of suburban sprawl. Ross Chapin provides a solution. After exploring neighborhoods through history, he finds contemporary examples of both pocket communities and the cohousing movement. Inspired by these, he suggests ways to upgrade existing communities, with site plans and a resources section.

**Mitchell Duneier, *Ghetto:
The Invention of a Place, the History of an Idea*, 2016.**
The concept of the ghetto began in 16th-century Venice. Mitchell Duneier traces it from there to the contemporary understanding of the term *ghetto* in American cities.

**Bradley M. Gardner, *China's Great Migration:
How the Poor Built a Prosperous Nation*, 2017.**
Bradley M. Gardner looks at China's economic boom and the migration of over 260 million people from rural areas and small cities to the largest, most economically vital urban areas that powered the boom. He reveals how this massive societal upheaval has changed China, through interviews with the people who lived it.

Jane Jacobs, *The Death and Life of Great American Cities*, 1961.
Jane Jacobs was a U.S.-born Canadian activist who wrote this classic criticism of urban planning in the 1950s. Her reflections on what makes functional cities and how to make them better for the citizens is both honest and indignant.

**Eric Klinenberg, *Palaces for the People:
How Social Infrastructure Can Help Fight Inequality,
Polarization, and the Decline of Civic Life*, 2018.**
While many blame social media, the news outlets, and societal narcissism for

American polarization, sociologist Eric Klinenberg has an alternative theory—it's caused mainly by social isolation. He proposes that shared community spaces like libraries, churches, and parks need to be fortified to help us strengthen our relationships, make friends, and solidify our communities.

BIOGRAPHY

James H. Jones, *Alfred C. Kinsey: A Public/Private Life*, 1997.

Alfred C. Kinsey, founder of the Institute for Research in Sex, Gender, and Reproduction, had a tremendous impact on how Americans viewed sexuality in the 20th century. James H. Jones presents a portrait of a man driven to save humanity from the psychological trauma he endured due to his upbringing.

309 [Unassigned]

Christopher Lasch, *The Culture of Narcissism: American Life in an Age of Diminishing Expectations*, 1979.

Historian Christopher Lasch was a contradictory figure in American academia. While he was often critical of liberal ideas, in the 1960s he became neo-Marxist who later advocated the equality of women. This book was a surprise bestseller by a man who warned that narcissism was coming to define American culture.

310 Collections of General Statistics

314 General Statistics of Europe

B. R. Mitchell, *European Historical Statistics, 1750–1970*, 1975.

In over 800 pages, this book covers the output of pig iron, beer, the number of students in universities, and many other sets of statistics covering 200 years of European history.

320 Political Science (Politics & Government)

Wendy Brown, *Undoing the Demos: Neoliberalism's Stealth Revolution*, 2015.

At this point in U.S. history, neoliberalism's tenets have infiltrated every aspect of our lives. As a result, everything in America—including the citizens—has been reduced to its economic value alone. American political theorist

Wendy Brown questions whether democracy in any form can survive the onslaught of strictly financial mandates above all other metrics.

Barry Goldwater, *The Conscience of a Conservative*, 1960.
While America was experimenting with big government in the years following the Great Depression, Arizona senator and businessman Barry Goldwater wrote this short book to argue for the value of conservative principles like freedom in modern politics. This book's influence on today's political landscape has been tremendous.

Chris Hedges, *Death of the Liberal Class*, 2010.
Chris Hedges argues that democracy is in peril because the liberal class, traditionally made up of the press, liberal religious institutions, labor unions, universities, and the Democratic Party, no longer fills its role as the nation's conscience. Its failure has provided a way for radical right politics and the corporate state to take over. He argues that its growing irrelevance will end our democracy.

Arlie Russell Hochschild, *Strangers in Their Own Land: Anger and Mourning on the American Right*, 2016.
Sociologist Arlie Hochschild left Berkeley, California, to spend some time in the conservative Louisiana bayou country. She wanted to understand people who seemed to be consistently voting against their own interests. What Hochschild found was not simple, and she genuinely liked the people she met there.

Zerlina Maxwell, *The End of White Politics: How to Heal Our Liberal Divide*, 2020.
America has had precisely one nonwhite male president and zero female presidents in over two centuries. Political analyst Zerlina Maxwell looks at what liberals are doing right and where they are messing up. She believes that growing demands for equity are signaling a power shift.

Thomas Paine, *The Rights of Man*, 1776.
Thomas Paine arrived in America at the right moment to publish his pamphlets *The Rights of Man* and *Common Sense*. His works stirred Americans to declare their independence from Great Britain. Paine advocated deism, free thought, and Christian doctrine.

Alan Ryan, *On Politics: A History of Political Thought from Herodotus to the Present*, 2012.
Alan Ryan introduces major philosophers from ancient Greece and explains what they believed and why they believed it. He reveals the effects their thought had in their times and the influence it still wields today.

Manning Marable, *Malcolm X: A Life of Reinvention*, 2011.
Through decades of detailed research, Manning Marable presents a previously unavailable portrait of the profoundly influential Malcolm X. Marable argues that Malcolm X was foremost an American constantly working to remake himself into something new. His assassination, at age 39, is also covered in accurate detail.

321 Systems of Governments & States

Joseph N. Abraham,
Kings, Conquerors, Psychopaths:
***From Alexander to Hitler to the Corporation*, 2018.**
Joseph N. Abraham argues that right-wing populists are not a problem. Throughout human history, they have always been with us, and that's unlikely to change. Instead, a problem occurs when other people follow them, ignore their outrageous behavior, and support them anyway. Abraham considers why this happens.

Anne Applebaum, *Twilight of Democracy:*
***The Seductive Lure of Authoritarianism*, 2020.**
Given a choice between democracy and authoritarianism, why would anyone choose the latter? Pragmatism, says journalist Anne Applebaum. If asked to choose between a system that keeps you outside and another that will reward your loyalty, many people will choose the rewards that benefit them and their families. Using examples from all around the world, Applebaum shows how nostalgia, polarization, and discontent lead some to yearn for a one-party state.

Hannah Arendt, *The Origins of Totalitarianism*, 1951.
After her forced exile from Germany in 1933, German-Jewish political philosopher Hannah Arendt explores totalitarianism from the rise of European anti-Semitism throughout the 19th century and into World War II. She believed that Nazi Germany and Stalinist Russia were the right and left sides of the same coin. Both used isolation, propaganda, and terror to further their causes.

Steven Levitsky and Daniel Ziblatt,
***How Democracies Die*, 2018.**
Looking at the history of democracies, Harvard professors Levitsky and Ziblatt argue that there are signposts along the way to their demise and that the election of Donald Trump is one we have already passed. Then they discuss how we can save our democracy.

322 Relation of State to Organized Groups

Joshua Bloom and Waldo E. Martin Jr., *Black Against Empire: The History and Politics of the Black Panther Party*, **2013.**
In 1966, the Black Panther Party arose in response to police brutality. They made no secret of their goal to combat the American empire. The party grew, despite governmental repression, but then it suddenly collapsed at the height of its influence. Joshua Bloom provides a scholarly look at the movement's rise and fall.

Claire Conner, *Wrapped in the Flag: A Personal History of America's Radical Right*, **2013.**
Claire Conner was the daughter of a national spokesman for the ultra-conservative John Birch Society. Her parents forced her to become a society member at age 13, but Conner later quit in disgust over prominent members' Holocaust-denying and White supremacist beliefs. She researches records and documents of the organization, uncovering contemporary and first-hand accounts that reveal the inside story of the JBS. The organization had many notable members, including Fred Koch, father of the billionaire Koch brothers, who have funded many fundamentalist and right-wing causes in recent decades.

Connor Towne O'Neill, *Down Along with That Devil's Bones: A Reckoning with Monuments, Memory, and the Legacy of White Supremacy*, **2020.**
When journalist Connor Towne O'Neill moved to Alabama, he came across citizens protecting a monument to Nathan Bedford Forrest in Selma. Learning that Forrest was a Confederate general and the first grand wizard of the Ku Klux Klan, he visited other monuments to Forrest across the South. What he finds exposes a history of White supremacy across the entire nation.

323 Civil & Political Rights

Taylor Branch, *Pillar of Fire: America in the King Years 1963–65*, **1998.**
This second part of Pulitzer Prize–winning author Taylor Branch's trilogy on the civil rights movement covers Martin Luther King Jr.'s leadership from 1963 in Birmingham, Alabama, to his acceptance of the Nobel Peace Prize. Branch clarifies how King's leadership made a monumental impact on the successes the movement achieved.

Colin G. Calloway, *The Indian World of George Washington: The First President, the First Americans, and the Birth of the Nation*, **2018.**
George Washington was a brilliant leader who was crucial to the nation's

formation. But there was a side to Washington's role in our founding that has been largely unexplored—his relationships with the Native American leaders whose land the nation needed to grow.

Erich Fromm, *The Sane Society*, 1955.

When social psychologist Erich Fromm looked at social systems to see how they affected mental health, he asked himself whether it were possible for a society, as a whole, to be sick. Looking at mid-20th century political and economic realities, Fromm concluded it can. He presented ideas to alleviate the alienation experienced by many.

Martha C. Nussbaum, *Liberty of Conscience: In Defense of America's Tradition of Religious Equality*, 2007.

While, in the U.S., freedom of religion is a pillar of government, Martha C. Nussbaum contends that the misunderstandings about the founding fathers' intentions give one particular segment of the nation's many religious traditions unequal access to its halls of power. She argues that not only is this an injustice but it also is an assault on our Constitution and puts our democracy at risk.

Thane Rosenbaum, *Saving Free Speech . . . from Itself*, 2020.

Free speech is weaponized on a routine basis. So what, if any, limits to free speech did the founding fathers have in mind? Thane Rosenbaum considers this question and points out that hate speech is illegal in many liberal democracies that seem to be doing fine. He looks at problems with unlimited free speech and what it's doing to society. Next, he considers what should be done about it.

Kai Strittmatter, *We Have Been Harmonized: Life in China's Surveillance State*, 2020.

China today has a degree of surveillance never seen before. There is nothing a Chinese citizen can hide from a government that uses facial recognition, GPS tracking, databases, and security cameras that even monitor faces for acceptable expressions. Kai Strittmatter warns this can happen anywhere.

BIOGRAPHY

Paula J. Giddings, *Ida: A Sword among Lions: Ida B. Wells and the Campaign Against Lynching*, 2008.

Ida B. Wells, child of slaves, led the first campaign against lynching in the U.S. Ignoring the resulting death threats and aspersions on her character, she was a suffragist, political activist, and journalist in Chicago. Paula J. Giddings declares Wells's personality and her life were as bold as they were effective.

Elisabeth Griffith, *In Her Own Right:* *The Life of Elizabeth Cady Stanton*, 1984.

Elizabeth Cady Stanton was one of the most important suffragists and women's rights activists in the 19th century. Elisabeth Griffith examines Stanton's role models and friendships and determines their influence on her decisions.

Kay Mills, *This Little Light of Mine:* *The Life of Fannie Lou Hamer*, 1994.

Kay Mills relates the biography of Black civil rights activist Fannie Lou Hamer, who risked everything she had for the civil rights movement. The Mississippi Freedom Democratic Party, which she cofounded, opposed the efforts of the local Democratic Party to block the Black vote. In addition, Hamer organized Freedom Summer to help Black Mississippians gain the vote. One of her projects when she became frustrated with her political efforts was a bank to help Black farmers.

324 The Political Process

Carol Anderson, *One Person, No Vote:* *How Voter Suppression Is Destroying Our Democracy*, 2018.

Carol Anderson demonstrates how the Shelby ruling in 2013 gutted the Voting Rights Act of 1965. She then traces the trail of voter suppression following in its wake and the activism fighting it.

Munir Moon, *The Beltway Beast:* *Stealing from Future Generations* *and Destroying the Middle Class*, abridged version, 2017.

Former financial industry executive Munir Moon explains why so many policies and ideas that dominate in Washington, D.C., are harmful to average citizens. He focuses on the older millionaires who control Congress that bend to lobbyists, multinational corporations, and others.

Johanna Neuman, *Gilded Suffragists: The New York* *Socialites Who Fought for Women's Right to Vote*, 2017.

Journalist Johanna Neuman looks at wealthy New York socialites of the late 19th and early 20th centuries who were essential in earning women's voting rights. These women were at the forefront of the Progressive Era. They also pressed for women's education, the right to pursue a career, and the right to sue for divorce.

325 International Migration & Colonization

Arthur Herman, *Gandhi & Churchill:* *The Epic Rivalry that Destroyed an Empire and Forged Our* *Age*, 2008.

After more than two centuries of British rule, Mohandas Gandhi, a middle-class man, led India's struggle for independence. He invented the nonviolent defiance that has become the model for social activism worldwide. Gandhi opposed Winston Churchill, the aristocratic British leader who stubbornly held on to the Indian subcontinent. But Herman argues the two men were more alike than different.

Kerby A. Miller, *Emigrants and Exiles: Ireland and the Irish Exodus to North America*, 1985.

The Irish potato famine precipitated an influx of Irish immigrants to America in the mid-19th century. Kerby A. Miller examines the letters, diaries, journals, memoirs, poetry, songs, and folklore of these people and the additional Irish following them.

Jia Lynn Yang, *One Mighty and Irresistible Tide: The Epic Struggle Over American Immigration, 1924–1965*, 2020.

In 1924, the U.S. Congress passed a quota system that ended large-scale immigration from southern and eastern Europe and cut off most from Asia. Jia Lynn Yang, a daughter of immigrants, tells how lawmakers, activists, and presidents abolished the law. The resulting 1965 Immigration and Nationality Act has changed the makeup of America.

326 Slavery & Emancipation

David Brion Davis, *The Problem of Slavery in Western Culture*, 1966.

David Brion Davis looks at how cultures from early recorded history through the 1770s viewed and used slavery to achieve economic and personal ends. He illustrates how slavery in America conflicted with the idealism and high principles championed by the young country.

Adam Hochschild, *Bury the Chains: Prophets and Rebels in the Fight to Free an Empire's Slaves*, 2005.

Adam Hochschild gives an account of the first grassroots movement in history to stop Britain's slave trade. The movement began in 1787 with 12 men who came together to change public opinion using methods like consumer boycotts that are still used today.

Simon Schama, *Rough Crossings: The Slaves, the British, and the American Revolution*, 2005.

Historian Simon Schama looks at a little-known part of the American Revolutionary War. When the last British governor of Virginia declared emancipation for any rebel-owned slave who served in the king's army, tens of thousands of escaped slaves went to British camps. Once the war was over,

these individuals found themselves in a precarious position, and many
fled to Nova Scotia, where they were betrayed and then shipped to
Sierra Leone.

Manisha Sinha, *The Slave's Cause: A History of Abolition*, 2016.

Manisha Sinha has effectively rewritten the history of abolition in the U.S.
She uses recently uncovered documents and letters to show that, rather than
being a movement of northern upper-class White reformers, it was a mass,
sweeping movement from all classes and races. In addition, Sinha looks at the
role slave uprisings had in the Haitian Revolution and ties abolition to other
causes such as feminism and the rights of labor.

327 International Relations

Ronen Bergman, *Rise and Kill First: The Secret History of Israel's Targeted Assassinations*, 2018.

Israeli journalist and military analyst Ronen Bergman gained the cooperation of members of the Israeli government to compile this account of Israel's
state-sanctioned use of assassination against its enemies since its formation
in 1948. It looks at the consequences for the nation and the individuals who
approved and carried out the attacks.

Thomas J. Christensen, *The China Challenge: Shaping the Choices of a Rising Power*, 2015.

China is not a threat to the current world order, says Thomas J. Christensen.
Instead, it is still a developing nation that faces too many problems at home
to challenge the U.S. for global domination. He sees China not as a competitor
but as a possible ally if approached correctly.

Glenn Greenwald, *No Place to Hide: Edward Snowden, the NSA, and the U.S. Surveillance State*, 2014.

Most people know the story of how 29-year-old Edward Snowden contacted
reporter Glenn Greenwald with evidence that the U.S. government was spying
on its citizens. Greenwald divulges how those meetings took place, along with
more revelations from material he obtained after Snowden escaped into exile.

Seymour M. Hersh, *The Price of Power: Kissinger in the Nixon White House*, 1983.

Pulitzer Prize–winning journalist Seymour Hersh looks at the terms of Henry
Kissinger, Richard Nixon's influential secretary of state. Kissinger had a con-
siderable impact on American foreign policy in the years comprising the end
of the Vietnam War, the resumption of relations with China, and the growing
threat in the Middle East.

Robert F. Kennedy, *Thirteen Days:*
A Memoir of the Cuban Missile Crisis, 1968.

During the Cuban Missile Crisis, Robert F. Kennedy was U.S. Attorney
General. Under his brother President John F. Kennedy, he was privy to all the
events of that tension-filled time. His detailed account is of historical value.

David Talbott, *The Devil's Chessboard:*
Allen Dulles, the CIA, and the Rise of America's
Secret Government, 2015.

Progressive journalist David Talbott offers this revealing look at the longest-
serving director of the CIA, Allen Dulles. Talbott provides evidence that
Dulles was not only brutal with foreign adversaries but with domestic ones
as well. Moreover, Dulles used his position to benefit himself and his wealthy
and powerful friends, viewing himself as above the law.

Tim Weiner, *The Folly and the Glory:*
America, Russia, and Political Warfare 1945–2020, 2020.

While the U.S. won the Cold War, foreign correspondent Tim Weiner relates
how Russia is coming out on top today. Along with Cold War history, Weiner
reveals Putin's undeniable influence on the American presidential election in
2016. Yet, he says, America is doing little to defend itself.

BIOGRAPHY

Kai Bird, *The Good Spy:*
The Life and Death of Robert Ames, 2014.

Pulitzer Prize–winning journalist Kai Bird tells of his childhood neighbor,
American CIA operative Robert Ames. Unlike most of the other agents of that
time and place, Ames built relationships with Arab intelligence figures. Bird
argues that had Ames not been assassinated, the current situation in the
Middle East would likely be quite different.

328 The Legislative Process

Richard A. Arenberg, *Congressional Procedure:*
A Practical Guide to the Legislative Process in the U.S.
Congress: The House of Representatives and Senate
Explained, 2018.

If you follow political news and find yourself baffled by talk of filibusters
and budget resolutions, this book is for you. Veteran Senate aide Richard A.
Arenberg provides a complete guide to how Congress works, with flowcharts
and a glossary of legislative terms.

Richard A. Arenberg and Robert B. Dove, *Defending the Filibuster: The Soul of the Senate*, 2012.

Arenberg and Dove argue that a filibuster is a necessary tool for the Senate and that without it, the U.S. would be entirely at the mercy of the majority party of the time. Moreover, it ensures the constitutional principle of checks and balances works. They back their argument with an explanation of the Senate's rules, procedures, and tactics. They also recount specific pieces of legislation that the filibuster has impacted.

Fergus M. Bordewich, *The First Congress: How James Madison, George Washington, and a Group of Extraordinary Men Invented the Government*, 2016.

Fergus M. Bordewich covers the consequential First Federal Congress of 1789–1791. At the time, the Constitution was a set of principles, and the nation still needed to establish a set method of government functioning. It was only through the bitter conflicts of some of our best-known founders that most of the issues were settled. Some, however, such as the balance between states' rights and those of the federal government, still confound us today.

330 Economics

Daron Acemoglu and James A. Robinson, *Why Nations Fail: The Origins of Power, Prosperity, and Poverty*, 2012.

Economists Daron Acemoglu and James A. Robinson based this book on their original research into societies from the past, such as ancient Rome, through present-day North and South Korea. They analyze what causes economic growth and what curtails or stops it. They reveal that politics and political institutions may have more responsibility than any other factor.

Milton Friedman, *Capitalism and Freedom*, 1962.

Milton Friedman considers how societies can have a responsive government while maintaining their citizens' economic and political freedoms. In 1976, Friedman won the Nobel Prize in Economics for his contributions to the field. He was a promoter of freedom, and he had a tremendous influence on modern conservative economic thought.

John Kenneth Galbraith, *The Affluent Society*, 1958.

Keynesian economist John Kenneth Galbraith, a proponent of liberalism and democratic socialism, wrote this classic work on the dangers of economic inequality. He saw the mid-20th century economy increasingly based on unnecessary consumption at the expense of public works that benefit all citizens.

Thomas Ramge and Jan Schwochow,
The Global Economy as You've Never Seen It:
99 Ingenious Infographics That Put It All Together, **2018.**
 Even economists can't entirely explain how the world economy works. It's
 too massive and complex to reduce to easily digestible concepts. But author
 Thomas Ramge and infographics expert Jan Schwochow do their best by
 providing 99 infographics that explain every part of the world economy from
 finance to labor.

Adam Smith, *An Inquiry into the Nature and Causes of the*
Wealth of Nations, **1776.**
 Scottish moral philosopher Adam Smith is the father of modern economic
 thought, particularly capitalism. His work is as applicable today as it was
 in 1776. He covers jobs, wages, government, business, education, and ethics,
 among other perennial concerns.

BIOGRAPHY

Zachary D. Carter, *The Price of Peace:*
Money, Democracy, and the Life of John Maynard
Keynes, **2020.**
 While most people know him today as one of the 20th century's most sig-
 nificant economic thinkers, the John Maynard Keynes journalist Zachary D.
 Carter introduces is a Renaissance man interested in just about everything.
 His friend Virginia Woolf said it would take 25 themes to capture his life and
 interests. At heart, Keynes was an anti-authoritarian thinker who sought to
 reinvent Enlightenment ideals.

331 Labor Economics

Jessica Bruder, *Nomadland:*
Surviving America in the Twenty-First Century, **2017.**
 Journalist Jessica Bruder has lived for years in her RV. She covers the plight of
 tens of thousands of mostly older Americans who have given up their perma-
 nent residences to travel the country from job to job while living in campers
 of various sorts. They can be found from Washington State to Florida and
 illustrate one trend that may grow more extensive. Bruder explains how our
 current economy has created the situation.

Matthew B. Crawford, *Shop Class as Soulcraft:*
An Inquiry into the Value of Work, **2009.**
 In the early 21st century, educational institutions placed a great deal of
 emphasis on knowledge-based jobs. Students were strongly encouraged to
 seek out college degrees despite a lack of desire on their part. Matthew B.

Crawford reexamines the role of manual labor in our society and the dignity it affords its practitioner. After all, he argues, *doing* does not preclude *thinking*.

Paul R. Daughtery and H. James Wilson, *Human + Machine: Reimagining Work in the Age of AI*, 2018.

After researching its role in over 1,500 organizations, Daughtery and Wilson explain how AI is no longer the future, it is now. They examine its current use and clarify why businesses must use it. Finally, they explain how to do so by describing six new roles every company needs to develop.

Philip Dray, *There Is Power in a Union: The Epic Story of Labor in America*, 2010.

American unions have been losing influence for decades. Philip Dray explains how and why they developed and rose in power before ceding ground to capital. He argues that they are needed even more today to aid the middle class.

Seth Holmes, *Fresh Fruit, Broken Bodies: Migrant Farmworkers in the United States*, 2013.

Medical doctor and anthropologist Seth Holmes lived and worked side by side with America's migrant farmworkers in all sorts of conditions. He explains how racism, anti-immigrant stances, and market forces keep migrant workers poor and how our insurance and healthcare system leaves them suffering in ways that a wealthy society profiting from them should find unacceptable.

332 Financial Economics

Ron Chernow, *The House of Morgan: An American Banking Dynasty and the Rise of Modern Finance*, 1990.

For over a century, four generations of J. P. Morgan's family ran secretive firms connected to the banking dynasty. In telling the story, Ron Chernow provides a revealing look at how banks operate.

Benjamin Graham, *The Intelligent Investor: The Classic Text on Value Investing*, 2006.

First published in 1949, Benjamin Graham's classic book on investing has guided generations of Americans. This revised edition has updated commentary by Jason Zweig, a financial journalist who helps readers understand how Graham's principles work today.

Michael Lewis, *Flash Boys: A Wall Street Revolt*, 2014.

When a group of Wall Street insiders left careers with seven-figure salaries to expose the corrupt and rigged market structure, they revealed a disturbing view of the American stock market.

Adam Tooze, *Crashed:*
How a Decade of Financial Crises Changed the World, 2018.

British historian Adam Tooze covers the global impact of the 2008 financial crisis. First, he traces how questions of the survival of capitalist democracy arose in its aftermath. He shows how recent political upheavals can be traced directly to it. Finally, he asks if we are out of danger a decade later.

BIOGRAPHY

Alice Schroeder, *The Snowball:*
Warren Buffett and the Business of Life, 2008.

Warren Buffett was the richest man in the world when his friend, insurance industry analyst Alice Schroeder, wrote this book. He gave her access to his papers, friends, and family so she could produce an accurate portrait of his principles and his integrity.

333 Economics of Land & Energy

Charles Fishman, *The Big Thirst:*
The Secret Life and Turbulent Future of Water, 2010.

After the city of Atlanta came to within 90 days of running out of drinking water in 2008, reporter Charles Fishman began researching our precarious water-dependent world. He reveals how we use water to maintain our environment, in industry, and for food production.

Nora Gallagher and Lisa Myers, eds.,
Tools for Grassroots Activists:
Best Practices for Success in the Environmental
Movement, 2016.

The folks at Patagonia give practical advice for running a grassroots campaign. Each chapter is written by an expert, while famous activists provide inspirational passages.

Joshua Horwitz, *War of the Whales:*
A True Story, 2014.

News stories of whales dying in large numbers after beaching themselves inspired Joshua Horwitz to investigate why some of the beachings occurred, the involvement of the U.S. Navy, and how they came to a stop.

Aldo Leopold, *A Sand County Almanac:*
And Sketches Here and There, 1949.

Conservationist, scientist, and philosopher Aldo Leopold finished this classic work before his death in 1948, recording the monthly changes on his farm in Wisconsin and in woodlands in Arizona, Manitoba, and other locations.

His writings inspired Annie Dillard and Edward Abbey, among other nature writers.

John McPhee, *Encounters with the Archdruid: Narratives About a Conservationist and Three of His Natural Enemies,* 1971.

Master nature writer John McPhee writes about four men and their relationships with each other and the various wilderness environments in which they find themselves.

Richard Rhodes, *Energy: A Human History,* 2018.

American historian Richard Rhodes looks at the sources of energy humans have used throughout history. He links energy consumption to the fates of businesses and nations. And then he considers whether renewable energy is the key to a better future.

Almir Narayamoga Suruí and Corine Sombrun, *Save the Planet: An Amazonian Tribal Leader Fights for His People, The Rainforest, and the Earth,* 2018.

Almir Narayamoga Suruí is an Amazonian tribal chieftain and global activist who seeks to save the rainforest despite death threats and large bounties placed on his life. He urgently proclaims the devastating consequences for the Earth if the rainforests are lost.

335 Socialism & Related Systems

Madeleine Albright, *Fascism: A Warning,* 2018.

Madeleine Albright, former U.S. Secretary of State, tells us why we need to be concerned about fascism today. The threat has grown globally in recent decades due to cultural, technological, and economic factors hollowing out the centers of political parties, providing traction for extremes on both the right and left. Knowledge, she asserts, is critical in fighting it.

Joshua Muravchick, *Heaven on Earth: The Rise and Fall of Socialism,* 2002.

For those opposed to it, the very word *socialism* evokes strong feelings. But it has been tried in many different guises, all over the world, for over two centuries. This book explains why it finally succeeded at the end of the 20th century for a very brief time.

Robert Service, *Comrades!: A History of World Communism,* 2007.

From Marx to Castro, Robert Service looks at the most critical figures in communist history. He argues that there was more to communism than repression and violence. He says some of its principles may still be helpful in today's world.

BIOGRAPHY

Jonathan Sperber, *Karl Marx: A Nineteenth-Century Life*, 2013.

According to historian Jonathan Sperber, people generally misunderstand Karl Marx. Sperber examines recently released collections of the work of both Marx and his disciple Friedrich Engels. He says Marx's sympathies are closer to Robespierre's than to today's Marxists.

336 Public Finance

Charles R. Morris, *The Cost of Good Intentions: New York City and the Liberal Experiment, 1960–1975*, 1980.

Charles R. Morris examines public policy in New York City's liberal years from 1960 through the return of fiscal conservatism in 1975. He looks at why it ended and what other governments can learn from it.

Steven R. Weisman, *The Great Tax Wars: Lincoln–Teddy Roosevelt–Wilson: How the Income Tax Transformed America*, 2003.

In 60 years, the U.S. went from an agrarian society to an industrial super-power. From Abraham Lincoln's income tax through World War I, the nation's elite and workers alike fought to establish the tax system that ultimately proved progressive. Steven R. Weisman looks at how these early battles fore-shadow some of the debates we still have today.

337 International Economics

Richard Dobbs, James Manyika, and Jonathan Woetzel, *No Ordinary Disruption: The Four Global Forces Breaking All the Trends*, 2015.

Our recent past has been called the Great Moderation, in which asset prices were going up, capital costs were going down, and labor and resources were abundant. Each new generation was expected to outperform its parents. But that time is over, and everything is reversing. What seemed evident to us in the past no longer applies. Richard Dobbs advises us on how to keep afloat through these difficult times.

Pankaj Ghemawat, *World 3.0: Global Prosperity and How to Achieve It*, 2011.

Economist Pankaj Ghemawat says globalization and deregulation are neither evil nor necessary. He debunks our assumptions about the topics and explains how globalization can help us all.

338 Production

Neil Barofsky, *Bailout:*
An Inside Account of How Washington Abandoned Main Street While Rescuing Wall Street, 2010.

Bush and Obama administration insider Neil Barofsky tells how the banks that caused the 2008 financial crisis were determined to be "too big to fail." It's an indictment of treasury secretary Timothy Geithner and his team, who catered to Wall Street executives while providing no incentives for them to change their practices. Instead, taxpayers bore the burden.

Steve Coll, *Private Empire:*
ExxonMobil and American Power, 2012.

Steve Coll examines an impressive amount of documentation to provide a look behind the curtain at ExxonMobil. The behemoth corporation has an outsized influence on the U.S. government through its lobbying efforts. And, in other countries where it conducts business, it has more impact than the U.S. embassies do. Coll looks at the workings of this corporation and at controversies that have followed it over the years.

Adam Fisher, *Valley of Genius:*
The Uncensored History of Silicon Valley (As Told by the Hackers, Founders, and Freaks Who Made It Boom), 2018.

Never has an industry risen to such global prominence in such record time as the tech giants of Silicon Valley. Adam Fisher tells the incredible stories shared by insiders about the rise of Apple, Google, and Facebook and how they came to occupy the place they are in today.

Barbara Kingsolver, *Animal, Vegetable, Miracle:*
A Year of Food Life, 2007.

American novelist Barbara Kingsolver decided to try an experiment. For one year, she and her family would refuse, as much as possible, to buy industrially produced food. Instead, they grew, wild-harvested, and slaughtered most of what they ate for an entire year. It's inspiring, but sometimes daunting, to read about how they made cheese and butchered roosters. The tenth-anniversary issue revisits the Kingsolver family, and each reflects on their year of self-sufficiency.

Kai-Fu Lee, *AI Superpowers:*
China, Silicon Valley, and the New World Order, 2018.

AI and China expert Kai-Fu Lee explores how Chinese artificial intelligence development has recently caught up with the U.S. Lee urges both countries to handle the astounding powers of AI with care, and he talks about the inevitable effect AI will have on global job markets. Finally, he predicts which jobs will be impacted and provides suggestions on how societies can cope with the changes.

Christopher Leonard, *Kochland:*
The Secret History of Koch Industries and Corporate Power in America, 2019.

The story of Koch Industries and the billionaire Koch brothers, Charles and David, parallels that of 20th-century America. Because their industries were involved in every aspect of American life, they had a tremendous impact on Americans' products. They also influenced the decline of unions and the lack of progress on climate change.

BIOGRAPHY

Ron Chernow, *Titan:*
The Life of John D. Rockefeller, Sr., 1998.

Ron Chernow presents a fascinating portrait of the first billionaire in history. He recounts the familiar story of how John D. Rockefeller amassed his fortune through the sometimes shady business practices of Standard Oil. But Rockefeller was also a religious man who gave away more money than anyone before him. Chernow also tells the story of the birth of corporations and their unparalleled rise to power.

David Nasaw, *Andrew Carnegie*, 2006.

One of the titans of the 19th-century industry was Scottish-born Andrew Carnegie, who founded Carnegie Steel. David Nasaw tells Carnegie's rags-to-riches story, beginning after he moved to Pittsburg when he was 13. At his death, he gave his money away to a wide variety of charities.

339 Macroeconomics & Related Topics

John Carreyrou, *Bad Blood:*
Secrets and Lies in a Silicon Valley Startup, 2018.

In this riveting story of Silicon Valley's high-stakes investment world, John Carreyrou follows the story of Elizabeth Holmes, a Stanford dropout whose company Theranos, a blood-testing business, was valued at nine billion dollars in 2014. The problem was, it was a fraud. The technology didn't work, and when the *Wall Street Journal* exposed the scam in 2015, the company's worth plummeted.

Clayton M. Christensen, Efosa Ojomo, and Karen Dillon,
The Prosperity Paradox:
How Innovation Can Lift Nations Out of Poverty, 2019.

Giving money and resources to poverty-stricken nations has proven, over and over, to be an ineffective strategy. Harvard Business School professor Clayton M. Christensen and his coauthors suggest that rather than tackling poverty from the top down, entrepreneurship and other economic development strategies should be tried to create growth from the ground up.

Matthew Desmond, *Evicted: Poverty and Profit in the American City*, 2016.

American sociologist Matthew Desmond follows eight families in Milwaukee who are desperately struggling to avoid homelessness. It's a heartbreaking look at poverty and economic exploitation. But it also offers solutions for the problem of homelessness in America.

Kathryn J. Edin and H. Luke Shaefer, *$2.00 a Day: Living on Almost Nothing in America*, 2015.

The 1.5 million American households surviving on less than $2.00 per person per day are hidden from view. Kathryn J. Edin explores how this devastating situation occurs. Through many interviews with the families themselves, she details how they manage to survive on such pitiful incomes, including selling their blood regularly.

Robert J. Gordon, *The Rise and Fall of American Growth: The U.S. Standard of Living Since the Civil War*, 2016.

Robert J. Gordon looks at the astounding economic growth between 1870 and 1970 in America. He concludes that the growth cannot continue and is, in fact, already dropping. Predicting that the decline will continue due to inequality, aging populations, and government debt, he calls on us to find new solutions for our children's future.

340 Law

Joel Carlson, *No Neutral Ground*, 1973.

Joel Carlson writes of his time in the 1950s and 1960s as a South African lawyer who worked to get justice for his Black clients. He details the "pass" system, examples of slave labor, and the torture of Black activists. Carlson left South Africa in 1970 after harassment and threats.

341 Law of Nations

David Luban, *Torture, Power, and Law*, 2014.

Philosopher and legal ethicist David Luban takes a thoughtful look at the use of torture in contemporary times. His essays cover the connection between torture, humiliation, and dignity. He also looks at the Obama administration's failure to punish perpetrators.

Mark Werts, *America's Simple Solutions:*
***A Visionary's Blueprint for a Better Tomorrow.* 2016.**

Mark Werts sets out to provide nonpartisan solutions to problems as
wide-ranging as education and healthcare by examining how other countries
handle them. He takes a fresh look at the words of our founding fathers and
notes that we have forgotten much of their legacy. He sees freedom, education,
and voting as the basis for many solutions.

342 Constitutional & Administrative Law

Samantha Barbas, *Newsworthy: The Supreme Court Battle*
***Over Privacy and Press Freedom,* 2017.**

Samantha Barbas uses the case of the Hill family to showcase how American
media grew to be such an outsized power. The Hill family were victims of
a bizarre crime in 1952. The family of seven was home when three escaped
convicts invaded their home and held them captive for 19 hours, finally taking
their car and clothes but leaving them unharmed. But the real problem for the
Hills began when a novel based on their story was published and made into
a movie, and when *Life* magazine covered their story. The family was embar-
rassed at the inaccuracies reported and sued for invasion of privacy. Richard
Nixon argued the case before the Supreme Court. The case still influences
privacy and freedom of the press issues today.

David J. Barron, *Waging War: The Clash Between Presidents*
***and Congress, 1776 to ISIS,* 2016.**

David J. Barron examines the history of wars in America and presidents'
efforts to either make them happen or avoid them. While the Constitution
gives only Congress the right to declare war, presidents, he finds, have often
been in charge of our armed conflicts.

Karen Blumenthal, *Jane Against the World:*
***Roe v. Wade and the Fight for Reproductive Rights,* 2020.**

In this book for young adults, acclaimed author Karen Blumenthal examines reproductive rights in America. Her well-researched history introduces the topic and its surrounding issues beginning with the *Roe v. Wade*
U.S. Supreme Court decision. Blumenthal looks at the roots of the debate
surrounding abortion and the repercussions for women.

Thomas Healy, *The Great Dissent:*
How Oliver Wendell Holmes Changed His Mind—and
***Changed the History of Free Speech in America,* 2013.**

Few Americans realize we did not have the right to peacefully protest in the
U.S. until conservative Supreme Court justice Oliver Wendell Holmes wrote
a court opinion in 1919 that formed the understanding of free speech we still
have today.

Charles L. Mee Jr., *Genius of the People*, 2013.

To say that the first session of Congress in 1787 was contentious would be an understatement. Historian Charles Mee outlines the issues dividing the two sides. First were those, like George Mason, who argued for states' rights and a government led by the people. On the other side were James Madison and Alexander Hamilton, who wanted a stronger federal government. We're still fighting over these issues today. Mee asserts that the founding fathers never meant the Constitution to be a narrowly and fundamentally interpreted document.

Laurence Tribe, *Uncertain Justice: The Roberts Court and the Constitution*, 2014.

The Supreme Court has been somewhat mysterious to most Americans, and its justices seem to be untouchable with their lifetime appointments. Law professor Laurence Tribe examines the court's decisions under Chief Justice John Roberts, including gay marriage and the Affordable Care Act. He argues that the court is in a unique position at this point in history to permanently shape our nation's future.

343 Military, Tax, Trade & Industrial Law

John Fabian Witt, *Lincoln's Code: The Laws of War in American History*, 2012.

Law professor John Fabian Witt examines how America's leaders, from George Washington to Abraham Lincoln, shaped international standards of wartime conduct. Then, focusing on the Lincoln administration's code, he demonstrates that our current controversies have been with us for a long time.

344 Labor, Social, Education & Cultural Law

Lowell E. Baier, *Inside the Equal Access to Justice Act: Environmental Litigation and the Crippling Battle over America's Lands, Endangered Species, and Critical Habitats*, 2015.

Environmental litigation expert Lowell E. Baier presents the history of the Equal Access to Justice Act, intended to support veterans, the disabled, and small businesses. But it has also served as a leash on public land management agencies. In this book, Baier examines the mixed record of the law.

Adam Cohen, *Imbeciles: The Supreme Court, American Eugenics, and the Sterilization of Carrie Buck*, 2016.

Adam Cohen chronicles the pseudoscience eugenics. In the 1927 *Buck v. Bell* case, the Supreme Court ruled that it was legal in the U.S. to sterilize "undesirable" citizens for the good of the nation as a whole. Towering figures in the nation's history, like former president William Howard Taft and Oliver Wendell Holmes Jr. were in the majority.

Richard Kluger, *Simple Justice: The History of Brown v. Board of Education and Black America's Struggle for Equality*, 1975.

The 1954 Supreme Court decision *Brown v. Board of Education* was a landmark in American history. It determined that Black Americans had a right to equal education under the law. Richard Kluger writes about the children it impacted and the Black legal establishment it helped form.

Randy T. Simmons, Ryan M. Yonk, and Kenneth J. Sim, *Nature Unbound: Bureaucracy vs. the Environment*, 2016.

Political scientist Randy T. Simmons and colleagues argue that current U.S. environmental laws often do more harm than good. They make the point that the very concept of wilderness is a bogus creation, so we should revisit the idea of nature to find a better path forward.

345 Criminal Law

John D. Bessler, *Cruel & Unusual: The American Death Penalty and the Founders' Eighth Amendment*, 2012.

Law professor John D. Bessler studies the Eighth Amendment and traces the history of capital punishment in America. After a thorough examination, he concludes that capital punishment should be declared unconstitutional.

James Goodman, *Stories of Scottsboro*, 1995.

In 1931, nine Black teenage boys traveling through Alabama by rail were accused of raping two White women on the train. James Goodman tells the story of the case that followed. The Supreme Court struck down the guilty verdict, not once but twice, and one of the women recanted her story.

Matthew LeRoy and Deric Haddad, *They Must Be Monsters: A Modern-Day Witch Hunt—The Untold Story Behind the McMartin Phenomenon: The Longest, Most Expensive Criminal Case in U.S. History*, 2018.

While many have forgotten it today, the national hysteria surrounding the Southern California McMartin Preschool in the 1980s had Americans seeing child abusers everywhere. Authors LeRoy and Haddad left school in the late 1980s to investigate the case. They interviewed hundreds of people in the upper-class community of Manhattan Beach, where it all began. Some have compared the episode to the Salem witch trials of 1692.

Stacy Schiff, *The Witches:*
Suspicion, Betrayal, and Hysteria in 1692 Salem, 2015.

Stacy Schiff reexamines the events in Salem, Massachusetts, in 1692. From the first case in which a minister's niece, seemingly under bewitchment, began to have attacks of convulsive screaming, members of the community started to turn on one another. Before it was over, 19 people accused of practicing witchcraft were executed.

Scott D. Seligman, *The Third Degree:*
The Triple Murder that Shook Washington and Changed
American Criminal Justice, 2018.

The Miranda rights, which are still in danger today, are not granted by the Constitution. Instead, as this true-crime thriller explains, they were obtained when a young Chinese immigrant, accused of murdering three diplomats in Washington, D.C., in 1919, was investigated for the crime.

346 Private Law

P. Mark Accettura, *Blood & Money:*
Why Families Fight Over Inheritance and What to Do About
It, 2011.

Elder law attorney P. Mark Accettura says that while families fight over inheritance for many reasons, it's rarely about greed. More often, the issue is about feeling important, loved, and secure. Mental illness and addictions exacerbate the problems. Using well-known cases, he advises how to preserve the family in the face of conflict.

Jo Becker, *Forcing the Spring:*
Inside the Fight for Marriage Equality, 2014.

Starting with Proposition 8 in California, which sought to ban gay and lesbian marriages, Jo Becker follows the story of how gay marriage was legalized in America. She follows the fight from Hollywood to Washington, D.C.

Orly Lobel, *You Don't Own Me:*
How Mattel v. MGA Entertainment
Exposed Barbie's Dark Side, 2019.

Law professor Orly Lobel discusses the war between Barbie doll maker Mattel and Bratz doll creator MGA. Lobel stresses the real issue was ownership of ideas, not toys.

Adam Winkler, *We the Corporations:*
How American Businesses Won Their Civil Rights, 2018.

The unknown civil rights movement for citizenship of corporations began while the Constitution was first being written. Adam Winkler follows the gains and losses of corporations from then to now. Currently, they are legal citizens with rights like any other individual, and they use those rights to push for business deregulation to the detriment of society.

347 Procedure & Courts

Kermit L. Hall, et al., eds., *The Oxford Companion to the Supreme Court of the United States*, 1992.

This reference has biographies of every justice that ever sat on the Supreme Court bench. It includes cases, judicial and legal terms, amendments to the Constitution, and a history of the court. The last print edition, released in 2005, is now available online for a fee.

Wil Haygood, *Showdown: Thurgood Marshall and the Supreme Court Nomination that Changed America*, 2015.

Thurgood Marshall was the first African American Supreme Court justice. Wil Haygood traces Marshall's ascent and tells of the many famous Americans who struggled to keep him off the bench.

Jane Mayer and Jill Abramson, *Strange Justice: The Selling of Clarence Thomas*, 1997.

Jane Mayer and Jill Abramson reveal suppressed evidence supporting Anita Hill's accusations of sexual misconduct by Clarence Thomas during his Supreme Court nomination hearings. They assert that the Republican-led judiciary committee misled America during the hearings and pushed the narrative that Anita Hill made up her televised testimony.

Jeffrey Toobin, *The Nine: Inside the Secret World of the Supreme Court*, 2007.

Jeffrey Toobin, a lawyer, and legal correspondent, gives a glimpse of what goes on in the U.S. Supreme Court chambers. His many interviews with the judges provide a peek at the future of law in America.

BIOGRAPHY

Jane Sherron De Hart, *Ruth Bader Ginsburg: A Life*, 2018.

Ruth Bader Ginsburg, champion of women's rights, was the first tenured female law professor at Columbia before becoming a Supreme Court justice. Jane Sherron De Hart spent 15 years researching this biography with Justice Ginsburg, her family, and her friends.

Melvin I. Urofsky, *Louis D. Brandeis: A Life*, 2009.

Progressive Supreme Court justice Louis D. Brandeis was instrumental in passing many of our most important laws, such as the Federal Reserve Act.

He helped establish the Federal Trade Commission and pioneered pro bono work in law practice. A secular Jew, Brandeis later became active in the American Zionist movement.

349 Law of Specific Jurisdictions & Areas

John D. Bessler, *The Birth of American Law: An Italian Philosopher and the American Revolution*, 2014.

American law scholar John D. Bessler examines how a little-known Italian philosopher named Cesare Beccaria influenced many of our founding fathers, including Thomas Jefferson, James Madison, George Washington, Dr. Benjamin Rush, and John Adams. As a result, he also impacted America's judicial system, Declaration of Independence, and Constitution.

350 Public Administration & Military Science

351 Public Administration

Randy T. Simmons, *Beyond Politics: The Roots of Government Failure*, 2011.

Randy T. Simmons asserts that practical concerns limit government power. In reality, governments can't solve all problems, and their efforts to do so often backfire, creating worse messes. Simmons suggests actions citizens can use to take responsibility for societal challenges when appropriate.

353 Specific Fields of Public Administration

James David Barber, *The Presidential Character: Predicting Performance in the White House*, 1972.

Political scientist James David Barber provided a method to predict what sorts of worldviews will be held by upcoming presidents. As remarkable as it sounds, he predicted the administrations of Nixon, Ford, Carter, Reagan, and H. W. Bush before they were elected. In addition, he analyzed how the predictions work. The 5th edition of this work was published in 2019.

Philip J. Hilts, *Protecting America's Health: The FDA, Business, and One Hundred Years of Regulation*, 2003.

Teddy Roosevelt created the U.S. Food and Drug Administration to halt the sale of contaminated meat and quack medicine. Before the formation of the FDA, there was little the government could do to keep harmful products from being sold to an unsuspecting public. In the years since, the administration has battled businesses and conservative politicians to continue its mission. Philip J. Hilts provides a passionate argument for ongoing support for the FDA.

Bryan Stevenson, *Just Mercy:*
***A Story of Justice and Redemption*, 2015.**
> The Equal Justice Initiative was founded by Bryan Stevenson in Montgomery, Alabama, to defend poor inmates. He tells the organization's history, from its founding to its successes, in combating cruel and unjust practices in our prison system.

355 Military Science

Andrew Bacevich, *Breach of Trust:*
How Americans Failed Their Soldiers
***and Their Country*, 2013.**
> History and international relations professor Andrew Bacevich argues that America must regain its view that civilians must fight wars, not a professional warrior class. He points out that most ordinary Americans feel entirely removed from the fighting in the war in Iraq and Afghanistan. The results, he says, are feelings of resignation about being at war that is hurting our national treasury and our moral standing as a nation.

Jerry Borrowman, *Compassionate Soldier:*
Remarkable True Stories of Mercy, Heroism,
***and Honor from the Battlefield*, 2017.**
> Jerry Borrowman tells of soldiers throughout history who demonstrated compassion and care amid war's horrors. He hopes that through reading his stories of soldiers behaving kindly and bravely, you will reexamine what glory and honor mean on the battlefield.

Rosa Brooks, *How Everything Became War and the Military*
***Became Everything: Tales from the Pentagon*, 2016.**
> Rosa Brooks gained a unique perspective on the current U.S. military system from her career as a former top Pentagon official and a human rights activist. She alerts us that the military's rapidly expanding role frequently has nothing to do with war and then stresses the threat this poses to us all.

Annie Jacobsen, *The Pentagon's Brain:*
An Uncensored History of DARPA, America's Top-Secret
***Military Research Agency*, 2016.**
> The controversial Defense Advanced Research Projects Agency (DARPA) is investigated by reporter Annie Jacobsen, who uses interviews, private documents, and declassified memos to penetrate what it's for and what it does. What she finds is fascinating and frightening.

Mary Roach, *Grunt:*
***The Curious Science of Humans at War*, 2017.**
> Science writer Mary Roach digs into what is involved in equipping soldiers

for battle. In doing so, she answers curious questions like "How is a wedding gown like a bomb suit?"

358 Air & Other Specialized Forces

Mike Moore, *Twilight War:*
***The Folly of U.S. Space Dominance*, 2008.**
Since the early space age, domination of military space weapons has been a U.S. priority. Mike Moore looks at the history of these efforts and surprisingly argues that unilateral military dominance by the U.S. would ultimately make Americans less secure.

359 Sea Forces & Warfare

Benjamin W. Larabee, et al., *America and the Sea:*
***A Maritime History*, 1970.**
Six maritime scholars relate the economic, political, and technological maritime history of the U.S., beginning with Native Americans and Vikings. They incorporate art, literature, and poetry to aid understanding.

James Stavridis, *Sea Power:*
***The History and Geopolitics of the World's Oceans*, 2017.**
U.S. Navy admiral James Stavridis looks at the history of naval forces and its past battles. He take you through world's oceans from an admiral's perspective, helping you understand how the shape of the oceans, along with military might, has sculpted the geopolitical world today.

360 Social Problems & Services; Associations

361 Social Problems & Services

Denis Dragovic, *No Dancing, No Dancing:*
***Inside the Global Humanitarian Crisis*, 2018.**
Denis Dragovic traveled to three humanitarian aid sites, in South Sudan, Iraq, and East Timor, to find out what happens in these vulnerable areas when the funds run out. Dragovic unveils the stories of the people there, and he tries to determine better ways to respond than by simply sending money.

Katrina Fried, *Everyday Heroes:*
50 Americans Changing the World One Nonprofit at a
***Time*, 2012.**
Katrina Fried and photographer Paul Mobley traveled America talking with activists and humanitarian workers. Their stories provide inspiration for anyone wishing to promote positive change in the world.

Frances Fox Piven and Richard A. Cloward,
Regulating the Poor:
The Functions of Public Welfare, 1971.

Piven and Cloward explained the welfare system as it existed in 1970s America. The updated 1993 edition examined the intervening erosion of welfare programs during the Reagan, Bush, and Clinton administrations. While considering why the U.S. has chosen to provide a flimsy social safety net compared with most other industrialized nations, they asked readers to reflect on the welfare system's role in society.

Theda Skocpol, *Protecting Soldiers and Mothers:*
The Political Origins of Social Policy in the United
States, 1992.

Government and sociology professor Theda Skocpol argues that the U.S. first introduced the concept of a social safety net when it provided generous benefits to the veterans of the Civil War. But in the aftermath of the war, women's groups began to influence legislative policy, resulting in more of the funds going to women and children. And this led to a decline in spending overall. In light of this history, Skocpol considers new ways to view America's social policy.

362 Social Problems & Services to Groups

Louise Aronson, *Elderhood:*
Redefining Aging, Transforming Medicine, Reimagining
Life, 2019.

Geriatrician Louise Aronson points out that ages 60–70 have been considered the decade when a person becomes "old" across cultures for thousands of years. If we stay with that metric, millions of people will now spend 40 years or more being elderly. She asks us to reimagine this time of life in a more humane and hopeful light.

Cris Beam, *To the End of June:*
The Intimate Life of American Foster Care, 2013.

Journalist and former foster parent Cris Beam looks at what removal from birth families does to foster kids. She follows a group of teenagers in New York who are preparing to leave the system. She asks, Where will they go? What will they do? Who will provide the types of emotional support most of us get from our families? These young people deserve better, and Beam looks at alternatives.

David Finkel, *Thank You for Your Service, 2013.*

Journalist David Finkel's previous book, *The Good Soldiers*, followed the U.S. 2-16 Infantry Battalion as they conducted the 15-month surge into Baghdad. In this book, Finkel contacts the soldiers after they return home and takes a close look at the war's effects on them and their families. He examines their difficulties in readjusting to civilian life. War, he concludes, is not something a person can just turn off.

John Geyman,
Profiteering, Corruption and Fraud in U.S. Health Care, 2020.

Our corporate, profit-driven healthcare system leaves physician John Geyman asking, "Who is our healthcare system for?" Is its purpose to make a few people very wealthy or to meet the needs of American citizens? Geyman supplies the facts needed to prove our broken system requires an overhaul.

Beth Macy, *Dopesick:*
Dealers, Doctors, and the Drug Company that Addicted
America, 2018.

Beth Macy traces the rise of the opioid crisis in America from the introduction of OxyContin in 1996 to the heroin epidemic that followed in its wake. From small-town communities in Appalachia to wealthy urban subdivisions, teenagers and adults alike fell victim to the allure of pain-numbing medications. Macy traces the role of pharmaceutical companies, doctors, and small-town criminals while also shining a light on economic factors that contributed.

David Oshinsky, *Bellevue:*
Three Centuries of Medicine and Mayhem
at America's Most Storied Hospital, 2016.

As America's oldest hospital, Bellevue, on New York City's East Side, is a patient treatment model today, but for years it was known for housing the mentally ill, the criminally insane, and sufferers of exotic diseases. This book traces its history from its opening in 1738 to its current role as a public safety net.

Rachel Louise Snyder, *No Visible Bruises:*
What We Don't Know About Domestic Violence
Can Kill Us, 2019.

Journalist Rachel Louise Snyder affirms that domestic violence is a problem we cannot ignore because the effects on society are too pervasive and devastating. Myths that blame the victims make the problem worse. Snyder explains that domestic violence is inseparable from the violence of the larger community because mass shootings and sexual assault often have their roots in hidden violence at home.

BIOGRAPHY

Michelle Bowdler, *Is Rape a Crime?:*
A Memoir, an Investigation, and a Manifesto, 2020.

In the early 1980s, a series of rapes terrorized the women of Boston. Michelle

Bowdler was the last to be assaulted during the spree. Yet, after one brief interview, she never heard from the police again. She later looked at how we treat rape in the U.S., where fewer than three percent of cases lead to convictions. Her book, part memoir and part investigation, is a plea for the crime to be treated as severe assault.

Ruth Coker Burks and Kevin Carr O'Leary, *All the Young Men: A Memoir of Love, AIDS, and Chosen Family in the American South,* **2020.**
Ruth Coker Burks first became aware of the AIDS epidemic while visiting a friend in the hospital. After seeing a red-painted door, with nurses outside drawing straws to see who must go in, she impulsively entered the room herself. A young man inside was dying and crying for his mother. Thus began her decades of work with people with AIDS, which she recalls in this memoir.

Rosayra Pablo Cruz and Julie Schwietert Collazo, *The Book of Rosy: A Mother's Story of Separation at the Border,* **2020.**
The decision to come to the U.S. with her two young sons was not easy for Rosy Cruz. But she felt life in Guatemala, with its gangs and chaos, left her no choice. Before they reached the U.S. border, they were dehydrated, exhausted, and starving. Then, at the Arizona border, the Department of Homeland Security seized her children under the nation's new zero-tolerance policy. With the help of her friend Julie Collazo, founder of Immigrant Families Together, she voices her heartbreaking yet hopeful story.

Judith Heumann, *Being Heumann: An Unrepentant Memoir of a Disability Rights Activist,* **2020.**
Judith Heumann has accomplished a lot since she became paralyzed from polio at 18 months. She fought to attend the grade school that had referred to her as a "fire hazard," she won a lawsuit to become a teacher in New York City, and she led the Section 504 sit-in at the U.S. Department of Health, Education, and Welfare in San Francisco. Heumann also led the campaign that resulted in the Americans with Disabilities Act. Her memoir insists that we all deserve an equal chance at life.

363 Other Social Problems & Services

Ben Austen, *High Risers: Cabrini-Green and the Fate of American Public Housing,* **2018.**
Chicago resident Ben Austen chronicles the history of America's attempts to provide public housing for its urban poor. Cabrini-Green was a housing project that was once home to 20,000 people. By 2011, all 23 towers were gone and the families relocated to make room for growing affluent, primarily White neighborhoods.

W. Fitzhugh Brundage, *Civilizing Torture:*
***An American Tradition*, 2019.**

Historian W. Fitzhugh Brundage looks at the history of torture in America, from the early settlers who came here to escape its threat in the Old World through today. He then explores society's disapproval of torture and the contradictory ability to tolerate it. And finally, Brundage discusses racial and legal issues that exacerbate its use.

Anna Clark, *The Poisoned City:*
***Flint's Water and the American Urban Tragedy*, 2018.**

Detroit journalist Anna Clark tells how Flint, Michigan, a city of 100,000 largely poor African Americans, came to have a water system poisoned with lead and other toxins. The state government switched the city's water supply to a source that corroded the lead pipes. For 18 months, complaints went unheard, and 12 people died before the city admitted the water was poisonous.

L. S. Gardiner, *Tales from an Uncertain World:*
What Other Assorted Disasters Can Teach Us About Climate
***Change*, 2018.**

Rather than contending that climate change is too large for individuals to impact, science educator L. S. Gardiner says examples of disaster response to earthquakes, fires, and floods can guide us to appropriate actions on a small scale to check climate change.

Eliza Griswold, *Amity and Prosperity:*
***One Family and the Fracturing of America*, 2019.**

The rural Pennsylvania town of Amity was excited when an energy company came to town and began paying off the residents. Single mother Stacey Haney was happy until domestic animals and pets began to die and people in her family became inexplicably sick. Haney began to investigate and took the case to court, after which her community began to fracture. This insider's story reveals the price and consequences of our energy infrastructure.

Daniel Okrent, *Last Call:*
***The Rise and Fall of Prohibition*, 2011.**

Daniel Okrent explores how the U.S. went from being a nation where liquor was cheaper than tea in the 1820s to one where alcohol consumption was illegal in 1920. By the time Prohibition ended, U.S. politics had changed forever through the government's expanded role in private lives.

Tatiana Schlossberg, *Inconspicuous Consumption:*
***The Environmental Impact You Don't Know You Have*, 2019.**

Most of us have no idea what impact our everyday habits have on the global environment. Science writer Tatiana Schlossberg helps you see how a sweater bought in the U.S. affects Mongolia and how watching Netflix depletes fossil

fuels. She makes these facts opportunities to learn what each of us can do to
save the planet.

364 Criminology

Carl Bernstein and Bob Woodward,
All the President's Men, 1974.

Investigative reporters for the *Washington Post* Carl Bernstein and Bob
Woodward would not let the 1972 story of the break-in at the Democratic
headquarters at the Watergate alone. Their investigations later brought the
Nixon presidency to an end.

Sarah Chayes, *Thieves of State:*
Why Corruption Threatens Global Security, 2015.

Kleptocracies have always been with us. But Sarah Chayes ties many of the
incendiary acts across the globe today to rampant government corruption
worldwide. She shows how large and small governments perpetrate crimes,
enraging their citizens to the point that the reaction outstrips the government
damage in ferocity and suffering. Chayes contends we must confront corruption to slow the resulting extremism that threatens us all.

Robert W. Fieseler, *Tinderbox:*
The Untold Story of the Up Stairs Lounge Fire and the Rise of
Gay Liberation, 2018.

Journalist Robert W. Fieseler details the event that ignited the gay rights
movement. In June of 1973, someone deliberately set fire to a gay bar in New
Orleans. Before it was extinguished, 31 men and one woman were dead, making it the largest mass murder in any gay community before the Pulse night-
club attack in Orlando in 2016. Fieseler exposes the prejudice the survivors
and families experienced in the fire's aftermath.

James Forman Jr., *Locking Up Our Own:*
Crime and Punishment in Black America, 2017.

Former D.C. public defender James Forman Jr. explains why the 1970s efforts
of African American leaders, including mayors, judges, and police chiefs in
Black communities, failed to prevent, and even contributed to, the mass incar-
cerations we see today. Forman reveals why their work backfired.

Philip Gourevitch, *We Wish to Inform You that*
Tomorrow We Will Be Killed with Our Families:
Stories from Rwanda, 1998.

Philip Gourevitch recounts the events from April 1994 when the Rwandan
government asked every member of the Hutu majority to slaughter all members of the Tutsi minority. By July, they had murdered over 800,000 Tutsis.
Gourevitch depicts the history that led up to the genocide and its aftermath.

Gerald Posner, *Case Closed:*
Lee Harvey Oswald and the Assassination of JFK, 1993.

Attorney and journalist Gerald Posner took a hard look at all the available evidence in John F. Kennedy's assassination. After years of speculation and controversial films, books, and accusations, Posner reached the only reasonable conclusion, which was corroborated by materials released since this book's publication.

Timothy B. Tyson, *The Blood of Emmett Till*, 2017.

Emmett Till has become an icon of the civil rights movement. The 14-year-old Chicago resident, visiting relatives in Mississippi, was lynched after a White woman accused him of flirting with her. Tyson examines all the available evidence to paint a horrific portrait of the treatment Till received. Making the tragedy even more outrageous, Till's accuser later admitted he was innocent.

365 Penal & Related Institutions

Anne Applebaum, *Gulag: A History*, 2003.

The Soviet Union was infamous for its gulags, a network of concentration camps for criminals and political prisoners alike. Threat of being sent to one was an effective way to terrorize the population into submission and squelch protests. Anne Applebaum gives the history of the gulags and chronicles their use from Stalin to glasnost.

Shane Bauer, *American Prison: A Reporter's Undercover Journey into the Business of Punishment*, 2018.

Private prisons are increasingly common in America. Investigative reporter Shane Bauer became a guard at one in Winnfield, Louisiana, for $9 an hour in 2014. In this book, Bauer shares his experiences and outlines the history of these institutions, particularly in the South where, since the Civil War, they have been part of the system to keep African Americans in their place.

Christopher P. Dum, *Exiled in America:*
Life on the Margins in a Residential Motel, 2016.

Sociologist Christopher P. Dum spent some time living in a residential motel, and he shares the stories of its residents—where they came from and why they wound up there. Most of them are the working poor, recently released prisoners, the addicted, the mentally ill, and people with disabilities. The conditions in which they live would be unimaginable for many of us. Dum suggests policy changes to help the vulnerable citizens who live in these places.

Heather Ann Thompson, *Blood in the Water:*
The Attica Prison Uprising of 1971 and Its Legacy, 2016.

Historian Heather Ann Thompson looks at the seldom-discussed civil rights issues of prisoners. In September of 1971, the prisoners in the Attica

Correctional Facility in upstate New York took over the prison for four days and nights, holding guards and civilian employees hostage while negotiating for improved living conditions. The situation ended in a brutal takedown in which prisoners and hostages alike were killed. Thompson looks at the aftermath and the lessons that we can all take away from it.

Christopher Zoukis, *Federal Prison Handbook: The Definitive Guide to Surviving the Federal Bureau of Prisons*, 2017.
Law student and former inmate Christopher Zoukis wrote this guidebook for anyone who finds themselves or a loved one in federal prison. He outlines prisoner rights, avoiding conflicts, available jobs, medical and religious services, and the underground economy. Prison is a harsh environment, and Zoukis aims to help those inside survive with dignity.

BIOGRAPHY

Albert Woodfox, *Solitary: Unbroken by Four Decades of Solitary Confinement. My Story of Transformation and Hope*, 2019.
Albert Woodfox tells how he survived over 40 years in solitary confinement in Louisiana's Angola Prison for a crime he didn't commit. Woodfox was alone in a six-by-nine-foot cell for 23 hours every day. His memoir provides a compelling argument against using solitary confinement in prisons everywhere.

366 Secret Associations & Societies

Adam Parfrey and Craig Heimbichner, *Ritual America: Secret Brotherhoods and Their Influence on American Society: A Visual Guide*, 2012.
Freemasons, Knights of the Pythias, and Skull and Bones are a few of the secret societies America has hosted. Parfrey and Heimbichner include symbols and images of these organizations and examine what they mean, shedding light on who the members are and why they exist.

368 Insurance

Theresa Barta, *Greed on Trial: Doctors and Patients Unite to Fight Big Insurance*, 2018.
Insurance law specialist Theresa Barta represents doctors terminated from their healthcare companies for placing patients' needs above the bottom line. In this book, Barta presents three cases she represented, questioning the outsized influence insurance companies have on our quality of healthcare in America.

Peter L. Bernstein, *Against the Gods:*
***The Remarkable Story of Risk*, 1996.**

Economic consultant Peter L. Bernstein examines the history of the stock
market. He also looks at the implications of risk and probability amid the bull
market of the late 20th century.

Eric Laursen, *The People's Pension:*
***The Struggle to Defend Social Security Since Reagan*, 2012.**

Social Security, a much-needed financial safety net for millions of Americans,
has been in perpetual danger since the 1980s. Eric Laursen, an independent
financial and political journalist, traces the story of a campaign of misinfor-
mation and lobbying from right-wing bankers, foundations, economists, and
politicians to cut Social Security. Laursen argues that the best solution may
be to take the system away from the government altogether and place it in the
hands of the people.

370 Education

Marilee Adams, *Teaching That Changes Lives:*
***12 Mindset Tools for Igniting the Love of Learning*, 2013.**

Burnout is particularly damaging when it happens to someone teaching
children. Marilee Adams helps teachers understand the power of mindsets,
or mental habits, and how they affect relationships with students, colleagues,
administrators, and the job. In addition, she lists online resources to help
teachers move through difficulties, making classrooms places of curiosity,
creativity, and caring.

Melba Pattillo Beals, *Warriors Don't Cry:*
A Searing Memoir of the Battle to Integrate Little Rock's
***Central High*, 1994.**

If you've ever seen footage or photographs of the Little Rock Nine, a group of
Black teenagers who entered the city's all-White high school in 1957, you have
a sense of the tension and terror those students faced. Melba Pattillo was one
of those students, and she shares what it was like to make her way through
a screaming mob intent on stopping them. She goes on to confide what that
school year and the years that followed were like.

John Holt, *How Children Learn*, **1967.**

Veteran teacher John Holt wrote this classic to help teachers and parents
understand how young children learn to talk, read, count, and reason.
"Learning," he said," is as natural as breathing." After becoming convinced
school reform was impossible, Holt later became an advocate of
homeschooling.

Marc Prensky, *Education to Better Their World:*
***Unleashing the Power of 21st-Century Kids*, 2016.**
Educator and futurist Marc Prensky offers a new model for educating the
world's youth. He argues that the focus on math, language arts, science, and
social studies is leaving most young people woefully unprepared for the
demands the world will place on them in the future. The alternative Prensky
proposes is a project-based system that would better serve students from
every walk of life.

Amanda Ripley, *The Smartest Kids in the World:*
***And How They Got That Way*, 2014.**
That America has been falling behind in educational metrics for decades is
old news. But investigative journalist Amanda Ripley explored the issue from
a new angle. She followed three American high school students as they made
their way through a year at three of the best performing school systems in the
world, in Finland, South Korea, and Poland. Ripley finds that while the school
system matters, societal attitudes toward growing up and learning are more
critical. Developing resilience by failing often and early, she finds, matters
more than sports and self-esteem.

George Stranahan, *A Predicament of Innocents:*
***Might the Schools Help?*, 2012.**
Surveying education after six decades of teaching experience, educator
George Stranahan delivers these essays on schooling from the students' perspectives. What do students want? What do they need? Stranahan feels traditional teaching methods stifle children's potential, and he offers new ideas to
foster a love of learning.

371 Schools & Their Activities; Special Education

Amye Archer and Loren Kleinman, eds.,
If I Don't Make It, I Love You:
***Survivors in the Aftermath of School Shootings*, 2019.**
School shootings are a tragic part of American life. Archer and Kleinman go
behind the headlines to bring us more than 60 stories that give first-hand
accounts of school shootings from the survivors of the 1966 University of
Texas at Austin tower shootings through the 2018 shootings in Santa Fe, New
Mexico.

Richard DuFour, *In Praise of American Educators:*
***And How They Can Become Even Better*, 2015.**
Richard DuFour argues that today's American teachers are not the overpaid
shirkers they are portrayed as. He says ill-advised reforms, not the quality of
educators, caused the plight of the nation's schools. He offers guidance to turn
things around, because today's teachers, he says, are the best we've ever had.

Steven Goodman, *It's Not About Grit:*
Trauma, Inequity, and the Power
***of Transformative Teaching*, 2018.**
Educator Steven Goodman takes a compassionate look at struggling and marginalized students to see how to help them. Many of these students deal with issues that more successful students are thankfully spared, such as poverty, racism, or family issues like separation or violence. Sharing stories from many of these students provides insight into problems that, if left hidden, can halt the educational process for the children involved.

E. D. Hirsch Jr., *The Making of Americans:*
***Democracy and Our Schools*, 2009.**
E. D. Hirsch argues that American schools are lagging behind many others globally because they have neglected content of subject-area teaching, especially in the earliest years of public schooling. Hirsch says it's only through standardized content that students from all socioeconomic backgrounds gain access to a level educational playing field. He outlines what, specifically, should be taught at each level.

Frederic H. Jones, *Fred Jones Tools for Teaching:*
***Discipline, Instruction, Motivation*, 2000.**
Teachers can't teach unless they can manage a classroom. In this book's third edition, Fred Jones provides a plan to reduce teacher stress while empowering students to listen, do, and learn.

Dale Russakoff, *The Prize:*
***Who's In Charge of Our American Schools?*, 2015.**
Dale Russakoff looks at what happens when a struggling public school district receives a financial windfall meant to help it improve. The problems come when people whose livelihoods are dependent on maintaining the status quo fight the change. In this case, influential figures like Mark Zuckerberg, Chris Christie, and Cory Booker are part of a story that demonstrates how politics and schools collide today.

372 Primary Education (Elementary Education)

Anne E. Cunningham and Jamie Zibulsky,
Book Smart:
How to Develop and Support
***Successful, Motivated Readers*, 2014.**
Cunningham and Zibulsky present this guide for parents of preschoolers who want to read with their children through the elementary grades. The lessons, activities, and stories included will help your child prepare for school and pave the way for lifelong learning. The authors explain why the love of reading is crucial to a child's success in life.

Michael Gramling,
The Great Disconnect in Early Childhood Education:
What We Know vs. What We Do, 2015.

Too often, policymakers have no classroom teaching experience with children. Michael Gramling argues that this accounts for the disconnect between what teachers are directed to do and what helps children learn. Teachers must challenge instructions that interfere with the process. And parents need to understand what teachers are required to do before they can see a teacher's position. Once parents understand this, they can become partners with the teacher in their children's education.

Margaret Berry Wilson,
The Language of Learning:
Teaching Students Core Thinking, Listening,
and Speaking Skills, 2014.

We all need excellent language skills, and it's far better if children learn them early on. Margaret Berry Wilson's guide helps you teach young students to listen and understand. They must learn specifically how to think about what they want to say, say what they mean, ask thoughtful questions, back up their opinions with reason, and disagree respectfully.

373 Secondary Education

Lorene Cary, *Black Ice*, 1991.

Lorene Cary recounts her time, starting in 1972, as a Black scholarship student in the previously all-White, all-male St. Paul's School's boot camp for future leaders. The book tells a coming-of-age story that deals with Cary's representing a minority in both race and sex. In addition, she shares what she learned about succeeding without selling out or betraying herself.

Brooke Hauser, *The New Kids:*
Big Dreams and Brave Journeys
at a High School for Immigrant Teens, 2011.

International High School at Prospect Heights in Brooklyn is a typical American high school in many ways, except for one: all its students have recently arrived as immigrants in the U.S. The stories these students tell are unforgettable (one made the trip to the states curled up in a suitcase). All are seeking the American dream.

Karyn Rashoff, *Parents in Highschooland:*
Helping Students Succeed in the Critical Years, 2013.

The teen years are challenging for many parents. As a guidance counselor with over three decades of experience, Karyn Rashoff offers help. She compiled these lessons from interactions with students and parents revolving around school, and she has isolated actionable tips to help you help your kids.

374 Adult Education

Kathleen Rooney, *Reading with Oprah:*
The Book Club that Changed America, 2005.
> Publisher and editor Kathleen Rooney explores the Oprah Book Club and the
> impact it has had on culture in America. She also tackles charges that the club
> has pandered to low tastes.

378 Higher Education (Tertiary Education)

Joseph E. Aoun, *Robot-Proof:*
Higher Education in the Age
***of Artificial Intelligence*, 2017.**
> Linguistics scholar Joseph E. Aoun says robots can now replace stock market
> analysts, legal researchers, and medical image interpreters. So should stu-
> dents be trained for jobs that may no longer exist in a few years? Aoun argues
> that a new discipline he calls *humanics*, which is dependent upon data literacy,
> technological literacy, and human literacy, is the answer. He says we need a
> humanities-rich education that focuses on communication and design skills
> so students will be ready to collaborate with machines in the future.

Derf Backderf, *Kent State:*
***Four Dead in Ohio*, 2020.**
> When Derf Backderf was 10, he saw members of the Ohio National Guard in
> his hometown. They were there on a mission to crush a trucker strike. A few
> days later, those same guardsmen went to Kent State University to put down
> a Vietnam War protest by unarmed college students. On May 4, 1970, the
> guardsmen opened fire on the crowd, killing four students and wounding nine.
> Backderf examines this troubling display of power deployed against dissent
> in America.

Kelly J. Baker, *Sexism Ed:*
Essays on Gender and Labor
***in Academia*, 2018.**
> Kelly J. Baker, fueled by the sexism and outright misogyny she experienced
> firsthand in academia, explores the fallout of battling patriarchy. She also
> urges other women to continue fighting.

William F. Buckley Jr.,
God and Man at Yale:
***The Superstitions of "Academic Freedom,"* 1951.**
> William F. Buckley published this scathing exposé about his alma mater, Yale
> University, at age 25. Among other things, Buckley criticized what he per-
> ceived as a united effort of faculty to turn students into believers in liberalism
> and secularism.

Andrew Delbanco, *College:*
***What It Was, Is, and Should Be*, 2012.**

Humanities professor Andrew Delbanco examines the increasing emphasis on
American colleges as *pre-professional* institutions—prep schools for careers
in law, medicine, and business. He defends the idea of a broad education with
a grounding in the humanities for any American who wishes it, arguing variety is essential for the nation's health.

Kent Garrett and Jeanne Ellsworth,
The Last Negroes at Harvard:
The Class of 1963 and the 18 Young Men
***Who Changed Harvard Forever*, 2020.**

In 1959, Harvard University recruited 18 "Negro boys" to begin affirmative action. Between that time and their graduation in 1963, the nation
had changed, and the young men had become African Americans. Kent
Garrett, one of the 18, reconnects with his classmates 50 years later. He
discloses where they have been, and together they muse on what their time at
Harvard meant.

Danny Iny, *Leveraged Learning:*
How the Disruption of Education Helps Lifelong Learners
***and Experts with Something to Teach*, 2018.**

Higher education in America is failing many of its students, says education
entrepreneur Danny Iny. Among the problems are high costs, outdated classes,
and the bureaucracies in charge. Iny says that in a world that is changing as
rapidly as ours is today, education should be agile to keep up. Lifelong learning is the key to success.

Hanna Rosin, *God's Harvard:*
***A Christian College on a Mission to Save America*, 2007.**

Patrick Henry College, a small Christian school outside Washington, D.C.,
is where Hanna Rosin spent a year and a half. She reports what happens to
the highly motivated, mostly homeschooled students who attend. The school
trains them to become high-profile members of the evangelical movement,
charged with taking back the country for God.

380 Commerce, Communications, Transportation

381 Commerce (Trade)

Eric Jay Dolin, *Fur, Fortune, and Empire:*
***The Epic History of the Fur Trade in America*, 2010.**

Eric Jay Dolin looks at how the fur industry in North America began in the early 17th century and only started to wane in the late 19th century. In the intervening nearly 300 years, it changed the face of America forever.

David Eltis and David Richardson, *Atlas of the Transatlantic Slave Trade*, 2010.

For over 350 years, the transatlantic slave trade thrived on capturing and enslaving approximately 12.5 million Africans and selling them in the U.S., the Caribbean islands, and Central and South America. Using 200 maps to illustrate their points, Eltis and Richardson estimate that around 80 percent of all voyages ever made involved these slaves. Their detailed atlas shows precisely where these people came from and where they wound up.

Anindya Ghose, *Tap: Unlocking the Mobile Economy*, 2017.

Mobile economy expert Anindya Ghose takes an optimistic look at what smartphones and other mobile technologies can do for the people who use them. Rather than focusing on the dark potential of these devices, Ghose stresses the time-saving and helpful aspects of the global mobile economy, including the Internet of things, virtual reality, and artificial intelligence.

Michael Mainelli and Ian Harris, *The Price of Fish: A New Approach to Wicked Economics and Better Decisions*, 2011.

Mainelli and Harris argue that we cannot continue to look at economics and commerce with the simple formulas we have been using. Instead, they present new systems like those developed by quantum physicists. They blend the factors of choice, economics, systems, and evolution to help us make better decisions for the world's most intractable problems.

BIOGRAPHY

Sam Walton, *Sam Walton: Made in America*, 1992.

Sam Walton reveals how he founded Walmart and Sam's Club, beginning with a small dime store in a decaying town. This instructive book on an ordinary man who made a fortune was published shortly before Walton died.

382 International Commerce (Foreign Trade)

Eric Jay Dolin, *When America First Met China: An Exotic History of Tea, Drugs, and Money in the Age of Sail*, 2012.

Eric Jay Dolin looks at how the fledgling United States of America and the Chinese empire, with its thousands of years of history, formed a trade and political relationship. The saga sheds light on a little-understood part of American history.

Dan Morgan, *Merchants of Grain: The Power and Profits of the Five Giant Companies at the Center of the World's Food Supply*, 1979.

This story of five multinational companies that largely control the entire planet's food supply is still relevant today. While their history goes back over a century, they continue to dominate. Note: An updated version is available that documents the changes with the companies since 1979: *Out of the Shadows: The New Merchants of Grain*, by Jonathan Kingsman.

384 Communications

Phil Lapsley, *Exploding the Phone: The Untold Story of the Teenagers and Outlaws Who Hacked Ma Bell*, 2013.

Phil Lapsley charts the history of the telephone system that had grown by the mid-20th century into an incredibly complex network that connected almost everyone. It was the Internet of its day. But an eclectic cast of characters made up of techies, teenagers, hippies, and outlaws who called themselves *phone phreaks* hacked the system. They considered it a lark until the FBI became involved.

Matt Richtel, *A Deadly Wandering: A Mystery, A Landmark Investigation, and the Astonishing Science of Attention in the Digital Age*, 2014.

Matt Richtel looks at human attention and how our connected devices affect it. To do so, he tells of the the tragic texting-while-driving accident in which college student Reggie Shaw hit and killed two rocket scientists on a Utah highway.

Tim Wu, *The Master Switch: The Rise and Fall of Information Empires*, 2010.

Law professor Tim Wu says every significant new communication industry beginning with the telephone was dominated by one monopoly. The dangers are apparent. Power over information equals control over world events. Wu sounds the alarm over the rise of Apple, Google, and even AT&T, the past telephone monopoly.

BIOGRAPHY

Robert V. Bruce, *Bell: Alexander Graham Bell and the Conquest of Solitude*, 1973.

Alexander Graham Bell accomplished more than the invention of the

telephone. While he was a very secretive individual who shunned the spotlight, he was also a phonetician, showman, and teacher of the deaf. Bruce's
biography looks at Bell's other inventions and his unhappiness with his
resulting fame.

385 Railroad Transportation

H. Roger Grant, *Railroads and the American People*, 2012.
H. Roger Grant looks at the golden age of railroads in America, from 1830 to
1930, and their impact on social history. He examines how trains changed
travel, how train stations became town centers, and railroads' heritage in our
art, folklore, and song.

**Richard White, *Railroaded:
The Transcontinentals and the Making
of Modern America*, 2011.**
Historian Richard White explores the economic and political impact railroads
had on America. Without them, we would never have become a world super-
power, but White also looks at the dark side of the railroading legacy.

387 Water, Air, Space Transportation

**Richard Holmes, *Falling Upwards:
How We Took to Air:
An Unconventional History of Ballooning*, 2013.**
In this history of hot air balloons and the aeronauts who piloted them,
Richard Holmes examines how they changed our view of the world and paved
the way for later air travel.

388 Transportation

**H. Roger Grant,
Transportation and the American People, 2019.**
Historian H. Roger Grant tells about America's transportation infrastructure
from its slow and dangerous beginnings through the airways, roadways, and
waterways we travel today. With each advance in technology, Grant recounts
the corresponding changes in the country's economic, political, and social life.

**Barry B. LePatner, *Too Big to Fall:
America's Failing Infrastructure
and the Way Forward*, 2010.**
Barry B. LePatner begins with the tragic collapse of the I-35W bridge in
Minneapolis in 2007 to examine the numerous design and funding problems
that imperil U.S. infrastructure. Then, he explains why our economic power
as a nation depends on keeping these systems reliable, as do our lives.

390 Customs, Etiquette, Folklore

391 Costume & Personal Appearance

Norberto Angeletti, and Alberto Oliva, *In Vogue: The Illustrated History of the World's Most Famous Fashion Magazine*, 2006.
Vogue, the iconic American fashion magazine, was launched in 1909 by Condé Nast, and its influence on the fashion industry has been tremendous. The history of *Vogue* is relayed here along with its photographers, artists, and illustrators.

Hafsa Lodi, *Modesty: A Fashion Paradox: Uncovering the Causes, Controversies and Key Players Behind the Global Trend to Conceal, Rather Than Reveal*, 2020.
Across the globe, mainstream fashion has been moving toward more modest attire. Partly influenced by women of faith and partly by feminists, high fashion like Gucci and mass labels like H&M integrate modesty into their designs. Hafsa Lodi looks at the people and companies leading the movement and the controversies surrounding it.

Doreen Yarwood, *The Encyclopedia of World Costume*, 1978.
Doreen Yarwood provides articles on clothing worn throughout history, in all cultures, from ancient times to the 20th century, in this one-volume encyclopedia.

392 Customs of Life Cycle & Domestic Life

Bill Bryson, *At Home: A Short History of Private Life*, 2010.
Writer Bill Bryson looked around the Victorian parsonage where he and his family lived and wondered about the story behind the everyday objects he found there. Then, going from room to room, he researched the things that he saw and in the process compiled a history of the average home.

Ann Cline, *A Hut of One's Own: Life Outside the Circle of Architecture*, 1998.
The global trend toward tiny houses had Ann Cline thinking about one-room human dwelling structures throughout history. Her examination shows primitive huts in times past and compares them with those in our own.

Shea Darian, *Living Passages for the Whole Family: Celebrating Rites of Passage from Birth to Adulthood*, 2008.
Starting and graduating from school are the only rites of passage to mark

milestones for many of today's children. Shea Darian seeks to increase rites of passages with 20 ceremonies that parents can use to help children through life events, heal past wounds, and empower them to take on new challenges.

Karl Schwantes, *Rock Her World: The Ultimate Guide to Choosing the Perfect Engagement Ring*, 2015.

Ring designer Karl Schwantes guides men through engagement ring selection. He considers questions such as "What ring will look best on my partner's hand?" and helps you understand the 4C's—cut, clarity, color, and carat. He also has suggestions for the perfect proposal.

394 General Customs

Mary Beard, *The Roman Triumph*, 2007.

Celebrated classics scholar Mary Beard brings you an eye-opening look at the Roman triumphal procession. When generals made it back to Rome after their most recent conquests, they held events to show off the soldiers, animals, prisoners, and bounty taken from the conquered lands. Beard also considers the dark side of the events and what they tell us about triumph, even in our own time.

Michael Harney, *The Harney & Sons Guide to Tea*, 2008.

As a buyer and blender at Harney & Sons, Michael Harney offers insight into the place of tea in world cultures and the agricultural factors that produce it. He discusses different types of tea and provides instructions on how to brew and appreciate each.

Karen Le Billion, *French Kids Eat Everything: How Our Family Moved to France, Cured Picky Eating, Banned Snacking, and Discovered 10 Simple Rules for Raising Happy, Healthy Eaters*, 2012.

Karen Le Billion expresses the shock she experienced on moving to northern France. There, children eat what adults eat and only at mealtimes. As a result, they will consume things most North American children would refuse. As a result, French children are slim, while obesity plagues even the young in the U.S. Le Billion shows Americans how they can raise healthier and happier children using French practices.

Peter Menzel and Faith D'Aluisio, *What I Eat: Around the World in 80 Diets*, 2010.

Peter Menzel travels the globe and reports on the one-day diets of 80 individuals. He provides photographs, calorie counts, and their ages and activity levels. The comparisons prove fascinating. In addition, famous writers and scientists discuss the impact of diets on health and the planet.

Inazo Nitobe, *Bushido:*
The Samurai Code of Japan, 1905.

The Samurai warriors of Japan had a code of ethics that guided their conduct and way of life. Inazo Nitobe looks at the traits Samurai lived by, such as courage, self-control, and benevolence. The book also examines their training and weapons.

395 Etiquette (Manners)

Josh Chetwynd, *The Book of Nice:*
A Nice Book About Nice Things for Nice People, 2013.

Whatever happened to nice? When did it go out of style? Never, says Josh Chetwynd; we still have polite practices embedded in our culture, from covering our mouths when we yawn to finding a perfect gift. Chetwynd says that they're more than just customs: these little niceties are what hold our society together.

Vicky Oliver, *301 Smart Answers*
to Tough Business Etiquette Questions, 2010.

While women no longer wear gloves and men don't tip their hats, manners matter just as much today as they ever did. But forms of etiquette change with time and place. Career coach Vicky Oliver helps workers understand everything from avoiding an unfortunate first impression to supply closet etiquette.

398 Folklore

Bruno Bettelheim, *The Uses of Enchantment:*
The Meaning and Importance of Fairy Tales, 1975.

Child psychologist Bruno Bettelheim's classic study of folk and fairy tales reveals what they unconsciously mean to children. He analyzes well-known stories, such as "Hansel and Gretel," for the Freudian meanings behind them, demonstrating how they help children make meaning of their lives.

Katherine M. Briggs, *An Encyclopedia of Fairies:*
Hobgoblins, Brownies, Bogies,
and Other Supernatural Creatures, 1971.

Katherine Briggs provides an exhaustive look at all sorts of legendary creatures. While the emphasis is on British folklore, she covers some from other places as well.

Italo Calvino, *Italian Folktales*, 1956.

Italian writer Italo Calvino presents 200 folktales from Italy, capturing their playfulness and mystery.

Adrienne Mayor, *The Amazons: Lives and Legends of Warrior Women Across the Ancient World*, 2014.
Adrienne Mayor explores the most recent archaeological evidence for the Amazons' existence. From the British Isles to China, Mayor searches for traces of these women-dominated warrior cultures.

Philip Pullman, *Fairy Tales from the Brothers Grimm: A New English Version*, 2012.
Of the hundreds of fairy tales recorded by the Brothers Grimm, Philip Pullman chooses 50, both well known and largely forgotten, to retell. He focuses on those tales that inspired him to develop his worldview and artistic vision.

Judith Roche and Meg McHutchison, eds., *First Fish, First People: Salmon Tales of the North Pacific Rim*, 1998.
Writers around the Pacific Rim, from Japan to Siberia to the U.S., share traditional and contemporary stories of the salmon that were once found everywhere in these regions but are now largely gone.

Malcolm South, ed., *Mythical and Fabulous Creatures: A Source Book and Research Guide*, 1987.
An invaluable source of information on mythological and legendary creatures from all over the globe, this work contains essays on each type, with glossaries, taxonomies, and extensive bibliographies.

Marina Warner, *Stranger Magic: Charmed States and the Arabian Nights*, 2011.
The Tales from the Arabian Nights became known in the West when translated into French and English during the early Enlightenment. At the time, the Middle East looked at them as a collection of folktales. But Marina Warner argues that the impact of the book has been far wider reaching than previously understood. The tales became a catalyst for imagination in the West, resulting in previously unimagined changes in society and science.

Eli Yassif, *The Hebrew Folktale: History, Genre, Meaning*, 1994.
Eli Yassif provides an exhaustive look at the central folk narratives in Jewish culture. He covers the major trends from each period.

Jane Yolen, *Favorite Folktales from Around the World*, 1986.
Folktales come from everywhere. Award-winning author Jane Yolen retells over 150 of them from Iceland to Papua New Guinea in this single volume.

CHAPTER 5

400–499

Languages

THE 400S MAKE UP THE smallest section in most libraries. Its books cover linguistics, grammar, dictionaries, and other language-related topics for every language globally. Because of the English-language and Eurocentric world in which Dewey operated, most numbers are devoted to English or other European languages. One section, 490–499, is where the system places every non-European language in the world. Unfortunately, I have very few non-European books in my portable library, because the lists I used yielded almost none.

400 Language

Kenneth Katzner, *The Languages of the World*, 1975.
Kenneth Katzner introduces all the world's language families at publication. They describe nearly 600 languages and provide 200 passages with English translations.

**Steven Pinker, *The Language Instinct:
How the Mind Creates Language*, 1994.**
Cognitive scientist Steven Pinker explains how language works, how children learn it, and how it evolved. The first edition was already considered a classic before the updated edition in 2000 reflected the latest scientific understandings.

401 Philosophy & Theory

**Diana Raffman, *Unruly Words:
A Study of Vague Language*, 2014.**
Language scholar Diana Raffman explains her theory on why vague words like *tall*, *rich*, and *old* are used and the problems they pose for disciplines as diverse as philosophy and law.

403 Dictionaries & Encyclopedias

David Crystal,
The Cambridge Encyclopedia of Language, **1987.**

Welsh English language and linguistics professor David Crystal wrote this
widely acclaimed reference on the history and use of the English language
around the globe. The revised version, published in 2003, has maps, illustrations, statistics, and suggestions for further reading. It's intended for a
general audience, helpful for students and language enthusiasts.

409 Geographic Treatment & Biography

James Turner, *Philology:*
The Forgotten Origins of the Modern Humanities, **2014.**

Philology encompassed the study of today's humanities, including classical
literature, the Bible, languages, other kinds of literature, history, culture, art,
and music. James Turner explores the past regard for the humanities and how
they became largely irrelevant. He also speculates on what we can gain by
exploring them once again.

410 Linguistics

R. R. K. Hartmann and F. C. Stork,
Dictionary of Language and Linguistics, **1972.**

Hartmann and Stork sought to clarify misunderstood or confusing terms for
both linguists and students.

413 Dictionaries

George A. Miller, *The Science of Words*, **1991.**

Cognitive scientist George A. Miller helped form the study of psycholinguis-
tics. In this work, he examines the word as the most basic unit of human
communication. He discusses the storage of words in memory and their use in
building ideas.

Kory Stamper, *Word by Word:*
The Secret Life of Dictionaries, **2017.**

Lexicographer Kory Stamper worked for Merriam-Webster, the publisher
of one of the most highly regarded dictionaries in the English language.
In this book, she offers a humorous peek into the world of dictionary
production. Of course, it's not simple. Language is constantly changing,
but how do you know which words merit a place in the dictionary because
they are here to stay? Stamper explains this along with other language
conundrums.

415 Grammar

Noam Chomsky, *Syntactic Structures*, 1957.
American linguist, activist, and intellectual Noam Chomsky published this
groundbreaking work on the science of language. It explores the rules that
govern spoken communication and how to study its internal structures. While
Chomsky is best known to recent generations as a political activist, he was
so influential in cognitive science that he is one of the most-cited authors in
scholarly indexes of the late 20th century.

419 Sign Languages

**Martin L. A. Sternberg,
American Sign Language Dictionary, 1998.**
Martin L. A. Sternberg provides this abridged version of the *American Sign
Language Dictionary*, which contains more than five thousand sign entries.
Illustrations and instructions accompany each.

420 English & Old English (Anglo-Saxon)

**Tom McArthur, ed.,
The Oxford Companion to the English Language, 1992.**
This reference covers every aspect of the English language, from its beginnings through late-20th-century dialects and slang. Entries detail the spoken
language, reading and writing, grammar, linguistics, rhetoric, and biographies of famous authors and the people who study languages.

Robert McCrum, *The Story of English*, 1986.
Robert McCrum traces the development of the English language from the
Anglo-Saxons through the Norman conquest, when the language underwent a
significant change, and up through the 20th century. He follows the language's spread worldwide as it became the dominant language of commerce
and culture. McCrum also examines terms incorporated from other languages
across the ages. Revised editions are available.

421 Writing System, Phonology, Phonetics

**David Crystal,
Spell It Out: The Singular Story of English Spelling, 2012.**
Spelling in the English language is tricky. And from grade school on, people tend to divide themselves into good and poor spellers. English language
expert David Crystal tries to explain the difficulty in 27 concise chapters. He
covers the early influence of Roman missionaries and moves on to theories of
where the language may be heading.

422 Etymology of Standard English

David Carroll, *The Dictionary of Foreign Terms in the English Language*, 1973.

David Carroll provides the definitions, usages, and origins of over four thousand words incorporated from foreign languages into English across many disciplines.

C. T. Onions, ed., *The Oxford Dictionary of English Etymology*, 1966.

Based on the original edition of the *Oxford English Dictionary*, this work examines the origins of common English words. These are updated with later discoveries where appropriate.

Leo Rosten, *The Joys of Yiddish*, 1968.

Scholar Leo Rosten covers Yiddish words incorporated into English in this classic work. Rosten explains the terms and phrases and explores their origins in folklore, the Bible, and other places, along with their pronunciations. A revised edition was released in 2000.

423 Dictionaries of Standard English

American Heritage Dictionary of the English Language, 1969.

This respected prescriptive dictionary was completely revised in 2018, adding 10,000 new entries and 4,000 color images, with revised definitions and etymologies based on the latest research. It is recommended for students.

Christine Ammer, *Have a Nice Day—No Problem!: A Dictionary of Clichés*, 1992.

Tired clichés are dark clouds hanging over the heads of most writers. You want to avoid those. Christine Ammer warns you of over 3,000 clichés, and she reveals their origins.

Theodore M. Bernstein, *Bernstein's Reverse Dictionary*, 1975.

Have you ever been stuck knowing the meaning of a word but not being able to bring the exact term to mind? Theodore M. Bernstein solves the problem in this alphabetically arranged dictionary. If you want an alternative to *stuffing*, you will find a list here.

Barbara Ann Kipfer, ed., *Roget's International Thesaurus*, 1962.

Roget's is the classic thesaurus of the English language. It was first published in 1911, and the eighth edition was released over a century later, in 2019, under lexicographer Barbara Ann Kipfer. The index and 50 new word lists make it easy to use.

Laurence Urdang,
Longman Dictionary of English Idioms, 1980.

Idioms, phrases that say one thing to mean another, can be confusing if you are not a native speaker of the language or dialect they come from. This dictionary, republished in 2000, provides over 4,500 idioms in English.

Webster's Third New International Dictionary of the English Language, Unabridged, 1961.

While this reference is available in many libraries, only the staunchest word fans would want to own a copy. At over four inches thick, it contains almost half a million entries. Every entry has pronunciation, definitions, usage, and meticulously researched etymologies.

Simon Winchester, *The Professor and the Madman: A Tale of Murder, Insanity, and the Making of the Oxford English Dictionary*, 1998.

Professor James Murray began to compile the *Oxford English Dictionary* in 1857. After calling for help gathering word citations, Murray was impressed by the research of Dr. W. C. Minor. However, when he travelled to honor Dr. Minor in person, Murray was shocked to discover that his contributor was an inmate in an asylum for the criminally insane. This story offers insight into the nature of 19th-century medicine, its treatment of the insane, and the making of one of the most remarkable reference works in the English language.

427 English Language Variations

Ramon F. Adams, *Western Words: A Dictionary of the American West*, 1981.

Ramon F. Adams catalogs and defines nearly 5,000 words and phrases commonly used by the cowboys of the American West during their peak. The book was revised in 1998 and would be a valuable source for writers and researchers of the time and place.

Daniel Cassidy, *How the Irish Invented Slang: The Secret Language of the Crossroads*, 2007.

The influx of Irish immigrants to the U.S. in the 19th century made profound changes in America. Daniel Cassidy examines the Irish words that entered the American lexicon and divulges how they shaped the language of America's criminal underworld and politics.

Gregory R. Clark, *Words of the Vietnam War:*
The Slang, Jargon, Abbreviations, Acronyms, Nomenclature,
Nicknames, Pseudonyms, Slogans, Specs, Euphemisms,
Double-talk, Chants, and Names and Places of the Era of
United States Involvement in Vietnam, 1992.

> Gregory R. Clark gathered these words and phrases from the soldiers who
> fought the Vietnam War, the politicians who made decisions affecting it,
> and protesters who fought against it. It also covers the terms used by the
> Vietnamese and Chinese peoples involved.

H. L. Mencken, *The American Language:*
A Preliminary Inquiry into the Development of English in the
United States, 1919.

> Influential 20th-century journalist H. L. Mencken defined *Americanism*, that
> is, the English language as the Americans of his time spoke and wrote it. He
> celebrated the language as it had developed naturally. He concluded that,
> rather than being inferior, American English is more colorful and creative
> than British English.

Hugh Rawson, *A Dictionary of Euphemisms and Other*
Doubletalk:
Being a Compilation of Linguistic Fig Leaves and Verbal
Flourishes for Artful Users of the English Language, 1985.

> Euphemisms are words or phrases used to refer to something while disguis-
> ing its meaning. Harmless examples are *bosom* and *privates*. They become a
> problem when used to cover up wrongdoing, such as calling a mass murder an
> *ethnic cleansing*. Rawson's work was completely revised and updated in 2003.

John Russell Rickford and Russell John Rickford, *Spoken*
Soul:
The Story of Black English, 2000.

> Poetic and original, Black English defines a people. Linguist John Russell
> traces its history and outlines its features.

428 Standard English Usage

Theodore M. Bernstein, *Miss Thistlebottom's Hobgoblins:*
The Careful Writer's Guide to the Taboos, Bugbears, and
Outmoded Rules of the English Language, 1971.

> Theodore M. Bernstein wrote this book to aid those suffering from trauma at
> the hands of overzealous elementary and middle school English teachers. He
> argues that the English language is too big and varied to fit into narrow rules.
> So instead, he challenges these rules through a series of letters to the fabled
> Miss Thistlebottom.

Denise Eide, *Uncovering the Logic of English: A Common-Sense Approach to Reading, Spelling, and Literacy*, 2011.

Reading and spelling can be a challenge for students who struggle because of brain differences. In this brief and insightful guide, Denise Eide reveals the principles governing the spelling of English words. Her lessons explain how to spell and why and will change the way you think about English.

Bryan A. Garner, *The Chicago Guide to Grammar, Usage, and Punctuation*, 2016.

Lexicographer Bryan A. Garner helps those who want their written communications to convey intelligence and correctness. He illuminates the history behind why certain forms are perceived as correct, tackles syntax, and explains traditional uses and changes in the usage over time. Garner ends the book with punctuation rules, a glossary, and a further reading list.

Mary Norris, *Between You & Me: Confessions of a Comma Queen*, 2015.

As a veteran of the notoriously exacting copy department at the *New Yorker*, Mary Norris advises how to properly follow a style manual to shape language. In this book, she dispenses advice, backing up her recommendations with witty examples.

Patricia T. O'Conner, *Woe Is I: The Grammarphobe's Guide to Better English in Plain English*, 1996.

Patricia T. O'Conner uses her experience as an editor at the *New York Times Book Review* in this brief and entertaining grammar guide. It's the perfect book for anyone wanting a grammar refresher without boredom.

430 German & Related Languages

433 Dictionaries of Standard German

Trevor Jones, ed., *Harrap's Standard German and English Dictionary*, 1964.

This original volume of *Harrap's Standard German and English Dictionary* covered only vol. 1 and the letters A–E. When completed, it was a three-volume set. In 1994, a one-volume concise edition was published.

439 Other Germanic Languages

Miriam Weinstein, *Yiddish: A Nation of Words*, 2001.

Miriam Weinstein tells the story of Yiddish, a language that grew out of

Jewish communities in Europe over the past millennium, blending Hebrew with various Romance, Slavic, and Germanic languages.

440 French & Related Romance Languages

443 Dictionaries of Standard French

**The New Cassell's French Dictionary:
French–English; English–French, 1962.**
New Cassell's dictionaries of foreign languages have been the gold standard for over a century. The most recent print version of the French dictionary was published in 2002.

450 Italian, Romanian & Related Languages

453 Dictionaries of Standard Italian

Barbara Reynolds, ed., The Cambridge Italian Dictionary, 1962.
Edited by lexicographer and scholar of Italian studies Barbara Reynolds, *The Cambridge Italian Dictionary* is intended for students and has separate Italian–English and English–Italian sections. It also has pronunciation and grammar guides to aid readers in their use. A concise volume was published in 1975.

460 Spanish, Portuguese, Galician

463 Dictionaries of Standard Spanish

**The American Heritage Larousse Spanish Dictionary:
English/Spanish, Espagñol/Inglés, 1986.**
This dictionary is set apart from other Spanish dictionaries by focusing on writers and speakers of American English and Latin American Spanish.

**Tana de Gamez, ed., Simon and Schuster's International Dictionary:
English/Spanish, Spanish/English, 1973.**
This dictionary was completely revised and updated in 1997 to cover commonly spoken words, technical and scientific terms, idioms, and geographic and biographic entries. There are also tables of irregular verbs and grammar, as well as pronunciation guides.

470 Latin & Related Italic Languages

473 Dictionaries of Classical Latin

P. G. W. Glare, *Oxford Latin Dictionary*, 1983.
This dictionary is the first that took its definitions directly from readings of original Latin sources. It contains roughly 40,000 words, along with quotations and definitions in English. Updated versions are available.

480 Classical Greek; Hellenic Languages

487 Preclassical & Postclassical Greek

Margalit Fox, *The Riddle of the Labyrinth: The Quest to Crack an Ancient Code*, 2013.
Linguist Margalit Fox has written a page-turning account of Arthur Evans and his discovery of an ancient civilization on Crete that predated Classical Greece by a thousand years. She reports discoveries of the people who lived in the age of Odysseus. And she exposes the mysterious events, including a suspicious death, surrounding the study of its artifacts in the 20th century.

490 Other Languages

491 East Indo-European & Celtic Languages

Kenneth Katzner, *English–Russian, Russian–English Dictionary*, 1984.
In 1994, this dictionary, based on American English, was revised to cover terms for post-Soviet Russia. It specifies irregularities in Russian declensions and conjugations for each word.

495 Languages of East & Southeast Asia

Peter X. Takahashi, *Jimi's Book of Japanese: A Motivating Method to Learn Japanese*, 2002.
If you're curious about the Japanese language or would like to develop basic Japanese speaking skills, Peter X. Takahashi makes it easy to learn. He provides pronunciation guides, tips on the basics, word lists with definitions, and charts to trace the characters of the Japanese language so you can learn to write Japanese as well.

CHAPTER 6

500–599

Natural Sciences & Mathematics

Tᴴɪꜱ ꜱᴇᴄᴛɪᴏɴ ʙᴇʟᴏɴɢꜱ ᴛᴏ ʙᴏᴏᴋꜱ that cover the sciences that exist in the natural world. Books about astronomy, animals, plants, and volcanoes would be shelved here. Likewise, mathematics—assumed to be discovered, not invented—is natural science.

500 Natural Sciences & Mathematics

Natalie Angier, *The Canon:*
***A Whirligig Tour of the Beautiful Basics of Science,* 2007.**
Science journalist Natalie Angier wishes to increase your overall scientific literacy. Using interviews with top scientists and her research, she takes you through every significant scientific discipline to explain how the world works.

Stephen J. Ceci, ed., *Why Aren't More Women in Science?:*
***Top Researchers Debate the Evidence,* 2006.**
Stephen J. Ceci presents 15 essays written by researchers with varied opinions on the impact of gender differences on scientific ability. All are based on empirical evidence and may lead you to question your assumptions.

Ben Goldacre, *Bad Science:*
***Quacks, Hacks, and Big Pharma Flacks,* 2010.**
Science writer and psychiatrist Ben Goldacre demonstrates how media can confuse and mislead us into thinking crazy things. He tells you what to watch for so you won't be fooled by bad science.

Mario Livio, *Brilliant Blunders:*
From Darwin to Einstein—Colossal Mistakes
by Great Scientists That Changed Our Understanding
***of Life and the Universe,* 2013.**
In, *Brilliant Blunders,* Mario Livio examines mistakes made by science greats like Charles Darwin, Lord Kelvin, Linus Pauling, Fred Hoyle, and Albert

Einstein. By sharing their missteps, he helps us see the role of mistakes in life and helps us understand that they open the path to truth.

Randall Munroe, *What If?: Serious Scientific Answers to Absurd Hypothetical Questions*, 2014.

Former NASA scientist Randall Munroe started getting all sorts of questions after beginning his *XKCD* web comic about life as a science geek. One example: "How fast can you hit a speed bump while driving and live?" His witty answers come from computer simulations, differential equations, and conversations with experts.

501 Philosophy & Theory

Thomas S. Kuhn, *The Structure of Scientific Revolutions*, 1962.

While Thomas S. Kuhn made his mark as a historian and philosopher, he was a physicist by training. His classic and influential work argues that the sciences weren't developed strictly through the scientific method. Instead, new beliefs took hold because of paradigm shifts. These, in turn, influenced complete changes in direction and study.

Melanie Mitchell, *Complexity: A Guided Tour*, 2009

Have you ever wondered how schools of fish form and stay together or how the brain's neurons work together to create thoughts? Computer science professor and complex systems specialist Melanie Mitchell delves into these questions using biological, technical, and social disciplines to frame her answers, providing an excellent introduction to complex systems science.

502 Miscellany

Marc J. Kuchner, *Marketing for Scientists: How to Shine in Tough Times*, 2011.

NASA astrophysicist Marc J. Kuchner explains to scientists why they shouldn't despair at the antiscience climate of the early 21st century. Rather than giving in to discouragement, he shows them how to leverage marketing knowledge to find a job, gain funding, and influence public debate.

504 [Unassigned]

Mary Holland, *Naturally Curious: A Photographic Field Guide and Month-by-Month Journey through the Fields, Woods, and Marshes of New England*, 2010.

Naturalist and wildlife photographer Mary Holland takes you into the forests, streams, and fields of New England across all four seasons. She helps you see things you may have missed without her expert guidance, including signs of animal habitation and insights into how the animals live.

506 Organizations & Management

Stephen Jay Gould, *Wonderful Life: The Burgess Shale and the Nature of History*, 1989.

American paleontologist, evolutionary biologist, and scientific historian Stephen Jay Gould examines a Canadian Rockies limestone quarry called the Burgess Shale. Using the fossils found there, Gould apprises what it teaches us about evolution and natural history.

508 Natural History

Bernd Heinrich, *A Naturalist at Large: The Best Essays of Bernd Heinrich*, 2018.

German-born American writer Bernd Heinrich spent his life studying the natural world in Maine and Vermont. He's also been a biology professor and a world-class ultramarathon runner. These essays cover everything from the ecological impacts of elephants and their relationship with mopane trees to the intelligence in ravens that his experiments have exposed.

Elizabeth Hennessy, *On the Backs of Tortoises: Darwin, the Galapagos, and the Fate of an Evolutionary Eden*, 2020.

The Galapagos Islands were a paradise before pirates, whalers, and settlers made their way there throughout the centuries. Geographer Elizabeth Hennessy focuses on the islands' giant tortoises. She says efforts of conservationists to restore both the tortoises and their environment to prehistoric conditions are futile. Instead, she proposes conservation that takes the past into account with no attempt to erase it.

John Muir Laws, *The Laws Guide to Nature Drawing and Journaling*, 2015.

If you admire Victorian and Edwardian nature journals, John Muir Laws can teach you how to create one of your own. As a naturalist, artist, and educator, he offers directions on observing nature, drawing it, and writing about it.

Amy Leach, *Things that Are: Encounters with Plants, Stars and Animals*, 2013.

Amy Leach expands your perceptions about nature in this debut collection of essays.

Barry Lopez, *Arctic Dreams*, 1986.

While Barry Lopez wrote this exploration of the Arctic Circle in the 1980s, it still captivates today. His straightforward portraits of the region's narwhals, polar bears, and native peoples help you picture its magnificence. But he also exposes the human destruction perpetrated on it.

Peter Wohlleben, *The Secret Network of Nature: The Delicate Balance of All Living Things*, 2018.

German forester Peter Wohlleben demonstrates how seemingly unrelated aspects of nature depend upon each other to keep our planet in balance. He reveals connections between trees and the Earth's rotation and explains why these connections, large and small, matter to the survival of both ecosystems and humans.

BIOGRAPHY

Edward O. Wilson, *Naturalist*, 1994.

Renowned American biologist Edward O. Wilson shares how he became obsessed with science as a child. His account of his tenure at Harvard, where his research changed the field of evolutionary biology, gives you a peek into how a scientist thinks and offers insights into late-20th century scientific thought.

509 History, Geographic Treatment, Biography

Fritjof Capra, *Learning from Leonardo: Decoding the Notebooks of a Genius*, 2013.

Leonardo da Vinci's genius impacted art, science, and math. Physicist Fritjof Capra isolates seven characteristics of Leonardo's genius and covers over 40 discoveries he made that went unrecognized in his own time. Capra then organizes the notebooks the way he believes Leonardo would have wanted them, were they ever to be published.

David Freedberg, *The Eye of the Lynx: Galileo, His Friends, and the Beginnings of Modern Natural History*, 2002.

The scientific organization called the Accademia dei Lincei (Academy of the Lynx-Eyed), founded in 1603, aimed to document and classify all of nature. The members used pictures not only of whole objects but of dissection and internal structure as well. When art professor David Freedberg discovered a cache of their drawings in Windsor Castle in the late 20th century, he decided to research and tell their story.

Deborah E. Harkness, *The Jewel House: Elizabethan London and the Scientific Revolution*, 2007.

Sir Francis Bacon and six other men and women who represent a prolific time of discovery are sketched by Deborah Harkness. Their contributions took us from medieval philosophical understanding to modern methods of inquiry.

Richard Holmes, *The Age of Wonder:*
How the Romantic Generation Discovered the Beauty and
***Terror of Science,* 2008.**
  Richard Holmes examines the lives of scientists at the turn of the 19th century
  in Britain. Their work remains influential even today.

Steven Weinberg, *To Explain the World:*
***The Discovery of Modern Science,* 2016.**
  American theoretical physicist and Nobel Prize winner Steven Weinberg looks
  at ancient and medieval scientific thought and explores how, even though
  incorrect, it led to discoveries that shape the way we see the world today.

BIOGRAPHY

Adrian Desmond, *Huxley:*
***From Devil's Disciple to Evolution's High Priest,* 1995.**
  T. H. Huxley (1825–1895) was a scientific genius who criticized Victorian
  culture while advocating scientific causes. He promoted Darwin's theory of
  evolution and an agnostic scientific worldview. Adrian Desmond explores
  Huxley's character and shows how he shaped our modern worldview.

Andrea Wulf, *The Invention of Nature:*
***Alexander von Humboldt's New World,* 2015.**
  Through his global exploration and scientific investigation, Alexander
  von Humboldt was profoundly influential for later thinkers from Darwin
  to Thoreau. Andrea Wulf's biography celebrates the achievements of von
  Humboldt's remarkable life.

510 Mathematics

Alex Bellos, *Alex's Adventures in Numberland:*
***Dispatches from the Wonderful World of Mathematics,* 2010.**
  Mathematician and freelance journalist Alex Bellos helps you see how fascinating mathematics can be. To illustrate his points, he travels from Germany
  to Japan, demonstrating how math influences our daily lives and makes
  them better.

Jeffrey Bennett, *Math for Life:*
***Crucial Ideas You Didn't Learn in School,* 2011.**
  Jeffrey Bennett demonstrates how math shapes the world and leads to better
  choices. After examining how math is taught in school, he offers solutions to
  help struggling students grasp the concepts.

Eugenia Cheng, *How to Bake a Pi:*
An Edible Exploration of the Mathematics
of Mathematics, 2015.

> While mathematics professor Eugenia Cheng provides examples of how math
> works in cooking, this book goes beyond to show that math is not just num-
> bers and formulas. She looks at the basis for metamathematics, which is how
> we think about and understand things.

Douglas R. Hofstadter, *Gödel, Escher, Bach:*
An Eternal Golden Braid, 1979.

> American scholar Douglas R. Hofstadter explains the ideas behind cognitive
> science, covering everything from logic to artificial intelligence.

Margot Lee Shetterly, *Hidden Figures:*
The American Dream and the Untold Story of the Black
Women Mathematicians Who Helped Win the Space
Race, 2016.

> Margo Lee Shetterly tells of a group of African American women who made
> the calculations that enabled the NASA space program to become a reality.
> While segregated from their White counterparts, these women continued to
> contribute with dignity and accomplishment.

BIOGRAPHY

Paul Hoffman, *The Man Who Loved Only Numbers:*
The Story of Paul Erdős and the Search
for Mathematical Truth, 1998.

> Paul Erdős, a mathematician and eccentric genius, was one of the greatest
> mathematical problem solvers of the 20th century. Paul Hoffman enumerates
> Erdős's many contributions to number theory and graph theory.

Sylvia Nasar, *A Beautiful Mind:*
The Life of Mathematical Genius and Nobel Laureate
John Nash, 1998.

> Brilliant mathematician John Nash contributed most heavily to game theory,
> which is foundational to current economic thinking. In this revealing and
> realistic biography, Sylvia Nasar shows how recurring bouts with schizophre-
> nia hindered his work.

512 Algebra

Simon Singh, *Fermat's Enigma:*
The Epic Quest to Solve the World's Greatest
Mathematical Problem, 1997.

> For over 350 years, mathematicians have been baffled by Fermat's Last

Theorem. British science writer Simon Singh tells the story of the efforts mathematicians have exerted to solve it.

516 Geometry

Mario Livio, *The Golden Ratio: The Story of Phi, the World's Most Astonishing Number*, 2002.
The golden ratio is phi, the mysterious number that has turned up in art, plants, galaxies, and economics. Mario Livio relates the history of phi, tracing it from Euclid to today's physicists. He then speculates on what the numbers tell us about the order of the entire universe.

519 Probabilities & Allied Mathematics

Jason Makansi, *Painting By Numbers: How to Sharpen Your BS Detector and Smoke Out the "Experts,"* 2016.
Given that dire consequences can result from misunderstanding numbers, including economic meltdowns, damaging medical trends, and faulty business decisions, Jason Makansi argues that we cannot afford to be numerically illiterate. He gives 12 commandments that you can apply to determine the truth of a situation using math.

Sarah Moss, *Probabilistic Knowledge*, 2018.
Credence, or plausibility, should have as much weight as full proof in our concepts of knowledge, says Sarah Moss. She ties probabilistic content to philosophy and language. In doing so, she demonstrates that statistical evidence is not enough for legal proof and that racial profiling violates epistemic norms.

Nate Silver, *The Signal and the Noise: Why So Many Predictions Fail—but Some Don't*, 2012.
American statistician and expert prognosticator Nate Silver shows why most predictions fail. Overconfidence, he finds, is a critical problem. In examining successful forecasters from meteorologists to sports predictors and then analyzing the cause of their success, Silver finds a command of probability techniques and a knack for teasing out key details to be critical factors.

520 Astronomy & Allied Sciences

Anil Ananthaswamy, *Through Two Doors at Once: The Elegant Experiment That Captures the Enigma of Our Quantum Reality*, 2018.
Most people have heard of the double-slit experiment first performed by Thomas Young in the early 19th century. The results contradict Newtonian

physics by demonstrating that light behaves like a wave even though it is composed of particles. In the years since, the ramifications of the experiment have puzzled scientists, the greatest of whom have disagreed about what it says about the material world. Anil Ananthaswamy explores the history surrounding the experiment and the questions it raises about reality.

Timothy Ferris, *Seeing in the Dark: How Backyard Stargazers Are Probing Deep Space and Guarding Earth from Interplanetary Peril*, 2002.

Amateur astronomer Timothy Ferris relates his adventures stargazing all over the planet. He discusses discoveries by amateurs like himself and makes recommendations for anyone wishing to join in the fun.

Carl Sagan, *Cosmos*, 1980.

Carl Sagan wrote this book as a companion to the PBS series by the same name. While it is dated today, Sagan's sense of the wonder and majesty of the cosmos is contagious, and his coverage of it is broad and deep.

Sidney C. Wolff, *The Boundless Universe: Astronomy in the New Age of Discovery*, 2016.

Astronomy may well be the last great physical frontier to explore. And scientists are making discoveries at a furious pace. Sidney C. Wolff's book explores recent research to find what it has to tell us about the cosmos.

522 Techniques, Equipment & Materials

Dava Sobel, *The Glass Universe: How the Ladies of the Harvard Observatory Took the Measure of the Stars*, 2016.

The "glass universe" comprises around 500,000 glass plates of photographs taken through telescopes at the Harvard Observatory from the mid-19th through mid-20th centuries and studied by the sisters, daughters, and wives of the scientists who were making the plates and joined later by recent female graduates from colleges like Vassar and Smith. Dava Sobel reveals how these women soon turned from making calculations about the plates to studying them and making original discoveries.

523 Specific Celestial Bodies & Phenomena

Mike Brown, *How I Killed Pluto and Why It Had It Coming*, 2010.

Astronomer Mike Brown describes how, in 2005, he achieved his dream, discovering another planet, Eris, far beyond Pluto but larger. The discovery itself would likely have been a welcome addition to our celestial knowledge. But the decision to demote Pluto to dwarf planet status created an uproar seldom seen in modern scientific history.

Richard Cohen, *Chasing the Sun:*
The Epic Story of the Star that Gives Us Life, 2010.

The sun has always been the touchstone around which time, the seasons, and even religion have revolved. Richard Cohen spent seven years traveling to 18 countries to explore the sun's role in language, mythology, art, and medicine. Cohen packs beautiful illustrations, facts, and stories into his ode to the sun.

Stephen Hawking, *A Brief History of Time*, 1988.

Superstar theoretical physicist Stephen Hawking wrote this blockbuster account of the origins and nature of the universe. In 1998, he updated it to include more-recent scientific findings that backed up his earlier assertions. The new edition also added a new chapter on wormholes and time travel.

Scott Hubbard, *Exploring Mars:*
Chronicles from a Decade of Discovery, 2012.

"Mars Czar" Scott Hubbard headed NASA's successful forays onto the Red Planet. He shows how his team decided to conduct the missions and develop the program, and he discloses the technological and political forces that shaped it.

Lawrence M. Krauss, *Atom:*
A Single Oxygen Atom's Odyssey from the Big Bang
to Life on Earth . . . and Beyond, 2001.

Internationally known theoretical physicist Lawrence M. Krauss takes you on a journey with one oxygen atom from the universe's beginnings to today. This tiny atom experiences a lot in its long life that will leave you amazed at the events that created you and the universe.

Jo Marchant, *The Human Cosmos:*
Civilization and the Stars, 2020.

Journalist Jo Marchant looks at portrayals of the past 20,000 years of human stargazing in art, religion, science, and biology. She points out that we have become increasingly disconnected from the sky's rhythms and cycles in recent centuries. In many places, it's no longer even visible due to light pollution.

Lisa Randall, *Dark Matter and the Dinosaurs:*
The Astounding Interconnectedness of the Universe, 2015.

Physics professor Lisa Randall argues that a piece of dark matter may have hit the Earth 66 million years ago, wiping out both the dinosaurs and around three-quarters of the other plants and animals. Randall makes complex scientific concepts accessible to a general reader as she explains her theory.

526 Mathematical Geography

Simon Garfield, *On the Map:*
A Mind-Expanding Exploration of the Way the World
***Looks*, 2012.**
> Simon Garfield traces the history of maps and mapmaking, while arguing that
> it was not language but mapmaking that caused us to evolve into our modern
> form. He provides all sorts of maps and points out how they have been used
> around the globe and throughout history.

Dava Sobel, *Longitude:*
The True Story of a Lone Genius Who Solved the Greatest
***Scientific Problem of His Time*, 1995.**
> Dava Sobel explains how John Harrison solved a problem that had bedeviled
> the greatest scientific minds of all time—how to navigate the sea. During the
> 18th century, the economic and political stakes wrapped up in ocean naviga-
> tion were high. Harrison used time to invent the chronometer, changing the
> course of navigation, clock-making, and history itself.

527 Celestial Navigation

Peter Ifland, *Taking the Stars:*
***Celestial Navigation from Argonauts to Astronauts*, 1998.**
> Peter Ifland gives the history of navigational instruments from ancient times
> to the present and explains how these instruments work.

529 Chronology

Frank Parise, ed., *The Book of Calendars*, 2002.
> While you can find some of this information quickly on the Internet, its
> usefulness is in the breadth of tables and conversions of dates across over 60
> ancient and modern calendars.

530 Physics

David Bodanis, *E=mc²:*
***A Biography of the World's Most Famous Equation*, 2000.**
> Most of us know that $E = mc^2$ was one of the most monumental scientific
> discoveries of all time. David Bodanis explains why science needed it, what it
> means, and its implications for our everyday lives.

Brian Greene, *The Hidden Reality:*
***Parallel Universes and the Deep Laws of the Cosmos*, 2011.**
> American theoretical physicist Brian Greene asks an audacious question, "Is

ours the only universe in existence?" His clear answers explain mind-bending concepts such as parallel universes, doppelgängers, and the multiverse. And he imaginatively speculates on what it all means.

Michael Hiltzik, *Big Science:* *Ernest Lawrence and the Invention That Launched* *the Military–Industrial Complex*, 2015.

Pulitzer Prize winner Michael Hiltzik relates the story of Ernest Lawrence, a young scientist living in the early 20th century in Berkeley, California. Lawrence invented the cyclotron, a device with a massive impact on subsequent physics. Hiltzik examines the industry and government interventions that followed and traces from the cyclotron's debut to our current military–industrial complex.

Carlo Rovelli, *Seven Brief Lessons on Physics*, 2014.

Italian theoretical physicist Carlo Rovelli's international bestseller makes an entertaining introduction to modern physics. Rovelli offers simple explanations of complex topics like quantum mechanics and the structure of the universe. The big picture, he says, is breathtaking.

Leonard Susskind, *The Black Hole War:* *My Battle with Stephen Hawking to Make the World* *Safe for Quantum Mechanics*, 2008.

Scientists don't exist in bubbles. Theoretical physicist Leonard Susskind details his real-life battle with the physics giant Stephen Hawking over the question of whether black holes permanently absorb everything in their vicinity. For decades Hawking contended they do, but Susskind was skeptical. He records their debate and relates how Hawking came to concede in 2004.

BIOGRAPHY

Kai Bird and Martin J. Sherwin, *American Prometheus:* *The Triumph and Tragedy of J. Robert Oppenheimer*, 2005.

Kai Bird and coauthor Martin J. Sherwin cover the life of J. Robert Oppenheimer, "father of the atomic bomb." They follow him from his education at the Ethical Culture school in New York City to the deserts of Los Alamos, New Mexico, where he led the American nuclear weapons laboratory. While Oppenheimer spearheaded the atomic age, he later opposed the development of these weapons of mass destruction.

Graham Farmelo, *The Strangest Man:* *The Hidden Life of Paul Dirac, Quantum Genius*, 2009.

Paul Dirac made scientific history with his contributions to quantum mechanics, for which he was the youngest theoretician in history to win a Nobel Prize.

But his unusual personality created social difficulties. Graham Farmelo, professor of physics, writes this compassionate and appreciative biography.

James Gleick, *Isaac Newton*, 2003.

Sir Isaac Newton had one of the greatest scientific minds of all time. James Gleick tells how Newton went from an impoverished childhood to become the founder of Newtonian physics and calculus. His intellect and leaps of logic were astounding.

Walter Isaacson, *Einstein: His Life and Universe*, 2008.

Journalist Walter Isaacson explores the personality and character traits that led Albert Einstein to become one of history's greatest scientists. Einstein's ideas and their impacts on our current world are also explained.

531 Classical Mechanics

Gavin Pretor-Pinney, *The Wavewatcher's Companion*, 2010.

After becoming mesmerized by waves washing onto a Cornwall beach, Gavin Pretor-Pinney embarked on a quest to understand waves, not just in the ocean but in everything. From our digestive systems to the Internet, waves drive everything that moves. He helps us appreciate these overlooked forces around us.

533 Pneumatics (Gas Mechanics)

Tom Zoellner, *The Heartless Stone: A Journey through the World of Diamonds, Deceit, and Desire*, 2006.

After being jilted by his fiancée, Tom Zoellner looked at the diamond ring she left behind and started wondering, What is it about this stone that drives fortunes and romance? So he decided to go on a global tour, searching for answers. From diamond mines to diamond merchants, Zoellner examined the history of its use as an engagement symbol and shares what he discovered.

535 Light & Related Radiation

Philip Ball, *Invisible: The Dangerous Allure of the Unseen*, 2014.

In writing about the world of microorganisms, British science writer Philip Ball seems to be spinning fantasy. From Shakespearean ghosts to nanoscience, he examines the fascination and reality of invisibility.

539 Modern Physics

Brian Cathcart, *The Fly in the Cathedral: How a Group of Cambridge Scientists Won the International Race to Split the Atom*, 2006.

Journalist Brian Cathcart investigates how two young researchers in

Cambridge raced against German and American scientists to split the atom, a feat that changed the course of history. Their accomplishment was astounding because they managed to find the answer using only pencil and paper, Plasticine, and their minds. The solution involved a bit of matter that is so small that finding it inside an atom is the spatial equivalent of finding a fly inside a cathedral.

Janna Levin, *Black Hole Blues and Other Songs from Outer Space*, 2016.

Physicist Janna Levin illuminates a century of history surrounding the gravitational waves predicted by Einstein in 1916 that were detected for the first time in a scientific experiment one hundred years later. She tells of the scientists and the scientific instrument, LIGO, that made it possible.

Claudia Marcelloni and Colin Barras, *Hunting the Higgs: The Inside Story of the ATLAS Experiment at the Large Hadron Collider*, 2014.

The Large Hadron Collider in Geneva, Switzerland, is legendary worldwide. Claudia Marcelloni and Colin Barras provide the history of CERN from its beginnings in the 1980s through its first years of operation. They include the famous experiment in 2012 that discovered a new particle thought to be the Higgs boson.

Craig Nelson, *The Age of Radiance: The Epic Rise and Dramatic Fall of the Atomic Era*, 2014.

Historian Craig Nelson discusses all facets of the Atomic Age, from the discovery of X-rays in the 1890s to Japan's nuclear plant meltdown in 2011, and its important figures, such as Marie Curie. He discusses how politicians like Ronald Reagan were involved in atomic power decision-making. He also looks at radiation in nature, revealing that even our bodies are radioactive.

540 Chemistry & Allied Sciences

Joe Schwarcz, *Let Them Eat Flax: 70 All-New Commentaries on the Science of Everyday Food & Life*, 2005.

Chemist Joe Schwarcz answers questions about our food supplies. Because one messed-up molecule can kill you, understanding these issues can be a matter of life and death.

Paul Strathern, *Mendeleyev's Dream: The Quest for the Elements*, 2001.

British writer Paul Strathern traces the history of chemistry and the periodic table. He reveals how we reached our modern chemical breakthroughs.

541 Physical Chemistry

Marie Boas Hall,
Robert Boyle and Seventeenth-Century Chemistry, 2014.

Seventeenth-century Irish scientist Sir Robert Boyle, best known for Boyle's Law, was also an early thinker in corpuscularism, which was replacing the beliefs of Aristotle and other classical Greek scientists. Marie Boas Hall tells about Boyle and his influence on modern chemistry.

John W. Servos,
Physical Chemistry from Ostwald to Pauling:
The Making of a Science in America, 1996.

In the early 20th century, physical chemistry was in its infancy. John W. Servos chronicles how scientists like A. A. Noyes and Linus Pauling worked in this field, which combined physics and chemistry in studies of chemical thermodynamics and aqueous solutions. While science has moved beyond physical chemistry, it had a massive impact on the modern world.

546 Inorganic Chemistry

Sam Kean, *The Disappearing Spoon:*
And Other True Tales of Madness, Love, and the History
of the World from the Periodic Table of Elements, 2010.

Rather than writing a history of the periodic table as a whole, science writer Sam Kean writes stories about the elements contained within the table.

John S. Rigden, *Hydrogen:*
The Essential Element, 2002.

Hydrogen is the simplest, most abundant element in the universe. John S. Rigden tells how scientists such as Linus Pauling and Paul Dirac experimented with the element to bring us inventions such as GPS.

550 Earth Sciences

Robert M. Hazen, *The Story of Earth: The First 4.5 Billion*
Years, from Stardust to Living Planet, 2012.

From the days when Earth was primarily fire and magma to today's biosphere, our planet has been through several completely different phases in its existence. Research scientist Robert M. Hazen takes us through them all, helping us understand Earth as it was and as it is, literally from the inside out.

John McPhee, *In Suspect Terrain, 1983.*

Celebrated nature writer John McPhee writes eloquently about the planet by discussing internationally renowned geologist Anita Harris and her research on plate tectonics, revealing a lot about the world's history.

Florian Schulz, *To the Arctic*, 2011.
Nature photographer Florian Schulz travels the Arctic every season, returning with breathtaking photos of the landscape, the animals, the seas, and the
rivers, even from underwater. Schulz also relates his adventures while taking
the photos.

Eric Scigliano, et al., *The Big Thaw:*
Ancient Carbon, Modern Science,
***and a Race to Save the World*, 2019.**
The permafrost of the world's polar regions holds four times the carbon found
in all the rest of the world's forests combined. Releasing this load will dev-
astate the planet. *The Big Thaw* introduces a team of scientists and students
urgently spreading the message of what we can do to save ourselves by saving
the permafrost.

Neil Shubin, *The Universe Within:*
Discovering the Common History of Rocks, Planets,
***and People*, 2013.**
Famous science writer Neil Shubin explores what our bodies have in common
with the universe. He looks at everything from the chemicals—the molecules
that make up our bodies—to why our bodies look and work the way they do.

551 Geology, Hydrology, Meteorology

Cynthia Barnett, *Rain:*
***A Natural and Cultural History*, 2015.**
Cynthia Barnett takes us from the first drops of rain falling on the planet to
our worries of drought and massive storm devastation today. She explores the
science of precipitation and relates its mythology, song, and history around
the globe.

Rachel L. Carson, *The Sea Around Us*, 1951.
People still enjoy Rachel Carson's classic work on the oceans for its lyrical
prose and moving images. Carson was a marine biologist who began her
career working for the U.S. Bureau of Fisheries. This book examines tides,
currents, and ocean life from plankton to sperm whales.

Donovan Hohn, *Moby-Duck:*
The True Story of 28,800 Bath Toys Lost at Sea
and of the Beachcombers, Oceanographers,
Environmentalists, and Fools, Including the Author,
***Who Went in Search of Them*, 2011.**
When Donovan Hohn heard about an accident in which thousands of bath
toys fell into the ocean, he interviewed people involved in the accident, then
followed leads to where they went. His discoveries shed light on affairs from
the global economy to ocean currents.

Robert Macfarlane, *Underland: A Deep Time Journey,* **2020.**
Renowned British nature writer Robert Macfarlane explores the areas underground both in reality and in myth. He looks at prehistoric cave art, even in undersea caves. And he uncovers the nuclear waste stored in an underground "hiding place." He reminds us that the underground spaces exist on the planet, but they also haunt our unconscious.

Lauren Redniss, *Thunder & Lightning:*
Weather Past, Present, Future, **2015.**
Lauren Redniss travels around the planet to show a wide variety of weather patterns and displays. She explains how the weather has impacted the history of humanity and explores the complicated sphere of climate change.

Elizabeth Rush,
Rising: Dispatches from the New American Shore, **2018.**
Elizabeth Rush examines the effects of climate change we are already experiencing. She narrates stories of lives and homes lost, and she profiles wildlife biologists and activists who are working to help with endangered and lost habitats.

Simon Winchester, *Krakatoa: The Day the World Exploded:*
August 27, 1883, **2003.**
Renowned journalist Simon Winchester depicts the eruption on the Java Island of Krakatoa in 1883, which killed over 40,000 people, with repercussions felt worldwide. The event also led to one of the first violent fundamentalist Islamic attacks in the modern world.

553 Economic Geology

Mark Kurlansky, *Salt: A World History,* **2002.**
Mark Kurlansky traces the role of salt in human history from its use as currency to its effect on world trade routes, wars, empires, and revolutions. Salts differ in composition and quality, and Kurlansky elaborates on how it has been valued, processed, and sold.

Michael Welland, *Sand: The Never-Ending Story,* **2008.**
Geologist Michael Welland explores tiny seemingly infinite sand, uncovering the science of sand and the people who study it. One story involves a vampire. This book will help you appreciate how sand impacts everyday life.

557 Earth Sciences of North America

John McPhee, *Basin and Range,* **1981.**
Basin and Range began John McPhee's series of books on geology and geologists. It covers the U.S. landscape from eastern California to eastern Utah,

examining the region's terrain and discussing the role of plate tectonics and the geologic time scale. *Basin and Range* is volume one of the Annals of the Former World series.

Wayne Ranney, *Carving Grand Canyon: Evidence, Theories, and Mystery*, 2005.
Geologist Wayne Ranney relates the history of the Grand Canyon while explaining that geologists often have to use theories to explain why the world lies as it does. The Grand Canyon, he says, still contains mysteries.

559 Earth Sciences of Other Areas

William E. Glassley, *A Wilder Time: Notes from a Geologist at the Edge of the Greenland Ice*, 2018.
In Greenland, William E. Glassley and two colleagues have discovered creatures and natural formations that enhanced their studies of plate tectonics and provided insights into the myths of creation. If that weren't enough, it also increased their appreciation of the limits of science.

560 Paleontology

Deborah Cadbury, *The Dinosaur Hunters: A True Story of Scientific Rivalry and the Discovery of the Prehistoric World*, 2000.
Award-winning British writer Deborah Cadbury describes the origins of paleontology. Set in Victorian England, the book describes the race between the villainous Richard Owen and the heroic Gideon Mantell to understand the meaning of uncovered dinosaur fossils.

Kirk Johnson, *Cruisin' the Fossil Coastline: The Travels of an Artist and a Scientist along the Shores of the Prehistoric Pacific*, 2018.
Kirk Johnson, curator at the Denver Museum of Nature and Science, writes this sequel to his first book, *Prehistoric Journey: A History of Life on Earth*. In this volume, he and Ray Troll continue the journey up the Pacific Coast from Baja California to northern Alaska, searching for fossils and clues about Earth's past along one of the oldest coasts in existence.

Paige Williams, *The Dinosaur Artist: Obsession, Science, and the Global Quest for Fossils*, 2018.
Investigative journalist Paige Williams relates the international fossil trade story of Eric Prokopi, an American amateur paleontologist who had built a career finding, preparing, and selling fossils to private collectors and museums worldwide. His work irritated and dismayed trained paleontologists

for years. Williams tells how trouble began for Prokopi when he smuggled
a mostly complete T. *bataar* skeleton out of Mongolia, where trafficking in
natural history is illegal.

565 Fossil Arthropoda

Richard Fortey, *Trilobite: Eyewitness to Evolution*, 2000.
Paleontologist Richard Fortey brings us an engaging look at trilobites, the
most common fossil in the world. Trilobites lived in the oceans over half a
billion years ago, surviving in water as frigid as the arctic and as warm as the
tropics. They came in many varieties and in all sizes. What they reveal about
the ancient global landscape is fascinating.

567 Fossil Cold-Blooded Vertebrates

**Stephen Brusatte, *The Rise and Fall of the Dinosaurs:
A New History of their Lost World*, 2018.**
One of the world's top paleontologists, Steve Brusatte delivers the most recent
dinosaur research. His narrative encompasses the entire age, from dinosaurs'
small beginnings in the Triassic period through the Cretaceous period, when
a devastating impact from space ended it. Brusatte introduces us to recently
discovered species and recounts his adventures in field research around
the globe.

**Elizabeth Kolbert,
The Sixth Extinction: An Unnatural History, 2015.**
Elizabeth Kolbert studies extinction events in the planet's history and argues
we are on the verge of another one. However, this time it will be caused
mainly through human activity. To prove her point, she travels the globe gathering evidence about species that are either already extinct or on the verge
of disappearing. She backs up her assertions with interviews with experts on
past and present ecosystems.

**Brian Switek, *My Beloved Brontosaurus: On the Road with
Old Bones, New Science, and Our Favorite Dinosaurs*, 2013.**
Brian Switek, like many kids, was fascinated with dinosaurs. Now a paleontologist, he writes this affectionate ode to these extinct creatures, in which
he imparts the latest scientific findings and emphasizes what's impressive
about them.

568 Fossil Aves (Birds)

**Pat Shipman, *Taking Wing:
Archaeopteryx and the Evolution of Bird Flight*, 1998.**
When the fossil of a creature that seemed half-bird and half-reptile was
discovered in Bavaria in 1861, many saw it as proof of Darwin's theory of

evolution and a definite link between the two animal classes. But in the intervening years, the skeleton has raised more questions than it has answered. Pat Shipman helps us understand the debate.

569 Fossil Mammalia

Mauricio Antón, *Sabertooth*, 2013.
Paleoartist Mauricio Antón presents science-backed art and facts about the sabertooth. While the book is a treat to look at, it also corrects common misunderstandings about these prehistoric creatures. For one thing, they weren't all big cats.

Darin A. Croft, *Horned Armadillos and Rafting Monkeys: The Fascinating Fossil Mammals of South America*, 2016.
South America contained some of the most distinctive prehistoric inhabitants on Earth. In this chronological survey, Darin A. Croft spotlights mammals such as sabertoothed marsupials and swimming sloths, helping us see their environments and understand how they lived.

570 Biology

Armand Marie Leroi, *The Lagoon: How Aristotle Invented Science*, 2014.
Biologist Armand Marie Leroi explores the work and influence of Aristotle, who was possibly the world's first biologist. He travels to Lesbos, Aristotle's home, to see firsthand what Aristotle saw. He looks at how Aristotle's scientific ideas were inseparable from his philosophy. This book provides an eye-opening look at the beginnings of science.

571 Physiology & Related Subjects

Stephen Blackmore, *Green Universe: A Microscopic Voyage into the Plant Cell*, 2012.
Botanist Stephen Blackmore explores the history of the plant cell, which first appeared on Earth more than three billion years ago. These microscopic entities make up all plants. Blackmore shows us the forms they take and how they affect the plants they compose.

David S. Moore, *The Developing Genome: An Introduction to Behavioral Epigenetics*, 2015.
Behavioral epigenetics is still in its infancy. David S. Moore is a psychologist who brings us the field's breakthroughs, sharing how our diets, environment, and early experiences may have more influence on what our genes do, and therefore what happens to us in life, than the genes we have at birth. As a result, the new science may revise our view of human nature.

Mary Roach, *Packing for Mars:*
The Curious Science of Life in the Void, **2010.**
Have you ever wondered what it would be like to live on a space station for
a year? NASA scientists have to consider the effects of life without gravity
on the minds, as well as the bodies, of astronauts. Mary Roach explains the
research that makes space exploration possible, from cadavers sitting in for
live people in crash tests to what happens if you lose your lunch in a helmet.

572 Biochemistry

Sean B. Carroll, *The Making of the Fittest:*
DNA and the Ultimate Forensic Record of Evolution, **2006.**
Molecular biology and genetics professor Sean B. Carroll traces the discovery
and study of DNA and how it has guided over three billion years of evolution
in this understandable history.

Sam Kean, *The Violinist's Thumb: And Other Lost Tales of*
Love, War, and Genius, as Written by Our Genetic Code, **2012.**
Science writer Sam Kean shows us how genes have influenced human life.
From cat ladies to our ancestors' trysts with Neanderthals, this book explains
why and how genes have influenced our past and will impact our future
as well.

Ben Miller, *The Aliens Are Coming! The Extraordinary*
Science Behind Our Search for Life in the Universe, **2016.**
Science writer Ben Miller looks at outer space with scientists searching for
signs of life out there. He raises questions about what, exactly, is life. From its
origins on Earth to our most recent discoveries of life in the cosmos, Miller
considers the question "Are we alone?"

BIOGRAPHY

Brenda Maddox,
Rosalind Franklin: The Dark Lady of DNA, **2002.**
When Maurice Wilkins, Francis Crick, and James Watson won the Nobel
Prize for discovering DNA in 1962, they omitted a crucial team member.
Rosalind Franklin was responsible for the data and photographs that led to
the discovery. Brenda Maddox rights this wrong, introducing us to this forgot-
ten scientist who had a massive impact on the modern world.

573 Specific Physiological Systems in Animals

Richard E. Leakey and Roger Lewin, *Origins:*
What New Discoveries Reveal about the Emergence
of Our Species and Its Possible Future, **1977.**
The Leakeys were a scientific dynasty of the 20th century. Father Louis and

mother Mary Leakey were renowned archaeologists. Brother Colin was a
botanist, and brother Richard was a paleontologist. In this work, Richard
explores the evolution of human beings from apelike ancestors. In 1992, he
published, *Origins Reconsidered: In Search of What Makes Us Human,*
in which he revisits earlier books in light of later discoveries by himself
and others.

574 [Unassigned]

John Madson, *Where the Sky Began: Land of the Tallgrass Prairie,* 1982.

The first edition of John Madson's book is considered a landmark in environmental literature. In it, he explores the tallgrass prairies, which, at the
time, were one of the world's rarest landscapes. In his 2004 revision, he offers
advice for those working on tallgrass prairie restoration.

Edwin Way Teale, *Autumn Across America,* 1956.

American naturalist and photographer Edwin Way Teale wrote four books,
all of which were award winners, about various trips across different regions
of the U.S., each focusing on a different season. They are all delightful to
read and look through. The other titles are *North with the Spring* (1951),
Wandering through Winter (1965), and *Journey into Summer* (1972).

Lewis Thomas, *The Medusa and the Snail: More Notes of a Biology Watcher,* 1974.

Physician and researcher Lewis Thomas uses a little jellyfish, the medusa,
which lives on a shelled sea slug's surface, as a metaphor for life and death
issues. He includes essays on everything from natural death to Montaigne.

James D. Watson, *The Double Helix: A Personal Account of the Discovery of The Structure of DNA,* 1968.

While their discovery of the structure of DNA won James Watson and
Francis Crick the Nobel Prize in 1962, Watson reveals the human events
behind the scientific work that led to the discovery of the Holy Grail of science. At only 24, Watson was up against science greats like Linus Pauling,
and he offers a personal peek into the exciting, high-pressure world of top
research scientists.

BIOGRAPHY

Kenneth R. Manning, *Black Apollo of Science: The Life of Ernest Everett Just,* 1983.

Ernest Everett Just was an African American biologist in early 20th-century
American academia. While Manning shares Just's private life and scientific
achievements, this book focuses on how he was hindered in his research and
denied recognition for his achievements by fellow scientists.

575 Specific Parts of & Systems in Animals

Ernst Mayr, *One Long Argument: Charles Darwin and the Genesis of Modern Evolutionary Thought*, 1991.

The publication of *On the Origin of Species* changed the world. It laid out Darwin's theories about all of life's descending from one common ancestor and introduced the radical thought that humanity was not created purposely for anything special. Darwin changed science at large by introducing the role of probability and chance. Evolutionary biologist Ernst Mayr seeks to explain Darwin's thought and the debates stemming from it.

576 Genetics & Evolution

Walter Alvarez, *T. Rex and the Crater of Doom*, 1997.

Geology professor Walter Alvarez synthesized the research of experts from a wide variety of fields to provide this blow-by-blow account of the enormous object that crashed into the Yucatan Peninsula over 65 million years ago. The resulting explosion had the impact of 100 million hydrogen bombs exploding. It obliterated much of the life on the planet, changing history and leading to the ascendancy of mammals.

Melanie Challenger, *On Extinction: How We Became Estranged from Nature*, 2011.

According to scientific research, the sixth extinction is on its way. While it may be too late to save some species, Melanie Challenger looks at the consequences of extinction itself. After all, it's nothing new in the history of the planet or even of humanity. Instead, it is the extinction of our cultures that Challenger is concerned about.

Charles Darwin, *On the Origin of Species by Means of Natural Selection, or, The Preservation of Favoured Races in the Struggle for Life*, 1859.

The influence of this book on modern science and culture has been thuge. Charles Darwin's five-year trip as a young man aboard the *Beagle* allowed him to study natural history. In his resulting scientific treatise, Darwin presents the evidence he found to support the theory of evolution, which posits all life, including human life, descended from a common ancestor.

Richard Dawkins, *The Selfish Gene*, 1976.

In this paradigm-shifting work, Richard Dawkins reversed the way scientists looked at genes. They went from thinking that organisms use genes to reproduce themselves to viewing genes as using the organisms to reproduce themselves. In other words, genes became considered the drivers of evolution. Dawkins's work has influenced other fields and given us the concepts of memes, which are self-reproducing ideas.

Sarah Stewart Johnson, *The Sirens of Mars:*
Searching for Life on Another World, **2020.**
   Planetary scientist Sarah Stewart Johnson explains how she became fascinated with Mars as a child in Kentucky. She recounts how she and her fellow
   scientists look for signs of life on the planet, the methods they use to find it,
   their failed attempts, and their successes. She says Mars serves as a mirror of
   Earth, reflecting our anxieties.

Carl Zimmer, *She Has Her Mother's Laugh:*
The Powers, Perversions, and Potential of Heredity, **2018.**
   How do our genes influence us? Not in the ways we might think, says science
   writer Carl Zimmer. Our genes do not come to us whole through our parents.
   Instead, we all carry bits and pieces of DNA from many ancestors. Zimmer
   explores how these influence our bodies and lives, but he also looks at how
   other factors, from microbes to our modern lifestyles, affect us.

577 Ecology

Alan Burdick, *Out of Eden:*
An Odyssey of Ecological Invasion, **2005.**
   Invasive species can be insects, reptiles, mammals, or plants. They get to
   the U.S. from everywhere, in airplane landing gear and ship ballast water, to
   name two ways. And the U.S. exports just as many of them to other lands in
   the same ways. As a result, invasive plant and animal species are upsetting
   the natural balance across many ecosystems. Science editor Alan Burdick
   shows you the consequences.

Sean Carroll, *The Big Picture:*
On the Origins of Life, Meaning, and the Universe Itself, **2016.**
   Quantum physics and the cosmic level are so startlingly different that it's
   difficult to comprehend. And what does either, really, have to do with us?
   Theoretical physicist Sean Carroll clarifies what science, particularly the discoveries of the past century, has to tell us about who we are, our place in the
   universe, and the purpose of it all.

Dan Egan, *The Death and Life of the Great Lakes,* **2017.**
   The Great Lakes hold 20 percent of the world's fresh water, and they make a
   tremendous contribution to life in the U.S. Reporter Dan Egan exposes how
   they are under severe threat from invasive species and "dead zones," which
   threaten to cover large sections of the lakes. But he also tells us what we can
   do to restore these treasures for the future.

David George Haskell, *The Forest Unseen:*
A Year's Watch in Nature, **2012.**
   Biologist David Haskell had a simple but brilliant idea, to visit a

one-square-meter section of Tennessee's old-growth forest almost daily for one year and record the changes he finds. He proclaims what these events tell us about nature and its history across the world.

Dahr Jamail, *The End of Ice: Bearing Witness and Finding Meaning in the Path of Climate Disruption*, 2019.

Dahr Jamail returned home after a decade as a war correspondent hoping to enjoy mountain climbing once again. But he found the once familiar landscapes wholly changed. So Jamail began traveling the planet looking at the devastation to wild habitats on land and underwater due to ice loss. He reaches the sad conclusion that we are on a dying planet, and he calls for us to protect the wild places we still have.

Menno Schilthuizen, *Darwin Comes to Town: How the Urban Jungle Drives Evolution*, 2018.

Evolutionary biologist Menno Schilthuizen says evolution is happening all around us—especially in cities. He provides examples of animal adaptation happening in real time due to the extremes of urban landscapes. From carrion crows that use traffic to crack nuts in Japan to lizards who are evolving feet that grip better to concrete in Puerto Rico, he offers the hopeful thought that nature may be okay after all.

578 Natural History of Organisms

Rob Dunn, *Every Living Thing: Man's Obsessive Quest to Catalog Life, from Nanobacteria to New Monkeys*, 2008.

Humans are curious and sometimes obsessive creatures. Biologist Rob Dunn tells of our struggles to catalog all life, the smallest to the most inaccessible, on this planet and the worlds beyond.

Pamela Frierson, *The Last Atoll: Exploring Hawai'i's Endangered Ecosystems*, 2012.

Hawai'ian resident Pamela Frierson spent ten years traveling to the far tiny islands in the northwestern end of Hawai'i. She tells of the ecosystems and history she finds there, including the Great Pacific Garbage Patch, which flows around the islands.

579 Microorganisms, Fungi & Algae

Irwin M. Brodo, Sylvia Duran Sharnoff, and Steven Sharnoff, *Lichens of North America*, 2001.

There are over a thousand varieties of lichens, products of symbiotic relationships between algae and fungi, detailed in this work by Canadian research scientists. The book provides photographs, distribution maps, and keys for identifying over 1,500 varieties. Included are English and

Latin names and notes that discuss lichens' biology, structure, uses, and significance.

Merlin Sheldrake, *Entangled Life: How Fungi Make Our Worlds, Change Our Minds & Shape Our Futures*, 2020.

Merlin Sheldrake examines the fascinating story of fungi, the microscopic lifeforms that have given us bread, medicines, and alcohol. They communicate and solve problems without a brain and are responsible for communication between plants. Scientists estimate we have only discovered ten percent of the fungi species. Still, technologies using the ones we have found may save us through their ability to digest toxins and other harmful materials.

Ed Yong, *I Contain Multitudes: The Microbes Within Us and a Grander View of Life*, 2016.

Trillions of microbes live inside us all. Science journalist Ed Yong humorously explains what these underappreciated microbes do for us and the planet. He uncovers how we may harm ourselves in our efforts to eradicate them and offers ways we may be able to use them to help ourselves out.

580 Plants

Maarten J. M. Christenhusz, Michael F. Fay, and Mark W. Chase, *Plants of the World: An Illustrated Encyclopedia of Vascular Plants*, 2017.

This one-volume reference to 450 vascular plant families has over 2,500 illustrations. Each entry also has descriptions, distribution, and evolutionary relationships.

Ruth Kassinger, *A Garden of Marvels: How We Discovered that Flowers Have Sex, Leaves Eat Air, and Other Secrets of Plants*, 2014.

In her earlier book *Paradise Under Glass,* Ruth Kassinger confides how she became obsessed with plants in her home conservatory. After becoming puzzled and frustrated about the failure of some plants to thrive, she sets out to learn everything she can about botany, with the hopes of becoming a better gardener. This book is the result.

BIOGRAPHY

Wilfrid Blunt, *Linnaeus: The Compleat Naturalist*, 1971.

Carl Linnaeus (1707–1778) was the founder of the Royal Academy of Sciences and the creator of the *Systema Naturae,* used to classify all known plants and animals. While Linnaeus was also a geologist, his particular interest was botany. British artist and curator Wilfrid Blunt presents this lively retelling of Linnaeus's remarkable life.

Hope Jahren, *Lab Girl*, 2016.

Paleobiologist Hope Jahren explains how her father's classroom labs served as her childhood playgrounds and relates her adult career as a scientist. Central to the book is her relationship with Bill, her lab partner and best friend. She recounts their scientific adventures, going rogue to travel to the Arctic and Hawai'i, where she currently lives.

581 Specific Topics in Natural History of Plants

Thor Hanson, *The Triumph of Seeds: How Grains, Nuts, Kernels, Pulses, & Pips Conquered the Plant Kingdom and Shaped Human History*, 2015.

Field biologist Thor Hansen urges you to appreciate seeds in his treatise. Our lives, he says, are inextricably intertwined with them. He looks at the history and uses of seeds through wonder-provoking stories.

Mike Krebill, *The Scout's Guide to Wild Edibles: Learn How to Forage, Prepare& Eat 40 Wild Foods*, 2016.

If you've ever considered becoming a forager, you would be wise to check out Mike Krebill's guide. He looks at 40 wild edible plants in North America, with photographs and identification tips for each. He also offers recipes to enjoy them in. His goal is to save you money, increase your range of nutrients, and get you and your loved ones outdoors.

A. W. Smith, *A Gardener's Book of Plant Names: A Handbook of the Meaning and Origins of Plant Names*, 2016.

First published in 1963, this classic reference contains over a thousand common plant names and their botanical names, definitions, origins of the terms, and historical and anecdotal information about the plants. The book also serves as an excellent identification guide.

Amy Stewart, *The Drunken Botanist: The Plants that Create the World's Great Drinks*, 2013.

Author Amy Stewart delivers the history of the plants that make up global spirits, from gin to Angostura bitters. She traces the history of our favorite drinks, telling stories of how molasses helped touch off the American Revolution and ergot may have led to the Salem witch trials. She also provides over 50 drink recipes alongside tips for gardeners.

Maia Toll, *The Illustrated Herbiary: Guidance and Rituals from 36 Bewitching Botanicals*, 2018.

Traditionally trained modern healer Maia Toll profiles 36 herbs, fruits, and flowers and offers ideas and rituals to help you with your physical and mental ailments. The book also includes a deck of oracle cards to allow you access your intuition.

582 Plants Noted for Characteristics & Flowers

Nancy Ross Hugo, *Seeing Trees: Discover the Extraordinary Secrets of Everyday Trees*, 2011.
Nancy Ross Hugo helps you understand what you see when you look at a tree. She describes the parts of trees and helps you understand what you can gain from getting to know these fellow living beings.

Hugh Johnson, *The International Book of Trees: A Guide and Tribute to the Trees of Our Gardens and Forests*, 1973.
While lawyer Hugh Johnson was not an expert in trees, his meticulously researched and widely respected work covers all trees from the common to the rare. Johnson added the newest tree varieties in the 2010 revised edition.

Gregory McNamee, *Trees: Between Earth and Heaven*, 2018.
Gregory McNamee travels six continents to bring us these beautiful portraits of trees with their stories, history, and cultural and spiritual significance.

Roger Tory Peterson and Margaret McKenny, *A Field Guide to Wildflowers of Northeastern and North-central North America*, 1968.
Peterson's Field Guide series are classics of field biology. They are intended to help you identify plants you come across or to find plants you are searching for. This guide has 1,293 species grouped by family, color, and characteristics.

Gordon Rowley, *The Illustrated Encyclopedia of Succulents*, 1988.
Gordon Rowley's book contains information on the classification and history of succulents and instructions on how to grow them.

585 Pinophyta

Richard Preston, *The Wild Trees: A Story of Passion and Daring*, 2007.
Richard Preston, the author of *The Hot Zone,* provides this study of California's coastal redwoods and the people who climb them. Through their stories, you come to understand the canopy of the trees as one of the planet's last unexplored ecosystems. Not only are the tops of the trees filled with branches and leaves, but they are also home to mosses, bushes, ferns, and even other trees.

589 [Unassigned]

Orson K. Miller, *Mushrooms of North America:*
A Comprehensive Guide to Finding, Identifying
and Collecting Edible Wild Mushrooms, **1972.**
   Orson Miller's field guide helps you identify and collect mushrooms. Scientific
   facts on 680 species are provided, with color photographs to aid identification.

590 Animals

Jane Goodall, *Through a Window:*
My Thirty Years with the Chimpanzees of Gombe, **1990.**
   For 30 years, world-renowned primatologist Jane Goodall lived among chimpanzees on the shores of Lake Tanganyika. She studied and got to know these
   inhabitants and their families, joys, and wars. This account of her research is
   one of the most important science books ever published.

Jennifer S. Holland, *Unlikely Friendships:*
47 Remarkable Stories from the Animal Kingdom, **2011.**
   Jennifer S. Holland documents cases of remarkable friendships between species. She speculates on why they occur, and the possibilities include a desire
   for nurturing. Sometimes, though, these relationships defy explanation, as in
   the case of Owen the hippo with Mzee the tortoise.

Steve Jenkins, *The Animal Book:*
A Collection of the Fastest, Fiercest, Toughest, Cleverest,
Shyest—and Most Surprising—Animals on Earth, **2013.**
   Steve Jenkins answers questions his children had about animals in this
   engrossing and beaurtifully illustrated book, which covers more than 300
   animals.

591 Specific Topics in Natural History of Animals

William DeBuys, *The Last Unicorn:*
A Search for One of Earth's Rarest Creatures, **2015.**
   William DeBuys travels with a conservation biologist to central Laos to find
   and photograph the saola, a large mammal only discovered in the West in
   1992. Even though their expedition was in largely uninhabited territory, they
   still encountered poachers.

Virginia Morell, *Animal Wise:*
How We Know Animals Think and Feel, **2013.**
   Animals are both more intelligent and emotional than we once thought.
   Science writer Virginia Morell examines scientific research that provides

insight into the minds and the hearts of wild and domesticated animals, including sea creatures, birds, and mammals.

Noble S. Proctor and Patrick J. Lynch, *A Field Guide to the Southeast Coast & Gulf of Mexico: Coastal Habitats, Seabirds, Marine Mammals, Fish, & Other Wildlife*, 2012.

Proctor and Lynch's guide will prove helpful to any beach visitor because it covers wildlife both underwater and the shore.

David Quammen, *The Tangled Tree: A Radical New History of Life*, 2018.

Are we direct biological descendants of our ancestors? Looking at the most recent discoveries in molecular biology, science writer David Quammen says no, not entirely. He tells of scientists who have discovered that much of our DNA is made of horizontal, as opposed to vertical, gene transfer. In these cases, we inherited genes from viral infections, not forebears. The implications for public health are immense.

BIOGRAPHY

Jonathan Weiner, *Time, Love, Memory: A Great Biologist and His Quest for the Origins of Behavior*, 1999.

Jonathan Weiner takes us to the CalTech labs of Seymour Benzer, a maverick scientist whose experiments with fruit fly genes revolutionized our understanding of DNA and animal and human behavior.

592 Invertebrates

David Attenborough, *Life in the Undergrowth*, 2006.

More than one million species of creatures with no backbones exist in the world. They've been here since the first forms of life made an appearance. Sir David Attenborough explores these creatures, from spiders to beetles, and he notes that children, who are closer in size to the invertebrates, seem to appreciate them the most.

593 Marine & Seashore Invertebrates

Juli Berwald, *Spineless: The Science of Jellyfish and the Art of Growing a Backbone*, 2017.

Ocean scientist Juli Berwald travels the world to study jellyfish. Unfortunately, explosions in their populations are wreaking havoc around the globe, even clogging power plants. Her efforts are tireless; in her quest, she even raised jellyfish in her dining room.

594 Mollusca & Molluscoidea

Elisabeth Tova Bailey, *The Sound of a Wild Snail Eating,* **2010.**
While Elisabeth Tova Bailey was bedridden from an illness, she had time to
watch a wild snail living on her nightstand. She discovered that the tiny creature had a full life despite its small size and limited environment. Her book
muses on what we can learn about the world and ourselves from nature.

Sy Montgomery, *The Soul of an Octopus:*
A Surprising Exploration into the Wonder
of Consciousness, **2015.**
Naturalist Sy Montgomery introduces her unlikely friends—a collection of
octopuses named Athena, Octavia, Kali, and Karma. She demonstrates how
each octopus has a unique personality, and the feats they are capable of indicate they have unsuspected intelligence.

595 Arthropoda

Anurag Agrawal, *Monarchs and Milkweed:*
A Migrating Butterfly, a Poisonous Plant, and Their
Remarkable Story of Coevolution, **2017.**
The evolutionary relationship between monarch butterflies and the milkweed
plant is not a love story. While the monarchs lay their eggs on milkweed
leaves every spring, the milkweed responds by trying to poison the young
monarchs. Anurag Agrawal researches why the monarch populations have
plummeted in recent years. Could it have anything to do with the milkweed?

Charley Eiseman and Noah Charney,
Tracks and Sign of Insects and Other Invertebrates:
A Guide to North American Species, **2010.**
Insects and invertebrates leave signs behind, just like birds, reptiles, and
mammals, but they are harder to see. Eiseman and Charney present photos
and descriptions of the tracks, egg cases, nests, webs, and burrows of beetles,
spiders, ants, flies, grasshoppers, millipedes, earthworms, wasps, and slugs,
among many others. With their guide, you discover the signs you've been
missing.

Bert Holldobler and Edward O. Wilson, *The Ants,* **1990.**
The Ants is a classic in scientific literature that provides the research of
renowned scientists Holldobler and Wilson. It's an introduction that covers
the anatomy, physiology, social organization, and natural history of ants.

Heather Holm, *Bees:*
An Identification and Native Plant Forage Guide, **2017.**
Heather Holm's comprehensive guide to the bees of the north-central and

eastern U.S. and southern Canada charts the life cycles, habitats, diets, nesting lifestyles, and native forage plants for 27 bee genera. It also offers detailed information on around 100 friendly plants for bee habitats so you can create a bee-friendly environment for yourself.

Sara Lewis, *Silent Sparks: The Wondrous World of Fireflies*, 2016.

You may have spent some childhood evenings chasing fireflies. But what do you really know about them? Biologist and firefly expert Sara Lewis enlightens us about the 2,000 or so species of fireflies. She delivers scientific research that has been done on them from all over the world and gives us an identification guide so we can study them too.

Lori Weidenhammer, *Victory Gardens for Bees: A DIY Guide to Saving the Bees*, 2016.

The mass death of bees has been a disturbing trend for decades. The fact is, we can't live without them. Lori Weidenhammer argues that a massive community effort is needed to save them. She presents ten garden plans with planting guides for gardens large and small that will provide sustenance for the bees. In addition, she provides projects for helping with nesting sites.

Wendy Williams, *The Language of Butterflies: How Thieves, Hoarders, Scientists, and Other Obsessives Unlocked the Secrets of the World's Favorite Insect*, 2020.

Science journalist Wendy Williams details the anatomy and the many species of butterflies, but she also explores their intelligence. And in talking with scientists who have spent lifetimes studying them, she learns how they inspire medical breakthroughs and how they impact the planet.

597 Cold-Blooded Vertebrates

Bruce Brown, *Mountain in the Clouds: A Search for Wild Salmon*, 1995.

Bruce Brown alerts us to the precarious position of wild Pacific salmon. Brown spent years wandering the Northwest, where he found environmental degradation that harmed the region's salmon and people.

Susan Casey, *The Devil's Teeth: A True Story of Obsession and Survival Among America's Great White Sharks*, 2005.

When Susan Casey made a trip to the islands off the San Francisco coast to visit with biologists Scot Anderson and Peter Pyle during shark season, her interest became obsession. Afterwards, she accepted an invitation to return the following year for the entire season. She had no idea what she had signed on for.

Kathleen Schmitt Kline, Ronald M. Bruch,
and Fred P. Binkowski, *People of the Sturgeon:*
***Wisconsin's Love Affair with an Ancient Fish*, 2009.**

Sturgeon, an ancient species of fish, like the wild Pacific salmon, were
once nearing extinction. This hopeful book relates to the efforts of the
Wisconsin Department of Natural Resources joining with researchers
and a group of spear fishers called Sturgeon for Tomorrow. Through their
efforts, Lake Winnebago now has one of the world's largest and healthiest
sturgeon populations.

David A. Steen, *Secrets of Snakes:*
***The Science Beyond the Myths*, 2019.**

Snakes inspire fear and awe worldwide. Wildlife biologist David A. Steen
wants you understand these creatures, including the latest scientific findings
about them. He tackles common snake myths and sets the record straight so
you will understand them better.

Patrik Svensson, *The Book of Eels:*
Our Enduring Fascination with the Most Mysterious
***Creature in the Natural World*, 2020.**

Eels are some of the most mysterious creatures on our planet. Patrik Svensson
uses his memories of eel fishing, literature, history, and science to examine
what is known and unknown about them. He reflects on more significant
issues facing all the planet's animals.

Emily Voigt, *The Dragon Behind the Glass:*
A True Story of Power, Obsession,
***and the World's Most Coveted Fish*, 2016.**

The dragonfish or Asian Arowana is the most expensive aquarium fish on the
planet. Investigative journalist Emily Voigt tells how collecting aquarium
fish first became a pastime. She narrates how captive breeding began for the
dragonfish. While the mass production of Asian Arowana helps meet demand,
its wild counterpart has become almost mythical.

Blair Witherington and Dawn Witherington, *Our Sea Turtles:*
A Practical Guide for the Atlantic and Gulf, from Canada to
***Mexico*, 2015.**

The Witheringtons help you understand why we should preserve the remarkable sea turtle in this field guide.

598 Aves

Jennifer Ackerman, *The Bird Way: A New Look at How Birds*
***Talk, Work, Play, Parent, and Think*, 2020.**

Science writer Jennifer Ackerman looks at discoveries about birds' brains in the latest research from avian scientists. Birds' brains are wired differently than ours, enabling a startling intelligence considering their size. She relates her field observations and those of others in demonstrating that this intelligence is genuine. You may never look at birds the same way again.

Paul Bannick, *Owl:*
A Year in the Lives of North American Owls, 2016.
Award-winning photographer Paul Bannick follows 19 species of owls found in the U.S. and Canada for an entire year, from spring through winter. His photos cover their activities from courtship through winter migrations.

Richard Crossley, Jerry Liguori, and Brian Sullivan,
The Crossley ID Guide: Raptors, 2013.
This guide covers all 34 diurnal raptors in North America (all the raptors except owls) with color plates depicting them both in flight and at rest. The maps covering their habitats and factors that aid or hinder identification are helpful for bird watchers and experts alike.

Paul R. Ehrlich, David S. Dobkin, and Darryl Wheye,
The Birder's Handbook:
A Field Guide to the Natural History
of North American Birds, 1988.
American biologist Paul Ehrlich provides this field guide to all the birds of North America. He helps you identify the various species and includes information about nesting, eggs, offspring care, food preferences, and foraging habits. Conservation and avian history are also covered.

Helen Macdonald, *H Is for Hawk*, 2015.
After her father, journalist T. H. White, suddenly died, Helen Macdonald turned to his book *The Goshawk* for comfort and guidance. In her grief, she decided to train a goshawk herself. But goshawks are known to be one of the world's most vicious predators, making her grief therapy dangerous.

Kevin Schafer, *Penguin Planet:*
Their World, Our World, 2013.
Photographer Kevin Schafer looks at every surviving species of penguin while simultaneously telling how they live. In this book's 2nd edition, he explores the effects of human activity and climate change on them and dispels myths about them.

Tom Stephenson and Scott Whittle, *The Warbler Guide*, 2014.
Fifty-six species of warbler live in the U.S. and Canada, and they are tricky to identify. This field guide helps by providing over a thousand color photos showing the birds from various angles. The guide has companion apps you can use to identify their songs and calls.

Jonathan Weiner, *The Beak of the Finch:*
***A Story of Evolution in Our Time*, 1994.**
  Peter and Rosemary Grant spent decades on a deserted Galapagos island
  studying the finches who lived there and the changes they underwent during
  their stay. The result is a dramatic vindication of Darwin's theory of evolution.

BIOGRAPHY

Tim Birkhead, *The Wonderful Mr. Willughby:*
***The First True Ornithologist*, 2018.**
  Francis Willughby was a 17th-century natural scientist who founded the field
  of ornithology. He collaborated with John Ray to write *Bird Sense* but then
  died before the book's completion. As a result, it was Ray who received the
  credit. Tim Birkhead corrects that oversight in this lively biography.

William Souder, *Under a Wild Sky:*
John James Audubon and the Making of
The Birds of America, 2005.
  While John James Audubon is rightly known for his breathtaking illustrations
  of wild birds and their habitats, his personal life was essentially a mystery.
  While he tried to present himself as both a frontiersman and an aristocrat, he
  reinvented himself often. William Souder relates how he managed to triumph
  despite his rejection by the scientific establishment.

599 Mammalia

Gunther Block, *The Pipestone Wolves:*
***The Rise and Fall of a Wolf Family*, 2016.**
  After five years of observing a wolf pack in Canada's Banff National Park,
  Gunther Block exposes the struggle for pack dominance and how mass tour-
  ism harms the wolves. His book debunks a few longstanding myths about wolf
  behavior and features photographs by John E. Marriott.

G. A. Bradshaw, *Elephants on the Edge:*
***What Animals Teach Us About Humanity*, 2009.**
  Can PTSD exist in animals? After extensive research, G. A. Bradshaw demonstrates that elephants, at least, can experience PTSD. Years of war, poaching,
  habitat loss, and captivity have broken down the ancient bonds of elephant
  societies worldwide. They display aggressive behavior similar to humans who
  have experienced genocide and other forms of social collapse. The situation
  isn't hopeless though, and Bradshaw details efforts to rehabilitate them.

Dian Fossey, *Gorillas in the Mist*, 1983.
  Dian Fossey lived with mountain gorillas in an African jungle for 13 years.
  She chronicles the experience along with her scientific research into the lives

of these endangered animals. Her work abruptly ended with her murder in 1985.

Karsten Heuer, *Being Caribou: Five Months on Foot with a Caribou Herd*, 2008.

Wildlife biologist Karsten Heuer and his wife spent five months tracking a caribou herd over Canadian and U.S. tundra, mountains, and frozen rivers. Their adventure included being stalked by grizzlies and wolves. They share both the beauty they found in the caribou and the dangers they faced.

Philip Hoare, *The Whale: In Search of the Giants of the Sea*, 2010.

As a child, Philip Hoare was captivated by a model of a blue whale in a natural history museum. Here, he explores the living whales of today. In addition, he traces humanity's troubled relationship with them in history and literature.

Sang-Hee Lee, *Close Encounters with Humankind: A Paleoanthropologist Investigates Our Evolving Species*, 2019.

Paleoanthropologist Sang-Hee Lee reconsiders the evolutionary development of the earliest *Homo sapiens*. He reports on recent scientific evidence about how they lived.

Doug Peacock and Andrea Peacock, *The Essential Grizzly: The Mingled Fates of Men and Bears*, 2006.

The Peacocks investigate the documented encounters of grizzly bears with humans. Using their experience with grizzlies and interviews with biologists and others who have encountered the bears, they help you appreciate the grizzly and how to explore their habitat respectfully.

Bruce L. Smith, *Life on the Rocks: A Portrait of the American Mountain Goat*, 2014.

Field biologist and photographer Bruce L. Smith captures the elusive American mountain goat in photographs. He delivers his observations of them through their long winters, precarious travel around cliffs, lack of food, predators, and human encroachment on their habitat. He also discovers they have a rich social life.

John Vaillant, *The Tiger: A True Story of Vengeance and Survival*, 2010.

In 1997, in the Russian Far East, a team of men and dogs tracked a Siberian tiger that had killed numerous people in a series of apparent revenge killings. While following them over snow and ice, John Vaillant looks at the history of these intimidating but beautiful creatures, who can grow to be up to ten feet long and weigh more than 600 pounds.

BIOGRAPHY

Jane Goodall, *In the Shadow of Man*, 1971.

Jane Goodall relates how she came to study the chimpanzees of Gombe, in Tanzania, what life with them was like, and she how she developed a personal relationship with them.

CHAPTER 7

600–699

Technology & Applied Sciences

THE SCIENCES IN THIS DIVISION were all developed by humans. Branches as diverse as medicine, engineering, homemaking, and business go in this section. If people had a role in creating a discipline for a practical purpose, it belongs in the 600s.

600 Technology (Applied Sciences)

David Macaulay,
The Way Things Work, 1989;
The New Way Things Work, 2000;
The Way Things Work Now, 2016.

For decades, David Macaulay has explained how the technology in our lives works. These three volumes provide a good record of how far technology has taken us from the 1980s to today. Macaulay created his books for children and teens, but they are appropriate for any age, with clear illustrations to accompany his explanations.

609 History, Geographic Treatment, Biography

Harold Evans, *They Made America:*
From the Steam Engine to the Search Engine:
Two Centuries of Innovators, 2006.

Journalist Harold Evans traces the history of the forgotten men and women whose inventions shaped American culture and aided its rise to global power.

Giles Slade, *Made to Break:*
Technology and Obsolescence in America, 2006.

Giles Slade discloses how planned obsolescence became a business model and way of life for our nation. He provides ample evidence of our disposable culture's harmful impact on the world.

610 Medicine & Health

Twila Brase, *Big Brother in the Exam Room:*
The Dangerous Truth about Electronic Health Records, 2018.

Twila Brase alerts us to the dangers of the government's electronic health record experiment. The HIPAA forms you sign in your doctor's office do not protect your health data. On the contrary, she says entire industries profit from it, and she reveals the steps you must take to protect your privacy and safety.

Cortney Davis, *The Heart's Truth:*
Essays on the Art of Nursing, 2009.

Only those with experience can understand the exhaustion, dedication, and joys of the nursing profession. Cortney Davis reflects on her three decades of experience, from nursing school to an inner-city ob-gyn clinic. Davis's inspirational essays explain why, despite the repetitiveness and grief that the job entails, nursing can also be a spiritual experience.

Martine Ehrenclou, *The Take-Charge Patient:*
How You Can Get the Best Medical Care, 2012.

Patient advocate Martine Ehrenclou interviewed over 175 doctors, nurses, pharmacists, medical billers, and patients to help you understand the best ways to handle situations you may face as a patient. When Ehrenclou became seriously ill, she used this book's advice, making this a tested guide.

Jerome Groopman, *How Doctors Think*, 2007.

Doctors are under tremendous pressure to make accurate decisions quickly. Studies show the average time it takes a physician to make a diagnosis is 18 seconds. Using research and interviews, physician Jerome Groopman helps you understand how doctors make these decisions so you can provide needed information to make their choices more effective.

Bhupendra O. Khatri, *Healthcare 911: How America's Broken Healthcare System is Driving Doctors to Despair, Depriving Patients of Care, and Destroying Our Reputation in the World*, 2018.

Even before COVID-19, America's healthcare system was in trouble. Bhupendra Khatri reveals how the physician suicide rate was already astronomical. Stress, depression, burnout, and physical ailments still plague many doctors, harming them and their patients.

BIOGRAPHY

Gillian Gill, *Nightingales:*
The Extraordinary Upbringing and Curious Life of Miss Florence Nightingale, 2005.

Scholar Gillian Gill narrates the life of Florence Nightingale, the woman credited with shaping modern nursing. Born to a wealthy family in Victorian England, Nightingale proved to be a maverick, rejecting her family's conventional expectations and becoming an international celebrity. But by 37, she was a recluse, confined to her bedroom and only seeing visitors by appointment.

Damon Tweedy, *Black Man in a White Coat: A Doctor's Reflections on Race and Medicine*, 2015.

Physician Damon Tweedy discloses the painful story of how a professor in medical school questioned his right to be a student because he was Black. He relates his experiences as a Black doctor in the U.S. Advocating for better health care for Black patients, Tweedy tells of his patients who suffer from diseases that are more common in Black Americans and how he is diagnosed with one of them himself. Tweedy looks at solutions to these problems.

611 Human Anatomy, Cytology, Histology

Lone Frank, *My Beautiful Genome: Exposing Our Genetic Future, One Quirk at a Time*, 2011.

Danish science journalist Lone Frank questions some claims about our genes, such as how they determine our personality and predict our likelihood of contracting diseases.

Jamie Roebuck, *Anatomy 360°: The Ultimate Visual Guide to the Human Body*, 2011.

Jamie Roebuck looks at the body from the outside in, and then from all angles, to show how your body works and why it behaves as it does.

Adam Rutherford, *A Brief History of Everyone Who Ever Lived: The Human Story Retold Through Our Genes*, 2016.

British geneticist Adam Rutherford reveals what genes tell us about who we are. He says genes read like an epic story, telling of humanity's wars, diseases, famines, and migrations rather than merely being a set of instructions for our life's unfolding.

612 Human Physiology

Edward Dolnick, *The Seeds of Life: From Aristotle to da Vinci, from Sharks' Teeth to Frogs' Pants, the Long and Strange Quest to Discover Where Babies Come From*, 2017.

Science writer Edward Dolnick chronicles the efforts of early scientists to understand the mechanics of how babies are made, in this true-life adventure story.

Sandeep Jauhar, *Heart: A History*, 2018.
Cardiologist Sandeep Jauhar explores the history of heart medicine and the technology used to treat the heart. He analyzes how our personal decisions affect our heart's health, looking at cases in his practice and his own family.

Joseph LeDoux, *The Deep History of Ourselves: The Four-Billion-Year Story of How We Got Conscious Brains*, 2019.
Neuroscientist Joseph LeDoux explores the earliest living organisms on the planet to teach us how our nervous systems evolved and our brains developed. He demonstrates how we have more in common with our one-celled ancestors than we realize.

Daniel E. Lieberman, *Exercised: Why Something We Never Evolved to Do is Healthy and Rewarding*, 2021.
Paleoanthropologist Daniel E. Lieberman says that moving our bodies is undoubtedly good for us and makes us feel better. But he disagrees that it is like a vitamin pill that we need daily to get benefits. Instead, he shows us how to make healthy movement more enjoyable while avoiding unnatural approaches and harmful exercise habits.

Mary Roach, *Gulp: Adventures on the Alimentary Canal*, 2013.
Fearless science writer Mary Roach explores our digestive system. She considers intriguing questions such as whether terrorists conceal bombs in their digestive tracts and whether or not it has been effective for exorcists to insert holy water into rectums.

Robert M. Sapolsky, *Behave: The Biology of Humans at Our Best and Worst*, 2017.
Internationally acclaimed biologist and neuroscientist Robert M. Sapolsky explores our behavior by going back in time. He chooses an action any one of us may do and goes back to a second before it, explaining the actions of hormones and the nervous system that caused it. He then pulls back even further to examine what in the environment influenced those internal events. Finally, continuing to pull back and review what he just explained through a broader, earlier lens, Sapolsky travels back millions of years to determine what evolutionary factors affect us today.

Matthew Walker, *Why We Sleep: Unlocking the Power of Sleep and Dreams*, 2017.
People tend to be proud of needing little sleep. But according to Matthew Walker, director of UC Berkeley's Sleep and Neuroimaging Lab, that is misguided. In this book, he looks at the most recent research into what happens when we sleep and how our lives are immeasurably impoverished and likely cut short without enough of it.

613 Personal Health & Safety

Richard P. Brown and Patricia L. Gerbarg,
The Healing Power of the Breath:
Simple Techniques to Reduce Stress and Anxiety,
Enhance Concentration, and Balance Your Emotions, 2012.
Two doctors share scientifically proven yoga, meditation, and qigong
techniques to help with anxiety, depression, insomnia, and other
stress-related issues.

Becky Feola, *The Eldercare Consultant:*
Your Guide to Making the Best Choices Possible, 2015.
Caring for an elderly relative is rarely simple. Eldercare expert Becky Feola
gives you practical advice on understanding when the elderly need help,
evaluating options for care, involving them in the care plan, and paying for it.
Through stories and research, she imparts hope and help.

Rory Miller, *Facing Violence: Preparing for the Unexpected:*
Ethically, Emotionally, Physically
(. . . and Without Going to Prison), 2011.
Much more is involved in self-defense than defense and counterattack moves.
Martial artist and corrections officer Rory Miller says that there are seven
areas you need to understand and consider to handle a violent attack successfully. He covers everything from understanding the legal implications to
dealing with the medical consequences.

Michael Moss, *Salt Sugar Fat:*
How the Food Giants Hooked Us, 2013.
Investigative reporter Michael Moss tells us how companies like Kraft, Coca-
Cola, Nestlé, and many others have manipulated their products to make us
crave their foods. He uncovers marketing techniques they use to redirect our
attention from negative press. These tactics help the industry make over a tril-
lion dollars a year in sales while harming the health of the billions of people.

Peter Ward, *The Clean Body: A Modern History,* 2019.
Our modern habits of bathing daily and wearing clean clothes have not always
been the norm. Peter Ward looks at hygiene practices in Europe and North
America to discover why we cleaned up our act.

614 Forensic Medicine; Incidence of Disease

Radley Balko and Tucker Carrington,
The Cadaver King and the Country Dentist:
A True Story of Injustice in the American South, 2018.
Radley Balko and Tucker Carrington unveil systemic and structural racism
in the Mississippi prison system. For nearly 20 years, two men, medical

examiner Steven Hayne and his friend dentist Michael West performed forensic and medical exams while hiring themselves out as experts for prosecutors in the state. Many of these resulting convictions were overturned later due to faulty forensics.

Deborah Blum, *The Poisoner's Handbook: Murder and the Birth of Forensic Medicine in Jazz Age New York*, 2010.

Pulitzer Prize–winning journalist Deborah Blum discloses how two forensic scientists in 1920s New York City pioneered chemical detective work to solve murders by poisoning. While investigating numerous other murders, they also uncovered cases of accidental deaths from ingestion or exposure to substances ranging from pesticides to morphine, which were legal and readily available at the time.

Debora MacKenzie, *COVID-19: The Pandemic that Never Should Have Happened and How to Stop the Next One*, 2020.

For the past three decades, Debora MacKenzie has provided a course on how viruses spread. Here she lays out what we've learned about them in recent history through battles with SARS, MERS, Zika, and Ebola. COVID-19, she says, would not have become a global pandemic if governments had heeded the information available from healthcare organizations.

Seth Mnookin, *The Panic Virus: The True Story Behind the Vaccine-Autism Controversy*, 2011.

Everyone from talk show hosts to Hollywood stars have pushed the idea that vaccines cause autism. Where did this idea come from? Seth Mnookin recounts how a British gastroenterologist published a paper in 1998 claiming that the measles–mumps–rubella shot might be responsible for the increase in autism diagnoses. After his theory was debunked and the paper was withdrawn, he lost his medical license. Yet many still believe it.

David Quammen, *Spillover: Animal Infections and the Next Human Pandemic*, 2013.

Before COVID-19, there were Ebola, SARS, and AIDS. All of them share an origin in wild animals that spilled over or leapt into human hosts. David Quammen exposes how this happens and what we are doing to combat it.

Meredith Wadman, *The Vaccine Race: Science, Politics, and the Human Costs of Defeating Disease*, 2017.

Many of us no longer remember the devastating effects of measles, rubella, polio, and rabies because of vaccines. Meredith Wadman traces their development and recounts the challenges they faced. Vaccines, she concludes, have served humanity well.

615 Pharmacology & Therapeutics

Ananta Ripa Ajmera, *The Ayurveda Way:*
108 Practices from the World's Oldest Healing System for
Better Sleep, Less Stress, Optimal Digestion, and More, 2017.
> Ayurveda is an ancient Indian medical tradition that perfectly complements a yoga practice. Certified Ayurveda Health Practitioner and yoga instructor Ananta Ripa Ajmera provides 108 essays that will help you improve your diet to aid digestion, relieve stress, and improve your sleep. She also shows how breathing exercises and massage improve your health.

Katherine Eban, *Bottle of Lies:*
The Inside Story of the Generic Drug Boom, 2019.
> Journalist Katherine Eban reveals how fraud, falsified data, and corner-cutting in the global generic drug industry are harming patients. Globalization itself is part of the problem because manufacturing takes place outside national regulations. Many generic drugs, she finds, are shams.

Burke Lennihan, *Your Natural Medicine Cabinet:*
A Practical Guide to Drug-Free Remedies
for Common Ailments, 2016.
> Burke Lennihan dispenses natural remedies for everything from acid reflux to emotional problems. He says that by using proper nutrition, we can clear up many ailments without prescription medications or a doctor visit.

Arielle Levitan and Romy Block, *The Vitamin Solution:*
Two Doctors Clear the Confusion
about Vitamins and Your Health, 2015.
> With so much conflicting information peddled about vitamins, how do we figure out which ones we need? Physicians Levitan and Block explain which may be helpful and for whom and which to avoid. They also offer advice on which vitamins might help specific ailments such as migraines.

Cheryl Pellerin, *Healing with Cannabis:*
The Evolution of the Endocannabinoid System and How
Cannabinoids Help Relieve PTSD, Pain, MS, Anxiety,
and More, 2020.
> Many people are now treating issues like anxiety with medical cannabis or CBD. Science writer Cheryl Pellerin explains how the endocannabinoid system works in the bodies of vertebrates to maintain balance in the body. Research shows how these substances treat issues from PTSD to cancer.

Michael Pollan, *How to Change Your Mind:*
What the New Science of Psychedelics Teaches Us
About Consciousness, Dying, Addiction, Depression,
and Transcendence, **2018.**

American journalist Michael Pollan explores psychedelics, which have
recently undergone a resurgence in medical research after being banned in
the 1960s. After offering himself as a test subject, Pollan reports what we've
discovered, occasionally from a first-hand perspective.

616 Diseases

Anil Ananthaswamy, *The Man Who Wasn't There:*
Tales from the Edge of the Self, **2015.**

Anil Ananthaswamy looks at the latest neuroscience findings about autism,
Alzheimer's disease, ecstatic epilepsy, and other brain differences that cause
unusual experiences. Then, in light of these revelations, he speculates on
where our sense of self comes from.

Bruce Fife, *Stop Alzheimer's Now!:*
How to Prevent and Reverse Dementia,
Parkinson's, ALS, Multiple Sclerosis,
and Other Neurodegenerative Disorders, **2011.**

Bruce Fife examines medical evidence that neurodegenerative disorders are
curable and preventable. He focuses on methods that prevent the diseases
because, while reversal is sometimes possible, in the case of Alzheimer's, 70
percent of the brain cells involved in memory have been destroyed before
symptoms appear. He released a second edition in 2016.

Stephan J. Guyenet, *The Hungry Brain:*
Outsmarting the Instincts that Make Us Overeat, **2017.**

Obesity researcher Stephan J. Guyenet presents recent research in neuroscience that reveals why we overeat. He uses these findings to give strategies to
help us be slim and healthy.

Robert Kolker, *Hidden Valley Road:*
Inside the Mind of an American Family, **2020.**

The Galvin family lived a comfortable middle-class life in Colorado. Their
12 children were born between 1945 and 1965. Robert Kolker discloses that
while they seemed to be the ideal family on the outside, behind the façade
there was violence and abuse. By the mid-1970s, six of the boys were diagnosed with schizophrenia. The family was not informed of countless studies
performed on them, including those involving their DNA.

Janet Maker, *The Thinking Woman's Guide to Breast Cancer:*
Take Charge of Your Recovery and Remission, **2017.**

When physician Janet Maker was diagnosed with breast cancer in 2011, she decided to use her research expertise to figure out the best possible treatment for herself. As a result, she learned a lot about the disease and its treatment. Her findings will help those struggling with the disease find the best treatment choices.

Siddhartha Mukherjee, *The Emperor of all Maladies: A Biography of Cancer*, 2010.

Siddhartha Mukherjee narrates the history of cancer through the stories of those who have it and those who treat it. Along the way, he explains what is going on inside someone who has cancer. Looking ahead, he considers possible future treatments.

Rebecca Skloot, *The Immortal Life of Henrietta Lacks*, 2010.

HeLa cells were the first human cells ever to be grown in culture. They revolutionized medical research and have been responsible for improving and saving millions of lives. And yet, before Rebecca Skloot wrote this book, few knew anything about the real woman who gave them without her permission. Skloot's book relates Henrietta Lacks's story and the impact her death, and her cells, have had on her children and on medicine.

BIOGRAPHY

Temple Grandin, *The Way I See It: A Personal Look at Autism & Asperger's*, 2008.

She didn't talk until she was three and a half. Her parents resisted the experts urging them to institutionalize her, and Temple Grandin went on to earn a Ph.D. in animal science. Grandin wrote this collection of essays, in which she outlines her views on autism and the best ways to work with children who are on the autism spectrum. They first appeared in *Autism Asperger's Digest*, an award-winning magazine.

Kay Redfield Jamison, *Robert Lowell, Setting the River on Fire: A Study of Genius, Mania, and Character*, 2017.

Celebrated American poet Robert Lowell (1917–1977) wrote profound poetry but led a turbulent life due to bipolar disorder. Clinical psychologist Kay Redfield Jamison interviews his daughter, Harriet Lowell, and examines his life in the context of the illness. In the process, Jamison explores the relationship between mental illness and creativity.

Paul Kalanithi, *When Breath Becomes Air*, 2018.

Paul Kalanithi was diagnosed with lung cancer when he was a 36-year-old on the verge of completing his training to become a neurosurgeon. After his diagnosis, he began writing this book to document his experiences of dealing with his imminent death while he worked to save the lives of others. At the same time, he was a new father. After his death in 2015, the publication of this book served as his affirmation of life.

Oliver Sacks, *On the Move: A Life*, 2016.
Renowned neuroscientist Oliver Sacks tells the story of his young adulthood
in this second memoir. He holds nothing back, sharing stories of his drug
addiction in California, his love affairs, his schizophrenic brother, and the
famous writers and scientists who influenced him.

617 Surgery & Related Medical Specialties

**Katherine Bouton, *Shouting Won't Help:
Why I—and 50 Million Other Americans—
Can't Hear You*, 2014.**
Hearing loss typically begins between ages 19 and 44, often for unknown
causes. So when *New York Times* editor Katherine Bouton faced hearing loss,
she decided to document the phenomenon and its effects on its sufferers. She
examines available treatment options.

**Linda Carroll and David Rosner, *The Concussion Crisis:
Anatomy of a Silent Epidemic*, 2011.**
Concussions occur fairly often in young children, teens, and adults on playing
fields in America. Linda Carroll reports that the effects can be devastating by
harming mental abilities and changing personalities.

**Lindsey Fitzharris, *The Butchering Art:
Joseph Lister's Quest to Transform the Grisly World
of Victorian Medicine*, 2017.**
Science historian Lindsey Fitzharris takes an unflinching look at 19th-century
surgical practices in this gruesome history. Surviving surgery was often
worse than living with the issue that required it in the first place. She details
how surgeon Joseph Lister figured out that germs were causing infection rates
to be so alarmingly high.

**Karen L. Smith, *Killing Heel Pain:
Your Final Freedom from Plantar Fasciitis*, 2017.**
Pain from plantar fasciitis is tough to deal with, and foot expert Karen L.
Smith explains how it develops and provides treatment options. Using illus-
trations, she explains why your case is unique and advises what to do about it.

618 Gynecology, Obstetrics, Pediatrics, Geriatrics

**Joanna Breyer, *When Your Child is Sick:
A Guide to Navigating the Practical and Emotional
Challenges of Caring for a Child Who is Very Ill*, 2018.**
After helping many parents deal with a seriously ill child, psychosocial counselor Joanna Breyer discusses how to cope with hospital settings, at-home
care, and long-term circumstances. She also touches on helping the other
children in the home while also attending to your own needs.

Jonathan Eig, *The Birth of the Pill:*
How Four Crusaders Reinvented Sex
and Launched a Revolution, **2015.**

> The birth control pill that touched off the sexual revolution of the 1960s has
> changed our entire social landscape. Jonathan Eig traces the four individuals
> responsible for its development—the radical feminist Margaret Sanger, the
> wealthy Katharine McCormick, the scientist Gregory Pincus, and the Catholic
> doctor John Rock. Their intertwined stories provide both a cultural and
> scientific history.

Becky Henry, *Just Tell Her to Stop:*
Family Stories of Eating Disorders, **2011.**

> Eating disorders can be deadly. They are also difficult to overcome. Becky
> Henry writes of her daughter's experience to help you understand how to
> support your loved one through these challenging diseases.

Alan Schwarz, *ADHD Nation: Children, Doctors, Big Pharma,*
and the Making of an American Epidemic, **2016.**

> While ADHD is a legitimate disorder that drugs can successfully treat, it is
> massively overdiagnosed in children and adults. Alan Schwarz looks at the
> history of this phenomenon and delivers stories of the dire consequences of
> medicating normal individuals with powerful drugs like Adderall.

Deborah Serani, *Depression in Later Life:*
An Essential Guide, **2016.**

> People often view depression as a normal part of aging. But Deborah Serani
> asserts this is a myth. Depression is both preventable and treatable in older
> adults. Serani offers stories to illustrate the forms depression may take, and
> she offers advice for treating it.

Benjamin Spock,
The Common Sense Book of Child and Baby Care, **1946.**

> Updated every few years, beloved American pediatrician Benjamin Spock's
> classic in American baby care provides practical advice for everything from
> feeding the infant to effective, caring discipline. The book is currently in
> its 10th edition, revised and updated by Robert Neelman, under the title *Dr.*
> *Spock's Baby and Child Care.*

620 Engineering & Allied Operations

Peter Forbes and Tom Grimsey, *Nanoscience:*
Invisible Powers Revealed, **2013.**

> Award-winning writer Peter Forbes and sculptor Tom Grimsey help you see
> the smallest bits of matter in this book about how nanoparticles improve
> our lives. Nanoscience is a fast-growing science that, among other things,

explains how butterfly wings get their color and provides cost-effective methods to desalinate seawater.

Lisa Osbeck, et al., *Science as Psychology:*
Sense-Making and Identity in Science Practice, 2011.

Research scientists study how other research scientists think and report what they learned here. How do patterns and relationships impact their results? What they learned teaches us about how we all think and relate.

Ainissa Ramirez, *The Alchemy of Us:*
How Humans and Matter Transformed One Another, 2020.

Materials scientist Ainissa Ramirez shows how inventions transformed our societies and our lives. She reveals how the stories we tell about new technologies are as transformative as the inventions themselves. Eight inventions including clocks and silicon chips illustrate her points.

Simon Winchester, *The Perfectionists:*
How Precision Engineers Created the Modern World, 2018.

Simon Winchester proves the Industrial Age in Great Britain could not have happened without precise, standardized measurements. Early engineers like John Wilkinson and Joseph Whitworth made discoveries that changed the world forever. And in the digital age, these breakthroughs are made globally. Winchester asks how precision and nature ultimately coexist.

621 Applied Physics

American Society of Mechanical Engineers,
Landmarks in Mechanical Engineering, 1996.

ASME's reference traces the history of mechanical engineering, from the invention of the steam engine through the end of the 20th century. Some of these inventions are no longer in use, but they were valuable in their time.

T. R. Reid, *The Chip:*
How Two Americans Invented the Microchip
and Launched a Revolution, 1984.

Before the invention of the silicon microchip, computers were huge and expensive. Only the wealthiest organizations could afford them. T. R. Reid tells how two young Americans, Jack Kilby and Robert Noyce, changed that with a discovery that led to the microchip. This book was revised in 2001.

Craig R. Roach, *Simply Electrifying:*
The Technology that Transformed the World,
from Benjamin Franklin to Elon Musk, 2017.

Electricity expert Craig R. Roach wrote this comprehensive history of electricity, including the early experiments, how scientists tamed it, and the outsized influence it has had on the world.

BIOGRAPHY

Matthew Josephson, *Edison: A Biography*, 1959.
Matthew Josephson's classic biography of Thomas Edison presents the genius without whom the world would be entirely different today. Though Edison's discoveries and inventions were monumental, he was a human being, and his unfortunate tendencies are documented in this book.

623 Military & Nautical Engineering

Joseph G. Bilby, *Civil War Firearms: Their Historical Background, Tactical Use and Modern Collecting and Shooting*, 1996.
Joseph G. Bilby delivers technical information on each Civil War firearm. In addition, he details their uses and advises on collecting them.

Diagram Group, *Weapons: An International Encyclopedia from 5000 B.C. to 2000 A.D.*, 1980.
This guide to weapons from early human history up through the end of the 20th century covers everything from clubs to stealth technology. An updated version, *The New Weapons of the World Encyclopedia*, was published in 2007.

Douglas Frantz and Catherine Collins, *The Nuclear Jihadist: The True Story of the Man Who Sold the World's Most Dangerous Secrets . . . and How We Could Have Stopped Him*, 2007.
Journalists Douglas Frantz and Catherine Collins expose how countries like Iran, North Korea, and Libya obtained nuclear secrets, blueprints, and weapon parts. Even though the international enterprise responsible was closed, the information is out there, ready to do harm.

Björn Landström, *The Ship: An Illustrated History*, 1961.
Björn Landström provides a pictorial history of ships based on extensive research on specific vessels, going back over 6,000 years to ancient Egypt and continuing through the nuclear submarines of the mid-20th century. He highlights particular ships and their place in history along with technical details about their construction.

David Macaulay, *Castle*, 1977.
Celebrated illustrator David Macaulay presents the architectural details of a medieval castle while outlining its construction step by step. It's a fascinating look at what life would have been like in one of these medieval fortresses.

Richard Rhodes, *The Making of the Atomic Bomb*, 1986.
Historian Richard Rhodes portrays the political and scientific milieu that

produced the atomic bomb. He describes the step-by-step and sometimes minute-by-minute account of its creation and detonations.

624 Civil Engineering

David McCullough, *The Great Bridge:*
The Epic Story of the Building of the Brooklyn Bridge, 1972.

American writer David McCullough relates the story of the Brooklyn Bridge, the most outstanding engineering achievement of its age. Washington Roebling, the chief engineer, and his wife Emily faced political obstacles while working on it, and a great and motley group of people shared in their drama.

Kevin Starr, *Golden Gate:*
The Life and Times of America's Greatest Bridge, 2010.

Historian Kevin Starr conveys the artistic merit of the Golden Gate Bridge while outlining its history and place in America.

628 Sanitary Engineering

Dan Fagin, *Toms River:*
A Story of Science and Salvation, 2013.

An environmental disaster unfolded in Toms Rivers, New Jersey. Science journalist Dan Fagin tells how an old chicken farm served as a toxic waste dump for decades, starting in 1971. When children nearby began to develop or be born with cancers, a legal fight ensued resulting in a $35 million settlement in 2001.

629 Other Branches of Engineering

Andrew Chaikin, *A Man on the Moon:*
The Voyages of the Apollo Astronauts, 1994.

Space historian Andrew Chaikin spent eight years researching the Apollo moon missions. He interviewed astronauts and shared the stories that culminate in Neil Armstrong and Buzz Aldrin's walks on the moon.

Joshua Davis, *Spare Parts:*
Four Undocumented Teenagers, One Ugly Robot,
and the Battle for the American Dream, 2014.

In a true-life David and Goliath story, Joshua Davis tells how, in 2004, four undocumented teenagers from an impoverished high school in Arizona competed in the Marine Advanced Technology Education Robotics Competition against some of the most elite collegiate engineers in the country and won. He follows them through the following years and reports how their experiences led to the DREAMers movement.

Paul Ingrassia, *Engines of Change:*
A History of the American Dream
***in Fifteen Cars*, 2012.**

Pulitzer Prize–winning journalist Paul Ingrassia tells the stories of 15 auto-
mobiles that shaped America's history and culture. Covering the Model T, the
Jeep, the Honda Accord, and others, he shows us the fascinating role these
cars have played in our lives.

Stephanie Nolen, *Promised the Moon:*
The Untold Story of the First Women
***n the Space Race*, 2004.**

Stephanie Nolen tells of 13 women chosen to be astronauts after they were
tested by a NASA doctor who believed that women are more physically suited
to space travel than men. These women trained intensively for two years
before the program was mysteriously canceled. It was later revealed that
John Glenn and one of their own undercut the program because they believed
women did not belong in space.

Mark Vanhoenacker,
***Skyfaring: A Journey with a Pilot*, 2015.**

Pilot Mark Vanhoenacker sheds light on the miracle of flight. He's not just
looking at the technical marvel of our ability to fly but also at the geographical,
cultural, and political consequences of taking to the skies.

BIOGRAPHY

A. Scott Berg, *Lindbergh*, 1999.

Twentieth-century aviator Charles Lindbergh was a legendary public figure.
A. Scott Berg presents a detailed account of Lindbergh, a profoundly private
man despite his fame. Berg presents a real human being, both the good and
the bad.

Beryl Markham, *West with the Night*, 1942.

Aviator, racehorse trainer, and celebrated beauty Beryl Markham writes
about her life of adventure in Kenya's Rift Valley and her years as a pilot.
In 1936, she was one of the first pilots to fly a nonstop solo flight across the
Atlantic against prevailing winds. This book, republished in 1983, brought her
renewed fame in her final years.

David McCullough, *The Wright Brothers*, 2015.

In 1903, two brothers from Ohio performed the first human-crewed flight
in history, in the Outer Banks of North Carolina. Wilbur and Orville Wright
were brilliant, courageous bicycle mechanics whose unlikely background
makes the book even more fascinating.

630 Agriculture & Related Technologies

Leah Penniman, *Farming While Black: Soul Fire Farm's Practical Guide to Liberation on the Land*, **2018.**
> While most of America's farmers are White, Leah Penniman, creator of the Black and Latino Farmers Immersion program, says it doesn't have to be that way. With guidelines for beginning to intermediate small-scale farmers, she offers advice for growing and running a small business, mixed with information on African-heritage farming. She also presents culturally relevant recipes using whole foods.

631 Techniques, Equipment & Materials

Michele Payn, *Food Truths from Farm to Table: 25 Surprising Ways to Shop & Eat Without Guilt*, **2017.**
> Farm and food advocate Michele Payn brings us 25 facts about our food and where it comes from. She brings together issues from both the farmer and consumer perspectives.

Janisse Ray, *The Seed Underground: A Growing Revolution to Save Food*, **2012.**
> Janisse Ray says that industrial farming and seed patenting have resulted in declining food choices. Fewer than one-fifth of seed choices have survived the past century. She considers seed-saving by ordinary gardeners who struggle to rectify the problem by preserving and eating old varieties of fruits and vegetables.

Mark Shepard, *Restoration Agriculture: Real-World Permaculture for Farmers*, **2013.**
> Mark Shepard explains how we can revive the perennial ecosystems that nature intended in our backyards, farms, and ranches. He says that nature's way is best.

Crystal Stevens, *Grow Create Inspire: Crafting a Joyful Life of Beauty and Abundance*, **2016.**
> Crystal Stevens's practical guide shows how to prepare seed-to-table meals, forage for food, make natural cleaning and beauty supplies, and preserve the food we grow or buy at farmers' markets. With this knowledge, she wants to inspire and empower you to be more self-reliant and planet friendly.

633 Field & Plantation Crops

Jorge Cervantes, *The Cannabis Encyclopedia: The Definitive Guide to Cultivation & Consumption of Medical Marijuana*, **2015.**
> Jorge Cervantes provides more than 2,000 pictures illustrating detailed

information on growing and harvesting medical marijuana, along with historical and legal information about medical cannabis.

634 Orchards, Fruits, Forestry

Philip Connors, *Fire Season: Field Notes from a Wilderness Lookout*, 2011.
Former *Wall Street Journal* editor Philip Connors spent half the year in a remote New Mexico fire tower with his dog, Alice, watching for smoke from behind the glass walls. He writes of his experiences in this area that gets hit by lightning, on average, around 30,000 times a year.

Susan Freinkel, *The American Chestnut: The Life, Death, and Rebirth of a Perfect Tree*, 2007.
In America's East Coast region, you can still find old fences and buildings made from the American chestnut. Susan Freinkel writes of the tree, preeminent for its beauty, size, and hardiness. She describes the heroic efforts to save the tree after it was decimated in the early 20th century by a blight that nearly drove it to extinction.

Norman Maclean, *Young Men and Fire*, 1992.
Norman Maclean was haunted for years by the Mann Gulch tragedy he witnessed in 1949. After jumping from a plane to battle a wildfire in the Montana wilderness, most of a team of 15 smoke jumpers died in a *blow-up*, an explosive firestorm of over 2,000 degrees. Only three survived, including the foreman who had thrown himself into an *escape fire*. Shortly after, accusations of murder surfaced.

Charles L. Sullivan, *Zinfandel: A History of a Grape and Its Wine*, 2003.
Through extensive research, Charles Sullivan tracked down the origins of the zinfandel grape. Here he examines the story of the grape and how it helped cement California's wine industry.

635 Garden Crops (Horticulture)

Zoe Ida Bradbury, et al., eds., *Greenhorns: The Next Generation of American Farmers: 50 Dispatches from the New Farmers' Movement*, 2012.
More than 5,000 farmers and activists who are committed to growing food in ways that respect the planet make up the Greenhorns. Fifty members of this movement contributed essays about their experiences working for social change and sustainability that range from inspirational to humorous.

Liz Druitt, *The Organic Rose Garden*, 1996.
Liz Druitt shows you how to grow a beautiful rose garden sustainably. She

contends that it's easier to raise roses organically than with chemicals, and she outlines how, from soil preparation to design.

Shaye Elliott, *Welcome to the Farm: How-To Wisdom from the Elliott Homestead*, 2017.

Shaye Elliott can show you how to grow your food in a small backyard or an apartment. She helps beginners optimize their space and take their first steps in growing plants and raising animals for dairy and chickens for eggs.

LaManda Joy, *Start a Community Food Garden: The Essential Handbook*, 2014.

LaManda Joy founded Chicago's Peterson Garden Project. She reveals how to raise a successful community garden that will provide members both healthy food and social interaction.

Susan Orlean, *The Orchid Thief: A True Story of Beauty and Obsession*, 2000.

Susan Orlean discloses her adventures in America's flower-selling subculture following John Laroche—an eccentric man determined to clone the rare ghost orchid, *Polyrrhiza lindenii*—through Florida's swamps, where he is helped by Seminoles and fought by law enforcement.

Sue Reed and Ginny Stibolt, *Climate-Wise Landscaping: Practical Actions for a Sustainable Future*, 2018.

Reed and Stilbolt help us figure out how to fight climate change. They show how to reduce our carbon footprint, cool off, and support pollinators and other wildlife in this guide to backyard gardening and sustainability.

Jack Turner, *Spice: The History of a Temptation*, 2005.

Jack Turner recounts the history of the spice trade. He tells of the men and women who sought the spices to season food or to use in magic or medicine. He discloses the history of individual spices such as cinnamon, pepper, and clove and tells why they proved to be irresistible lures that reshaped the world.

636 Animal Husbandry

Melissa Berryman, *People Training for Good Dogs: What Breeders Don't Tell You and Trainers Don't Teach*, 2011.

Former animal control officer Melissa Berryman has witnessed tragedies when dogs were mishandled. She shows how to increase your control over your canine for the safety of your community, your family, and your pet. The key is understanding that dogs are not people and cannot be motivated by the things that inspire us.

Pete Freyburger, *Vetting:*
***The Making of a Veterinarian*, 2009.**
> Small-animal veterinarian Pete Freyburger recounts his experiences in vet
> school and his later efforts to support his community and his animal patients.

Allan J. Hamilton, *Lead with Your Heart:*
***Lessons from a Life with Horses*, 2016.**
> Neurosurgeon and horse-trainer Allan J. Hamilton reveals what his studies
> and experiences have taught him about both working with horses and living a
> fulfilling life.

Meredith Hodges, *Training Mules and Donkeys:*
***A Logical Approach to Longears*, 2013.**
> Meredith Hodges, the producer of the DVD training series *Training Mules
> and Donkeys,* provides this companion textbook that outlines the information
> and training program covered in the videos.

Maryn McKenna, *Big Chicken:*
The Incredible Story of How Antibiotics
Created Modern Agriculture and Changed the Way
***the World Eats*, 2017.**
> Until the recent past, chicken was a locally grown food and a rare treat. But
> industrial farming methods and antibiotics have changed the chicken into
> one of the most highly consumed animals in the world. Health journalist and
> *National Geographic* contributor Maryn McKenna shows how this happened
> and its effects on both our health and the planet's health.

Debra Rosenman, *The Chimpanzee Chronicles:*
***Stories of Heartbreak and Hope from Behind the Bars*, 2020.**
> In 25 stories, primatologists, sanctuary directors, veterinarians, and others
> who work with captive chimpanzees reveal what life is like for these animals.
> The reasons for their captivity vary, from biomedical research to the exotic
> pet trade. While some of the stories are heartbreaking, they help us under-
> stand that these animals need compassion.

637 Processing Dairy & Related Products

Gianaclis Caldwell, *Mastering Artisan Cheesemaking:*
The Ultimate Guide for Home-Scale
***and Market Producers*, 2012.**
> Master cheesemaker Gianaclis Caldwell leads beginner and expert home chee-
> semakers through the science and art of developing everything from a simple
> mozzarella to unique inventions. By explaining not just the how but the why,
> she equips you to explore cheesemaking confidently.

638 Insect Culture

Alison Gillespie, *Hives in the City:*
***Keeping Honey Bees Alive in an Urban World*, 2014.**
Alison Gillespie details how to practice beekeeping in unusual ecosystems—
urban environments where laws and people aren't always friendly to the
practice. If you'd like advice on how to raise honeybees in the city, this book
can show you the way.

639 Hunting, Fishing & Conservation

Dyan deNapoli, *The Great Penguin Rescue:*
40,000 Penguins, A Devastating Oil Spill,
and the Inspiring Story of the World's Largest
***Animal Rescue*, 2010.**
Dyan DeNapoli was placed in charge of the largest penguin rescue mission
in history when an iron ore carrier foundered off the coast of South Africa in
2000. Over 75,000 penguins along the South African coast are now endangered due to the resulting oil spill.

Eric Jay Dolin, *Leviathan:*
***The History of Whaling in America*, 2007.**
For over 200 years, the whaling industry provided the world's light through
whale oil. It also contributed to industrial lubricants and perfume. Eric Jay
Dolin tells of the industry from the failed whaling expedition of Captain John
Smith in 1614 through its decline in the late 19th and early 20th centuries as
disasters and discoveries gradually replaced the need for whale oil.

Anders Halverson, *An Entirely Synthetic Fish:*
How Rainbow Trout Beguiled America
***and Overran the World*, 2010.**
Discovered in northern California in the late 19th century, rainbow trout are
now stocked all over the U.S. and Canada. In other places where they have
damaged local ecosystems, scientists are working on eradicating them. This
exhaustive history of the rise of the rainbow trout also provides a window to
our relationship with nature.

Rachael Lanicci,
Garden Secrets for Attracting Birds:
***A Bird-by-Bird Guide to Favored Plants*, 2010.**
If you'd like to attract more birds to your garden, Rachael Lanicci shows
you how to turn gardens and yards into specific bird habitats with the right
plants and trees. She also has a guide with illustrations to different
species of birds.

Earl Swift, *Chesapeake Requiem:*
A Year with the Watermen of Vanishing Tangier Island, **2018.**
Chesapeake Bay blue crabs have provided a living for the small community
who have lived on Tangier Island since America's Revolutionary War era.
Separated from the North American shore by 12 miles of estuary water, the
islanders have a proud history. But two-thirds of the island has been sub-
merged since the 1850s. Experts estimate that the island may be uninhabit-
able within a quarter century. Author Earl Swift spent two years living on the
island, and he sheds light on the people and life there still.

Ian Urbina, *The Outlaw Ocean:*
Journeys Across the Last Untamed Frontier, **2019.**
In some ways, our oceans are similar to *Waterworld*, the 1995 sci-fi film star-
ring Kevin Costner. Most of them are under no authority, and they are prey to
criminal activity and exploitation. After five years of investigation, author Ian
Urbina brings us a disturbing picture of oil dumpers, poachers, pirates, and
slave traders.

640 Home & Family Management

Amy Barickman, *Amy Barickman's Vintage Notions:*
An Inspirational Guide to Needlework, Cooking, Sewing,
Fashion, and Fun, **2010.**
When Amy Barickman began collecting vintage homemaking and decora-
tive guides, she discovered the work of Mary Brooks Picken, the founder of
the Women's Institute of Decorative Arts. Exploring Picken's work inspired
Barickman to make this practical guide to creating a beautiful life for yourself
with a vintage twist.

Eknath Easwaran, *Take Your Time:*
The Wisdom of Slowing Down, **2006.**
A beloved teacher of Indian spiritual classics and English literature, Eknath
Easwaran imparts his techniques for improving everything from your health
to your productivity. From his perspective, peace isn't found through what we
do but rather how we think.

Derek Fagerstrom and Lauren Smith, *Show Me How:*
500 Things You Should Know:
Instructions for Life from the Everyday to the Exotic, **2008.**
We all need to know practical skills like packing a suitcase, but if you ever
wondered how to fight a shark, Fagerstrom and Smith tell you that too. While
everything they share may not be on your to-do list, you will find their
instructions entertaining.

Sarah Kallio and Stacey Krastins, *The Stocked Kitchen:*
One Grocery List . . . Endless Recipes, 2009.

Kallio and Krastins aren't providing a cookbook but a system. They share a
list of ingredients to always have on hand, then give over 300 recipes in which
to use them. The result is less stressful mealtimes.

David Toht, *Backyard Homesteading:*
A Back-to-Basics Guide to Self-Sufficiency, 2011.

David Toht covers raising fruits and vegetables in spaces of all sizes. You get
an introduction to laws and regulations for raising livestock in populated
areas. And he dispenses methods to use and preserve your harvests.

641 Food & Drink

Dominique Ansel, *Everyone Can Bake:*
Simple Recipes to Master and Mix, 2020.

If you dream of creating unique baked desserts, renowned pastry chef
Dominique Ansel shows you how to do it. After becoming a baker's appren-
tice in France at 16, he achieved celebrity for creating frozen s'mores and the
Cronut, among other desserts. Ansel provides step-by-step instructions and
helpful baking tips that will have you baking like a pro.

Michael Biddick, *43 Wine Regions:*
A Practical Guide to the Top Regions
and Vintages Around the World, 2018.

Michael Biddick determines the best wine regions and recent vintages using
data on climate, consumer reviews, critic scores, and quality systems. He
relates his tastings and conversations with winemakers from all around the
world in this practical guide.

Mark Bittman, *How to Cook Everything:*
Simple Recipes for Great Food, 1998.

Mark Bittman makes cooking everything as simple as possible in this classic
work. He explains why specific techniques and ingredients work better than
others. By providing suggestions for variations on almost every recipe, he
encourages you to experiment and have fun with cooking. The revised version
was published in 2019.

Jennifer Clair, *Six Basic Cooking Techniques:*
Culinary Essentials for the Home Cook, 2018.

Culinary instructor Jennifer Clair declares that you will be an outstanding
home cook if you know the proper way to handle a knife, cook meat, prepare
pan sauces, and make great vegetables. She shows how to accomplish these
tasks and tells you which ingredients you need for top-notch results.

Mollie Katzen, *The Heart of the Plate:*
***Vegetarian Recipes for a New Generation*, 2013.**
 Mollie Katzen's cookbook for vegetarian home cooking has simple, satisfy-
 ing dishes that are easy to prepare. Katzen dispenses her trademark wit and
 unique take on cooking and eating, along with variations in the illustrated
 book's recipes.

Samin Nosrat, *Salt, Fat, Acid, Heat:*
***Mastering the Elements of Good Cooking*, 2017.**
 Cooking instructor Samin Nosrat asserts that if you can master the use of salt,
 fat, acid, and heat in your cooking, you will make delicious food every time,
 even without a recipe. Mastering these four elements is crucial. With over 100
 recipes and variations, she shows you where to begin.

Michael Pollan, *Cooked:*
***A Natural History of Transformation*, 2013.**
 Michael Pollan takes cooking lessons from masters and distills the knowledge
 he gleans in this book. He isolates four elements—fire, water, air, and earth—
 that are crucial in the cooking process and masters one recipe at a time by
 looking at how these elements play a role in the process.

Irma S. Rombauer, *The Joy of Cooking*, 75th ed., 2019.
 First published in 1931 by Irma S. Rombauer, this classic American cookbook
 instructs you on how to cook everything. Irma's great-grandson John Becker
 worked with his wife, Megan Scott, to develop this 75th edition with over 600
 new recipes, in addition to updating and improving older offerings. A new
 chapter outlines how to save time and money while avoiding waste.

BIOGRAPHY

James Birdsall, *The Man Who Ate Too Much:*
***The Life of James Beard*, 2020.**
 James Beard transformed the way the world eats. Born in 1903, Beard was a
 failed actor who became one of the world's most influential cookbook writers
 and one of the first cooking show hosts. Birdsall explores Beard's personal life
 and motivations. Beard transformed American cooking from second-rate into
 an international cuisine.

642 Meals & Table Service

Lora Arduser and Douglas Robert Brown, *The Professional*
Caterer's Handbook: How to Open and Operate
***a Financially Successful Catering Business*, 2006.**
 Arduser and Brown tell you everything you need to know about starting a

catering business. Their guidebook will help you set up a kitchen, handle your employees, and navigate legal requirements.

Diane Phillips, *Perfect Party Food: All the Recipes and Tips You'll Ever Need for Stress-Free Entertaining from the Diva of Do-Ahead*, 2005.

When you throw a party, you don't want to be stuck in the kitchen while everyone else is having fun. Diane Phillips helps you enjoy your guests by preparing everything ahead of time, no matter what type of event you are hosting. She has menus, decorating tips, and bar guides for every affair from a neighborhood barbeque to a dressy cocktail party.

643 Housing & Household Equipment

Teri B. Clark, *301 Simple Things You Can Do to Sell Your Home and For More Money Than You Thought: How to Inexpensively Reorganize, Stage, and Prepare Your Home for Sale*, 2006.

Teri B. Clark delivers small, inexpensive tips you can implement to sell your home quickly and for more money. Learn the secrets of highlighting the home's positive features while minimizing the negative through the use of color and items like candles that you may already have on hand. The book's updated 2016 2nd edition is by Michael J. Cavallaro.

Bee Wilson, *Consider the Fork: A History of How We Cook and Eat*, 2012.

Award-winning British food historian Bee Wilson unveils how kitchen technology, even something as simple as a fork, changed our relationship to cooking and food. She looks at modern tools like stainless steel pots but also provides information on devices no longer used, such as the cider owl.

644 Household Utilities

Stephen Hren and Rebekah Hren, *The Carbon-Free Home: 36 Remodeling Projects to Help Kick the Fossil-Fuel Habit*, 2008.

When the Hrens upgraded their 1930s urban home to reduce their energy consumption, they decided to share their experiences so others could do the same. In addition to demonstrating how to use renewable energy for home heating, they also share tips for sustainable transportation and gardening.

646 Sewing, Clothing & Personal Living

Darin Colucci, *Everything I Never Learned in School: A Guide to Success*, 2016.

Darin Colucci's practical guide shows how to achieve your goals and dreams by exploring these stories and lessons. Success and happiness are often the same things, and Colucci brings out not-so-common wisdom on both.

Laynee Gilbert, *So What?:*
A Single Mom's Guide to Staying Sane in the 21st Century (*Not Just for Single Moms),* 2012.

Counselor Laynee Gilbert seeks to comfort those who may beat themselves up over their failure to be the perfect parent to their children. Single parenting is difficult, and this lighthearted read will provide comfort and reassurance.

Linda Lee, *Sew Easy:*
The Essential Guide to Getting Started, 2005.

Linda Lee's 64-page board book is part of a kit in a case containing single-project cards that you can choose from to create and practice simultaneously. The book shows and explains how to do specific sewing tasks. The idea is do it precisely the first time, then follow her encouragement to do it your way the next time.

Don MacMannis and Debra Manchester MacMannis,
How's Your Family Really Doing?:
10 Keys to a Happy Loving Family, 2011.

The MacMannises consider the family as a whole rather than a collection of individuals. They demonstrate how to identify family unit strengths and weaknesses through using ten essential keys, having constructive conversations, and overcoming damaging influences. With tips and tools, it's a handy family reference from prewedding through empty nesting.

Susan Yellin and Christina Cacioppo Bertsch,
Life After High School: A Guide for Students with Disabilities and Their Families, 2010.

While students in the U.S. have legal support from the Individuals with Disabilities Education Act and other laws, they encounter a different world once they leave the public school system. Yellin and Bertsch show how they can get the support they need in college and the workplace. They also provide further resources to help with the transition.

647 Management of Public Households

Stephen Fried, *Appetite for America:*
Fred Harvey and the Business of Civilizing the Wild West— One Meal at a Time, 2010.

Ray Kroc and J. Willard Marriott did not create the service industry in America; they capitalized on it. The first true national service empire was created by Fred Harvey, who, from the 1880s through World War II, owned and managed a chain of restaurants and hotels along the Atchison, Topeka, and Santa Fe railroad line. American life is still profoundly influenced by Harvey's innovations.

648 Housekeeping

Bettina Deda, *Downsize with Style: A 5-Step Process to Create a Happy Home and Refine Your New Lifestyle*, 2014.
   Bettina Deda guides you through downsizing or moving into a smaller space from start to finish by providing practical advice and making the process and the results a life-enhancing experience.

Marie Kondo, *The Life-Changing Magic of Tidying Up: The Japanese Art of Decluttering and Organizing*, 2014.
   World-famous Japanese organizing expert Marie Kondo provides a step-by-step method to help you declutter your home by tackling categories of clutter. In the process, you will make your life more peaceful, easier to manage, and happier.

649 Child Rearing & Home Care of People

Laura Berman, *Talking to Your Kids about Sex: Turning "The Talk" into a Conversation for Life*, 2009.
   Therapist Laura Berman believes that sex education is one of the most important things children need to learn, and they don't get enough of it in schools. Parents must help their children develop correct understandings and healthy attitudes toward sex. But this doesn't need to be an uncomfortable burden. She teaches you how to talk with your children from their earliest years through adolescence with frankness and humor.

Julia A. Bucher, ed., *American Cancer Society Complete Guide to Family Caregiving: The Essential Guide to Cancer Caregiving at Home*, 2011.
   Taking care of a cancer patient at home can be a difficult task. But this book can guide you through the process, from setting up your home to dealing with insurance. There are checklists with questions to ask doctors, symptoms to pay attention to, and where to get help when you need it.

Deborah Gilboa, *Get the Behavior You Want—Without Being the Parent You Hate!: Dr. G's Guide to Effective Parenting*, 2014.
   Parenting expert Deborah Gilboa has created a reference for parents of children aged 18 months to 12 years. She isolates typical behavior issues and instructs on how to deal with them effectively without creating resentment. In addition, Gilboa focuses on how to encourage behaviors you do want, from table manners to risk assessment.

Jennifer Harvey, *Raising White Kids: Bringing Up Children in a Racially Unjust America*, 2018.
   In a society full of racial tensions, Jennifer Harvey shows parents, churches,

and educators committed to equity and justice how to start a conversation
and honestly discuss race.

Laura M. Ramirez, *Keepers of the Children: Native American Wisdom and Parenting*, 2004.

Laura M. Ramirez says Native Americans cherished their children for their
unique spirits. She imparts their methods for uncovering children's strengths
so they can make valuable contributions to the world.

Wendy Thomas Russell, *Relax, It's Just God: How and Why to Talk to Your Kids About Religion When You're Not Religious*, 2015.

Award-winning journalist Wendy Thomas Russell explores the unique challenges encountered by nonreligious people when they become parents. Many
of them want their children to be religiously tolerant without indoctrination.
They want to comfort their children in difficult times without resorting to
religious language. This book gives guidance on these issues and many others.

650 Management & Auxiliary Services

Jenny Blake, *Pivot: The Only Move that Matters is Your Next One*, 2016.

Change is certain. But the stakes can be high when your career is on the line.
Career strategist Jenny Blake helps you determine the best next move.

Ray Dalio, *Principles: Life and Work*, 2017.

After growing up in a middle-class Long Island home, Ray Dalio began the
investment firm Bridgewater Associates. Since its inception, the company has
grown, according to *Fortune* magazine, into the fifth most important private
company in the U.S. Dalio shares the secrets of his firm's success, which he
believes will help anyone make better decisions for life and business.

Richard Dodson and Nancy Burke, *Power Your Career: The Art of Tactful Self-Promotion at Work*, 2016.

Understanding how to put yourself forward is critical to avoid getting left
behind. After interviewing thousands of people about how they work to get
noticed, Burke and Dodson outlined the actions anyone can take to promote
themselves without being pushy or creating anxiety.

Fran Hauser, *The Myth of the Nice Girl: Achieving a Career You Love Without Becoming a Person You Hate*, 2018.

Women have often felt caught between two alternatives: to please others and
be considered nice, or to assert, please themselves, and be considered, well . . .
not nice. But what if there is another way? Fran Hauser shows us that women

can be themselves, be nice, and be successful all at the same time. And she says it's possible to rise above double standards.

Melanie A. Katzman, *Connect First: 52 Simple Ways to Ignite Success, Meaning, and Joy at Work*, 2019.
People, says Melanie Katzman, are what ultimately matter in business. A focus on data can distract from that. So instead, she provides simple actions you can take to make sure you connect with others in ways that help you and them.

651 Office Services

Connie Dieken, *Talk Less, Say More: 3 Habits to Influence Others and Make Things Happen*, 2009.
Time is money, the saying goes, and Connie Dieken can help you save it while ensuring you get essential messages out.

652 Processes of Written Communication

Jason Fagone, *The Woman Who Smashed Codes: A True Story of Love, Spies, and the Unlikely Heroine Who Outwitted America's Enemies*, 2017.
Few have heard of Elizabeth Smith, who, along with her husband, invented the modern science of cryptology. Early on, Smith used her skills to capture criminals in the U.S. Later, in World War II, she pitted her wits against Hitler's Enigma while her husband did the same with Purple, Japan's version of the code. The couple's story makes a fantastic account of communication systems.

Simon Singh, *The Code Book: The Science of Secrecy from Ancient Egypt to Quantum Cryptography*, 2000.
Science writer Simon Singh delivers the history of codes and how they have made and broken individuals, wars, and nations. While he explains how codes work in accessible language, he also focuses on the people who wrote and cracked them.

657 Accounting

Gregory Mostyn, *Basic Accounting Concepts, Principles, and Procedures*, Vols. 1 and 2, 2008.
Gregory Mostyn's textbook is designed for self-learners and provides an easy-to-understand introduction to financial accounting. It contains practice tests and problems with detailed answers in an included CD-ROM. The second volume is a reference for bookkeepers, managers, and investors who wish to understand basic accounting and financial reports. The book was revised in 2017.

658 General Management

William Ammerman, *The Invisible Brand: Marketing in the Age of Automation, Big Data, and Machine Learning*, 2019.

While you probably know that AI is targeting you for the advertisements you see, you may not be aware of how these powerful algorithms are changing the marketing landscape in real time. Technologist William Ammerman has been at the vanguard of digital marketing for decades, and he will help you see it at work in places you didn't expect. He also shows you how to harness its power for your business.

Jason Barron, *The Visual MBA: Two Years of Business School Packed into One Priceless Book of Pure Awesomeness*, 2019.

In the course of receiving his MBA from the Brigham Young Marriot School of Business, Jason Barron sketched out notes for each class to capture all the essential points he needed to learn for each. He has edited those notes to help others understand what he learned in much less time and with much less expense. It makes a great companion to classes or a springboard for self-education in business.

Jonah Berger, *Contagious: Why Things Catch On*, 2013.

Marketing professor Jonah Berger describes six principles you need to understand in order for your ideas to go viral for a product or a service.

Drew Boyd and Jacob Goldenberg, *Inside the Box: A Proven System of Creativity for Breakthrough Results*, 2013.

Hundreds of major corporations use systematic inventive thinking or SIT to make creativity a part of their culture. Thinking outside the box is commonly recommended, but Boyd and Goldenberg say research demonstrates that advice is misguided. Instead, using templates within the familiar is how creative thinking works best for all of us.

Tim Calkins, *How to Wash a Chicken: Mastering the Business Presentation*, 2018.

Presentation skills can make or break businesses and careers. Marketing professor Tim Calkins shows how to maximize your presentations to get your point across and make your idea compelling.

Patrick Schwerdtfeger, *Anarchy, Inc.: Profiting in a Decentralized World with Artificial Intelligence and Blockchain*, 2018.

We are living in unstable times. With increasingly sophisticated technology and trends toward decentralization, estimates are that 40 percent of Fortune 500 companies will no longer be in business by 2030. But Patrick

Schwerdtfeger says if you understand these trends and work with, not against, them, you can come out ahead.

Michael L. F. Slavin, *One Million in the Bank:*
How to Make $1,000,000 with Your Own Business, Even If
You Have No Money or Experience, 2015.

Michael L. F. Slavin writes from personal experience. After going from broke to millionaire, he shares how he did it. The idea is not to get rich quickly but to build your business step-by-step with a good business model, sound money habits, and a bounty of excellent business advice.

659 Advertising & Public Relations

Jackson Lears, *Fables of Abundance:*
A Cultural History of Advertising in America, 1994.

American cultural historian Jackson Lears looks at the history of advertising, from the European peddler to the 20th-century American corporation. He reflects on the ways it has affected American society.

Mike Smith, *Targeted:*
How Technology is Revolutionizing Advertising and the Way
Companies Reach Consumers, 2014.

When the digital age began, it ushered in a shift in the methods advertisers used to gain our attention. Mike Smith shows how digital advertising works and how it is microtargeted, and he stresses why it's essential for businesses to keep up with the changes.

Roy H. Williams, *The Wizard of Ads:*
Turning Words into Magic and Dreamers into
Millionaires, 1998.

Roy H. Williams provides a basic education in effective advertising, with plenty of examples of what works and what doesn't. He wishes to help you live a balanced, healthy, happy life while attracting business. His book was republished in 2012.

660 Chemical Engineering

Marcus Wohlsen, *Biopunk:*
Solving Biotech's Biggest Problems in Kitchens and
Garages, 2011.

Marcus Wohlsen introduces us to men and women who are working on their own to manipulate DNA to create all sorts of improbable developments. While they have benevolent intentions, from working on cancer drugs to protecting the global food supply, Wohlsen also warns of possible destructive uses of the technology.

663 Beverage Technology

Peter H. Gleick, *Bottled and Sold:*
***The Story Behind Our Obsession with Bottled Water*, 2010.**
Renowned scientist and freshwater expert Peter H. Gleick tells the story of how water, once accessible to all, became big business. He exposes the damage the industry is doing to our environment and the rest of the planet.

Cameron M. Ludwick and Blair Thomas Hess,
***The State of Bourbon: Exploring the Spirit of Kentucky*, 2018.**
This travel guide offers a historical and present-day trip through Kentucky's distilleries, restaurants, and hotels; and it provides a peek at the sights along the Kentucky Bourbon Trail.

Victoria Redhed Miller, *Craft Distilling:*
***Making Liquor Legally at Home*, 2016.**
Victoria Redhed Miller shows how to make legal liquor safely, with step-by-step recipes. And she takes you through the licensing process in both the U.S. and Canada.

664 Food Technology

Tom Mueller, *Extra Virginity:*
***The Sublime and Scandalous World of Olive Oil*, 2011.**
Tom Mueller uncovers the fraudulent world of fake olive oil. It's nothing new. Fake olive oil was with us in ancient times, and it's still with us today. Anyone who cares about their food needs to read about how America's lack of consumer protections defrauds us. Mueller uncovers how even toxic products can be perfectly legal.

Kari Underly,
The Art of Beef Cutting:
A Meat Professional's Guide
***to Butchering and Merchandising*, 2011.**
Kari Underly presents the perfect resource for grocery store owners, restaurateurs, and home butchers. While covering the fundamentals of international beef cuts and cooking styles, she also recommends cutting tools and demonstrates step-by-step cutting techniques.

666 Ceramic & Allied Technologies

Helen McKearin and Kenneth M. Wilson,
***American Bottles & Flasks and Their Ancestry*, 1988.**
McKearin and Wilson's guide to antique bottles and flasks has photographs and drawings with descriptions of both. Information on composition and history is also provided, along with details on reproductions.

668 Technology of Other Organic Products

Antonia Fraser, *A History of Toys*, 1966.
Renowned writer Antonia Fraser provides this history of toys, which was republished in 1972. She covers the earliest toys and the German toy industry of the 17th and 18th centuries and beyond.

669 Metallurgy

Cyril Stanley Smith, *A History of Metallography: The Development of Ideas on the Structure of Metal Before 1890*, 1988.
Cyril Stanley Smith provides the foundational textbook on the history and structure of metals and alloys, from the earliest understandings through the late 19th century.

670 Manufacturing

674 Lumber Processing, Wood Products, Cork

Martyn Bramwell, ed., *The International Book of Wood*, 1976.
Martyn Bramwell's guide to the trees of the world details the wood they produce and the qualities and characteristics of each type. Harvesting techniques and materials that are manufactured from them are also covered.

676 Pulp & Paper Technology

Mark Kurlansky, *Paper: Paging Through History*, 2017.
After searching the role of paper from ancient times until today, Mark Kurlansky concludes we will never become completely paperless. He speculates about the warnings every new technology brings and reminds us that paper was once new itself.

677 Textiles

Susan W. Greene, *Wearable Prints, 1760–1860: History, Materials, and Mechanics*, 2012.
The Industrial Revolution brought us the technology that made printing fabric possible. Susan W. Greene covers the process of printing and dyeing cloth with examples of contemporary historical manuscripts and publications on the topic. With over 1,600 color images of many types of samples, her scholarly history is accessible to the casual reader.

Kassia St. Clair, *The Golden Thread:*
***How Fabric Changed History*, 2019.**
> In a narrative going back over 30,000 years, Kassia St. Clair relates what we
> know about fabric history. She covers the stories behind acclaimed fabrics like
> silk and materials made to help people survive in harsh climates like outer
> space. In addition, the clothmaking industry and the social and economic
> impacts fabrics have had on humanity worldwide are examined.

Isabel B. Wingate, *Fairchild's Dictionary of Textiles*, 1979.
> This book was completely revised and expanded in 2009, but this earlier 6th
> edition contains 14,000 definitions of fibers. Isabel B. Wingate also covers
> regulations, inventors, and business terms relevant to textiles.

680 Manufacture of Products for Specific Uses

681 Precision Instruments & Other Devices

David S. Landes, *Revolution in Time:*
***Clocks and the Making of the Modern World*, 1983.**
> Economics professor David S. Landes looks at how we have measured time
> through the ages. The book's 2000 revision looks at clock-making technology
> from the past through the end of the 20th century.

Tan Le, *The NeuroGeneration:*
The New Era in Brain Enhancement That Is Revolutionizing
***the Way We Think, Work, and Heal*, 2020.**
> Inventor Tan Le goes around the globe to share the latest developments in
> artificial intelligence. She shows how AI is helping people overcome disabili-
> ties like paralysis, control objects with their minds, and so much more.

682 Small Forge Work (Blacksmithing)

Randy McDaniel, *A Blacksmithing Primer:*
***A Course in Basic and Intermediate Blacksmithing*, 2004.**
> Randy McDaniel introduces the essential information and techniques of the
> ancient craft of blacksmithing. Over 400 drawings illustrate the instructions.

683 Hardware & Household Appliances

Thomas Thwaites, *The Toaster Project: Or a Heroic Attempt*
***to Build a Simple Electric Appliance from Scratch*, 2011.**
> Thomas Thwaites constructs a toaster from scratch. In the process, he uncov-
> ers surprising and disturbing information about what goes into making our
> most common products.

684 Furnishings & Home Workshops

John Wilson, *Making Wood Tools: Traditional Woodworking Tools You Can Make in Your Own Shop*, 2014.
Since the late 1800s, most woodworking tools have been made in metal shops. Before that, woodworkers made their tools from wood as part of their training. John Wilson revives the earlier tradition. He shows you how to make these tools, use them, and collect them.

686 Printing & Related Activities

Sue Astroth, *Make Spectacular Books: Fabulous Fabric, Skewer & Folded Books*, 2006.
If you'd like to delve into book making, crafter Sue Astroth shows you 19 projects using three different techniques. The projects vary in size and composition.

Allan Haley, et al., *Typography Referenced: A Comprehensive Visual Guide to the Language, History, and Practice of Typography*, 2012.
In this reference source, you will find illustrated typography in design, the history of specific typefaces, definitions of typographical terms, and the effects of technology on typefaces.

688 Other Final Products & Packaging

John Baichtal and Joe Meno, *The Cult of LEGO*, 2011.
Braichtal and Meno celebrate LEGO bricks and the people who love them. They share photographs and the stories behind those who use LEGO bricks to recreate everything from World War II battleships to M. C. Escher lithographs.

Daniel Imhoff, *Paper or Plastic: Searching for Solutions to an Overpackaged World*, 2005.
Daniel Imhoff exposes all the materials in packaging and the destructive ways packaged goods affect society. But he ends with eco-friendly laws, ways to reduce the packaging we consume, and technological breakthroughs that make packaging more environment-friendly.

690 Construction of Buildings

David Johnston and Scott Gibson, *Green from the Ground Up: Sustainable, Healthy, and Energy-Efficient Home Construction*, 2008.
To leave the smallest environmental impact possible, David Johnston provides new home builders and architects with explanations of what green

building is. His instructions show how to purchase the best materials, install eco-friendly water and energy systems, and more. The updated 2014 edition is also helpful as a guide for remodeling.

S. Peter Lewis, *Treehouse Chronicles:* *One Man's Dream of Life Aloft*, 2008.

S. Peter Lewis narrates his adventure of building his treehouse in Maine. He celebrates both the experience and the wildlife he encounters while working.

David Macaulay, *Pyramid*, 1976.

David Macaulay's books provide illustrations of technological marvels. In this book, he presents images to help you visualize ancient Egypt during the construction of the pyramids. He also explores what these structures meant to the people who created them.

Mike Oehler, *The Earth-Sheltered Solar Greenhouse Book:* *How to Build an Energy free Year-Round Greenhouse*, 2007.

Mike Oehler lays out his revolutionary techniques for building greenhouses that require no extra energy, even in winter. He explains how to make the greenhouse you want and customize it for your unique landscape and climate, with plenty of illustrations, diagrams, charts, and drawings. Oehler also provides helpful tips and tricks, including information on how to find free building materials and how to grow everything organically.

693 Specific Materials & Purposes

Bart Kaltenbach, et al., *Sun Sticks and Mud:* *1000 Years of Earth Building in the Desert Southwest*, 2012.

Bart Kaltenback looks at the history of earth building in the desert Southwest of the U.S. He also features modern architects who use these techniques to create beautiful, comfortable, and environmentally sustainable homes.

694 Wood Construction

Jeremy Bonin, *Timber Frames:* *Designing Your Custom Home*, 2007.

In this reference, Jeremy Bonin helps you create an energy-efficient timber-frame home while introducing you to the basics of timber-frame terminology and revealing surprising possibilities.

695 Roof Covering

Joseph Jenkins, *The Slate Roof Bible:* *Everything You Need to Know About the World's* *Finest Roof*, 2003.

Joseph C. Jenkins shows you everything you need to know about slate roofs, from their history to safely installing and recycling them. He provides over 300 photos, charts, and line drawings, making the book useful for architects, roofers, designers, homeowners, and historians.

697 Heating, Ventilating & Air-Conditioning

**Greg Pahl, *Natural Home Heating:
The Complete Guide to Renewable Energy Options*, 2003.**
Although dated, Greg Pahl's book on renewable home heating options still provides a good analysis of the options to heat a home, along with the advantages and disadvantages of each.

CHAPTER 8

700–799

Arts & Recreation

I F PEOPLE MANIPULATE ANYTHING, BE it landscapes, soundwaves, or paper, to make it more attractive or entertaining, a book about it belongs in this division. Examples include books on design, painting, and sculpture. Likewise, works on the performing arts such as music, dance, and theater go here. And finally, in 790–799, you can find books on games and sports of all sorts.

700 The Arts

Marc Aronson, *Art Attack:*
***A Short Cultural History of the Avant-Garde*, 1998.**
  Marc Aronson defines *avant-garde* as those people or creations on the cutting edge of any type of art. He charts the history of avant-garde movements, artists, and art from the 19th century forward.

Wil Haygood, et al., *I Too Sing America:*
***The Harlem Renaissance at 100*, 2018.**
  Historian Wil Haygood's survey of the art, literature, music, and social history of the Harlem Renaissance is based on decades of scholarly research. Thematic chapters present the vast array of genius concentrated in its time and place. Haygood also highlights the impacts of various works on larger U.S. culture.

Michael Kimmelman, *The Accidental Masterpiece:*
***On the Art of Life and Vice Versa*, 2006.**
  If you've ever wished for an artistic life, *New York Times* critic Michael Kimmelman argues that you already have one. By instructing you how to appreciate art, he reveals how to find it in everyday life. With attention, curiosity, and courage, he says you can be an artist yourself.

Olivia Laing, *The Lonely City:*
***Adventures in the Art of Being Alone*, 2016.**
  When editor and critic Olivia Laing moved to New York City in her

mid-thirties, she was surprised to find herself feeling lonely despite the people all around. Curious, she began seeking art that renders loneliness in the city. She considers works that capture the feeling and finds that loneliness is a universal human experience, no matter our circumstances.

Donald H. Ruggles, *Beauty, Neuroscience & Architecture: Timeless Patterns & Their Impact on Our Well-Being*, 2019.
Architect Donald H. Ruggles reports recent findings in neuroscience relating to the human need for beauty. Using these as a springboard, he reflects on the implications for architecture. By looking at fields as diverse as fractal geometry and psychology, Ruggles help us understand the importance of patterns in our lives and surroundings.

BIOGRAPHY

Jenny Uglow, *Mr. Lear: A Life of Art and Nonsense*, 2018.
Jenny Uglow acquaints us with beloved British poet and artist Edward Lear. While many of us know "The Owl and the Pussy-Cat" and his many paintings, the man himself was much more complicated than these famous works suggest.

701 Philosophy of Fine & Decorative Arts

Cat Bennett, *Making Art a Practice: 30 Ways to Paint a Pipe (How to Be the Artist You Are)*, 2013.
Artists need more than technique and good ideas. Personal habits of mind and character, like courage, keep an artist on the creative path. Cat Bennett's handbook will take you through experiments that make you more self-aware and develop essential qualities you need to produce works of art.

E. H. Gombrich, *Art and Illusion: A Study in the Psychology of Pictorial Representation*, 1960.
Globally renowned art historian E. H. Gombrich explores image-making. With respect for the creative capacity of humanity, he rigorously examines questions of style, psychology, imitation, tradition, and expression. The sixth edition of this classic was published in 2002.

703 Dictionaries of Fine & Decorative Arts

Edward Lucie-Smith, *The Thames & Hudson Dictionary of Art Terms*, 1984.
British art critic Edward Lucie-Smith provides over 2,000 entries and 375 illustrations in this concise dictionary of terms used in all the significant fields of art—the fine arts, architecture, decorative arts, and the applied and graphic arts from all around the globe, from antiquity to the late 20th century.

704 Special Topics in Fine and Decorative Arts

Margaret McCann, ed., *The Figure: Painting, Drawing, and Sculpture*, 2014.
Centering on the influential New York Academy of Art, Margaret McCann showcases figurative art produced by the artists, instructors, and alumni of the academy. Famous artists like Jenny Saville and Will Cotton provide essays and examples of their work. In addition, the book traces the evolution of figurative art techniques.

Hiroshi Unno, *The Art of Fantasy, Sci-Fi and Steampunk*, 2018.
Globally recognized writer Hiroshi Unno traces how fantasy art has evolved across art and literature over the past two centuries. With examples from Mary Shelly's *Frankenstein* to Walt Disney films, this book will please anyone interested in the world of imagination.

Marina Warner, *Forms of Enchantment: Writings on Art & Artists*, 2018.
In this anthology, British historian and literature professor Marina Warner explores a diverse group of artists, primarily women, and examines the stories and symbols alluded to in their works.

707 Education, Research & Related Topics

Kelly Baum, et al., *Unfinished: Thoughts Left Visible*, 2016.
Kelly Baum looks at over 100 works of unfinished art throughout history. She goes back 2,000 years using case studies that incorporate commentary from critics and scholars. Interviews with today's artists about recent unfinished works reveal what they say about present-day art.

708 Galleries, Museums & Private Collections

William Kloss, *Art in the White House*, 2018.
Art historian William Kloss catalogs the 500 or so works of art in the White House. The works, which belong to the nation, have a special meaning for each presidential family. Kloss also presents the collection of presidential portraits, along with critical essays and commentary. It is now in its third edition.

Wu Tung, *Tales from the Land of Dragons: 1,000 Years of Chinese Painting*, 1997.
In this scholarly look at the collection of Chinese painting from the Museum of Fine Arts in Boston, Wu Tung examines their historical contexts. Calligraphy and other forms of art are examined along with the development of techniques and traditions across the years.

709 History, Geographic Treatment, Biography

Ian Chilvers, ed., *Art that Changed the World: Transformative Art Movements and the Paintings That Inspired Them*, 2013.

The social, historical, and cultural milieu that produced art movements, styles, artists, and works is explored in this book.

Alisa LaGamma, *Kongo: Power and Majesty*, 2015.

The ancient kingdom of Kongo covered a vast portion of Central Africa. Alisa LaGamma tells how the European explorers, missionaries, and slave traders who arrived in the 15th century caused a massive upheaval in the region. She appraises the effects on the region's art.

Maya Lin, *Maya Lin: Topologies*, 2015.

American architect and public artist Maya Lin is best known for the Vietnam Veterans Memorial in Washington, D.C. Her entry won the most prominent design competition in American history and is the most visited memorial in the U.S. capital. The simplicity of her art forms obscures their impact. In this book, Lin walks you through the design process of 50 of her projects.

Carol Strickland, *The Annotated Mona Lisa: A Crash Course in Art History from Prehistoric to Post-Modern*, 3rd ed., 2007.

Amazingly, Carol Strickland covers 25,000 years of art history with illustrations, sidebars, and brief essays to clarify her points in just over 200 pages. She touches on art terminology, movements, artists, and museums.

Jen Townsend and Renée Zettle-Sterling, *Cast: Art and Objects Made Using Humanity's Most Transformational Process*, 2017.

Townsend and Zettle-Sterling's anthology of writings on casting provides a history of the art, possibilities for its application, and the different media with which to cast. It would be useful for artists, craftspeople, historians, and designers and enlightening for anyone else who is interested.

Lawrence Weschler, *Everything that Rises: A Book of Convergences*, 2006.

Lawrence Weschler sees connections everywhere he goes, often in the most unlikely places. While delving into art, geography, science, and time, he finds that everything has a link to pretty much everything else.

BIOGRAPHY

Blake Gopnik, *Warhol*, 2020.

American art critic Blake Gopnik bases this biography of revolutionary

20th-century artist Andy Warhol on archival research and hundreds of inter-views with the people who knew him. He looks at Warhol's humble beginnings, his famous paintings, his celebrity, his love life, and the Art Factory, where he worked and entertained the glitterati of his time. Warhol's private life, Gopnik finds, was quite different from his public persona.

Deborah Solomon, *Utopia Parkway: The Life and Work of Joseph Cornell*, 2004.

Art critic Deborah Solomon recounts the story of Joseph Cornell, an unusual 20th-century artist who created three-dimensional shadow boxes. Living in a small house with his mother and invalid brother in Queens, New York, Cornell spent his nights making art, which he called an intersection of Surrealism, Abstract Expressionism, and Pop Art. His relationships with major artists such as de Kooning and Warhol and romantic links to Susan Sontag and Yoko Ono were just as interesting as his art.

Mark Stevens and Annalyn Swan, *de Kooning: An American Master*, 2006.

Abstract expressionist painter Willem de Kooning was one of the most influential painters of the 20th century. A Dutch native, de Kooning came to America as a stowaway in 1926 after completing classical art training in Rotterdam. During the Depression, he worked for the Works Progress Administration and gained renown for his work. His life was legendary for its intensity, influence, and accomplishment.

710 Area Planning & Landscape Architecture

711 Area Planning (Civic Art)

Dianne Aprile, ed., *A Landscape and Its Legacy: The Parklands of Floyds Fork*, 2012.

Dianne Aprile and artist Julius Friedman present the story of Floyds Fork in Louisville, Kentucky. Frederick Law Olmsted's work inspired the 4,000-acre park. Aprile provides a history of Floyds Fork, including the people who were instrumental in producing it, along with Friedman's beautiful photographs of the property.

712 Landscape Architecture (Landscape Design)

Marilyn Raff, *The Intuitive Gardener: Finding Creative Freedom in the Garden*, 2002.

When Marilyn Raff began to turn her suburban yard from an expanse of grass into a beautiful garden, she was a complete beginner. Rather than follow the rules, she followed her inner voice. Her results were so stunning they touched off a new career for Raff in garden design. She tells you how to turn your patch of earth into the garden of your dreams.

Randle Siddeley, *The Garden: Before & After*, 2019.

Internationally acclaimed garden designer Randle Siddeley, 4th Baron Kenilworth, presents the gardens he has designed. Before and after photos starkly contrast the spaces. He examines the gardens he has worked on for the rich and famous worldwide.

Andrea Wulf, *Founding Gardeners: The Revolutionary Generation, Nature, and the Shaping of the American Nation*, 2011.

America's founding fathers, from George Washington to James Madison, were keenly interested in their gardens. Andrea Wulf researched the gardening interests of this group of men to help you understand how their great love of gardening, botany, and agriculture influenced their actions in all arenas.

BIOGRAPHY

Witold Rybczynski, *A Clearing in the Distance: Frederick Law Olmsted and America in the Nineteenth Century*, 2000.

Nineteenth-century American landscape architect Frederick Law Olmsted designed many of America's great parks, and he was also a central figure in the period's history. While his work survives from New York's Central Park to the Stanford University campus, he also cofounded *The Nation* and the Red Cross. And those were just a few areas he influenced.

717 Structures in Landscape Architecture

Pat Sagui, *Landscaping with Stone: Create Patios, Walkways, Walls, and Other Landscape Features*, 2005.

After outlining the foundations of using stone in landscape design, Pat Sagui inspires you to incorporate it into your own spaces. He then provides tips to help you work with stone and implement specific projects.

719 Natural Landscapes

Sharon A. Receveur and Tavia P. Cathcart, *Bernheim Arboretum and Research Forest*, 2010.

Isaac Wolfe Bernheim lived the American dream. A German immigrant, he made his fortune in a Kentucky-based whisky business. As a work of philanthropy, he purchased over 14,000 acres in Kentucky, occupied by subsistence farmers, that had been largely shorn of trees. Archivist Sharon A. Recenveur shows how Bernheim transformed the area into a stunning wildlife preserve with trails, formal gardens, and native ecosystems, which he then donated to the people of Kentucky.

720 Architecture

Janey Bennett, *The Fantastic Seashell of the Mind: The Architecture of Mark Mills*, 2017.

Frank Lloyd Wright's statement that seashells are nature's perfect architecture inspired his student Mark Mills. Janey Bennett recounts how Mills used the idea in his house designs, where roofs and ceilings formed the centerpieces. Below them, partitions made the ceiling structure visible from the entire interior. Through these features, the houses became like shells for their occupants.

Alain de Botton, *The Architecture of Happiness*, 2006.

Philosopher Alain de Botton discusses what many architects are reluctant to talk about—beauty in design. Rather than look at beauty as a frivolous add-on, he argues it is crucial to our happiness because our surroundings influence our feelings and self-concepts.

Matthew Frederick, *101 Things I Learned in Architecture School*, 2007.

Architecture school needn't be so pedantic, argues architect Matthew Frederick. In this book, he provides short lessons on the ideas and skills necessary for architecture students to grasp. From how to draw a line to understanding color theory, his book makes an excellent resource for anyone interested in design.

James F. O'Gorman, *ABC of Architecture*, 1997.

This nontechnical introduction to architecture is perfect for anyone who wants to understand its basics. James F. O'Gorman covers its structure, history, and criticism as well as the elements that make up a building. In addition, practical information such as how to read plans and how architects play with space and light is provided.

Boyce Thompson, *Designing for Disaster: Domestic Architecture in the Era of Climate Change*, 2019.

Climate change, Boyce Thompson says, has made the designs of years gone by impractical. He offers homeowners, architects, and builders 16 examples of homes that will prove resilient against earth, wind, fire, and water threats. Additional resources are also provided.

Leyla Uluhanli, Jai Imbley, eds., *Mosques:*
Splendors of Islam, **2017.**

This celebration of mosque architecture features over 60 historic Islamic monuments. Expert-written essays accompany the illustrations and examine the history of the buildings while tracing the stylistic changes between them.

BIOGRAPHY

Brenden Gill, *Many Masks:*
A Life of Frank Lloyd Wright, **1987.**

American architectural genius Frank Lloyd Wright is famous for his masterpieces in diverse settings, such as Fallingwater, the Johnson Wax Building, and the Guggenheim Museum. He is also widely known for his colorful personal life. Writer Brendan Gill was a friend of Wright's and uncovers the facts by stripping away embellishments that Wright encouraged.

Mark Lamster, *The Man in the Glass House:*
Philip Johnson, Architect of the Modern Century, **2018.**

Philip Johnson had a massive impact on urban architecture in 20th century America. Known for his contributions to what has been called starchitecture, he designed steel-and-glass skyscrapers and trained younger architects to do the same. Mark Lamster relates the contradictory private life of a deeply flawed man whose foibles mirrored those of American society.

721 Architectural Materials & Structure

Lew French, *Sticks & Stones:*
The Designs of Lew French, **2016.**

Natural builder Lew French divulges how he used stonemasonry to create amazing fireplaces, outdoor walls, sculptures, and other works in the U.S. and Brazil without using a chisel. His work is displayed here in beautiful photographs.

724 Architecture from 1400

Randolph C. Henning, *Aaron G. Green:*
Organic Architecture Beyond Frank Lloyd Wright, **2017.**

Aaron G. Green, a student of Frank Lloyd Wright, went on to design organic commercial, industrial, religious, and municipal buildings all over the globe. Randy Henning tells of his career, including the 1999 award he received for a school design in Greensboro, North Carolina, which features the world's largest single geothermal loop system.

725 Public Structures

William Seale, *A White House of Stone:*
Building America's First Ideal in Architecture, **2017.**
  Historian William Seale writes in extensive detail about the stonemasonry
  underlying the white paint on 1600 Pennsylvania Avenue. He delves beneath
  the layers to see the shapes, placement, and carvings on the stone and
  explores the abandoned quarry down the river that yielded them, now unused
  for centuries.

Robert C. Trumpbour and Kenneth Womack,
The Eighth Wonder of the World:
The Life of Houston's Iconic Astrodome, **2016.**
  The Astrodome changed the face of American sports. Trumpbour and
  Womack chart its history from the fanfare surrounding its opening in 1965 to
  its challenges, such as its use in the Hurricane Katrina disaster. They reflect
  on its role in the long-lasting changes in user experiences that sports fans
  came to expect.

726 Buildings For Religious & Related Purposes

Thomas Barrie, *Spiritual Path, Sacred Place,* **1996.**
  Architecture professor Thomas Barrie explores religious buildings around the
  globe and examines how specific design features represent the spiritual. He
  also considers how contemporary spaces reflect those concerns.

Joan Breton Connelly, *The Parthenon Enigma:*
A New Understanding of the West's Most Iconic Building
and the People Who Made It, **2014.**
  The Parthenon has largely been destroyed by fire and war and was disman-
  tled by the British to obtain the Elgin Marbles. Joan Breton Connelly examines the remaining pieces to uncover unexpected revelations about ancient
  Greek society.

Ross King, *Brunelleschi's Dome:*
How a Renaissance Genius Reinvented Architecture, **2001.**
  Celebrated writer Ross King tells of Brunelleschi, a goldsmith and clockmaker
  instrumental in the construction of the dome of Florence Cathedral. The revolutionary period of Renaissance Florence is the backdrop for Brunelleschi's
  contributions, which include the machines he invented that made the
  building possible.

Nan Shunxun and Beverly Foit-Albert,
China's Sacred Sites, **2007.**
  Nan Shunxun and Beverly Foit-Albert explore over 50 ancient sites in China.

They illuminate how the sites' designers sought to blend architecture and nature to harmonize with the Chinese philosophies of Buddhism, Taoism, and Confucianism.

728 Residential & Related Buildings

**Gill Heriz, *A Woman's Shed:
She Sheds for Women to Create, Write, Make,
Grow, Think, and Escape*, 2021.**
> Artist Gill Heriz looks at sheds belonging to 70 diverse women. Photos from Nicolette Hallett reveal what the women do in their huts, from puppetry-making to writing.

**William J. Hirsch,
*Designing Your Perfect House:
Lessons from an Architect*, 2008.**
> Master architect William J. Hirsch helps you design your own perfect house in 12 lessons. He starts with big picture ideas like design philosophy and then moves on through practical issues like budgets and contractors. Relevant illustrations help you understand his points.

**Witold Rybczynski,
The Most Beautiful House in the World, 1989.**
> Architect Witold Rybczynski takes us through the process he underwent when he accidentally began building his own house. The building, originally intended to be a simple work shed, was slowly expanded until it became a livable house. He reveals his train of thought, helping us understand how architects think. The result emphasizes the importance of buildings in our lives.

**Thomas Durant Visser, *Field Guide to New England
Barns and Farm Buildings*, 1997.**
> At the time this book was published, Vermont had been losing around a thousand old barns and outbuildings a year to fires, neglect, or bulldozers. Historic barn preservationist Thomas Durant Visser traveled to six New England states taking pictures of remaining structures. This book contains over 200 of them.

**Lynda Waggoner, *Fallingwater:
Frank Lloyd Wright's Romance with Nature*, 1996.**
> Fallingwater is one of America's best-known private residential buildings. Located in the Pennsylvania forest, it feels as though it rose from the landscape around it. In this book, Wright scholar Lynda Waggoner introduces Frank Lloyd Wright's masterpiece and examines his architectural philosophy and influences.

730 Sculpture & Related Arts

David Finn, *How to Look at Sculpture*, 1989.
David Finn examines classical sculpture from ancient Egypt to the late 20th century. If you want to increase your appreciation of the art form, Finn can help.

Michael Maharam, ed., *Irving Harper: Works in Paper*, 2013.
This study of mid-20th century designer Irving Harper presents his iconic furniture and other home goods. Harper also produced fantastic paper sculptures in his spare time. This book examines all aspects of his work.

Jed Perl, *Calder: The Conquest of Space: The Later Years: 1940–1976*, 2020.
This second of a two-volume work on 20th-century sculptor Alexander "Sandy" Calder and his wife, Louisa, shares the couple's years during and after World War II, when they entertained artists and writers who had fled Europe to stay in America. Jed Perl looks at Calder's public sculptures and examines the influence they had on the art form. He concludes with Calder's death in 1976 and the retrospective of his work at the Whitney Museum in New York.

731 Processes, Forms, Subjects of Sculpture

Dorcas Adkins, *Simple Fountains for Indoors & Outdoors: 20 Step-by-Step Projects*, 1999.
Dorcas Adkins demonstrates how to make fountains for tabletops and yards. With easy-to-follow instructions, you can build and personalize your own with accessories like shells and fish.

736 Carving & Carvings

Chris Alexander, *Star Wars Origami: 36 Amazing Paper-Folding Projects from a Galaxy Far, Far Away. . . .*, 2012.
Chris Alexander provides instructions on how to make 36 *Star Wars* origami projects from the super-easy to the tricky. Be aware that the folding paper included will likely be absent if you purchase a used copy.

Malcolm Wells, Connie Simó, and Kappy Wells, *Sandtiquity: Architectural Marvels You Can Build at the Beach*, 1999.
An architect, a sculptor, and a photographer join forces to show how to create impressive buildings, from amphitheaters to ziggurats, using only damp sand and any tool with a straight edge.

737 Numismatics & Sigillography

Richard G. Doty, *The Macmillan Encyclopedic Dictionary of Numismatics*, 1982.
Richard G. Doty delivers this comprehensive reference on coins. He covers their terminology and history through the late 20th century.

738 Ceramic Arts

Don Davis, *Wheel-Thrown Ceramics: Altering, Trimming, Adding, Finishing*, 1998.
Written for all skill levels, Don Davis's manual provides everything on ceramics from the basics of throwing clay to tips for collecting international pottery.

Robert Piepenburg, *The Spirit of Ceramic Design: Cultivating Creativity with Clay*, 2009.
Rather than focus on specific techniques to produce ceramics, Robert Piepenburg examines the relationship between artists' sense of spirituality and their designs. He gives insight into using the spiritual to realize an artistic vision.

739 Art Metalwork

Harold Newman, *An Illustrated Dictionary of Jewelry*, 1981.
Jewelry collector Harold Newman provides this extensive, illustrated guide to making and collecting jewelry. Covering the history of famous jewels and biographies of famous designers and jewelry makers, he traces global jewelry making from the Renaissance to the late 20th century.

740 Graphic Arts & Decorative Arts

741 Drawing & Drawings

Lynda Barry, *Making Comics*, 2019.
In cartoonist Lynda Barry's book *Syllabus*, she reveals what she teaches her students at the University of Wisconsin—Madison. This follow-up provides exercises to help you construct your own comics. With her insistence that anyone, even you, can draw, Barry will help you surprise yourself with your creations.

Betty Edwards, *Drawing on the Right Side of the Brain*, 1979.
Now in its fourth edition, Betty Edwards's classic book for beginning and practicing artists helps you tap into the creative areas of your brain,

enhancing both your drawing and your life.She demonstrates how drawing can also be used for problem-solving.

Sean Howe, *Marvel Comics: The Untold Story*, 2012.

It would be difficult to overestimate the influence of Marvel Comics on American popular culture. Sean Howe tells how the corporation started, rose to prominence, and weathered failures and controversies. With details about Martin Goodman and Stan Lee's leadership and the artists, writers, editors, and characters who made Marvel possible, it's a treat for fans.

John Lewis, *March: Book One+Two+Three 2013 2015 2016*, 2016.

U.S. Congressman and civil rights activist John Lewis narrated a first-person account of the civil rights movement in America with coauthor Andrew Aydin and artist Nate Powell. While the struggle for civil rights in America has been a brutal battle that isn't over yet, we would not be as far along as we are without the activism retold in this graphic series. Note: This serious nonfiction book is in this section because of its format, not its content.

Charles Solomon, *Enchanted Drawings: The History of Animation*, 1989.

Charles Solomon narrates the history of animation beginning with 18th-century magic lantern shows. With stunning illustrations, it traces the development of the art up through Disney's animated version of *The Lion King*.

Art Spiegelman, *The Complete Maus*, 2003.

This classic work of graphic art combines *Maus I: A Survivor's Tale* and *Maus II*. In it, Art Spiegelman relates his parents' experiences in Nazi Europe. While unveiling their trauma, Spiegelman explores how such horrific events affect even the children of the survivors. Note: This serious nonfiction book is in this section because of its format, not its content.

BIOGRAPHY

Brian M. Kane, *Hal Foster: Prince of Illustrators— Father of the Adventure Strip*, 2001.

Hal Foster was one of the most influential illustrators of the 20th century. In this biography, Brian M. Kane confirms that Foster's drawings of Tarzan and Prince Valiant influenced both the character of Superman and the painter James Bama.

Selma G. Lanes, *The Art of Maurice Sendak*, 1980.

Beloved children's author and illustrator Maurice Sendak is celebrated in this biography filled with memorable illustrations from works like *Alligators All*

Around and *Where the Wild Things Are*. Selma G. Lanes looks at Sendak's creative processes as revealed in his interviews and quotes.

Elizabeth K. Wallace and James D. Wallace, *Garth Williams, American Illustrator: A Life*, 2016.

Artist and illustrator of 20th-century children's books Garth Williams lived a cosmopolitan life. The Wallaces disclose how he rubbed shoulders with some of the most prominent figures of his era, including Winston Churchill, Laura Ingalls Wilder, and E. B. White, among many others. His illustrations for *Charlotte's Web*, the *Little House* books, and *The Cricket in Times Square* are beloved today.

745 Decorative Arts

Judith Blacklock, *Flower Arranging: The Complete Guide for Beginners*, 2012.

Judith Blacklock shows you how to arrange flowers from the simple to the contemporary. It's the perfect book for anyone who wants to learn the basics of arranging blooms gathered from shops or gardens.

Mel Byars, *The Design Encyclopedia*, 2005.

With over 3,000 entries, Mel Byars's reference covers decorative design from the 19th to the 21st century. He profiles designers, firms, movements, styles, and materials. A list of exhibitions and fairs is included.

Marc Michael Epstein, ed., *Skies of Parchment, Seas of Ink: Jewish Illuminated Manuscripts*, 2015.

Jews are sometimes called the People of the Book, and this volume has numerous illustrations from their books and manuscripts going back over 500 years. Contributions from experts explore the history of the manuscripts, their interpretations, and how they overlapped and differed from Christian, Islamic, and other bookmaking traditions of the time.

Christian Heck and Rémy Cordonnier, *The Grand Medieval Bestiary: Animals in Illuminated Manuscripts*, 2012.

Heck and Cordonnier explore the representations of animals, both accurate and not, in medieval manuscripts. With nearly 600 images from all over Europe, they present visions of the domestic, the wild, and the mythical. The book highlights not just art history, but medieval thought about the place of fauna in creation.

Genevieve Layman, *Gather & Make: Plant-Based Projects for All Seasons*, 2018.

For every month of the year, Genevieve Layman gives instructions for three easy, affordable projects using plants. She also provides tips for planting and taking care of the plants featured in them.

Emily K. Neuburger, *Journal Sparks: Fire Up Your Creativity with Spontaneous Art, Wild Writing, and Inventive Thinking*, 2017.

Journals aren't just for writers. Emily K. Neuburger presents 60 writing prompts combined with art instructions to help ignite your creativity. Her book gives everyone a chance to play and explore.

746 Textile Arts

Anthony Berlant and Mary Hunt Kahlenberg, *Walk in Beauty: The Navajo and Their Blankets*, 1977.

Using full-color plates and black-and-white images of Navajo blankets, Berlant and Kahlenberg trace their history and how events dictated changes in both colors and materials. The authors unveil what makes these blankets works of art, how they represent the spirit of their creators, and what they tell us about Navajo society.

Deb Brandon, *Threads Around the World: From Arabian Weaving to Batik in Zimbabwe*, 2019.

Textiles are used for creative expression worldwide because of their versatility in materials, styles, and uses. Deb Brandon spent years researching textiles from 25 cultures around the globe and presents photographs of textile artisans and their unique designs.

Alison Cole, *The Embroiderer's Little Book of Hints and Tips: For Everyone Who Loves to Stitch*, 2016.

Alison Cole gives tips and hints to help anyone embroider, from beginners to experts. She demonstrates everything from how to set up a proper workbasket to framing creations. With its soft, workbasket-sized cover, you can keep it nearby and add your own notes to the blank pages included for them.

Priscilla A. Gibson-Roberts and Deborah Robson, *Knitting in the Old Way: Designs and Techniques from Ethnic Sweaters*, 2005.

Spinner and scholar Priscilla Gibson-Roberts and fiber arts editor Deborah Robson provide 15 sweater shapes from various ethnic and traditional cultures. While discussing color and texture, they impart techniques you can use to create your own.

Elizabeth Hartman, *The Practical Guide to Patchwork: New Basics for the Modern Quiltmaker*, 2010.

For quilters of all levels, Elizabeth Hartman describes how to change colors and fabrics for different looks, how to organize your workspaces, and ways to improve your skills. Her straightforward approach and instructions makes quilting relaxing and fun.

Yuki Morishima and Rie Nii, *Kimono Refashioned: Japan's Impact on International Fashion*, 2018.

This global exploration of the kimono traces the history of the garment and its massive influence on fashion design in the East and West. From the Cincinnati Art Museum to the Kyoto Costume Institute, collections demonstrate motifs and creative reimaging of kimonos throughout the world for both men and women.

Linda Parry, *William Morris Textiles*, 1985.

Textiles expert Linda Parry examines the work of William Morris with particulars about both their design and manufacture. She delves into the embroideries, prints, and weaves used to make his carpets, textiles, and tapestries, with color photos to illustrate.

Heather Thomas, *A Fiber Artist's Guide to Color & Design: The Basics & Beyond*, 2012.

Artist and quilting instructor Heather Thomas presents 12 workshop lessons to demonstrate color principles such as application, dominance, temperature, and complexity. She also explains design elements like line, shape, and form.

BIOGRAPHY

Lesley Frowick, *Halston: Inventing American Fashion*, 2014.

This monograph details the style and influence of American fashion designer Roy Halston Frowick (1932–1990) and his rise to international prominence as a fashion designer. His iconic pillbox hat worn by Jackie Kennedy is just one example. Here his niece and confidant Lesley Frowick recounts her interviews with the famous personalities who admired and worked with him.

747 Interior Decoration

Kerri McCaffety, *The Chandelier Through the Centuries: A History of Great European Styles*, 2007.

Kerri McCaffety brings us the ultimate reference on chandeliers, with their histories, timelines, charts, and diagrams. The 200 photographs help you appreciate their beauty.

Donald M. Rattner, *My Creative Space: How to Design Your Home to Stimulate Ideas and Spark Innovation*, 2019.

Architect Donald M. Rattner explores how space and its contents contribute to our creativity. Using over 500 photographs of everyday items, like furniture and cookware, he explains how our minds and imaginations are activated through interactions with our surroundings.

Roberta Sandenbergh, *Small Space Living:*
Expert Tips and Techniques on Using Closets, Corners,
***and Every Other Space in Your Home*, 2018.**
As homes become more expensive, many live in smaller places, from tiny
homes to studio apartments. Small space architect Roberta Sandenbergh
shows how to find storage spots in the often overlooked areas of your home,
such as over doors and in closets. She also gives practical advice on dividing
spaces to accommodate extra people.

748 Glass

Mary Lou Bertucci and Joanna Hill,
Tiffany's Swedenborgian Angels:
Stained Glass Windows Representing the Seven Churches
***from the Book of Revelation*, 2011.**
Bertucci and Hill share the hidden meaning behind a set of seven stained-
glass windows that the Louis Comfort Tiffany studios were commissioned to
create in the early 20th century. Each window depicts one of the seven angels
in the book of Revelation.

C. S. Lambert, *A Passion for Sea Glass*, 2008.
C. S. Lambert helps you see all the ways artists are using sea glass. The beauty
of sea glass windows is astonishing. Other examples may inspire you to create
your works of art.

749 Furniture & Accessories

Joseph Aronson, *The Encyclopedia of Furniture*, 1939.
The final edition of this classic reference was published in 1965. Over 2,000
photographs covered furniture from every era and architectural style, with a
glossary and index.

Helen Comstock, *American Furniture: Seventeenth,*
***Eighteenth, and Nineteenth Century Styles*, 1963.**
This classic guide to American furniture places pieces in their historical and
decorative contexts illustrated with over 700 photographs. The styles are
presented chronologically with information on the designers and craftspeople
who created them. In addition, Helen Comstock highlights the innovations of
each period.

Ralph and Terry Kovel,
***American Country Furniture, 1780–1875*, 1966.**
Rather than focusing on fine furniture, this book looks at American styles
from all ethnic backgrounds and regions of the country, such as the Shaker,
Pennsylvania, and spool styles. It features furniture and useful household
items of every type.

750 Painting & Paintings

Robert Cumming, *Annotated Art:*
The World's Great Paintings Explored and Explained, 1995.

Robert Cumming dissects 45 global masterpieces, symbol by symbol, to help
you understand the artist's intended meaning. For each painting, he gives
background information from the author's life and times that bears on the
interpretation. By following his examples, you will learn to unlock the meanings for yourself.

751 Techniques, Equipment, Materials & Forms

Steve Grody, *Graffiti L.A.: Street Styles and Art*, 2007.

Graffiti has gained fans worldwide. Steve Grody traces the art form's beginnings in 1930s Los Angeles to today. He interviews famous (and infamous)
graffiti artists and unveils a diversity of cultures and styles.

Karen Richardson,
Watercolour Toolbox: Essentials for Painting Success, 2013.

Canadian artist Karen Richardson uses her 35 years of both creating and
teaching art to isolate what hinders people from learning to paint. She identifies each problem and provides solutions. Using her approach, you can learn
to paint flowers, buildings, landscapes, and more.

757 Human Figures

Charlotte Mullins, ed.,
Painting People: Figure Painting Today, 2006.

Artist Charlotte Mullins explores the work of prominent figure artists from
all over the world, providing illustrations, interviews, and commentary. She
includes a wide range of styles.

758 Nature, Cityscapes & Other Subjects

Sabine Adler, *Lovers in Art*, 2005.

Sabine Adler examines renderings of kisses, mythological love stories, and
everyday couples by famous artists throughout history. The book is organized
in relationship stages from first meetings through marriage and covers a full
range of human emotions.

Barbara Novak, *Nature and Culture:*
American Landscape Painting, 1825–1875, 1985.

Barbara Novak uses examples from literature, journals, and art to illustrate
ideas artists have projected onto America's natural landscape. The pictures

they conveyed were neither small nor simple, and they led to the belief in American destiny.

759 History, Geographic Treatment, Biography

Kenneth Clark, *An Introduction to Rembrandt*, 1979.
Dutch artist Rembrandt Harmenszoon van Rijn is considered one of the greatest Western painters in history. British art historian Kenneth Clark analyzes his most famous works and reveals what they tell us about the man himself.

Lawrence Gowing, *Vermeer*, 1960.
British artist and curator Lawrence Gowing presents classic, scholarly studies of Dutch painter Johannes Vermeer's beloved works such as *Christ in House of Martha and Mary* and *Girl with a Pearl Earring*.

Donelson F. Hoopes, *Winslow Homer Watercolors*, 1969.
Using the Brooklyn Museum and the Metropolitan Museum of Art collections, Donelson F. Hoopes presents beautiful landscape watercolor paintings from famous American watercolor painter Winslow Homer.

Ross King, *Leonardo and The Last Supper*, 2012.
While Leonardo da Vinci may have been one of the greatest intellects in the history of the world, he was also a human being who doubted his abilities. Ross King examines how Leonardo painted *The Last Supper* against obstacles of war and lack of self-confidence. While reviewing the methods of painting large-scale frescoes, King also reveals a lot about the painting's symbolism and Leonardo's religious beliefs.

Ross King, *Mad Enchantment: Claude Monet and the Painting of the Water Lilies*, 2016.
Master of French Impressionism Claude Monet created his beloved *Water Lilies* while dealing with World War I, the loss of his wife and eldest son, and his fading eyesight due to cataracts. In addition, young artists like Henri Matisse and Pablo Picasso were challenging the supremacy of Impressionism as an artistic style. King explores how Monet managed to overcome all doubts to achieve these sublime paintings.

Barbara Buhler Lynes, et al., *Georgia O'Keeffe and New Mexico: A Sense of Place*, 2004.
Three authors tell the story of artist Georgia O'Keeffe and her paintings of the landscapes around New Mexico. Barbara Buhler Lynes is a curator of the Georgia O'Keeffe Museum. Frederick W. Turner writes of her personality and art colony. And Lesley Poling-Kempes provides geological information of the region and traces O'Keeffe's experiences there. Their book features

50 of O'Keeffe's paintings along with photographs of the sites in which she painted them.

Anne Marie O'Connor, *The Lady in Gold: The Extraordinary Tale of Gustav Klimt's Masterpiece, Portrait of Adele Bloch-Bauer*, 2012.

Reporter Anne Marie O'Connor tells the broad story of Austrian artist Gustav Klimt and his painting of Jewish society figure Adele Bloch-Bauer. The lives of the artist and subject were terrific stories on their own, but when the Nazis stole the portrait and the heirs had to go all the way to the U.S. Supreme Court to determine its fate, the story became worthy of a Hollywood movie.

Debora Silverman, *Van Gogh and Gauguin: The Search for Sacred Art*, 1992.

Many know of Vincent Van Gogh's self-severed ear lobe but don't know the connection to Paul Gauguin. The two artists shared a yellow house at Arles, hoping to help one another in a small artist-brother community. Van Gogh's dramatic act brought the attempt to an end. Debora Silverman exposes how their contradictory religious beliefs fed their works and inspired their different paths to create new sacred art.

Miles J. Unger, *Picasso and the Painting that Shocked the World*, 2018.

When *Les Demoiselles d'Avignon* first appeared, it was considered a monstrosity, likely a work of insanity. Miles J. Unger tells how Pablo Picasso came to Paris from Spain as an 18-year-old and became a central figure in the drug-fueled bohemian movement. It reveals how he used Cubism to deal with the fragmented reality the world had become.

BIOGRAPHY

Jonathan Brown, *Velázquez: Painter and Courtier*, 1986.

Diego Veláquez painted in the Spanish 17th-century court of Philip IV. As an artistic genius, he found painting portraits financially lucrative but artistically confining. How he coped with these tensions while staying inside the court's parameters is the subject of Jonathan Brown's well-researched biography.

Chuck Close, *Chuck Close: Face Book*, 2012.

American painter and photographer Chuck Close discloses struggles that stemmed from his childhood dyslexia and on to the collapsed spinal artery that nearly paralyzed him at age 48. He details his artistic techniques. And an engaging, interactive section where you can mix and match parts to create unique portraits adds to the book's appeal.

**Benita Eisler, *The Red Man's Bones:
George Catlin, Artist and Showman*, 2013.**

George Catlin was not the first White man to paint Native Americans nor the first to paint west of the Mississippi. But, while he wanted to capture the native peoples before they disappeared through what he himself referred to as genocide, he also began exploiting them by taking them on tour for live shows. Benita Eisler charts the story of his paintings and his checkered life.

**Andrew Graham-Dixon,
Caravaggio: A Life Sacred and Profane, 2011.**

Michelangelo Merisi da Caravaggio (1571–1610) produced realistic paintings of his troubled life and times. Italy was filled with contradictions where the religious and the secular fought for the soul; that Caravaggio lived on the dark side is evident in his paintings. Andrew Graham-Dixon spends a large portion of this book on Caravaggio's murder of a pimp, which likely led to his suspicious death.

Shelia Hale, *Titian: His Life*, 2012.

The life of 16th-century Venetian artist Tiziano Vecelli, or Titian, was largely undocumented except for his work. In this meticulously researched portrait, Titian expert Shelia Hale bases the story on contemporary records and interpretations of Titian's paintings set against the backdrop of Venice, which was a world powerhouse during his time.

**Jane Kamensky, *A Revolution in Color:
The World of John Singleton Copley*, 2017.**

While he is best known for his portraits of American Revolutionary War figures such as Samuel Adams and Paul Revere, John Singleton Copley left America for London, seeking his fortune at the beginning of the war for independence. He paid for his decision to remain neutral. Jane Kamensky tells the story of his life and his work.

Richard Meryman, *Andrew Wyeth: A Secret Life*, 1990.

Richard Meryman exposes the dark secrets behind the painter of *Christina's World*, one of America's most beloved paintings. While Andrew Wyeth carefully concealed his obsessions and pain, they managed to come through the surface of his paintings. Meryman uses interviews with Wyeth and his family, friends, and critics and strives to convey the man and his art in all their complexity.

David Michaelis, *N. C. Wyeth: A Biography*, 1998.

N. C. Wyeth, father of painter Andrew Wyeth, was a world-renowned artist and illustrator. His illustrations for Scribner Illustrated Classics are pinnacles in a career that produced painted landscapes, portraits, and murals. But despite his wild successes, he counted himself a failure because he wanted to be a fine artist and considered illustrations unimportant. David Michaelis depicts the story of the elder Wyeth from beginning to end.

Hilary Spurling,
Matisse the Master:
A Life of Henri Matisse, The Conquest of Colour,
1909–1954, 2007.

This second part to *The Unknown Matisse* tells of the painter's later years. Hilary Spurling reveals Matisse's self-doubt and desperation as he dealt with the effects of two world wars. His paintings were an attempt to deal with the intense pain the violence caused. Spurling also looks at the influential women in his life who were all as interesting as the artist himself.

760 Printmaking & Prints

Robert Hughes, *Goya*, 2006.

Robert Hughes documents Spanish artist Francisco José de Goya y Lucientes's career. From his early church work through his middle years in the court to the dark works of his later years, Goya's life takes us through the stormy history of late-18th- through early-19th-century Spain, from Holy Inquisition through war.

769 Prints

W. Raife Wellsted, Stuart Rossiter, and John Flower,
The Stamp Atlas, 1986.

The authors cover almost 500 stamps from all over the world. They help you identify stamps through the late 20th century by geographic, historical, or philatelic context.

Carl Zigrosser and Christa M. Gaehde,
A Guide to the Collecting and Care of Original Prints, 1965.

If you've ever considered collecting prints as a hobby or vocation, Zigrosser and Gaehde will help. They trace the history of prints and how to tell originals from reproductions. A glossary of terms and techniques and information on print restoration are also included.

770 Photography, Computer Art, Cinematography

Catherine Anderson, *The Creative Photographer*, 2011.

Catherine Anderson shows you how to turn any photo or group of photos into works of art suitable for giving to others or treasuring yourself.

Errol Morris, *Believing is Seeing:*
***Observations on the Mysteries of Photography*, 2011.**
Academy Award–winning director Errol Morris examines how documentary
photographs portray truth. To do so, he travels to the places photographed to
investigate what, exactly, is shown. How photographers manipulate their photos tells us about the human desire to see things from a particular perspective.

Martin W. Sandler,
***Photography: An Illustrated History*, 2002.**
Martin W. Sandler examines 150 years of historical photographs to demonstrate technological developments across time. He highlights famous photographers and affirms the impacts photography has had on fields from the
military to medicine.

Anne Tucker, *The History of Japanese Photography*, 2003.
While the technical capabilities of Japanese photography mirror technical
developments in the West, the artistic sensibility is quite different. Anne
Tucker writes scholarly essays on the evolution of photography in Japanese
culture and the interplay between photography and other Japanese art forms.

BIOGRAPHY

Ansel Adams, *Ansel Adams: An Autobiography*, 1985.
One of America's most beloved photographers, Ansel Adams told his life story
with his own black-and-white photographs illustrating the events. In addition
to photography, Adams shared his experiences as a conservationist, teacher,
and musician.

Ren and Helen Davis,
Landscapes for the People: George Alexander Grant,
***First Chief Photographer of the National Park Service*, 2015.**
America's National Parks are treasures for all its people. George Alexander
Grant began visiting all the parks in 1929 to document the stunning land-
scapes with his camera. Ren and Helen Davis survey his artful images of
Yosemite, Yellowstone, battlefields, monuments, historical sites, and more.

Timothy Egan, *Short Nights of the Shadow Catcher: The Epic*
***Life and Immortal Photographs of Edward Curtis*, 2012.**
Pulitzer Prize–winning author Timothy Egan brings us the story of Edward
Curtis, a handsome and charismatic man with a grade school education who
mingled with presidents, vaudeville stars, and the leading thinkers of his
day. At age 32, he left everything behind to begin documenting the cultures
of Native Americans. Curtis spent the next 30 years gaining the trust of
these peoplesand documenting their lives and rituals. He finally became

their passionate advocate. In his 40,000 photos and 10,000 audio recordings, Curtis preserved a record of their vanishing cultures.

Philip Gefter, *What Becomes a Legend Most: A Biography of Richard Avedon*, 2020.

Twentieth-century portrait photographer Richard Avedon was famous for his bold minimal style. But while his influence and talent were significant, he was often dismissed as a "celebrity photographer." Photography critic Philip Gefter discloses what influenced Avedon's work, gossip from the artistic circles he ran in, and how he finally got the recognition he deserved with his exhibit in the Metropolitan Museum of Art in the late 1970s.

Vicki Goldberg, *Margaret Bourke-White: A Biography*, 1986.

While Margaret Bourke-White was working for *Life* magazine, she took pictures at every important world event. She was on the front lines at armed conflicts and even interviewed Gandhi right before his assassination. Vicki Goldberg tells of this complex trailblazer for women's opportunities.

778 Specific Fields & Kinds of Photography

David Hall, *Beneath Cold Seas: The Underwater Wilderness of the Pacific Northwest*, 2015.

Photographer David Hall takes you underwater from just off the coast of California to Alaska. He presents a diverse range of plants and animals, some of which exist nowhere else. Using innovative techniques, he combines scenes from above the water and below to reorient those most acquainted with the land.

Art Wolfe, *Earth is My Witness: The Photography of Art Wolfe*, 2014.

The renowned photographer Art Wolfe delivers a sampling of his pictures taken worldwide over four decades. Most document landscapes, cultures, and animals that are in danger of disappearing. His goal is to help us treasure the world we have before it disappears. Wade Davis puts this collection in context in the introduction.

779 Photographic Images

Alex Bernasconi, *Blue Ice*, 2015.

The continent of Antarctica has the harshest climate in the world. Award-winning photographer Alex Bernasconi provides panoramic views of the landscape while sharing the diverse creatures it harbors. British glaciologist Julian Dowdeswell explains the continent's geography and discusses the effects of climate change on it. And British Antarctic Survey team member

Peter Clarkson relates the history of Antarctic exploration and what it was like to study and live there.

Jim Brandenburg,
Chased by the Light: A 90-Day Journey, 2001.

Celebrated nature photographer Jim Brandenburg took one picture every day between the autumnal equinox and the winter solstice near his home in the Minnesota north woods. He presents the photographs here, capturing both the waning light and his thoughts from the journal he kept at the time. He concludes with photos of the landscape after a devastating windstorm upended the area the following summer.

Annie Griffiths, *Simply Beautiful Photographs*, 2010.

Award-winning photographer Annie Griffiths chooses some of the most beautiful photographs from National Geographic Image Collection. Using these, she explores the elements that make up a beautiful photograph, such as light, motion, and wonder. And she provides quotes from scholars and poets to further highlight each feature.

Nathan Myrhvold,
The Photography of Modernist Cuisine, 2013.

Nathan Myrhvold presents singular artistic photographs, like the inside of a blueberry and a jar of vegetables photographed from the inside as they are boiling for canning. The stories and techniques used for each photo are revealed at the back of the book.

David F. Noyes, *The Photographing Tourist:*
A Storyteller's Guide to Travel and Photography, 2015.

David F. Noyes shows you how to improve your travel photography with stellar photographs and thoughtful documentation. His goal is to help you appreciate and learn from what you encounter on the road.

780 Music

Aaron Copland, *Copland on Music*, 1963.

American classical music composer Aaron Copland questioned why Americans seemed to value art so little. In this deeply thoughtful work, he probed the crucial role of music and how America could increase its role in society.

John Eliot Gardiner,
Bach: Music in the Castle of Heaven, 2013.

Composer, musician, and historian John Eliot Gardiner takes the few facts we know about Johann Sebastian Bach's life and combines them with a study of the era's broader history. His analysis of Bach's music helps us understand Bach himself.

Vivian Perlis, *Composers' Voices from Ives to Ellington: An Oral History of American Music*, 2005.

Using the Oral History of American Music archives at Yale University, Vivian Perlis offers interviews with great American composers from the first half of the 20th century. She also included a CD of their works.

Charles Rosen, *The Romantic Generation*, 1995.

Rosen turns his expertise to the music of the 19th century's Romantic period. While looking at the unique contributions of significant composers such as Schubert and Liszt, he also considers the cultural events from art, literature, science, and philosophy that tied the era together.

Alex Ross, *The Rest is Noise: Listening to the Twentieth Century*, 2008.

Alex Ross examines how modern and postmodern composers often sought to defy the conventions of their predecessors and how they succeeded in doing so. He also articulates the impact their music has had on mass culture through cinema and pop music.

Nate Sloan and Charlie Harding, *Switched on Pop: How Popular Music Works and Why It Matters*, 2019.

Musicologist Nate Sloan and songwriter Charlie Harding join forces to study 16 21st-century pop songs to illustrate musical concepts required to fully appreciate modern popular music. From Taylor Swift to Outkast, there is something here for everyone.

BIOGRAPHY

Judith Chernaik, *Schumann: The Faces and the Masks*, 2018.

Nineteenth-century Romantic composer Robert Schumann presented many facets or faces to the world throughout his life. Judith Chernaik brings him to life in this scholarly study of his contradictions.

Carlos Santana, *The Universal Tone: Bringing My Story to Light*, 2014.

Grammy award–winning guitarist Carlos Santana tells of his abusive, poor childhood in Mexico and his ascent to the top of rock stardom in America. Santana discusses his obvious mystical communion with his music.

Sylvie Simmons, *I'm Your Man: The Life of Leonard Cohen*, 2012.

Canadian-born musician, composer, and ordained Buddhist monk Leonard

Cohen was a study in contradictions. Sylvie Simmons traces the twists and turns of his life from Montreal to Mumbai, sharing his loves, vision, and music in this portrait.

Maynard Solomon, *Mozart: A Life*, 1995.

Music producer Maynard Solomon writes this biography of Wolfgang Amadeus Mozart from his life as a young musical prodigy through his death. While there are many stories about Mozart, Solomon reports, many are not accurate.

Jan Swafford,
Beethoven: Anguish and Triumph: A Biography, 2014.

Musical scholar Jan Swafford presents Western classical music's magnificent composer Ludwig van Beethoven in this biography. During the waning years of the Enlightenment, Beethoven moved to Vienna after growing up in Bonn. His contemporaries sometimes misunderstood his music, and he struggled against the deafness that gradually erased his hearing.

781 General Principles & Musical Forms

Robert Christgau, *Is It Still Good to Ya? Fifty Years of Rock Criticism, 1967–2017*, 2018.

Rock critic Robert Christgau writes this salute to rock 'n' roll music at the end of his five decades writing for the *Village Voice*. He provides a history of popular music through the ages, then focuses on the teen music of the 1950s that later evolved into this art form. After considering where the music will go next, he ends with obituaries of the genre's great musicians.

Scott DeVeaux,
The Birth of Bebop: A Social and Musical History, 1999.

With its roots in jazz, bebop arose in the early 1940s with talented young Black performers like Charlie Parker, Dizzy Gillespie, and Thelonious Monk. Scott DeVeaux captures the historical and cultural environment which spawned the art form and linked it to the civil rights movement in the U.S.

James Fraher, *The Blues is a Feeling:*
Voices & Visions of African-American Blues Musicians, 1998.

After interviewing and photographing celebrated blues musicians like John Lee Hooker and Sunnyland Slim, James Fraher relates their stories and celebrates their music.

Gary Giddins, *Visions of Jazz:*
The First Century, 1998.

Jazz critic Gary Giddins writes this history of jazz, drawing on his decades of writing for the *Village Voice*. He considers the genre's greats, from Louis Armstrong to Duke Ellington. He also covers artists

sometimes mocked as jazz derivatives like pop stars Rosemary Clooney
and Frank Sinatra.

Peter Guralnick, *Lost Highway: Journeys and Arrivals of American Musicians*, 1979.

Music critic Peter Guralnick examines country, rockabilly, and the blues
from their beginnings and their spread by traveling musicians. He depicts
American popular culture while highlighting stars of the genres such as
Ernest Tubb and Sleepy LaBeef.

Greg Milner, *Perfecting Sound Forever: An Aural History of Recorded Music*, 2009.

Without recording technology, musical stars would never achieve fame and
popularity. Greg Milner explores the history of this technology, from Thomas
Edison's recordings to the predominantly synthesized music of today.

Mark Zwonitzer, *Will You Miss Me When I'm Gone? The Carter Family and Their Legacy in American Music*, 2002.

When an Appalachian family of musicians—A. P., Sara, and Maybelle Carter—
went into a studio in Bristol, Virginia, to record their music, they did more
than just capture a music tradition. They began the modern folk, country, and
bluegrass movement that continues to this day.

BIOGRAPHY

Terry Teachout, *Duke: A Life of Duke Ellington*, 2013.

Edward Kennedy "Duke" Ellington has been at the apex of American jazz
since the form reached its height. Yet, while his music was a hit from Harlem
clubs to Carnegie Hall, Ellington was a private man who revealed little to
anyone. Cultural critic Terry Teachout provides a peek at the man behind the
persona to reveal the truth about this creative genius.

Terry Teachout, *Pops: A Life of Louis Armstrong*, 2009.

Using previously unavailable material, Terry Teachout paints a portrait of
beloved American jazz musician Louis Armstrong both backstage and after
hours. Armstrong was more than a musician. He was a complex and reflective
genius whose talents in writing and art are not often appreciated.

782 Vocal Music

Rich Cohen, *The Sun and the Moon and the Rolling Stones*, 2016.

Throughout the 1970s, *Rolling Stone* reporter Rich Cohen went on tour
with the band the Rolling Stones getting to know all the members. While he
chronicles the band's story from the 1961 meeting of Mick Jagger and Keith

Richards through the 21st century, he concentrates on the band's height of popularity from 1968 to 1972.

Angela Y. Davis, *Blues Legacies and Black Feminism: Gertrude "Ma" Rainey, Bessie Smith, and Billie Holiday*, 1998.

Scholar and political activist Angela Y. Davis analyzes the lyrics and performances of three iconic Black female blues musicians. Using the historical, social, and political backdrops of their times, she demonstrates how each stood against conventional expectations. In the process, Davis shows how blues music serves as entertainment and is an art form capable of raising the collective consciousness.

Jonathan Gould, *Can't Buy Me Love: The Beatles, Britain, and America*, 2007.

Author Jonathan Gould, a musician, looks at the songwriting and talent that created the Beatles' songs of timeless appeal. He examines the band members' lives and the cultural influences that impacted them, and he also looks at the cultural and historical events that helped propel the band to superstardom.

Alan Paul, *One Way Out: The Inside History of the Allman Brothers Band*, 2014.

Alan Paul put together this oral history of the Allman Brothers Band from 1969 through the book's publication. Using interviews with band members and many associates, he uncovers details about the band unavailable elsewhere. Also included is a discography of Paul's essential Southern rock albums.

Todd S. Purdham, *Something Wonderful: Rodgers and Hammerstein's Broadway Revolution*, 2018.

Musical theater fans know about the 20th century's big-name musical theater shows from *Oklahoma!* to *The Sound of Music* resulting from the collaboration of Richard Rodgers and Oscar Hammerstein II. Todd S. Purdham looks at the emotionally distant relationship between these two men. And he considers their failures as well as their phenomenal successes.

Paul Robinson, *Opera & Ideas: From Mozart to Strauss*, 1985.

Using six operas and two song cycles, Paul Robinson connects contemporary intellectual ideas with the music. He shows that like most popular artistic forms, operas express what is relevant to people in their time and place.

Tricia Rose, *Black Noise: Rap Music and Black Culture in Contemporary America*, 1994.

Professor of Africana studies Tricia Rose takes a serious look at the lyrics and rhythms of rap music to examine the issues and debates it has yielded from the use of musical technology to the cultural politics that shaped it. She also looks at individual artists who were popular in its first decade.

BIOGRAPHY

Marian Anderson,
My Lord, What a Morning: An Autobiography, 1956.

Marian Anderson was the first African American to perform at the Metropolitan Opera. Her immense talent was both honored and disrespected. Yet, through it all, Anderson displayed grace and warmth, concentrating on those who helped her achieve.

John Carter Cash,
House of Cash: The Legacies of My Father, Johnny Cash, 2011.

The profile of Johnny Cash by his son and namesake, John Carter Cash, uses family archives for illustrations. He reveals what the Man in Black was like in private, the values Cash strove to impart and live by, what he liked to read, and his spiritual life.

Roger Daltrey,
Thanks a Lot, Mr. Kibblewhite: My Story, 2018.

Roger Daltrey, founder and lead singer of The Who, tells his life story, which is entwined with the band's. He's equally frank in sharing tales of drummer Keith Moon's mayhem and reveals how they began smashing their instruments to end their shows.

Gary Giddins, *Bing Crosby:*
Swinging on a Star: The War Years, 1940–1946, 2017.

Twentieth-century singer Bing Crosby was the preeminent American performer during the years surrounding World War II. Cultural critic Gary Giddins uses his second volume to tell how Crosby encouraged both the war's soldiers and the folks they left at home. In the process, he redefined entertainment and popular culture.

Robert Gordon,
Can't Be Satisfied: The Life and Times of Muddy Waters, 2003.

Muddy Waters was perhaps the most influential blues guitarist from America's Mississippi Delta in the early 20th century. After making his way to Chicago and taking up the electric guitar, Waters impacted everyone from Jimi Hendrix to the Rolling Stones. Robert Gordon tells the story against its social and political backdrop.

Malka Marom, *Joni Mitchell: In Her Own Words*, 2014.

From 1966 to 2012, journalist Malka Marom befriended and interviewed singer–songwriter, Joni Mitchell. The result is a book about Mitchell's life, both the good and the bad. Sifting through the material she had gathered, Marom realized Mitchell's defining element was creativity.

Dolly Parton, *Dolly Parton, Songteller: My Life in Lyrics*, 2020.

Dolly Parton presents illustrations from her archives and uses lyrics from 175 of her songs to share stories of her life. The book covers over six decades in the music business and conveys why Dolly is so popular among music fans of all stripes.

Bruce Springsteen, *Born to Run*, 2016.

Bruce Springsteen's songs are poetic sketches of vignettes from ordinary lives. In his autobiography, he details his story from his small-town beginnings in Freehold, New Jersey, to his performance in the Super Bowl's halftime show in 2009 and beyond. His life story will inspire anyone who dreams of following their inner song.

Karen Tongson, *Why Karen Carpenter Matters*, 2019.

Karen Tongson was named after American pop star Karen Carpenter and she wrote this combined memoir of her own life and biography of Carpenter, shedding light on both. The Carpenters, the music duo of Karen and her brother Richard, ended when Karen died of anorexia at age 32. Tongson reflects on the perfectionism that led to Carpenter's death and her music's impact on people of color, LGBT+ communities, and others outside the mainstream who find a voice through Carpenter's music.

784 Instruments & Instrumental Ensembles

Stephanie Stein Crease, *Music Lessons: Guide Your Child to Play a Musical Instrument (And Enjoy It!)*, 2006.

Studies have shown children's brain development is enhanced when they learn to play an instrument. Stephanie Stein Crease looks at different musical instruments and musical schools and enables you to decide which is best for you and your child. She then guides you through the frustrations of ongoing practice and shows how to celebrate achievements, however small.

Matthew Guerrieri, *The First Four Notes: Beethoven's Fifth and the Human Imagination*, 2012.

Music critic Matthew Guerrieri highlights the impacts of Beethoven's Symphony No. 5 on Beethoven himself and the ways the work has influenced culture worldwide.

Joseph Horowitz, *Understanding Toscanini: A Social History of American Concert Life*, 1987.

Music conductor Toscanini was a cultural icon as famous in his day as major sports figures are now. Joseph Horowitz presents this man's story and his extraordinary rise to fame by combining cultural history and musical criticism.

Jon Wiederhorn and Katherine Turman,
Louder Than Hell: The Definitive Oral History of Metal, **2013.**
Based on over 250 interviews with musicians and associates, this book traces the oral history of heavy metal music. While metal music is unappreciated by many, it has stood the test of time. To its fans, it is often more lifestyle than entertainment.

785 Ensembles With One Instrument Per Part

Lewis Lockwood, et al., *Inside Beethoven's Quartets:*
History, Performance, **Interpretation, 2009.**
Music professor Lewis Lockwood provides an analysis of three of Beethoven's quartets. In addition, he provides a recording performed by members of the Julliard String Quartet.

786 Keyboard & Other Instruments

Charles Rosen, *Piano Notes: The World of the Pianist*, **2002.**
Master pianist Charles Rosen educates us about the piano and why it is in danger of becoming obsolete. We learn how the piano makes its distinctive sounds, how it has shaped Western music, and how it affected great composers of the past. He speculates on the place of the piano in the future of music.

James A. Strain, *A Dictionary for the Modern Percussionist*
and Drummer, **2017.**
James A. Strain's reference for percussionists and music educators uses over 300 examples to distinguish the many varieties of percussion instruments and their uses in various styles of music, from classical to popular.

BIOGRAPHY

Robin Kelley, *Thelonious Monk:*
The Life and Times of an American Original, **2009.**
History and ethnicity scholar Robin D. G. Kelley tells the story of Thelonious Monk, the man who brought us bebop. By pushing the boundaries on what was acceptable in music, Monk remained true to his unique musical sound and changed the face of jazz music. While his personality was admired and attacked by turns, there is no doubt he was a great artist.

Annik LaFarge, *Chasing Chopin:*
A Musical Journey Across Three Centuries,
Four Countries, and a Half-Dozen Revolutions, **2020.**
By concentrating on Frédéric Chopin's "Funeral March" and the three years it took him to compose it (1837–1840), Annik LaFarge uses the composition

to illustrate the themes of Chopin's life. His attachment to his native Poland, his relationship with George Sand, the technological advances in the piano, and his life in 1830s Paris are all threads woven into his music, especially the Opus 35 sonata. LaFarge says the man behind the music is not the sad, romantic composer often portrayed.

787 Stringed Instruments (Chordophones)

Mike Abbot, *The Guitar & Amp Sourcebook: An Illustrated Collection of the Axes and Amps that Rocked Our Guitar World*, 2012.

This ode to the guitar and amp has photos of the world's most popular models as well as brand comparisons between Fender and Gibson. Mike Abbot recounts the history of these and other pieces and sketches the musicians who used them. He also gives beginners advice on choosing equipment.

BIOGRAPHY

Oliver Craske, *Indian Sun: The Life and Music of Ravi Shankar*, 2020.

The Indian sitar became known worldwide because of Ravi Shankar, the instrument's master who traveled to take classical Indian music to the world. He taught Beatle George Harrison to play the sitar, introducing it to another generation of music lovers. He later blended Western classical music and jazz with Indian compositions. Through his music, Shankar became an ambassador of Indian culture in the West.

Charles R. Cross, *Room Full of Mirrors: A Biography of Jimi Hendrix*, 2005.

Rock music journalist Charles R. Cross tells the story of Jimi Hendrix, from his difficult childhood to his death at 27 from a drug overdose. While Hendrix lived a life of sex, drugs, and rock 'n' roll, Cross finds that Hendrix really craved ordinary family life.

Kent Gustavson, *Blind But Now I See: The Biography of Music Legend Doc Watson*, 2009.

Kent Gustavson follows the life of legendary North Carolina native Doc Watson in this comprehensive biography. The book was completely revised and re-released as a second edition in 2012.

788 Wind Instruments (Aerophones)

BIOGRAPHY

Miles Davis, *Miles: The Autobiography*, 1990.

In his autobiography, Miles Davis speaks honestly about his climb to the top and the musicians he played with along the way, including Charlie Parker, Dizzy Gillespie, and John Coltrane. In addition, he reveals why he kept a vow of silence for five years, his drug problems, and his thoughts on racism in both the music business and society at large. This book includes a Davis discography and photos.

Ben Ratliff, *Coltrane: The Story of a Sound*, 2007.

Jazz writer Ben Ratliff relates John Coltrane's biography in two sections. The first part looks at the musician's life, focusing on the last ten years when his compositions obtain a religious quality. The second part considers the influence Coltrane had on jazz and social history from the mid-1950s onward.

Ross Russell, *Bird Lives! The High Life and Hard Times of Charlie (Yardbird) Parker*, 1973.

Ross Russell, a true fan, eulogizes American saxophonist and composer Charlie Parker. He looks at the world that produced Bird and his magnitude of personality, which was as legendary as his sound.

790 Recreational & Performing Arts

Martin Duberman, *Paul Robeson: A Biography*, 1990.

Scholar and playwright Martin Bauml Duberman writes for young adults about one of the most internationally well-known actors, singers, and activists of the 20th century, Paul Robeson. The son of a formerly enslaved person, Robeson was a graduate of Columbia Law School who quickly rose to stardom on stage. But his outspoken ideas on race and fairness caused him to become an outcast from the entertainment industry.

791 Public Performances

Graeme Burk and Robert Smith, *Who is the Doctor: The Unofficial Guide to Dr. Who: The New Series*, 2012.

Burk and Smith capture why *Dr. Who* has captivated fans for decades. Throughout the history of the series, there have been eight different stars playing the lead role. All the primary actors and characters are covered, along with backstories. And they summarize every episode of the six seasons of the series that began in 2005.

John Dunning, *Tune in Yesterday: The Ultimate Encyclopedia of Old-Time Radio, 1925–1976*, 1976.

The golden age of radio broadcasting was the 1930s, '40s, and '50s, before television became ensconced in most homes. John Dunning presents 1,500 radio shows in alphabetical order. He provides the history, time slot, producers, actors, writers, sound effects people, and advertisers for each program.

Dunning also lists the names of the theme songs. Larger sections include themes like the news broadcasts, providing a complete reference on the topic.

Mark Harris, *Pictures at a Revolution: Five Movies and the Birth of the New Hollywood*, 2008.

In 1967 five movies were nominated for Best Picture. They were *Guess Who's Coming to Dinner*, *The Graduate*, *In the Heat of the Night*, *Doctor Dolittle*, and *Bonnie and Clyde*. Movie critic Mark Harris explores how each of these movies represents a part of larger cultural upheavals.

Thomas S. Hischak, *Musicals in Film: A Guide to the Genre*, 2016.

Beginning with *The Jazz Singer* in 1927, Thomas S. Hischak's reference work gives an overview of musicals on the silver screen up through 2015. He presents them chronologically, looking at each version's era and discussing the changes.

Robert Matzen, *Errol & Olivia: Ego & Obsession in Golden Era Hollywood*, 2010.

One of the first great romantic couples of Hollywood's golden age, Errol Flynn and Olivia de Havilland were massive stars in their own right. Robert Matzen tells the story of their relationship and the equally fascinating stories of each individually.

Salvador Jimenez Murguía, ed., *The Encyclopedia of Racism in American Films*, 2018.

This scholarly reference analyzes racism in films and the film industry. It contains articles by critics, scholars, and activists who discuss individual movies, tropes, fantasies about minority lives, and the lack of roles for actors of color. The adverse effects on society include a disconnect from reality and the erasure of the true stories.

Andrew Sarris, *The American Cinema: Directors and Directions, 1929–1968*, 1996.

Auteur theory posits that the artistic vision of its director largely determines a film's greatness. Film critic Andrew Sarris was a major proponent of the theory and, through this work, managed to elevate directors to artistic status. The book covers over 200 American directors and contains a chronology of the most important films and Sarris's most influential essays on filmmaking.

BIOGRAPHY

Patricia Bosworth, *Jane Fonda: The Private Life of a Public Woman*, 2011.

Jane Fonda, the daughter of movie legend Henry Fonda, lived in the public eye from the start. Her early family life was both public and heartbreaking. Jane rose to superstardom in films in the 1960s. Her political activism and support for her husband Tom Hayden's career were linked to the exercise video empire she created. She later abandoned all that when she married entrepreneur and philanthropist Ted Turner, which ushered in a completely different phase of her life.

Simon Callow, *Orson Welles: Volume 3: One-Man Band*, 2015.

Orson Welles's long career in film, radio, theater, and television both awed and baffled audiences and critics alike. Simon Callow's third volume of a four-volume series on the actor covers Welles's career from his self-imposed exile from America in 1947 to 1964. Welles completed some of his greatest works during this era.

Scott Eyman, *Empire of Dreams: The Epic Life of Cecil B. DeMille*, 2010.

Cecil B. DeMille, best known for epic blockbuster movies like *The Ten Commandments* and *King of Kings*, started as a silent film director in Hollywood's earliest years. Despite the biblical basis of his most successful films, DeMille was no Bible thumper. But his politics later shifted to the right, and he supported the McCarthy-era anticommunist hysteria. Scott Eyman provides a well-researched story of one of Hollywood's most influential figures.

Scott Eyman, *John Wayne: The Life and Legend*, 2014.

John Wayne once said, "I've played the kind of man I'd like to have been." And millions still love the kind of man he portrayed. Scott Eyman interviewed Wayne before his death and more than 100 family members, co-workers, and friends. In the process, he reveals how Wayne lived up to his aspirations and how he failed. In addition, Eyman examines how Wayne's conservative political views contributed to his audience and the types of characters he played.

Neal Gabler, *Walt Disney: The Triumph of the American Imagination*, 2006.

Neal Gabler tells how Walt Disney used his imagination and hard work to invent a world to his liking. While his private life remained unhappy, he changed cartoons into an art form, reinvented the amusement park, and pioneered a marketing model that bound film, television, print, music, theme parks, and merchandising and that is still widely used today.

Brian Jay Jones, *George Lucas: A Life*, 2016.

Award-winning author Brian Jay Jones looks at the career of George Lucas, who became an international superstar with the release of the first *Star Wars* movie in 1977 and later created the *Indiana Jones* series. Jones looks at the technology Lucas used and the famous entertainment industry figures who helped him.

William J. Mann,
The Contender: The Story of Marlon Brando, **2019.**
   Through his movie roles in *A Streetcar Named Desire* and *On the Waterfront*,
   Marlon Brando defined what it means to be an actor in American culture.
   William J. Mann says he also was an outspoken critic of racism in society and
   the increasing monetization of everything. Mann explores what inspired and
   motivated Brando.

David Robinson, *Chaplin: His Life and Art*, 1985.
   Charlie Chaplin, the comedic genius whose career took place mainly in the
   silent films of the early 20th century, was a troubled and complex man. David
   Robinson relates how Chaplin was the lonely and perfectionist son of an alco-
   holic father and a mentally disturbed mother. While he kept America laughing
   through hard times, America forced him to leave during the anticommunist
   McCarthy years.

792 Stage Presentations

Adrian Brine and Michael York,
A Shakespearean Actor Prepares, **2001.**
   For actors, a Shakespearean performance is the pinnacle of accomplishment.
   Adrian Brine and Michael York do not provide a list of dos and don'ts. Instead,
   they point out what actors must *understand* about the plays to help them
   tap into their creative potential and create something unique and fresh for
   the parts.

Jenna Fischer, *The Actor's Life: A Survival Guide*, 2017.
   Before playing Pam Beesley on *The Office*, Jenna Fischer struggled to make
   it as an actress for nearly a decade. When she moved to Hollywood from
   St. Louis, she had no idea how hard it was to break into the industry. In this
   guide, Fischer helps the young actors who follow behind her. She offers honest,
   helpful advice on everything from getting a headshot to avoiding scams.

Frank Hauser and Russell Reich, *Notes on Directing:*
***130 Lessons in Leadership from the Director's Chair*, 2003.**
   When Russell Reich received notes from his mentor Frank Hauser, culled
   from decades of directing theater and cinema, he expanded the typewritten
   document to a book filled with wisdom, techniques, and advice on directing. Hauser was a British director who worked with everyone from Sir Alec
   Guinness to Kevin Spacey. The lessons in his book will help directors, actors,
   and audiences understand the craft.

Jennifer Homans, *Apollo's Angels: A History of Ballet*, 2010.
   As a former dancer and current historian and critic, Jennifer Homans
   provides the first cultural history of ballet. Unlike other art forms, ballet is
   handed down through generations with no text or standard notation. Every

nation has its unique gestures and expression that spring directly from their histories. Homans will help you appreciate the nuances of the form.

Lin-Manuel Miranda and Jeremy McCarter, *Hamilton: The Revolution: Being the Complete Libretto of the Broadway Musical, with a True Account of Its Creation, and Concise Remarks on Hip-hop, the Power of Stories, and the New America*, 2016.

Composer, lyricist, star, and creator of *Hamilton*, Lin-Manuel Miranda and Jeremy McCarter, a cultural critic and theater artist who helped develop it, together tell the story behind the smash stage production. Alexander Hamilton, one of the founding fathers of the U.S., was a poor immigrant from the Caribbean. His story is told through a fusion of hip-hop, pop, and R&B. The musical uses Hamilton as a template for the mix of immigrants that followed, forming America as we know it today.

Kliph Nesteroff, *The Comedians: Drunks, Thieves, Scoundrels and the History of American Comedy*, 2015.

Comedy historian Kliph Nesteroff covers the early 20th century American vaudeville circuit through early 21st century comedy superstars. He demonstrates how comedians serve as social commentators and how changes in their style and content reveal a lot about society.

Brian Seibert, *What the Eye Hears: A History of Tap Dancing*, 2015.

Brian Seibert's entertaining guide to the history of American tap dancing tells how the art form sprang up from both the jigs and clog dances of the British Isles and the dances of African slaves. Seibert speaks of both famous and forgotten tap dancers and their contributions to the form's style.

BIOGRAPHY

Deborah Jowitt, *Jerome Robbins: His Life, His Theater, His Dance*, 2004.

American choreographer Jerome Robbins redefined the role of dance in musical theater. Deborah Jowitt's biography provides anecdotes and photographs that give a peek into the 20th-century dance world. Many consider Robbins the top American-born ballet choreographer in history.

Steve Martin, *Born Standing Up: A Comic's Life*, 2008.

While Steve Martin only spent four years in standup comedy, those years were unparalleled in terms of commercial success. Here he tells how he started at age ten working at Disneyland and later worked at the Bird Cage Theatre at Knott's Berry Farm. Martin's dedication paid off professionally, but he reveals the personal cost.

Sam Wasson, *Fosse*, 2013.
Bob Fosse, a celebrated director, choreographer, and actor, was responsible for some of the biggest box office hits in American stage and screen
history, from *The Pajama Game* to *Chicago*. In addition, he presented
a larger-than-life persona that has inspired generations of performers
and audiences. But despite his success, Fosse was seldom satisfied with
his accomplishments.

Richard Zoglin, *Hope: Entertainer of the Century*, 2014.
Author Richard Zoglin argues that Bob Hope was the most important entertainer of the 20th century. Before his death at age 100, he performed in vaudeville, radio, television, standup comedy, and the cinema. In addition, his work
with troops on active duty was a massive success. But a darker side of Hope is
also explored.

793 Indoor Games & Amusements

Sid Fleischman, *Escape! The Story of the Great Houdini*, 2006.
Sid Fleischman wrote this book for young adults about magician Harry
Houdini's astounding story. Fleischman used insider information and uncov-
ered secrets about the Great Houdini.

794 Indoor Games of Skill

Van Burnham, *Supercade:
A Visual History of the Videogame Age, 1971–1984, 2001.**
Videogames changed the face of technology. Van Burnham narrates their
history from the earliest days at the Brookhaven National Labs and MIT, from
Pac-Man to *Zaxxon*. Then she covers the games' development and the impact
they've had on society.

R. A. Dyer, *Hustler Days:
Minnesota Fats, Wimpy Lassiter, Jersey Red,
and America's Great Age of Pool, 2003.**
R. A. Dyer tells of the world popularized by the 1961 movie *The Hustler*, the
world of high-stakes pool, which started in the 1930s and ended with a crash
after the 1969 tournament. That's when police arrested tournament winner
Jersey Red and 80 other hustlers in this world of bitter rivalries and danger.

**Michael Weinreb, *Game of Kings: A Year Among the Geeks,*
Oddballs, and Geniuses Who Make Up America's Top High
School Chess Team, 2007.**
Located in Brooklyn, New York, Edward R. Murrow High School, one of the
top high schools in the nation, serves primarily an immigrant and minority
population. Sportswriter Michael Weinreb follows the school's stellar

chess team through one season, while tagging behind them from games in Washington Square Park to the national championships in Nashville.

795 Games of Chance

Maria Konnikova, *The Biggest Bluff: How I Learned to Pay Attention, Master Myself, and Win*, 2020.

Erik Seidel, a Poker Hall of Fame inductee, didn't want to take Maria Konnikova on as a pupil. She wasn't interested in money, she told him. Instead, she was interested in poker academically; as a human behavior researcher, Konnikova wanted to know what it could teach her. But as she applied Seidel's lessons, she began to earn big money, wound up on television, and even developed a fondness for Las Vegas. Here she shares the surprising insights about life that she gleaned from her foray into high-stakes poker.

796 Athletic & Outdoor Sports & Games

Reed Albergotti and Vanessa O'Connell, *Wheelmen: Lance Armstrong, the Tour de France, and the Greatest Sports Conspiracy Ever*, 2013.

Lance Armstrong won seven Tours de France, several while fighting cancer. In America, he came to symbolize hope and resilience. But after admitting he lied about everything on the *Oprah* show, including blood doping, *Wall Street Journal* reporters Albergotti and O'Connell investigated his story. They uncovered what Armstrong omitted—an international conspiracy to help American cyclists reach the top of the sport.

George Dohrmann, *Play Their Hearts Out: A Coach, His Star Recruit, and the Youth Basketball Machine*, 2010.

Pulitzer Prize–winning journalist George Dohrmann explores the cutthroat world of youth basketball by telling two stories. The first is of AAU coach Joe Keller, who dreamed of finding the next LeBron James. And the second is of Demetrius Walker, a talented, fatherless kid whom Keller hoped to propel to stardom. Through their experiences, Dohrmann unveils the hopes, exploitation, and corruption that feed on children, parents, and coaches alike.

The Editors of *Sports Illustrated*, *The Story of Baseball: In 100 Photographs*, 2018.

The editors of *Sports Illustrated* sketch baseball's history using 100 archival photos that capture baseball's most significant moments. From the earliest days through one-handed pitcher Jim Abbott's 1993 no-hitter, this book is a treat for any fan.

Marshall Jon Fisher, *A Terrible Splendor: Three Extraordinary Men, a World Poised for War, and the Greatest Tennis Match Ever Played*, 2009.

In 1937, just a few years away from World War II, Wimbledon hosted the greatest tennis match of the time to decide the Davis Cup winner. German Baron Gottfried von Cramm, ranked number two, played against American Don Budge, ranked number one. Sportswriter Marshall Jon Fisher explores the background politics and history between Germany and America and the part each nation played behind the scenes of the match.

David Goldblatt,
The Age of Football: Soccer and the 21st Century, 2020.

The most popular competitive team sport in the world today is known as soccer in the U.S. but elsewhere as football. Sportswriter David Goldblatt reveals how the sport became so dominant that it has affected politics, economics, and social divisions everywhere. Without understanding football, he says, you can't understand the world today.

S. C. Gwynne, *The Perfect Pass:*
American Genius and the Reinvention of Football, 2016.

How did American football go from a run-dominated sport to a pass-dominated one? It wasn't gradual; it was the result of the audacious coaching of Hal Mumme, a football coach at Iowa Wesleyan, a school with an overlooked team, and his offensive line coach Mike Leach. Together, they concocted a game-changing strategy that other teams were forced to emulate, changing the game forever.

Jon Krakauer, *Into Thin Air:*
A Personal Account of the Mt. Everest Disaster, 1997.

When American writer and mountaineer Jon Krakauer was standing on the summit of Mt. Everest in May 1996, he noticed clouds assembling but was unconcerned about them. Before the approaching storm left them behind, five of Krakauer's fellow climbers were dead and many more guilt-stricken and haunted by the events. Krakauer tells the harrowing story here.

A. J. Liebling, *The Sweet Science*, 1949.

From boxing's heyday, celebrated journalist A. J. Liebling paints portraits of its legends and events from the sidelines. From Sugar Ray Leonard to Joe Louis, Liebling brings the stories to life. *Sports Illustrated* named this book "the best American sports book of all time."

Christopher McDougall, *Born to Run:*
A Hidden Tribe, Superathletes, and the Greatest Race
the World Has Never Seen, 2009

American author and journalist Christopher McDougall decided to explore the secrets of long-distance running. The search took him from science labs at Harvard to Mexico's Tarahumara, who live in the Copper Canyon region. This reclusive people has superhuman running abilities, and they perform amazing feats with ease. While studying the group's methods, McDougall trained himself to reach the same heights. With the right knowledge, he says any of us can do the same.

BIOGRAPHY

Allen Barra,
***The Last Coach: A Life of Paul "Bear" Bryant*, 2005.**
Like many public figures, Bear Bryant, the famed Alabama Crimson Tide foot-ball coach, was controversial. To some, he represented the best of American sport by standing up for values like courage, discipline, loyalty, and grit. But for others, he represented the worst of college football—authoritarianism, fanaticism, and brutality. Allen Barra portrays Bryant as a complex mixture of good and bad.

John Branch,
***Boy on Ice: The Life and Death of Derek Boogaard*, 2015.**
Reporter John Branch tells the tragic story of the National Hockey League's Derek Boogaard. His death at age 28 from a drug and alcohol overdose drew international attention to the injuries and concussions that played a part in his demise.

Glen Denny, *Valley Walls:*
***A Memoir of Climbing & Living in Yosemite*, 2016.**
American rock climbing owes much of its popularity to a group of innovators who got their start on Yosemite's rock walls in the 1960s. Throughout that period, climber Glen Denny was there and recorded it all in photographs. He chronicles their heart-stopping escapades and achievements.

Jonathan Eig, *Ali: A Life*, 2017.
The greatest, according to Muhammad Ali, was himself. Using inexhaustible research to uncover the truth about one of the 20th century's most famous athletes, Jonathan Eig tells the unforgettable story of how Cassius Clay from Louisville become a larger-than-life figure who gained international celebrity.

Gordon Kirby, *Mario Andretti: A Driving Passion*, 2001.
Driver Mario Andretti was renowned for his ability to win in any race car. Gordon Kirby interviews Andretti, his family, and his race associates to tell Andretti's story and uncover the secrets of his success.

Charles Leerhsen, *Ty Cobb: A Terrible Beauty*, 2015.
The legendary Ty Cobb, first player inducted into the Baseball Hall of Fame, remains a controversial figure. His ruthless style of creating mental distress for his opponents earned admirers and enemies. But after his death, when it was rumored he was both a racist and misogynist, his reputation took a hit. Charles Leerhsen researched Cobb's story to expose the man behind the hype.

Henry Yunick, *Best Damn Garage in Town:*
***The World According to Smokey*, 2001.**
Henry "Smokey" Yunick, a founder of stock car racing, wrote this

three-volume history of the sport. The books cover Smokey's early life and
how he got involved in the so-called low-class sport of stock car racing in its
early days. Smokey provides a unique and colorful insider's look at the sport.

797 Aquatic & Air Sports

Daniel James Brown, *The Boys in the Boat: Nine Americans and Their Epic Quest for Gold at the 1936 Berlin Olympics*, 2013.

Americans from the West Coast were underdogs in the sport of rowing in 1936.
But a team of nine young men, sons of blue-collar workers, first beat teams
of premier rowers from elite American East Coast schools and then British
teams of the same pedigree. Finally, they went up against Hitler's German
rowing crew. Daniel James Brown interviewed and used journals of the team
to share the tale.

Bob Fisher, et al., *Sailing on the Edge: America's Cup*, 2013.

The America's Cup is one of the most sought-after prizes in the world of
sailboat racing. The authors provide a history of the race and the technology
changing it today. Focusing on the 2013 34th cup, they describe the science,
the shipbuilding, and the skippers that made it possible.

Peter Heller, *Kook: What Surfing Taught Me About Love, Life, and Catching the Perfect Wave*, 2010.

In surfing lingo, a, *kook* is a beginner. And every kook wants to become a
shredder, which is no small feat. Peter Heller sets out to accomplish this goal
in one year. He tells of his quest in the company of his girlfriend and members
of the surfing subculture he encounters. He also discloses the techniques and
science that make their feats possible.

Ken Whiting, et al., *Whitewater Kayaking: The Ultimate Guide*, 2008.

If you've ever wanted to tackle the most challenging waters for kayakers, this
guide covers basic to advanced skills needed to run the rapids unscathed
and exhilarated.

BIOGRAPHY

Vince Welch, Cort Conley, and Brad Dimock, *The Doing of the Thing: The Brief, Brilliant Whitewater Career of Buzz Holmstrom*, 1998.

Buzz Holmstrom was one of America's greatest river runners. In 1937, using
boats he built himself, his was the first solo run of the Green and Colorado
Rivers. But his brilliant career was cut short with his mysterious death on the
Grande Ronde River at age 37.

798 Equestrian Sports & Animal Racing

Judi Daly, *Trail Training for the Horse and Rider*, 2004.
If you'd like to ride trails on horseback, you will find Judi Daly's book useful. Daly explores the qualities that make a good trail horse, the equipment needed, safety considerations, troubleshooting, and problems you may encounter, from crossing streams to emergencies. Of course, if your horse has a temperament problem, that's covered too.

Laura Hillenbrand, *Seabiscuit: An American Legend*, 1999.
Laura Hillenbrand tells of the racehorse Seabiscuit and the electrifying story of his 1938 win. With incredible odds against his success, Seabiscuit, a cheap horse with crooked legs, was transformed into a winner by the combined efforts of the millionaire who bought him, a mysterious mustang breaker, and a failed boxer with one blind eye who was half-crippled himself.

Debbie Clarke Moderow,
Fast into the Night: A Woman, Her Dogs,
***and Their Journey North on the Iditarod Trail*, 2016.**
Debbie Clarke Moderow reveals how she came to race, not once but twice, on Alaska's Iditarod Trail while in her late forties. Through losing control of her team and then finding it again, she relates what she learned about the connection between humans and dogs.

799 Fishing, Hunting, Shooting

Rob Beattie, *The Fishing Handbook:*
***An Illustrated Guide for Anglers*, 2007.**
Dedicated fisherman Rob Beattie explores a pastime that defies simple explanations or even definitions. Becoming successful at fishing, he says, may take a lifetime to unravel.

Don Currie, *Mastering Sporting Clays*, 2018.
Shooting sporting clays can be enjoyed both competitively and just for fun. Don Currie shows you how to begin the sport, but he also discloses tactics used by advanced shooters that help them conquer problem areas and become more successful on the course.

John Gierach, *A Fly Rod of Your Own*, 2017.
Fly fishing hall of famer John Gierach celebrates fishing with those who are as passionate as he is. He discusses his trips to remote fishing lodges and discloses why most people who fish care just as much about four-wheel-drive vehicles as they do about rods and lures.

Scott Null and Joel McBride, *Kayak Fishing:*
The Ultimate Guide, **2nd ed., 2011.**
   No matter your skill level at kayak fishing, Null and McBride have tips to
   share. They will help you stay safe and form a foundation for your practice.
   In addition, the book is full of photographs and contributions from kayak
   angling professionals.

Thomas R. Pero, ed., *A Passion for Grouse:*
The Lore and Legend of America's Premier Game Bird, **2017.**
   In this illustrated book on hunting ruffed grouse, Thomas R. Pero relates
   conversations with legends of the sport, grouse biologists, and dog and gun
   experts. In addition, there are tips, strategies, and tactics.

Tom Rosenbauer, ed., *Salt: Coastal and Flats Fishing,* **2014.**
   Renowned outdoor photographer Andy Anderson presents an album of photos
   from his fishing adventures in the world's coastal hot spots, highlighting the
   American coast and nearby islands. Editor Tom Rosenbauer tells the stories of
   the trips the pictures were taken on.

CHAPTER 9

800–899

Literature

Books containing examples of exceptionally well-written language belong in the 800s. Here, you will find books on rhetoric, fine literary fiction, poetry, humor, and essays. As I used to tell students, this section is for "art made from words." Books of literary criticisms go here too. As with the 400s, this division is arranged by the author's language. The available numbers are overwhelmingly devoted to English and Eurocentric literature, but there is a place for every other language in the 890–899 subdivision. For more information about this division, see the Introduction on page 3.

800 Literature (Belles-lettres) & Rhetoric

801 Philosophy & Theory

Milan Kundera,
***The Curtain: An Essay in Seven Parts*, 2005.**
Czech-born writer Milan Kundera looks at the novel's purpose in this essay. He uses the metaphor of a curtain as a magic fabric comprised of legends. Cervantes tore through this fabric when he wrote the first modern novel, *Don Quixote*. Kundera examines the ways writers have borrowed across cultures ever since. Great novelists, he says, pierce our veils of preconceptions to teach us something new about ourselves.

Archibald MacLeish, *Poetry and Experience*, 1961.
American poet and former Librarian of Congress Archibald MacLeish examines how poetry is used as a vehicle to convey meaning. He assesses four poets—Dickinson, Yeats, Rimbaud, and Keats—to demonstrate how their styles produce different outcomes.

Daniel Mendelsohn, *Waiting for the Barbarians:*
***Essays from the Classics to Pop Culture*, 2012.**
Over 15 years, Daniel Mendelsohn wrote a series of essays for *The New York Review of Books*, which built his reputation as one of today's greatest

critics. In these 24 essays, Mendelsohn touches on everything from *Avatar* to Rimbaud's poems.

803 Dictionaries & Encyclopedias

William Rose Benét, *The Reader's Encyclopedia*, 1965.

Most recently published in 1998 as *Benét's Reader's Encyclopedia*, by Bruce Murphy, the fourth edition of this one-volume reference work is regarded as the best of its type. It covers literature from all around the world through the end of the 20th century and includes, among other topics, biographies of writers, literary schools, movements, myths, awards, and plot summaries.

Catherine Lewis, *Thrice Told Tales: Three Mice Full of Writing Advice*, 2013.

Writing professor Catherine Lewis provides this whimsical and quirky set of lessons, intended to entertain while sharpening your writing skills.

808 Rhetoric & Collections of Literature

Margaret Atwood, *Negotiating with the Dead: A Writer on Writing*, 2002.

Canadian author Margret Atwood writes six essays, each of which explores a different topic of contemplation for writers. Atwood, best known for *The Handmaid's Tale* and *Oryx and Crake*, is one of the 20th century's most respected writers.

Thomas C. Foster, *How to Read Literature Like a Professor: A Lively and Entertaining Guide to Reading Between the Lines*, 2014.

English professor Thomas C. Foster shows you how to uncover the hidden meaning in the poetry and prose you read. A red dress, for example, is seldom just a garment. Instead, it may signify all sorts of messages that, without Foster's guidance, you might be oblivious to.

Edward Hirsch, *How to Read a Poem: And Fall in Love with Poetry*, 2000.

American poet Edward Hirsch wants you to love poetry as much as he does. In looking at verses from great writers like Sylvia Plath and Charles Baudelaire, Hirsch brings their messages to life and teaches you to do the same with the poems you read.

Tracy Kidder and Richard Todd, *Good Prose: The Art of Nonfiction*, 2013.

Tracy Kidder began his collaborations with Richard Todd at the *Atlantic Monthly* while still an unknown writer. They first worked together on *The*

Soul of a New Machine, which won a Pulitzer Prize. Here they provide a concise discussion of successful writing for those working with narratives, essays, or memoirs.

Steven Pinker, *The Sense of Style: The Thinking Person's Guide to Writing in the 21st Century,* 2014.

Linguist and cognitive scientist Steven Pinker's brief guide to writing with clarity and style acknowledges that language changes. He offers rationales for breaking some older rules, but he also explains why others are best adhered to. He demonstrates good writing by comparing it with unsuccessful writing.

Rick Reichman, *20 Things You Must Know to Write a Great Screenplay: A Thorough Primer for Screenwriters,* 2008.

Screenwriting teacher Rick Reichman shows screenwriters for film and television how to format a screenplay before submitting it. He gives the technical writing information needed to pitch a script, and much more.

John Rember, *MFA in a Box: A Why to Write a Book,* 2011.

John Rember helps you improve your creative writing efforts by digging deep into your past to uncover your stories. His goal is to help you write literature, not ordinary prose.

809 History, Description & Criticism

Harold Bloom, *The Western Canon: The Books and School of the Ages,* 1994.

American literary critic Harold Bloom surveys Western literature from the Old Testament through Freud, Kafka, and Beckett. He analyzes why the works are considered significant, and he comments on attempts to determine which is best.

Northrop Frye, *The Great Code: The Bible and Literature,* 1981.

Canadian literary critic and ordained minister Northrop Frye examines the role the Bible has played in the art and literature of the West. He also looks at its place in Western imagination overall. While he says the Bible is no longer central to our society, it still has a monumental place in our collective psyche.

Lynn Marie Houston, ed., *Literary Geography: An Encyclopedia of Real and Imagined Settings,* 2019.

The alphabetically arranged entries in this reference help you understand the importance of settings in the literary works you read. By looking at the scene's historical, political, and cultural elements, you enrich the meaning of the text and enhance your understanding of themes. A further reading section provides information on mapping, geography, ecocriticism, and nature in literature.

Ken Jennings,
Planet Funny: How Comedy Took Over Our Culture, 2018.

Kenneth Wayne Jennings gained fame as the holder of the longest winning streak in *Jeopardy!* history. In this history of comedy, Jennings traces how we wound up in a nation where people get their news from comedy shows and presidents can be elected based on showmanship.

Lisa Kröger and Melanie R. Anderson,
Monster, She Wrote: The Women Who Pioneered Horror & Speculative Fiction, 2019.

From Mary Shelley's *Frankenstein* to Helen Oyeyemi, women have been frightening their readers for centuries. Kröger and Anderson provide reading lists to enlarge your to-be-read pile, but they also share sketches of the equally entertaining lives of the books' creators.

Seth Lerer, *Children's Literature:*
A Reader's History, from Aesop to Harry Potter, 2008.

Comparative literature professor Seth Lerer provides a one-volume history of children's literature across its many genres. His work points out the qualities shared by the books children love.

Frank M. Robinson, *Science Fiction of the 20th Century:*
An Illustrated History, 1999.

American science fiction author Frank M. Robinson traces the history of the 20th century's sci-fi genre in pulp magazines and films.

Susan Sontag,
Against Interpretation, and Other Essays, 2001.

Since Susan Sontag's initial 1966 publication of this classic collection of essays on culture and art, it has never been out of print. The republished version from 2001 has an additional piece in which Sontag defends her ethical stances.

810 American Literature in English

Paula Gunn Allen, ed., *Spider Woman's Granddaughters:*
Traditional Tales and Contemporary Writing
by Native American Women, 1990.

Native American poet and literary critic Paula Gunn Allen researched why the writings of Native Americans, particularly women, have been omitted from the literary canon. She emphasizes the oversight with examples of extraordinary traditional and contemporary works by Native American women.

Paul Elie, *The Life You Save May Be Your Own: An American Pilgrimage*, 2004.

Paul Elie explores the works and relationships of three mid-20th century American writers who used their writings to explore their Catholic faith. The three—Trappist monk Thomas Merton, short story writer Flannery O'Connor, novelist and philosopher Walker Percy—were dubbed the School of the Holy Ghost. Through the years, they corresponded and read one another's works.

Ralph Ellison, *Shadow and Act*, 1964.

Scholar and author of *Invisible Man*, Ralph Ellison used his literary talents to analyze the literature, music, and culture, both Black and White, that influenced him and his writing. He refused to use stereotypes to define what an African American writer should be.

James D. Hart, *The Oxford Companion to American Literature*, 5th ed., 1983.

James D. Hart completed the first five editions of *The Oxford Companion to American Literature* on his own. The sixth edition was published after his death with the help of co-editor Phillip Leininger. The book contains entries on authors, historians, naturalists, literary critics, and others of note involved in American literature, in over 5,000 entries. It also provides summaries of various works, historical backgrounds, commentaries, awards, and other issues involved in American writing.

A. Robert Lee, *Multicultural American Literature: Comparative Black, Native, Latino/a and Asian-American Fictions*, 2003.

British author A. Robert Lee examines American multicultural fiction and autobiographical writings. He particularly notes the ways politics, popular culture, and race issues influenced these writers.

811 American Poetry in English

Jennifer Bartlett, et al., eds., *Beauty is a Verb: The New Poetry of Disability*, 2011.

Beauty is a Verb contains poetry about disabilities by American poets and essays that delve into the relationship between the poems and their creators. The poems represent many styles, and the disabilities discussed include everything from blindness to multiple sclerosis.

Joseph Bruchac, ed., *Breaking Silence: An Anthology of Contemporary Asian-American Poets*, 1983.

Since this book's publication in 1983, there have been many more Asian American poets of note. But still, this volume is a vital contribution featuring poets from Hawai'ian, Korean, Chinese, Japanese, and Filipino backgrounds.

E. E. Cummings, *95 Poems*, 1958.

E. E. Cummings, one of the giants of 20th-century poetry, was known for his experimental punctuation, sentimentality, and sexual openness. Cummings also received two Guggenheim Fellowships and an Academy of American Poets Fellowship. *95 Poems* was his last published book of poetry.

Emily Dickinson, *The Complete Poems of Emily Dickinson*, 1890.

Though she was mostly unknown in her lifetime, Emily Dickinson has since reached the apex of revered American poets. Her reclusiveness and originality gave her the freedom to experiment with form. This book provides the original texts of all of her 1,775 poems.

Robert Frost, *The Poetry of Robert Frost*, 1949.

American farmer-turned-poet Robert Frost was one of the 20th century's most famous poets. Best known for "Stopping by Woods on a Snowy Evening" and "The Road Not Taken," Frost was a four-time Pulitzer Prize winner. This book, republished in 1979, contains the 350 poems he wrote, plus annotations.

Nikki Giovanni, *The Collected Poetry of Nikki Giovanni, 1968–1998*, 2003.

Celebrated American poet and activist Nikki Giovanni has received numerous accolades for her poetry's ability to expose the essence of what it is like to be Black in America. Despite the title, this volume does not contain all her poems, as she continued to write after it was published.

Theodore Roethke, *The Far Field*, 1965.

Theodore Roethke's last published volume of poems contains poetry collected from journals and magazines in which it previously appeared, such as *The Atlantic Monthly*, *The New Yorker*, and *The Partisan Review*. His work is celebrated for its stunning imagery and depth of meaning.

Kevin Young, ed., *African American Poetry: 250 Years of Struggle & Song*, 2020.

Covering 250 African American poets from America's colonial period through today, Kevin Young provides poems by an enslaved person, Phillis Wheatley, through well-known poets of the 20th century like Langston Hughes and Lucille Clifton. Young is both a poet and a scholar, and he makes a point of celebrating voices that are distinctly Black American.

21ST CENTURY

The list below contains a tiny sample of noteworthy poetry collections published in the 21st century. While all these volumes have won awards for outstanding merit, they are included only as places to start exploring contemporary poetry for yourself.

Fatimah Asghar, *If They Come for Us: Poems*, 2018.

Mei-Mei Berssenbrugge, *A Treatise on Stars*, 2020.

Reginald Dwayne Betts, *Bastards of the Reagan Era*, 2015.

Billy Collins, *Sailing Alone Around the Room:
New and Selected Poems*, 2002.

Stephen Dunn,
What Goes On: Selected and New Poems 1995–2009, 2010.

Terrance Hayes,
American Sonnets for My Past and Future Assassin, 2018.

Layli Long Soldier, *Whereas: Poems*, 2017.

Jamaal May, *Hum*, 2013.

Sharon Olds, *Stag's Leap*, 2012.

José Olivarez, *Citizen Illegal*, 2018.

BIOGRAPHY

Justin Kaplan, *Walt Whitman: A Life*, 1980.
Justin Kaplan brings you this biography of one of America's greatest poets, Walt Whitman. Through poems such as "Song of Myself," Whitman's emotional and sexual openness and his exuberance changed the face of poetry forever.

Linda Leavell, *Holding On Upside Down:
The Life and Work of Marianne Moore*, 2013.
Scholar Linda Leavell reveals the complex story of the great 20th-century American poet Marianne Moore. At the heart of the story is Moore's relationship with her mother, with whom she lived for 60 years. It was a relationship of both love and confinement, and understanding it is a key to understanding Moore's poetry. After her mother's death, the reclusive Moore reinvented herself to become a modern celebrity.

Dianne Wood Middlebrook,
Anne Sexton: A Biography, 1991.
Twentieth-century poet Anne Sexton wrote sublime poetry despite the mental illness and alcoholism that plagued her for most of her life. While this book received criticism for using tapes of Sexton's psychiatric sessions, it gets to the

heart of her tragic life, which went from abused person to abuser and ended with her suicide.

812 American Drama in English

Stella Adler, *Stella Adler on America's Master Playwrights: Eugene O'Neill, Thornton Wilder, Clifford Odets, Tennessee Williams, William Inge, Arthur Miller, Edward Albee*, 2012.

Acting instructor to the stars Stella Adler offers her lectures on America's best-known plays and playwrights. With her insistence on understanding the truth beneath the words, she strives to make actors interpret what a play means to them before they act in it. She also insists they understand both the playwrights and the times in which the plays were written.

William Blackwell Branch, ed., *Black Thunder: An Anthology of Contemporary African American Drama*, 1992.

African American playwright William Blackwell Branch brings together nine plays by Black Americans writing about their cultural experiences. The plays, written between 1975 and 1990, were by playwrights George C. Wolfe, Leslie Lee, Steve Carter, Amiri Baraka, P. J. Gibson, William Branch, Alexander Simmons, Ed Bullins, and August Wilson.

BIOGRAPHY

Arthur and Barbara Gelb, *O'Neill: Life With Monte Cristo*, 1962.

After writing Eugene O'Neill's biography just nine years after his death in 1953, the Gelbs continued to research the playwright's life for the next 38 years. Using the massive amount of information they uncovered, they completely revised the biography for this new edition, released in 2002. O'Neill was the only American playwright ever to receive a Nobel Prize. The new edition is three volumes, with this being the first.

John Lahr, *Tennessee Williams: Mad Pilgrimage of the Flesh*, 2014.

Drama critic John Lahr writes this candid picture of one of America's greatest playwrights, Tennessee Williams. He reveals Williams's childhood family's complex and contradictory influences and his unconventional sex life. Lahr also talks about the plays and writes candidly about the backstage antics that ensued while producing them.

Arthur Miller, *Timebends: A Life*, 1987.

Arthur Miller, whose plays *The Crucible* and *Death of a Salesman* are still studied worldwide, relates in his autobiography the saga of his refusal to cooperate with the McCarthy-era House Un-American Activities Committee's demands for evidence against others in the entertainment industry. He also discusses his marriage to entertainment icon Marilyn Monroe.

Imani Perry, *Looking for Lorraine: The Radiant and Radical Life of Lorraine Hansberry*, 2018.

Lorraine Hansberry wrote the celebrated play *A Raisin in the Sun*. But after her early death at 34, she was largely overlooked. Imani Perry tells of Hansberry's unconventional life and her confrontations with power, for which she paid. She also tells of Hansberry's relationships with celebrated figures of her time, such as Malcolm X and Langston Hughes.

813 American Fiction in English

Brian Carpenter and Tom Franklin, eds., *Grit Lit: A Rough South Reader*, 2012.

Carpenter and Franklin gathered this anthology of writing that paints the darker, poorer side of the American South. They promise no romanticism or nostalgia but offer unvarnished views from an often overlooked fiction genre.

Bernard A. Drew, *Black Stereotypes in Popular Series Fiction, 1851–1955: Jim Crow Era Authors and Their Characters*, 2015.

Even the most celebrated and well-meaning fiction authors from the Jim Crow era (1900–1955) misrepresented Black characters, relying on racial stereotypes in their portrayals. Using examples from Booth Tarkington to Octavus Roy Cohen, this book profiles 29 writers and their Black characters. There are also 72 brief entries on others.

Melanie Rehak, *Girl Sleuth: Nancy Drew and the Women Who Created Her*, 2006.

For almost a century, Nancy Drew has enthralled girls. But for years, the author of the series was, well, a mystery. Finally, Melanie Rehak solves it for us by sharing the character's creation and the two women who penned the stories. She also tells how Nancy and her influence evolved with society.

Catherine M. Roach, *Happily Ever After: The Romance Story in Popular Culture*, 2016.

People sometimes criticize romance novels as unrealistic, with too much emphasis on heterosexual relationships. Scholar Catherine Roach, who also writes romance as Catherine LaRoche, examines the genre to see why it is so popular and what it tells us about love, sex, and American popular culture.

Ilan Stavans, ed., *Becoming Americans: Four Centuries of Immigrant Writing*, 2009.

For over 400 years, immigrants have been coming to America. Award-winning author Ilan Stavans gathers nearly 100 poems, stories, novel excerpts, diary entries, memoirs, and letters that share their thoughts and firsthand experiences in chronological order.

Margaret Earley Whitt, ed., *Short Stories of the Civil Rights Movement: An Anthology*, 2006.

These stories, written by Black and White, young and old, and known and unknown writers, all have the backdrop of the civil rights movement of the 1960s in common. The works are arranged by subjects such as school desegregation, marches, and violence. Twenty writers are featured, of whom eleven are Black and nine are White.

BIOGRAPHY

Valerie Boyd, *Wrapped in Rainbows: The Life of Zora Neale Hurston*, 2002.

Zora Neale Hurston is one of the most acclaimed writers of 20th century America. She influenced generations of Black writers, particularly Maya Angelou, Toni Morrison, and Alice Walker. Journalist Valerie Boyd researched Hurston's story, from her youth spent in America's first incorporated, all-Black town to her connections to Harlem Renaissance figures like Langston Hughes. Hurston's purported involvement in vodou makes her personal life as interesting as her novels, short stories, and plays.

David Herbert Donald, *Look Homeward: A Life of Thomas Wolfe*, 1987.

Scholar David Herbert Donald narrates the story of Thomas Wolfe, one of the giants of 20th-century American fiction. Donald maintains that, contrary to portrayals, Wolfe was not an unconscious genius dependent on editor Max Perkins to shape his work. Instead, he was an experimental artist akin to William Faulkner.

Caroline Fraser, *Prairie Fires: The American Dreams of Laura Ingalls Wilder*, 2017.

Caroline Fraser presents the real life of Laura Ingalls Wilder. Famous for her children's book series, *The Little House* books, Wilder only began writing the books in her 60s after she lost nearly everything in the Great Depression. As a result, she garnered fame and fortune. But Fraser shows that Wilder's childhood was far more grueling and poverty-stricken than the books depict.

Barry Gifford and Lawrence Lee, *Jack's Book: An Oral Biography of Jack Kerouac*, 1978.

American writer Jack Kerouac was a profound influence on mid-20th-century America's literary landscape. After Kerouac's death at age 47, Gifford and

Lee interviewed his friends and lovers to compose this portrait of the writer whose life had become a legend.

R. W. B. Lewis, *Edith Wharton: A Biography*, 1975.

Acclaimed literary critic R. W. B. Lewis used extensive research from Edith Wharton's archives at Yale to bring us the life story of the American novelist. From her childhood in a wealthy family in New York City to her service in France during World War I, Wharton wrote of the world she knew unsentimentally in novels like *The Age of Innocence*.

Kenneth S. Lynn, *Hemingway: Life & Work*, 1987.

Ernest Hemingway's life was legendary in 20th-century America. Kenneth S. Lynn writes about the man behind the larger-than-life stories to help us understand these works that changed American fiction.

Charles J. Shields, *Mockingbird: A Portrait of Harper Lee*, 2006.

This biography was revised and updated after the publication of *Go Set a Watchman* in 2016. Years after her death, Harper Lee's story was still ongoing, with arguments between family and a former agent over copyright and the release of this previously unknown prequel of *To Kill a Mockingbird*.

Amy Tan, *Where the Past Begins: A Writer's Memoir*, 2017.

Celebrated American author Amy Tan writes about how she came to write her novels through uncovering memories of her troubled childhood. In this memoir, she outlines how the writing process works for her. While the story is interesting on its own, other writers can also use her methods to build a platform for themselves.

Brenda Wineapple, *Hawthorne: A Life*, 2003.

Nathaniel Hawthorne, the writer of *The Scarlet Letter* and *The House of Seven Gables*, was an enigma to those who knew him. Handsome but aloof unless approached first, he was considered a genius by his contemporaries. He mingled with some of the most revered figures of his time, including Emerson, Thoreau, Melville, and Franklin Pierce, 14th president of the U.S. But with changing times, some of his activities are now viewed unfavorably.

Richard Wright, *Black Boy*, 1945.

Growing up in the Jim Crow South, Richard Wright was brilliant, desperate, and determined. With unflinching honesty, this autobiography exposes the brutality, poverty, and hunger he suffered while growing up. After Wright escaped the world of his youth and headed for Chicago, he began his extraordinary literary career.

814 American Essays in English

Alexander Chee,
How to Write an Autobiographical Novel: Essays, 2018.

Award-winning American author Alexander Chee reflects on how his lifetime of copious reading and writing and his eclectic background have shaped him as a person. He was born in the U.S. and raised in South Korea, Guam, Truk, and Maine. His various identities as Korean American, son, artist, gay man, and activist, and his colorful assortment of past jobs make his perspective unique.

Joan Didion, *Slouching Towards Bethlehem*, 1967.

Journalist Joan Didion dissected American society in the 1960s in a way few others have done. She covers the events of the day, from bombings to mass murders, and reflects on what it tells us about our morals and wholesomeness.

Toni Morrison, *The Source of Self-Regard:*
Selected Essays, Speeches, and Meditations, 2019.

While acclaimed author Toni Morrison is best known for her novels such as *The Bluest Eye, Tar Baby,* and, *Beloved,* she was also an editor and professor who wrote essays, speeches, and commentary on society. She spent four decades writing this collection of nonfiction.

Lia Purpura, *All the Fierce Tethers: Essays*, 2019.

American poet and educator Lia Purpura examines topics as varied as slugs and prayer. However, the essay "My Eagles" is considered astonishing in its breadth, as it uses multiple facets of the birds as a species and symbol.

Claudia Rankine, *Citizen: An American Lyric*, 2014.

American poet and playwright Claudia Rankine presents essays, poetry, and images that detail the ways racism is endemic in American society today. She sees racial aggressions in everyday life between people and the media. But, she says ignoring the problem will hurt us because we will inevitably lose out on the talents and contributions of an unvalued segment of society.

Gore Vidal, *United States: Essays, 1952–1992*, 1993.

American writer Gore Vidal was a celebrity writer of novels, essays, and plays. He was also an astute political critic who used these essays to examine America from Eisenhower to Clinton.

David Foster Wallace, *A Supposedly Fun Thing I'll Never Do*
Again: Essays and Arguments, 1997.

Author David Foster Wallace once won an award just for being a genius. As the author of *Infinite Jest*, he has legions of followers for his amusing, thoughtful, and seemingly effortless prose. In this collection of essays, he

covers everything from David Lynch films to traveling on a Caribbean
cruise ship.

BIOGRAPHY

Lawrence Buell, *Emerson*, 2004.
Ralph Waldo Emerson was the first celebrity intellectual in American history.
His essays on individuality and what it means to be an American have shaped
the nation's view of itself for the past 150 years. Scholar Lawrence Buell examines the impact of Emerson's work on American ideals.

815 American Speeches in English

BIOGRAPHY

Rebecca Solnit, *Recollections of My Nonexistence*, 2020.
Rebecca Solnit writes of growing up in California and coming of age as a
poor woman with little voice in San Francisco. She recounts the violence she
endured and witnessed and the lack of caring she got from authority figures.
Finally, Solnit tells how she found her voice through the books she read and
the gay men she met, who helped her discover new ways of living and loving.

817 American Humor & Satire in English

David Rakoff, *Half Empty*, 2010.
David Rakoff exposes how our contemporary culture lies to us. He says contrary to what many believe, all our wildest dreams will not come true, and all
people are not good at heart. He examines the moments in his own life when
he was forced to face reality and finds that most things are a mixture of good
and bad.

818 American Miscellaneous Writings

Wendell Berry, *The World-Ending Fire: The Essential Wendell Berry*, 2017.
Wendell Berry is a holdout from an earlier time. Refusing to succumb to the
onslaught of modern technology and consumerism, he has lived simply on his
farm in rural Kentucky for decades while cultivating his fields with horses
and mules. Berry continues to use pencil and paper to write novels and essays
on the environment and agriculture. In this collection of essays, he stresses
why we can't continue to live the way we currently do. He offers a hopeful
vision of how we can restore our land, our relationships, and ourselves.

Annie Dillard, *The Writing Life*, 1989.
Annie Dillard, author of *Pilgrim at Tinker Creek* and *An American Childhood*,

poet, and literary critic confronts the difficulty of writing and why she writes in spite of it.

Norman Mailer, *The Armies of the Night: History as a Novel, the Novel as History*, 1969.

This example of creative nonfiction by one of the genre's pioneers is based on Norman Mailer's experiences in the 1967 March on the Pentagon in Washington, D.C. That day, between 100,000 and 200,000 protesters marched to end the Vietnam War. In his reporting, Mailer used fiction techniques to make the story an unforgettable immersive experience.

Peter Orner, *Am I Alone Here?: Notes on Living to Read and Reading to Live*, 2016.

Novelist Peter Orner examines stories and writers who have influenced him. Some of those included are Zora Neal Hurston, Franz Kafka, Eudora Welty, and Václav Havel.

Henry David Thoreau, *Walden*, 1854.

Henry David Thoreau was a transcendentalist and a close friend of Ralph Waldo Emerson. For two years, he lived alone in a cabin he built on Walden Pond near Concord, Massachusetts. Then Thoreau published this book, giving an account of his cabin building, the bugs and other creatures who shared his home, and his visits to neighboring humans. The result is a deep contemplation on life and the state of the world as he saw it.

BIOGRAPHY

Maya Angelou, *I Know Why the Caged Bird Sings*, 1969.

Maya Angelou's inspiring memoir of the triumph of good over adversity has influenced millions of people worldwide. From her early abandonment by her parents, her endurance of racism, and her molestation at age eight, she learns that she must love herself and be kind to others. Through reading great authors, Angelou finds herself and her spirit.

Earle Labor, *Jack London: An American Life*, 2013.

Jack London scholar Earle Labor tells how, early in life, London made his way working as an oyster pirate, a hobo, and a prospector. After he began making money on his books *The Call of the Wild* and *White Fang*, London became an early activist for social justice. While not critically appreciated by his contemporaries, today he is regarded as one of America's great writers.

Benjamin Moser, *Sontag: Her Life and Work*, 2019.

Benjamin Moser profiles Susan Sontag after studying her restricted archives and interviewing people worldwide who knew her. He looks at her high-profile trips covering the Cuban Revolution and Sarajevo and the writings she produced. He found her life reflected the time in which she lived, even as she rebelled against it.

Arnold Rampersad, *Ralph Ellison: A Biography*, 2007.

When Ralph Ellison published *Invisible Man* in 1953, the book's critical success propelled him to national prominence. Literary critic Arnold Rampersad spent years going through Ellison's papers to bring us this portrait of his complicated life. While Ellison never published a second novel, his life was nevertheless full of essay writing and interviews. His closest friends were men like Saul Bellow, Richard Wright, and John Cheever. While he saw the racism and problems with America, he kept a consistent faith in the country's moral strength, which outraged some Black nationalists.

Marion Rodgers, *Mencken: The American Iconoclast*, 2005.

As a fearless wit and outspoken iconoclast, journalist H. L. Mencken covered the Scopes monkey trial, crusaded against Prohibition, and fought for free speech. Marion Rodgers tells these well-known stories and covers the controversy over Mencken's racial views and his difficulties as a German American around the two world wars.

Gertrude Stein, *The Autobiography of Alice B. Toklas*, 1933.

Gertrude Stein wrote this work about her lover, Alice B. Toklas, to make money. With its gossipy stories of artists Cezanne, Matisse, and Picasso and writers like T. S. Eliot, Sherwood Anderson, and Ernest Hemingway, the book was a commercial success, but some people were angry with its depictions.

Mark Twain, *My Autobiography*, 1910.

Over the last four years of his life, Mark Twain dictated this work to his biographer Albert Payne. He tells of his remarkable life, from riverboat pilot on the Mississippi River to his worldwide celebrity as an author. A later three-volume edition titled *Autobiography of Mark Twain*, edited by Harriet E. Smith, et al., is also available.

William Carlos Williams, *The Autobiography of William Carlos Williams*, 1951.

As a physician who was an equally talented poet, William Carlos Williams practiced medicine for 40 years of the 20th century while simultaneously publishing more than 30 books. Williams maintained that each career pursuit benefited, rather than conflicted, with the other.

820 English & Old English Literatures

Virginia Blain, Isobel Grundy, and Patricia Clements, *The Feminist Companion to Literature in English: Women Writers from the Middle Ages to the Present*, 1990.

Written and compiled by scholars, this reference contains almost 3,000 entries that cover women from all over the world who wrote primarily in English.

Margaret Drabble, ed., *Oxford Companion to English Literature*, 2006.

The Oxford Companion to English Literature is a standard reference for scholars and students of English literature. The resource covers topics from around the globe, including writers, genres, literary theory, allusions, and characters. The sixth edition was published in 2000. Updated versions are available online by subscription.

Paul Fussell, *The Great War and Modern Memory*, 1975.

World War I had a profound and irreversible effect on the generation who lived through it. American historian Paul Fussell explores the ways the war changed British society. He sketches the writers who wrote about the war as journalism, history, and literature.

Dominic Head, ed., *The Cambridge Guide to Literature in English*, 2006.

The third edition of this international survey of English literature details works written in Old English up through the early 21st century, providing a comprehensive survey.

Rob Nixon, *Slow Violence and the Environmentalism of the Poor*, 2011.

Rob Nixon examines environmental activist literature written by the poor in the Global South. While industrial nations are slowly destroying the planet, people often ignore the outcomes, except for these vulnerable inhabitants who see the effects most plainly. By making their words visible to a broader audience, Nixon hopes to draw attention to our planet's plight.

Richard Tillinghast, *Finding Ireland: A Poet's Explorations of Irish Literature and Culture*, 2008.

As a transplant to Ireland, American poet Richard Tillinghast writes about Ireland today. He looks at past writers and poets, of course, and guides us through their readings, but he also celebrates today's Irish music, architecture, and garden design.

William H. Wilde, Joy Hooton, and Barry Andrews, *The Oxford Companion to Australian Literature*, 1987.

The second edition of this volume, published in 1996, is a comprehensive reference source to all Australia's major published fiction and nonfiction works. With over 3,000 entries on genres, literary topics, authors, and key historical events, the book, written in accessible language, is a useful source for scholars, students, and general readers.

Philip Zaleski and Carol Zaleski,
The Fellowship: The Literary Lives of the Inklings:
J. R. R. Tolkien, C. S. Lewis, Owen Barfield,
Charles Williams, **2015.**
> C. S. Lewis, J. R. R. Tolkien, Owen Barfield, and Charles Williams called themselves the Inklings. They met weekly in Oxford pubs for three decades to discuss their work, literature, ideas, and religion. Their discussions sharpened their writing, leading to the cultural influences of their work.

821 English Poetry

T. S. Eliot, *The Waste Land,* **1922.**
> T. S. Eliot's masterpiece is the poem "The Wasteland." In this W. W. Norton Company edition of the poem, the entire text is provided, with notes Eliot supplied for the original American edition published by Boni & Liveright. Many of Eliot's notes require explanations themselves. This edition also has 25 reviews and critical essays written at the poem's publication with the contemporary reactions to it.

Robert Graves, *Collected Poems, 1966,* **1966.**
> While Robert Graves had his most commercial success with the biography *I, Claudius* and the memoir *Goodbye to All That,* he considered his poems his most significant work. For this volume, he discarded the ones from his earlier life that he said "no longer pass muster," keeping only the best.

Thomas Hardy, *The Complete Poems,* **1925.**
> Thomas Hardy is best known today for his novels *Far from the Madding Crowd* and *Tess of the D'Urbervilles.* But he considered himself primarily a poet, and his poems are well respected. While he was a naturalist, his poems display elements of romanticism and Enlightenment ideas.

Seamus Heaney,
Open Ground: Selected Poems 1966–1996, **1999.**
> Mythic and meditative, Seamus Heaney, Northern Ireland's most celebrated poet, takes you on a journey through the past—both his past and that of his homeland. Using an archaeological dig as a metaphor, he pierces through layers of history, story, and legend to find the truth. But he is also aware of the power of words to cut and do damage.

James Kinsley, ed., *The Oxford Book of Ballads,* **1969.**
> James Kinsley gathered 150 ballads from England and Scotland, from the early to the recent. Tunes accompany over half of them. Kinsley attempted to find the earliest sources of each to ensure the works presented are faithful to the originals.

Christina Rossetti, *The Complete Poems of Christina Rossetti: A Variorum Edition*, 1980.

Widely accepted as the greatest female poet of the Victorian era, Christina Rossetti wrote over a thousand poems before her death in 1894. The first volume of her collected poems was first published in 1980 by Louisiana State University Press. Her works cover varying themes from fantasy to religious devotion.

William Shakespeare, *The Sonnets*, 1999.

While generally considered the top English language writer, William Shakespeare is best known for his plays. Nevertheless, this collection of 154 sonnets has been scrutinized by scholars wanting to explore the nature of these love poems, whether or not they were autobiographical, and who he wrote them for. While originally published in 1609, more recent editions including the 1999 Signet Classics edition, edited by William Burto, are available.

Dylan Thomas, *The Collected Poems of Dylan Thomas, 1934–1952*, 1952.

Welsh poet Dylan Thomas was appreciated internationally for his poems, scripts, and public performances. He is best known for the radio drama, later adapted for stage and film, "Under Milk Wood" and for the poem "Do not go gentle into that good night."

BIOGRAPHY

Jonathan Bate, *Ted Hughes: The Unauthorized Life*, 2015.

Twentieth-century poet Ted Hughes left a significant mark on popular culture. Known for his charismatic personality and his first marriage to American poet Sylvia Plath, Hughes published prose, poetry, and children's books. Scholar Jonathan Bate spent five years in the Hughes archive and wrote this critical biography that considers his work and his life, which was marked by brilliance and scandal.

Leo Damrosch, *Eternity's Sunrise: The Imaginative World of William Blake*, 2015.

Leo Damrosch chronicles the life of one of British literature's most enigmatic writers, William Blake. Blake forces you to see the world in a completely new light with his fantastic etchings and engravings that complement his otherworldly poems. He believed our consciousness here and now touches on eternity, and we can access it for ourselves if we will only open to it. Damrosch attempts to help us share Blake's vision.

Richard Holmes, *Coleridge: Darker Reflections, 1804–1834*, 2000.

Acclaimed biographer Richard Holmes writes this second volume of his biography on 19th-century poet Samuel Taylor Coleridge. In poems such as "Kubla

Khan" and "The Rime of the Ancient Mariner," Coleridge mastered metaphor and imagery. However, he was equally well known for his talkativeness and drug use.

Donald R. Howard,
Chaucer: His Life, His Work, His World, 1989.

Fourteenth-century author Geoffrey Chaucer was the son of a wealthy London vintner. While not a nobleman, Chaucer served in the courts of Edward III and Richard II, which gave him access to the political turmoil and upheaval that would inspire his later writings in *The Canterbury Tales* and *Troilus and Criseyde*. Donald R. Howard presents the private and public life of the father of English poetry.

Brenda Maddox,
Yeats's Ghosts: The Secret Life of W. B. Yeats, 2000.

Nobel Prize–winning poet W. B. Yeats was one of Ireland's most revered 20th-century poets. Critic Brenda Maddox reveals how his private life was a complicated mix of passionate love affairs that were often unrequited. Yeats's early toying with the supernatural influenced his life and obsessions with the mystical, including hauntings by his ancestors.

Robert Bernard Martin, *Tennyson: The Unquiet Heart*, 1980.

Sir Alfred Lord Tennyson served as England's poet laureate during the Victorian age. While his poems have fallen from critical favor, Tennyson was an important figure in his time. Robert Bernard Martin shows him to have been a miserable man, despite his fame.

Stanley Plumly,
Posthumous Keats: A Personal Biography, 2008.

Romantic poet John Keats died at age 25. American poet Stanley Plumly closely examines his work to see if Keats achieved the poetic immortality he craved through his poems. This book is, at heart, an ode to the poet.

822 English Drama

Note: Using the criteria I set out in the Introduction, only books on Shakespeare were available for this section. Please explore the many other English playwrights.

David Crystal and Ben Crystal, *Oxford Illustrated Shakespeare Dictionary*, 2016.

David and Ben Crystal's unique dictionary alphabetically lists all the words anyone reading Shakespeare's poetry or plays would need to know. It defines the terms from his works, but it also defines terms and topics from Elizabethan Age theater and everyday life to help you understand them.

Marjorie Garber, *Shakespeare After All*, 2005.

Author Marjorie Garber provides a perfect introduction to all 38 of Shakespeare's plays in this engaging look at each one of them individually.

Using information pulled from her lectures at Yale and Harvard, she weaves in details about his life and times.

James Shapiro,
Contested Will: Who Wrote Shakespeare? 2010.

Did William Shakespeare of Stratford-upon-Avon write the poems and plays attributed to him or not? Shakespearean scholar James Shapiro examines the history of the debate—when and why it began and the famous people convinced that Shakespeare did not write the works attributed to him. Shapiro also discusses what the controversy tells us about our views on brilliance.

BIOGRAPHY

Stephen Greenblatt, *Will in the World: How Shakespeare Became Shakespeare*, 2004.

Throughout the years, some have argued that a young man with limited education from a small town in England couldn't have written the plays attributed to William Shakespeare. But distinguished literature professor Stephen Greenblatt explains precisely how it *was* possible in the context of the times.

823 English Fiction

Kevin Birmingham, *The Most Dangerous Book: The Battle for James Joyce's* Ulysses, 2014.

The novel that ushered in the modern era, James Joyce's *Ulysses,* intimidates many readers today. Literary historian Kevin Birmingham tells the story of Joyce's early years of writing and follows through the struggle to get *Ulysses* published with the help of Bennett Cerf, cofounder of Random House, and Morris Ernst, founder of the American Civil Liberties Union. Not only is this a study of censorship, it will also help you understand the novel and why it is considered the most remarkable of the 20th century.

Alan Burton,
Historical Dictionary of British Spy Fiction, 2016.

Alan Burton provides over 200 entries on the authors, characters, stories, films, filmmakers, TV shows, and subgenres of British spy fiction. The reference also has cross-references, a chronology, appendices, and a bibliography.

Katherine Frank, *Crusoe: Daniel Defoe, Robert Knox and the Creation of a Myth*, 2011.

Most of us have heard of *Robinson Crusoe*, but few of us know the story of Robert Knox. Katherine Frank exposes the link between Robert Knox and the novel. She relates how an accurate account of Knox's captivity on the island of Ceylon (now Sri Lanka) was published 40 years before Defoe's masterpiece. Defoe had a copy of the Knox account in his possession. As Frank relates,

Defoe most likely kept it handy while writing the celebrated novel of the
resourceful man long stranded on another island.

Claudia L. Johnson, *Jane Austen's Cults and Cultures*, 2012.

Even though she only completed six novels, Jane Austen inspires passion and
adoration from her fans. Claudia L. Johnson looks at the history of Austen's
place in the world throughout history to see why her very name represents a
specific set of feelings about life.

BIOGRAPHY

Sybille Bedford, *Aldous Huxley: A Biography*, 1973.

Celebrated novelist Sybille Bedford wrote this biography of her close friend
Aldous Huxley. She details the social and historical setting in which he wrote,
in addition to more private details.

Quentin Bell, *Virginia Woolf: A Biography*, 1974.

There are other biographies of Virginia Woolf, but this one by Woolf's nephew
Quentin Bell covers her life from start to finish. Bell discusses her relationships with T. S. Eliot, Katherine Mansfield, and Vita Sackville-West.

Richard Ellmann, *James Joyce*, 1959.

Richard Ellmann captures the life of James Joyce, author of *Ulysses*,
and shares the genius and foibles of one of the towering figures of
20th-century literature.

Patrick French, *The World Is What It Is:*
The Authorized Biography of V. S. Naipaul, 2008.

Novelist V. S. Naipaul wrote some of the most important British novels of the
20th century. British historian Patrick French used Naipaul's private papers
and personal memories to share his genius, work, and life.

P. N. Furbank, *E. M. Forster: A Life*, 1978.

E. M. Forster asked his friend P. N. Furbank to write this biography. Furbank
complied and used their letters, Forster's diaries, and their conversations in
which Foster reminisced about his past. Despite their friendship, Furbank is
honest in his portrayal. Originally published as two volumes, it is also available as one.

Elizabeth Gaskell, *The Life of Charlotte Brontë*, 1857.

The Brontë family invited Elizabeth Gaskell to write the official biography
of Charlotte Brontë, the author of *Jane Eyre* and *Villette*. This is a first
biography of a female author by her friend, another female novelist, when
female novelists were rare. Gaskell drew on her memory of Brontë, conversations with those close to her, and complete access to Brontë's letters.

Selina Hastings,
The Secret Lives of Somerset Maugham: A Biography, 2010.

While the author of *The Razor's Edge* and *Of Human Bondage* was one of the most widely read authors of the 20th century, he was also an enigmatic figure whose personal life was largely unknown. British journalist Selina Hastings tells of Maugham's lonely upbringing by unloving relatives after his parents' deaths. And she details his affairs with men and women and his years working with British secret intelligence during both world wars.

Alister McGrath, *C. S. Lewis—A Life:*
Eccentric Genius, Reluctant Prophet, 2013.

Distinguished theologian Alister McGrath writes this biography of beloved novelist and Christian apologist C. S. Lewis. McGrath uses recently published letters of Lewis as a prism through which to examine the significant events of Lewis's life. He details Lewis's conversion to Christianity from atheism and reexamines his works in light of this new information.

Claire Tomalin, *Charles Dickens: A Life*, 2011.

Charles Dickens's memorable characters, like Ebenezer Scrooge, made his novels hugely successful. But their author was a bundle of contradictions. Award-winning author Claire Tomalin examines Dickens's life with appreciation and honesty.

824 English Essays

Kate Briggs, *This Little Art*, 2018.

Translator Kate Briggs writes a meditation on the work and art of translation. Then, using her own experiences for illumination, she examines the relationships of other translators to their subjects.

Teju Cole, *Known and Strange Things: Essays*, 2016.

Teju Cole writes over 40 essays, including "The White Industrial Savior Complex," previously published in the *Atlantic*, and covers diverse topics like Virginia Woolf and Barack Obama. His Nigerian upbringing gives him a different perspective on global events than those commonly encountered in North America and Europe.

William Hazlitt, *Selected Writings*, 1991.

Early 19th-century scholar William Hazlitt is seldom read today despite his reputation as one of the greatest British essayists. He was a philosopher, biographer, political commentator, polemicist, and grammarian. In addition, he was a widely respected art, drama, and literary critic. But his progressive views on politics gave him trouble with conservatives.

BIOGRAPHY

Fred Kaplan, *Thomas Carlyle: A Biography*, 1983.

Scottish essayist Thomas Carlyle was one of the Victorian era's most famous writers. Fred Kaplan captures the times in which Carlyle lived and the complexities of his life.

825 English Speeches

Joan Webber,
Contrary Music: The Prose Style of John Donne, 1986.

While John Donne's poetry receives a great deal of critical attention and study, his sermons are neglected. Joan Webber sets out to correct that imbalance in this analysis of Donne's homilies.

828 English Miscellaneous Writings

James Boswell, *The Life of Samuel Johnson*, 1790.

The Life of Samuel Johnson is one of the earliest and most lauded English language biographies. Written in the 18th century, its author, James Boswell, tells of his relationship with Samuel Johnson, the most renowned poet, lexicographer, and critic of his day. Boswell based it on the minutely detailed journals he kept of his travels with and observations of Samuel Johnson.

Jon Godden and Rumer Godden,
Two Under the Indian Sun, 1966.

The Godden sisters, who grew up to be writers, tell of five crucial years living with their father, a steamship captain, in India, beginning when Jon was seven and Rumer was only six. They bring to life the India they knew from 1914 to 1919 with its sights, smells, and tastes. They also write of the near-universal experience of childhood as "a time when everything was clear: each thing was itself: joy was joy, hope was hope, and fear and sorrow were fear and sorrow."

Charlotte Gordon, *Romantic Outlaws: The Extraordinary Lives of Mary Wollstonecraft & Mary Shelley*, 2015.

Charlotte Gordon looks at Mary Wollstonecraft, the author of *The Vindication of the Rights of Women*, a seminal and still influential work of feminism, who lived a life of adventure, chasing pirates and observing the French revolution. She died when her daughter Mary was only one week old. But the parallels of their lives are astounding. Mary wrote *Frankenstein*, one of the most influential English novels, and edited her husband Percy Shelley's poetry, sealing his fame. Her life was as adventure-filled as her mother's.

Richard Holmes,
Footsteps: Adventures of a Romantic Biographer, **1985.**
Richard Holmes traveled extensively to research his biographies of Robert Louis Stevenson, Mary Wollstonecraft, and Percy Shelley. He recounts those journeys and the things he discovered from them. Along the way, he conveys the joys and labor involved in writing an exemplary biography.

BIOGRAPHY

Leo Damrosch, *Jonathan Swift: His Life and His World*, 2013.
Jonathan Swift, the author of *Gulliver's Travels*, cultivated a public image that Leo Damrosch's extensive research found misleading. Damrosch uses his findings to showcase Swift in a new light.

Richard Ellmann, *Oscar Wilde*, 1988.
Oscar Wilde's life was just as legendary for its drama as his plays, novels, stories, and poetry. American literary critic Richard Ellmann captures Wilde's complicated life and cultural influence with sensitivity to its beauty and tragedy.

Norman Ian MacKenzie and Jeanne MacKenzie,
H. G. Wells: A Biography, **1973.**
The MacKenzies examine the critical reception of H. G. Wells's writing up through the late 1960s, combined with his life story.

James Pope-Hennessy, *Robert Louis Stevenson*, 1974.
Robert Louis Stevenson was a 19th-century novelist, poet, and travel writer from Scotland. Best known for novels such as *Treasure Island*, Stevenson garnered recent attention for his entertaining travelogues. This biography combines his life with a critical appraisal of his works.

829 Old English (Anglo-Saxon) Literature

Seamus Heaney, *Beowulf: A New Verse Translation*, 2001.
Nobel Prize–winning author Seamus Heaney gives a new translation of one of the oldest narratives in the English language, *Beowulf*. His translation makes it clear that this is not just a tale of archaic heroism; it is a tale that still resonates today.

830 Literatures of Germanic Languages

Henry and Mary Garland, eds.,
The Oxford Companion to German Literature, **1976.**
This Oxford Companion covers the literature of German-speaking countries from the mid-8th century through the end of the 20th century. Authors,

works, dialects, and more make up this scholarly reference. The third edition of the print volume of this work was published in 1997. It is available online as well.

Thomas Mann, *Last Essays*, 1959.

In this collected work, Thomas Mann, the 20th-century Nobel Prize–winning writer of novels, short stories, and critical essays, analyzes the European and German soul after World War II. These essays were published upon Mann's return to Switzerland after fleeing the Nazis in World War II.

833 German Fiction

BIOGRAPHY

Gunnar Decker, *Hesse: The Wanderer and His Shadow*, 2018.

Counterculture icon Herman Hesse is best known today for his novels *Siddhartha* and *Steppenwolf*. Using recently released correspondence of Hesse with Stefan Zweig and psychoanalyst Josef Lang, Gunnar Decker provides a new critical interpretation of Hesse's work in this translation by Peter Lewis.

Ernst Pawel, *The Nightmare of Reason: A Life of Franz Kafka*, 1984.

German-born novelist Ernst Pawel tells of the tragic life of Franz Kafka, the genius behind *The Metamorphosis* and *The Trial*. Pawel details the harsh events of Kafka's life and their influence on his disturbing work.

839 Other Germanic Literatures

Sholom Aleichem, *Old Country Tales*, 1966.

Sholom Aleichem (his pen name is Hebrew for "peace be unto you") wrote over 40 volumes of Yiddish literature. His stories are of shtetl life in Eastern Europe before World War II.

Örnólfur Thorsson, ed., *The Sagas of Icelanders: A Selection*, 2000.

The Viking men and women who settled in Iceland at the turn of the first millennium CE were the sources of these literary epics. The sagas contain archetypal hero adventures and explore psychological issues with a realism that modern readers easily understand.

BIOGRAPHY

Sue Prideaux, *Strindberg: A Life*, 2012.

Prolific 19th-century Swedish writer August Strindberg wrote over 60 plays,

18 novels, three volumes of poetry, and nine autobiographies before his death in 1912. While he was as famous for his wild lifestyle as for his writing, he completely changed the nature of drama by introducing the elements of psychological warfare to his plays. English novelist and playwright Sue Prideaux helps us see the links between Strindberg's life and works.

840 Literatures of Romance Languages

Daniel Levin Becker, *Many Subtle Channels: In Praise of Potential Literature*, 2012.

OuLiPo, founded in 1960 and based in Paris, is a collective of writers, artists, and mathematicians who follow agreed-upon rules and constraints to produce works that confound and amaze. One example is the Georges Perec novel *A Void,* written entirely without the letter *e.* When Daniel Levin Becker earned a Fulbright grant, he chose to study the group in Paris and write this book about his findings.

BIOGRAPHY

Graham Robb, *Victor Hugo: A Biography*, 1999.

Graham Robb writes of 19th-century French Romantic novelist and playwright Victor Hugo, best known for his novels *Les Misérables* and *The Hunchback of Notre-Dame.* But Hugo was also a well-regarded painter, architect, political thinker, and visionary who communicated with Virgil, Shakespeare, and Jesus.

841 French Poetry

BIOGRAPHY

Graham Robb, *Rimbaud: A Biography*, 2001.

The life of 19th-century French poet Arthur Rimbaud was remarkable for multiple crimes, drug use, gay activity, and anarchism. His poetry was largely unknown when he died. But in the years since, starting in the early 20th century, he became a significant influence for artists from Picasso to Patti Smith.

842 French Drama

BIOGRAPHY

Deidre Bair, *Samuel Beckett: A Biography*, 1978.

Deidre Bair's celebrated and scholarly work tells of Nobel Prize–winning

Samuel Beckett's life from his upper-middle-class life in Ireland through his involvement in the French Resistance in the Second World War, his private correspondence, and writings. Beckett was known for his novels and plays, such as *Waiting for Godot.*

843 French Fiction

Emmanuel Carrère, *97,196 Words: Essays*, 2019.

French writer Emmanuel Carrère wrote most of his fiction and nonfiction about identity, illusion, and reality. This shorter collection of essays introduces his work to an English-speaking audience, demonstrating how he explores the themes of his other works and his own eccentric life.

Voltaire, *Candide*, 1759.

Jesuit-educated Enlightenment philosopher, historian, and satirist Voltaire wrote the tale of the hapless Candide, a man who insists that the widespread optimism of his day, that we live in "the best of all possible worlds" is a fact. However, through a series of outrageous events, Candide eventually discovers that, despite his beliefs, things don't always turn out for the best.

Caroline Weber, *Proust's Duchess: How Three Celebrated Women Captured the Imagination of Fin-de-Siècle Paris*, 2018.

In *The Remembrance of Things Past,* Marcel Proust wrote of the Duchesse de Guermantes. But few know that the character was a composite of three women who were superstars of French high society: Geneviève Halévy-Bizet-Straus, Laure de Sade, and Élisabeth de Riquet, comtesse de Caraman-Chimay. These women were unhappily married to wealthy, well-connected men and hosted salons that attracted and inspired writers, artists, composers, designers, and journalists. Proust, enamored with them when young, got to know them later in life and used them to create his unforgettable character.

BIOGRAPHY

Frederick Brown, *Flaubert: A Biography*, 2006.

In 1856, Gustave Flaubert stood trial for the lewd behavior portrayed in his recently published novel *Madame Bovary.* His honest portrayal of adultery and female sexuality was not yet acceptable. Frederick Brown details Flaubert's life of contradictions along with his famous friendships with Turgenev, Zola, and de Maupassant, as well as his various mistresses from France, England, and Egypt.

Graham Robb, *Balzac: A Biography*, 1996.

Nineteenth-century French Realism novelist and playwright Honoré de Balzac was known for his skillful character development and plots that were partially autobiographical, across his many novels, such as *Cousin Bette*. Robb considers how the escapades of Balzac influenced his extensive body of work and how it, in turn, has influenced artists ever since.

848 French Miscellaneous Writings

BIOGRAPHY

Deirdre Bair, *Simone de Beauvoir: A Biography*, 1990.

Deirdre Bair examines the existentialist philosopher, activist, and feminist Simone de Beauvoir and her life with Jean-Paul Sartre. Bair bases her book on interviews with the author that took place over five years.

Sarah Bakewell, *How to Live, Or, A Life of Montaigne in One Question and Twenty Attempts at an Answer*, 2011.

Renaissance essayist Michel Eyquem de Montaigne is considered one of the world's greatest essayists and the first modern individual. His essays are as enjoyable today as they were in his own time. Acclaimed biographer Sarah Bakewell relates the life of Montaigne and the questions he pondered in this engaging biography.

Leo Damrosch, *Jean-Jacques Rousseau: Restless Genius*, 2005.

Leo Damrosch takes the events of 18th-century philosopher and political thinker Jean-Jacques Rousseau's life and weaves them with his writings to illuminate each. Rather than a passé thinker, Rousseau's ideas have taken hold and still have a great deal of influence, particularly in the U.S.

Jean-Paul Sartre, *The Words*, 1963.

When Existentialist philosopher, novelist, and playwright Jean-Paul Sartre was 59, he wrote this autobiography in which he analyzes his first ten years of life. His childhood was loving and steeped in the printed word. This autobiography not only retells his life but evaluates the use of books and language in human life.

Francis Steegmuller, *Cocteau: A Biography*, 1970.

Poet, novelist, playwright, and filmmaker Jean Cocteau was a scandalous figure in the 20th-century art world. By turns charming and brutal, while also opium-addicted and homosexual, Cocteau nevertheless managed to enter the conservative Académie Française. Francis Steegmuller covers it all in this page-turning account.

Judith Thurman, *Secrets of the Flesh: A Life of Colette*, 1999.

Colette lived a life that combined literary giftedness with scandal. After an early marriage, she grew tired of her husband's dominance and began a public lesbian affair with Napoleon's niece. At age 40, Colette gave birth to her first child, for whom she cared little. Then, at 47, she seduced her teenaged stepson. Later, Colette flirted with Nazis in Paris while the Gestapo held her third husband, a Jew. Throughout all this, she wrote, first, the early Claudine novels and then on through *Gigi, Cheri,* and *Break of Day.*

850 Italian, Romanian & Related Literatures

851 Italian Poetry

Mary Jo Bang, tr., Dante Alighieri, *Inferno*, 2013.
This ambitious project by poet Mary Jo Bang brings *Inferno* into modern English while preserving Dante's original message. She adds allusions to more recent poets, like T. S. Eliot and Gerard Manley Hopkins, and inserts rock and jazz lyrics and references to modern life such as swimming pools and roulette tables. As a result, the original poem becomes understandable to modern readers through an overlay of contemporary life.

853 Italian Fiction

Giuseppe di Lampedusa, *The Leopard*, 1958.
This classic novel, set in the 1860s, tells of a corrupt and dying aristocracy threatened by democracy and revolution. The action centers around Don Fabrizio, who is a charismatic Sicilian prince. Colorful and intriguing characters surround him from all economic and social strata with varying political beliefs and motives.

Primo Levi, *If Not Now, When?* 1982.
Renowned writer Primo Levi was both a chemist and a writer who spent 11 months in Auschwitz before his liberation in 1945. He was one of few Italian Jewish survivors. He based this novel on a true story of Russian, Polish, and Jewish individuals trapped behind enemy lines in World War II.

854 Italian Essays

Primo Levi, *The Periodic Table*, 1975.
Primo Levi presents 21 essays, each named after one element on the periodic table. Each renders his experience as a Jewish-Italian chemist in the years before, during, and after his time in Auschwitz. It was named the best science book in the history of the world by the Royal Institution of Great Britain.

856 Italian Letters

Italo Calvino, *Italo Calvino: Letters, 1941–1985*, 2013.
Not only was Italo Calvino considered one of the most influential novelists of the post–World War II era, but he was also an influential literary critic and

editor. This book pulls together roughly 650 of his letters, translated into English, with annotations. His correspondence includes exchanges with literary greats such as Umberto Eco, Natalia Ginzberg, and Gore Vidal.

860 Spanish & Portuguese Literatures

Philip Ward, ed.,
The Oxford Companion to Spanish Literature, 1978.

This comprehensive and cross-referenced guide to the languages of Spain and Central and South America could use an update, but it would nevertheless be helpful for its earlier information.

861 Spanish Poetry

Pablo Neruda, *The Heights of Macchu Picchu*, 1967.

Chilean poet Pablo Neruda is considered one of the greatest poets of the 20th century. *The Heights of Macchu Picchu* is his most famous long poem. Inspired by a trip to the Incan city's ruins in the Andes, it represents an interior journey exploring his inner life and the history of Latin America and its breathtaking landscape.

863 Spanish Fiction

Jorge Luis Borges, *Fictions*, 1944.

This collection of stories by Argentine writer Jorge Luis Borges was unlike anything that had ever come before. They are perfect examples of Surrealist literature. Perhaps the best known of these stories is "The Library of Babel," where an infinite library contains every possible book. It is a book containing dreams within dreams.

BIOGRAPHY

Gerald Martin, *Gabriel García Márquez: A Life*, 2008.

Nobel Prize–winning Colombian writer Gabriel García Márquez authored the celebrated magical realism novels *One Hundred Years of Solitude* and *Love in the Time of Cholera*. His private life, as with many writers, was complicated. Gerald Martin provides the story.

864 Spanish Essays

Jorge Luis Borges, *Selected Non-Fictions*, 1999.

While Jorge Louis Borges is best known for his fiction and poetry, most of his actual writing was nonfiction, consisting of essays, reviews, prologues, lectures, and notes on culture. He presents a sampling here.

868 Spanish Miscellaneous Writings

BIOGRAPHY

Ian Gibson, *Federico García Lorca: A Life,* **1985.**
Award-winning author Ian Gibson tells the story of Federico García Lorca, who was executed in 1936 at age 38 by anti-republican rebels in the Spanish Civil War. Internationally renowned, he is still considered the most significant Spanish poet and playwright of the 20th century.

870 Latin & Related Italic Literatures

871 Latin Poetry

Gilbert Highet, *Poets in a Landscape,* **1957.**
Classical scholar Gilbert Highet discusses the great Latin poets such as Virgil and Horace, looking at their world and lives. He also provides modern translations of their best work, making this an excellent introduction to classical poets.

873 Latin Epic Poetry & Fiction

Ted Hughes, *Tales from Ovid: Twenty-four Passages from the* **Metamorphoses, 1997.**
British poet laureate Ted Hughes created a stir when he published this retelling of *The Metamorphoses of Ovid,* one of the great works of classic poetry. Hughes translates 24 of the stories in this critically acclaimed volume.

879 Literature of Other Italic Languages

Dorothy Curley and Arthur Curley, comps and eds., *Modern Romance Literatures,* **1967.**
Scholars Dorothy and Arthur Curley compiled this list of essential modern romance authors and their works. They include short selections of the pieces with recommended reading lists for each.

880 Classical Greek & Hellenic Literatures

Michael Grant, *Greek and Latin Authors, 800 BC–AD 1000: A Biographical Dictionary,* **1980.**
English classicist Michael Grant provides 376 biographical sketches of Greek and Latin authors covering over 1,000 years of writing. It includes a chronological list of the authors and a separate list of works of doubtful attribution.

882 Classical Greek Dramatic Poetry & Drama

Richmond Y. Hathorn, *Crowell's Handbook of Classical Drama: A Modern Guide*, 1967.
Richard Yancey Hathorn's reference book contains entries on the plays, playwrights, summaries, criticisms, and related terms and topics of classical theater. Topics, arranged alphabetically, also deliver information on fragmentary and lost plays.

883 Classical Greek Epic Poetry & Fiction

Adam Nicolson, *Why Homer Matters: A History*, 2014.
Homer's epic poems tell us about much more than the mythology of the ancient Greeks of 4,000 years ago. The origins of the *Iliad* and the *Odyssey*, says Adam Nicolson, go back much further to the steppes of Eurasia, where their earliest versions are lost. Nicolson says they hold a unique place in our collective psyche and culture as the myths uniting the Western world.

889 Modern Greek Literature

Nikos Kazantzakis, *The Odyssey: A Modern Sequel*, 1938.
Greek writer Nikos Kazantzakis tells the story of Odysseus after he finally returns to Ithaca from the Trojan War. Finding the reality of home unlike his memory, Odysseus leaves again, searching for answers to his questions on God.

890 Literatures of Other Languages

Isaac Babel, *The Complete Works of Isaac Babel*, 2001.
This volume gathers the works of 20th-century playwright and short story author Isaac Babel, author of *Tales of Odessa*, who was executed in 1940 after he was declared a Trotskyist terrorist and foreign spy in Stalin's Great Purge.

Elif Batuman, *The Possessed: Adventures with Russian Books and the People Who Read Them*, 2010.
Elif Batuman examines the place of the novel in the lives of fans. She looks at the great Russian writers and travels the globe to explore how their lives, culture, and writing impacted their readers.

Isaiah Berlin, *The Hedgehog and the Fox: An Essay on Tolstoy's View of History*, 1953.
Philosopher Isaiah Berlin, using Tolstoy's views on history as a springboard, wrote this essay about the distinction between two groups of people: the foxes who spend their time and energy on the diversity of life and the hedgehogs who pull everything together in one central, all-embracing system.

Donald Fanger, *The Creation of Nikolai Gogol*, 1979.
Nikolai Gogol is considered Russia's greatest comic writer. While the facts about Gogol's life have been sparse, Donald Fanger uses contemporary sources, his works, letters, and even drafts to explain the genius behind this iconic writer.

Peter Finn and Petra Couvée, *The Zhivago Affair: The Kremlin, the CIA, and the Battle Over a Forbidden Book*, 2014.
Doctor Zhivago was the only novel written by Russian poet Boris Pasternak. Although it was censored in the Soviet Union, Pasternak gave a copy of the original manuscript to a visiting Italian talent scout in 1956, who published it on returning home. The novel became an international bestseller. Later, the CIA smuggled copies of the Russian language version back into the Soviet Union, and it quickly became an underground sensation. Finn and Couvée narrate the story, which includes both spies and dissent.

Victor Terras, ed., *Handbook of Russian Literature*, 1990.
With 1,000 entries covering 1,000 years, this reference for English-speaking students of Russian literature includes authors, genres, movements, period studies, and journal reviews.

BIOGRAPHY

Manoranjan Byapari and Sipra Mukherjee, *Interrogating My Chandal Life: An Autobiography of a Dalit*, 2017.
Writer Manoranjan Byapari translates this memoir of Itibritte Chandal Jivan's life of poverty and struggle. It begins with Jivan's childhood spent in West Bengal and Dandakaranya refugee camps, his exploitation while seeking employment, and the gang warfare of the Naxalite movement. While in prison, he learned to read at age 24, which opened an entirely new world for him. His memoir brings into sharp focus the gap between the comfortably well-off and the world's desperately poor.

Joseph Frank,
***Dostoevsky: The Seeds of Revolt, 1821–1849*, 5 vols. 1979.**
Slavic and comparative literature professor Joseph Frank wrote the definitive biography, in five volumes, of the great 19th-century Russian novelist Fyodor Dostoevsky. To research this work, Frank learned Russian and did a thorough study of the cultural and political events of Dostoevsky's time. He then set about placing the novels within their contemporary milieu.

V. S. Pritchett,
***The Gentle Barbarian: The Life and Work of Turgenev*, 1977.**
V. S. Pritchett used English and French translations of the materials surrounding Russian novelist and short story writer Ivan Sergeyevich Turgenev's life to write his biography.

Michael Scammell, *Solzhenitsyn: A Biography*, 1984.
Aleksandr Solzhenitsyn grew up in concert with the Soviet Union. His life, and his outlook on his government, parallel the events of the nation almost perfectly. So in telling his life story, Michael Scammell also relates the history of Soviet communism and the attitudes of the intellectuals of Solzhenitsyn's day.

Alexandra Tolstoy, *Tolstoy: A Life of My Father*, 1953.
Widely considered one of the greatest novelists globally, Lev (Leo) Tolstoy is best known for his novels *War and Peace* and *Anna Karenina*. However, he was also well known for his complex personal life and somewhat extreme views on morality and ascetics. His daughter and private secretary, Alexandra, wrote this biography.

892 Afro-Asiatic Literatures

**Amos Oz, *Dear Zealots:*
Letters from a Divided Land, 2019.**
Internationally recognized Israeli writer, journalist, and intellectual Amos Oz wrote these three essays for his grandchildren and their generation. They deal with the nature of fanaticism, suggestions for tempering it, the Jewish roots of humanism, and the political place of Israel in the Middle East and internationally. In reading the essays, you gain a broad view of Israel's history, religion, and politics.

895 Literatures of East & Southeast Asia

**Donald Keene, *Dawn to the West:*
Japanese Literature in the Modern Era, 1984.**
Donald Keene, an authority on Japanese translation and scholar of Japanese culture and literature, wrote a trilogy of the history of modern Japanese literature. *Dawn to the West* is the final volume.

Hualing Nieh, *Mulberry and Peach: Two Women of China*, 1976.
This novel tells how a woman named Mulberry fled post–World War II China, in the wake of the Japanese occupation, to go to the U.S. Once there, she experiences troubles maintaining her Chinese cultural and ethical roots. To cope with her problems, she creates Peach, an alter ego who is fearless and sexually uninhibited. China banned the book after its publication in 1976. The novel highlights both the plight of the disaffected and an examination of psychological disintegration.

Hiroaki Sato and Burton Watson, eds., *From the Country of Eight Islands: An Anthology of Japanese Poetry*, 1986.
Hiroaki Sato and Burton Watson, both of whom have lived in Japan and are fluent in the language, translated this survey of Japanese literature.

CHAPTER 10

900-999

Geography, Biography, History

SINCE IT COVERS SUCH A massive amount of information, this division has the most titles in this book. The geography books are primarily travel writing. The biography books assigned to subdivision 920 by the LOC were generally written decades ago or didn't belong under a specific subject. For example, a recently written biography of Albert Einstein would more likely be in the physics section (530) instead of the 920s. Finally, the history books are arranged by continent.

900 History & Geography

901 Philosophy & Theory of History

Francis Fukuyama,
***The End of History and The Last Man*, 1992.**
  American political economist Francis Fukuyama argues that liberal democracy is the high point of human governmental frameworks. Using the fall of the Soviet Union, he argues free-market capitalism is the only viable economic system. By analyzing religious fundamentalism, politics, scientific progress, and war, he reaches conclusions that are still hotly debated. The book was updated and reprinted in 2006.

902 Miscellany of History

Bernard Grun, *The Timetables of History:*
***A Horizontal Linkage of People and Events*, 1991.**
  Bernard Grun's reference covers over 7,000 years of history in a table format to present a massive, continuous timeline. The book divides events into the following categories: history, politics, literature, theater, religion, philosophy, learning, visual arts, music, science, technology, growth, and daily life. The most recent print version, the fourth edition, was published in 2005.

James Trager, *The People's Chronology: A Year-by-Year*
***Record of Human Events from Prehistory to the Present*, 1979.**
  This reference covers historical events in chronological order with entries

under each year that provide the significant developments in 30 categories, such as politics, economics, and technology.

904 Collected Accounts of Events

David Eggenberger,
Dictionary of Battles: From 1479 BC to the Present, 1967.
While David Eggenberger initially published the 1967 version of this book as a dictionary, it has been revised several times as *The Encyclopedia of Battles*. With over 1,500 conflicts covering more than 3,000 years, the book contains entries listed in alphabetical order on each battle.

907 Education, Research & Related Topics

John Clive, *Not by Fact Alone:*
Essays on the Writing and Reading of History, 1991.
English author and actor John Clive explores great and influential historians from the past. He finds that history writing is often not solely dependent on the events but also on the historian.

Barbara W. Tuchman,
Practicing History: Selected Essays, 1981.
Perhaps best known for *In a Distant Mirror*, a history of the Middle Ages, and *The Guns of August*, a history of World War I, self-taught historian Barbara W. Tuchman writes about the craft of historical writing in this collection of essays. Her way of looking at history and the lessons she draws from it is unique.

909 World History

Neal Ascherson, *Black Sea*, 1995.
Scottish historian Neal Ascherson provides a study of the Black Sea region, in which Asia and Europe meet. Over the past several thousand years, encounters between ancient and modern cultures in Russia, Ukraine, the Caucasus, Turkey, and Greece have shaped the world's religions, languages, and trade. The work provides a necessary backdrop from which to understand world history.

Will Durant, *The Reformation: The Story of Civilization*, 1957.
This history of the world is vol. 6 in the classic 11-volume set *The Story of Civilization*. In it, Will Durant, in collaboration with his wife Ariel, writes of the history of Europe from 1300–1564 CE.

Yuval Noah Harari, *Sapiens:*
A Brief History of Humankind, 2011.
Internationally renowned Israeli historian Yuval Noah Harari examines the

rise of our species when other humanoids occupied the planet 100,000 years ago. By considering what the fields of biology, anthropology, paleontology, and economics can reveal to us, he traces our path to the present and speculates on where the future may take us.

Charles C. Mann, *1491:*
***New Revelations of the Americas Before Columbus*, 2005.**
Science writer Charles C. Mann uses the most recent discoveries of archaeology and history to demonstrate that indigenous peoples had produced some of the largest cities and most technologically advanced societies in the world before Europeans arrived in the Americas.

Callum Roberts, *The Unnatural History of the Sea*, 2007.
Scientist Callum Roberts traces the history of commercial fishing. He concludes that the oceans have been overfished and exploited at least since medieval times. Our current ocean crises did not begin with the Industrial Revolution as is commonly thought. Roberts suggests ways to restore our oceans to their former glory through restraint and intelligent management.

Simon Schama, *The Story of the Jews:*
***Finding the Words: 1000 BC–1492 AD*, 2013.**
Celebrated historian Simon Schama writes the epic history of the Jews from their earliest beginnings until the late Middle Ages. He finds that rather than a people always set apart, their ability to integrate into many civilizations across time and geography is amazing.

Peter Watson, *The Modern Mind:*
***An Intellectual History of the 20th Century*, 2000.**
Internationally educated and recognized scholar Peter Watson covers all the significant writers, artists, scientists, and philosophers of the 20th century to provide a clear map of humanity's journey from the 19th to the 21st century. This fascinating work covers accomplishments, ideas, schools of thought, and worldwide counter-cultural movements.

910 Geography & Travel

Ibn Battúta, *The Travels of Ibn Battúta: Explorations of the Middle East, Asia, Africa, China and India from 1325 to 1354: An Autobiography*, 1929.
We know about Marco Polo, but few in the West know about Ibn Battúta, a Berber scholar who set out from Tangier at age 21 on a pilgrimage to Mecca. For almost 30 years, he traveled the known world, covering more than 40 countries still in existence today. He writes of his travels, including the various societies and individuals he encounters. He sketches the history, plants, and cuisines as well.

Jason Lewis, *Dark Waters: True Story of the First Human-Powered Circumnavigation of the Earth*, 2012.

Modern-day adventurer Jason Lewis writes about his adventures as the first human to circumnavigate the globe using only the power of his own body. He came close to death in different countries under various circumstances involving everything from disease to crocodile attacks. *Dark Waters* is the first volume of three in the Expedition series.

John Muir, *My First Summer in the Sierra*, 100th Anniversary Edition, 2011.

Early environmental activist John Muir wrote many letters, books, and essays about his experiences in nature, particularly in California's Sierra Nevada. Muir's words are combined with Scot Miller's photography to describe the area that is now Yosemite National Park.

Dervla Murphy, *Full Tilt: Ireland to India with a Bicycle*, 1965.

Dervla Murphy, an Irish touring cyclist and author of travel adventure books, wrote this story of her trip in 1963 across Europe, Persia, and Afghanistan, and then across the Himalayas and Pakistan and ending in India. Amazingly, most of the trip was on a bicycle in the depths of a nasty winter.

Rick Steves, *Travel as a Political Act*, 2015.

Television personality and travel writer Rick Steves explores how travel can help bring humanity closer together through exposure to other cultures. Through increased familiarity, different cultures can become understandable and give us a better lens through which to view our own. He shares stories from his extensive worldwide travels over decades. And in this second edition of the book, Steves encourages us to view travel as an antidote to xenophobia and nationalism.

911 Historical Geography

J. F. Ade Ajayi and Michael Crowder, *Historical Atlas of Africa*, 1985.

Ajayi and Crowder's atlas contains three types of maps that illustrate events, historical processes, and numerical data. Ample explanatory text accompanies each map.

Geoffrey Barraclough, ed., *The Times Atlas of World History*, 1989.

This chronological atlas presents the history of the world from the earliest times to the most recent. Students and general readers are the intended audiences, and it contains more than 600 maps with commentary from over 100 historians, a glossary, and an index. The most recent print edition is from 2009.

Lester J. Cappon, ed., *Atlas of Early American History: The Revolutionary Era, 1760–1790*, 1976.
This atlas contains maps from the periods of just before, during, and after the Revolutionary War. It was a collaboration between the Institute of Early American History and Culture in Williamsburg, Virginia, and the Newberry Library in Chicago. Some maps draw from data taken from the 1790 census.

Martin Gilbert, *Atlas of Russian History*, 1972.
Historian Martin Gilbert's atlas, spanning 2,000 years of Russian history, provides maps covering wars, famines, monarchies, politics, industry, society, trade, and cultures.

Francis Robinson, *Atlas of the Islamic World Since 1500*, 1982.
Francis Robinson covers Muslim history and society on a global scale. While some of the information may be outdated, much of it is still relevant.

912 Maps & Plans of Surface of Earth

Rand McNally Atlas of the Oceans, 1977.
Scholars from over 20 academic institutions created the *Rand McNally Atlas of the Oceans*, last updated in 1994. It covers the oceans themselves, in addition to explorations, marine life, resources, and maps.

Joel Makower, ed., *The Map Catalog: Every Kind of Map and Chart on Earth and Even Some Above It*, 1986.
Last revised in 1992, this reference is different from others in that it aims to contain every *kind* of map, not just those related to a specific subject or geographical region. It has historical, road, aerial, geological, weather, nautical, military, census, and astronomical maps, to name a few. Map making techniques have changed since it was last published, but it provides a good introduction to the history of mapmaking nonetheless.

John Noble Wilford, *The Mapmakers: The Story of the Great Pioneers in Cartography— from Antiquity to the Space Age*, 1981.
Science writer John Noble Wilford provides this global history of maps and mapmaking. The 2001 revised edition of the book updates information on the ways maps are made for everything from the universe to the human brain.

David Zurick and Julsun Pacheco, *Illustrated Atlas of the Himalaya*, 2006.
Zurick and Pacheco's comprehensive atlas covers the entire Himalayan

region's geography, economics, politics, and culture. It has over 300 maps of the whole area from northern Pakistan to northeast India.

913 Geography of & Travel in Ancient World

Yigael Yadin,
***Masada: Herod's Fortress and the Zealots' Last Stand*, 1945.**
Yigael Yadin documents his excavation of the hill fort of Masada. His work both confirmed the historical account of the event by Josephus and also turned up amazing discoveries and artifacts that added greatly to the historical understanding of the time and place.

914 Geography of & Travel in Europe

Jay Ben Adlersberg, *Ireland: In Word and Image*, 2013.
If you're planning a trip to Ireland or wish you could, this book can help prepare you for what you may see. With beautiful poetic language and over 200 photographs, Jay Ben Adlersberg exposes Ireland's captivating history, culture, and beauty, north to south and ancient to modern.

Nick Inman, *A Guide to Mystical France:*
***Secrets, Mysteries, Sacred Sites*, 2016.**
Nick Inman explores France's hidden places, such as the prehistoric cave paintings, the ley lines, the Carnac stone alignments, and haunting cathedrals such as Chartres and monasteries such as Mont-Saint-Michel. Through exploring the covert in France, he helps you appreciate the visible.

Robert D. Kaplan,
***Balkan Ghosts: A Journey Through History* 1993.**
The Balkans have played a significant role in world history. Robert D. Kaplan leads us through the modern history of this area, from the assassination of Archduke Franz Ferdinand, which began World War I, through the ethnic wars in Serbia, Bosnia, and Croatia in the final years of the 20th century. The second edition, published in 2005, contains six additional essays covering developments between 1996 and 2000.

Robert Macfarlane, *Landmarks*, 2015.
Acclaimed British nature writer Robert Macfarlane explores the way words and language shape our sense of place. Through his study of nature literature and his travels around the British Isles, Macfarlane imparts a unique way of coming to know and understand the landscape.

Stephen Spinder, *Ten Years in Transylvania:*
***Traditions of Hungarian Folk Culture*, 2007.**
Outside the legends of Dracula and stories of Vlad the Impaler, the wider world often overlooks Transylvania. Stephen Spinder wants to rectify this

neglect by looking at the region's ancient culture, still largely intact. Over 140 photographs capture the beauty of the landscape and the colorful folk culture of this Hungarian region.

915 Geography of & Travel in Asia

Saul Bellow,
To Jerusalem and Back: A Personal Account, 1976.

One of the 20th century's most celebrated writers traveled to Jerusalem to record the viewpoint of current Jewish residents, including political leaders, journalists, and average citizens. To these, he added his perspectives as a Jewish American. Taken together, they comprise a portrait of Jewish thought in the late 20th century.

Abby Denson, *Cool Tokyo Guide:*
Adventures in the City of Kawaii Fashion, Train Sushi,
and Godzilla, 2018.

Cartoonist Abby Denson takes you on a graphic tour of the streets of Tokyo in this entertaining travel guide. She introduces you to unusual and colorful restaurants, shops, and museums and counsels on sharing etiquette, handling confusing toilets, and journey preparation.

Jason Elliot,
An Unexpected Light: Travels in Afghanistan, 1999.

In the years before 9/11, Jason Elliot traveled through the countryside of Afghanistan and reported on a country that is sadly no longer there. Leaving the safety of Kabul, he traveled by foot, horseback, and hitchhiking, traversing the length and breadth of the country. Along the way, he explored the history of this mysterious land.

Eric Hansen,
Stranger in the Forest: On Foot Across Borneo, 1988.

Travel writer Eric Hansen recorded his travels across the entire 1,500 miles of Borneo, which he traversed on foot in the company of small bands of nomadic Penan hunters. From this disappearing world, he introduces plants and animals that sound fantastical.

Heinrich Harrer, *Seven Years in Tibet*, 1953.

After escaping from an English internment camp in India in 1943, Austrian mountaineer Heinrich Harrer spent seven years hidden away in Tibet in the days before the Chinese annexed the country. He records the daily life, religion, and politics of a lost time and place.

Kate Harris,
Lands of Lost Borders: A Journey on the Silk Road, 2018.

Canadian writer Kate Harris biked the entire length of the ancient Silk Road with her friend Mel Yule. She tells of their adventures while weaving in the history of science and exploration in this travelogue.

Peter Hessler, *River Town: Two Years on the Yangtze*, 2001.

Peter Hessler moved to the small Chinese city of Fuling as a Peace Corps volunteer in 1996. At the time, he was its first American resident in over 50 years. He got a unique glimpse at the ancient practices and ways of life of the locals whom the Communist Party had educated. After the book's publication, the Three Gorges Dam construction partially flooded the city, as had long been planned, dislocating over a million residents.

Eric Newby, *A Short Walk in the Hindu Kush*, 1958.

Eric Newby was an unhappy London fashion-industry worker when he decided he wanted a change. So after taking a four-day walking training course in Wales, he tackled the Hindu Kush.

916 Geography of & Travel in Africa

Tim Butcher,
Blood River: A Journey to Africa's Broken Heart, 2007.

After becoming obsessed with the idea of retracing the steps of explorer Henry Morton Stanley, British journalist Tim Butcher began the trek along the Congo for 2,500 miles. He relates the region's history while narrating his experiences.

James T. Campbell, *Middle Passages:*
African American Journeys to Africa, 1787–2005, 2006.

Over 12 million Africans were brought to the Americas against their will in the slave trade following Columbus. Early in the 18th-century, groups of these African Americans managed to recross the "middle passage" back to Africa. In the years since, many more, often well-known Black Americans have made the trip. James T. Campbell explores the impacts of these journeys.

Geoffrey Moorhouse, *The Fearful Void*, 1974.

While this book is about confronting fear, it is also about traversing all 3,600 miles of the Sahara Desert by camel and on foot. English journalist Geoffrey Moorhouse tells of his journey, which began in October 1972 and ended in March 1973, just 300 miles shy of his goal.

Paul Theroux, *The Last Train to Zona Verde:*
My Ultimate African Safari, 2013.

Celebrated travel writer Paul Theroux takes one last journey through his favorite continent, which he calls "the kingdom of light." After leaving Cape Town in South Africa, he heads north along Africa's little-traveled west to Angola. Then, passing "the Red Line," he runs into an impoverished, sunbaked central area, where he begins to question why he made the trip at all.

Elizabeth Marshall Thomas, *The Harmless People*, **1959.**
The San of the Kalahari Desert in Botswana and South West Africa (Namibia today), called Bushmen when the book was written, are well-known hunter–gatherers. In the 1950s, Elizabeth Marshall Thomas went to live with them and wrote this classic work of anthropology as a result. In the 1980s, she revisited the San several times and later updated this work to record how they coped with contacts with the modern world.

BIOGRAPHY

Tim Jeal, *Stanley:*
The Impossible Life of Africa's Greatest Explorer, **2007.**
While history has portrayed Henry Morton Stanley as a callous opportunist who paved the way to African exploitation, biographer Tim Jeal reveals a different man through his access to previously closed family archives. Jeal presents a poverty-stricken and neglected young man forced to make his way in the world.

917 Geography of & Travel in North America

Stephen E. Ambrose, *Undaunted Courage:*
Meriwether Lewis, Thomas Jefferson, and the Opening
of the American West, **1997.**
American historian and biographer Stephen E. Ambrose narrates the story of the Lewis and Clark Expedition. When Thomas Jefferson charged Meriwether Lewis and William Clark with exploring the newly acquired Louisiana Territory, the three-year journey proved challenging yet awe-inspiring.

Bill Bryson, *A Walk in the Woods:*
Rediscovering America on the Appalachian Trail, **1998.**
Entertaining travel writer Bill Bryson recounts his adventures hiking the Appalachian Trail, which stretches from Georgia along the mountain chain up through Maine. He depicts the sights, the history, and the characters he travels with along the way.

Wade Davis, *Grand Canyon, River at Risk*, **2008.**
Eminent anthropologist Wade Davis records a trip he took down the Colorado River by raft with Robert F. Kennedy Jr., a water conservation advocate. Davis weaves scientific explanations into their journey and points out areas where conservation and restoration are possible. He also reflects on what was lost when we diverted the river from its natural path.

P. G. Downes, *Sleeping Island:*
The Story of One Man's Travels in the Great Barren Lands
of the Canadian North, **2006.**
Schoolteacher P. G. Downes traveled alone in the Great Barren Lands of the

Canadian North on his summer vacations in the early 20th century. This book chronicles one such trip to the unmapped Nueltin Lake. His respect for the region, its wildlife, and its inhabitants make this book a moving portrait of a now vanished place.

Michael Joseph Oswald, *Your Guide to the National Parks: The Complete Guide to All 58 National Parks*, 2012.

This practical travel guide by award-winning travel writer Michael Joseph Oswald covers the 58 U.S. national parks. He explores every park's hiking trails, campgrounds, and essential gear while offering kid-friendly suggestions. He also provides information on restaurants, places to stay, and nearby attractions.

Lauret Savoy, *Trace: Memory, History, Race, and the American Landscape*, 2015.

In this sweeping history of North America, from deep time to the present, Lauret Savoy traces the creatures and humans who have lived on the continent. Savoy herself is of African American, European American, and Native American descent, and she uses her body to represent these races who lived on and shaped the land.

918 Geography of & Travel in South America

Bruce Chatwin, *In Patagonia*, 1977.

British novelist and travel writer Bruce Chatwin spent six months in Patagonia, at the tip of South America, with only his dog for company. When he published his account of his time there, the book became a classic. However, residents of the region later asserted his depiction of events wasn't wholly factual.

John Gimlette, *At the Tomb of the Inflatable Pig: Travels Through Paraguay*, 2003.

You seldom find Paraguay represented in literature. John Gimlette seeks to make up for the inattention with this exploration of Paraguay's natural beauty and hair-raising history. In addition, the quirkiness of this country makes for entertaining reading.

David Grann, *The Lost City of Z: A Tale of Deadly Obsession in the Amazon*, 2009.

Legends of the lost kingdom of El Dorado have inspired explorers to tackle the Amazon seeking gold, then later, scientific and archaeological glory. David Grann's book centers around the expedition in 1925 with British explorer Percy Fawcett and his 21-year-old son. The expedition vanished without a trace.

Candice Millard, *The River of Doubt:*
Theodore Roosevelt's Darkest Journey, **2005.**
When Theodore Roosevelt lost the election of 1912, he distracted himself
by setting out to traverse and map a dangerous, uncharted tributary of the
Amazon, the River of Doubt, with his son Kermit and Cândido Mariano da
Silva Rondon, a famous Brazilian explorer. Candice Millard provides this
account of the dangerous trip, on which three men died and Roosevelt came
close to suicide.

919 Geography of & Travel in Other Areas

Jim Bell, *The Interstellar Age:*
Inside the Forty-Year Voyager Mission, **2015.**
In 2012, the Voyager One spacecraft left our solar system. Its first mission was
to explore the solar system itself, beyond the moon, past Saturn, and possibly
into interstellar space. Jim Bell, a scientist who worked on the mission, details
the people and science behind this historic feat.

Bill Bryson, *In a Sunburned Country,* **2001.**
Bill Bryson gives us his ode to Australia, an equally hospitable and dangerous
country and continent. He appreciates the clean cities with their cheerful
inhabitants. But he also enjoys its spectacular coastlines and deserts and
takes you into these beautiful but brutal regions.

Robyn Davidson, *Tracks,* **1980.**
Born in Queensland, Australia, Robyn Davidson decided to walk across the
Australian Outback, with only four camels and a dog for companions, after
attending college in Brisbane. She shares her trials and adventures in this
memoir of crossing the continent and finding herself.

Julian Dowdeswell and Michael Hambrey,
The Continent of Antarctica, **2019.**
Earth's least understood and explored continent, Antarctica, is examined in
this book by two authors who have spent time in fieldwork both on the land
and in the oceans surrounding it. We now recognize Antarctica as a driver in
our environment's balance. Dowdeswell and Hambrey discuss the threats it
faces as well as its biology and history.

Fergus Fleming,
Ninety Degrees North: The Quest for the North Pole, **2001.**
Before the race to the moon, there was the race to the North Pole. Fergus
Fleming traces the trips Americans, Britons, Scandinavians, and Italians
made to reach it first and the catastrophes that resulted from many of them.
After the dust settled, others made efforts to get there by balloon, ski, airship,
and even motorbike. And these days, the brave set out on foot.

920 Biography, Genealogy, Insignia

Marie Arana, *Silver, Sword, and Stone: Three Crucibles in the Latin American Story*, 2019.

Three lives in Latin America taken together capture the history of the area across a thousand years. The first is Leonor Gonzáles of Peru, who works as a gold miner to survive, just like her late husband. The second is Carlos Buergos, a Cuban who fought in the civil war in Angola. And the third is Xavier Albró, a Jesuit priest who immigrated to Bolivia from Barcelona and worked with the Indigenous people of the area. Marie Arana sees each representing a different component as crucial to understanding Latin American history—wealth, violence, and religion.

Diana Bowder, ed., *Who Was Who in the Greek World, 776 BC–30 BC*, 1983.

A chronological table at the beginning of the book places the highlighted individuals into historical context. Then biographical sketches, written by scholars, describe figures in literary and historical ancient Greece.

Diana Bowder, ed., *Who Was Who in the Roman World, 753 BC–AD 476*, 1980.

As in the book above, the reference contains a chronological table of the figures included. The articles, written by scholars, feature philosophers, poets, military figures, politicians, and other ancient Romans of note.

Franklin W. Knight and Henry Louis Gates Jr., eds, *Dictionary of Caribbean and Afro–Latin American Biography*, 2016.

Using original, extensive research, scholars summarize the lives of notable Caribbean and Latin American individuals of African descent.

921 Optional

Richard Marius, *Thomas More: A Biography*, 1984.

American scholar Richard Marius writes of Thomas More, the "Man for all Seasons," the Tudor lord chancellor of England, who was beheaded for refusing to accept Henry VIII as the head of the Church of England. But while often eulogized for his principles, More was also a human with faults.

Theodore Rosengarten, *All God's Dangers: The Life of Nate Shaw*, 1974.

In 1969, Theodore Rosengarten, a graduate student from Massachusetts, learned of Nate Shaw, a survivor of the defunct radical organization the Alabama Sharecroppers Union. After tracking down the 84-year-old man near Tuskegee, Rosengarten recorded Shaw's story. Though illiterate, Shaw had an

astounding intellect and memory that he used to tell the disturbing experiences of many Black Americans.

923 Optional

Esther Forbes, *Paul Revere and the World He Lived In*, 1942.
Historian and prolific writer Esther Forbes wrote this biography of one of
America's founding fathers and Revolutionary War heroes, Paul Revere.

Paul Murray Kendall, *Richard the Third*, 1955.
American scholar Paul Murray Kendall wrote this classic study of the life of
one of England's most controversial and reviled kings.

Booker T. Washington,
***Up From Slavery: An Autobiography*, 1901.**
Though he was born a slave, Booker T. Washington became head of the
Tuskegee Institute, a teacher's college for Black Americans. He gave speeches
urging the White community to aid African Americans in educating themselves so they could become meaningful contributors to society. This classic
autobiography articulates his life and works.

925 Optional

Henry Guerlac, *Lavoisier—the Crucial Year:*
The Background and Origin of His First Experiments
***on Combustion in 1772*, 1972.**
The role Antoine-Laurent de Lavoisier played in the history of science should
be considered as important as those of Newton and Darwin, says Henry
Guerlac. He relates Lavoisier's discovery of the role of air in combustion and
how it tipped off the chemical and industrial revolutions.

927 Optional

Lawrence and Elisabeth Hanson,
***The Noble Savage: A Life of Paul Gauguin*, 1955.**
Biographers Lawrence and Elisabeth Hanson based this classic work on
French artist Paul Gauguin on his letters and previously unavailable material.

Giorgio Vasari, *The Lives of the Artists*, 1550.
Sixteenth-century Italian painter and architect Giorgio Vasari wrote this collection of biographical sketches of the great artists. The biographies scan the
beginning, middle, and end of the Renaissance period. The work also presents
an influential theory of Renaissance art. The Oxford University Press edition
from 1971 includes 36 sketches, including Giotto, Brunelleschi, Leonardo,
and Michelangelo.

928 Optional

Pearl S. Buck, *My Several Worlds: A Personal Record*, 1954.

American Nobel Laureate Pearl Buck writes this memoir of her life, the first half of which was primarily spent in China, where her parents were missionaries. Most of her books, including *The Good Earth*, are set there. However, the China she portrays is now long gone.

Frank McCourt, *Angela's Ashes: A Memoir*, 1996.

While Frank McCourt's autobiography has wrenching descriptions of poverty and cruelty, it will inspire you with its beautiful language and dignity of spirit. Once you've read it, you won't forget it.

Vladimir Nabokov, *Speak Memory: An Autobiography Revisited*, 1951.

Twentieth-century master writer Vladimir Nabokov's autobiography chronicles his life from his birth in St. Petersburg to his immigration to the U.S., where he wrote *Lolita* and other significant novels. He provides insights into his works and discusses teaching literature at Wellesley, Stanford, Cornell, and Harvard.

Ernest Samuels, *Henry Adams*, 1989.

In 1989, Belknap Press released a one-volume edition of the biography of Henry Adams that was initially published as a set of three volumes. Henry Adams wrote his autobiography, *The Education of Henry Adams*, but Samuels's work provides a more objective view of the celebrated journalist and scholar.

Ernest J. Simmons, *Chekov: A Biography*, 1962.

Anton Chekov was one of the 19th century's literary giants. Ernest J. Simmons's biography details Chekov's life, including his marriage to an actress and his career as a physician and writer.

929 Genealogy, Names & Insignia

J. P. Brooke-Little, *An Heraldic Alphabet*, 1985.

Heraldry refers to family coats of arms or genealogies. For either the casual enthusiast or the expert, Richmond herald of arms John Philip Brooke-Little's dictionary of heraldry and heraldic terms gives a comprehensive overview of the topic and over 300 drawings to illustrate the subjects.

Fox Butterfield, *All God's Children: The Bosket Family and the American Tradition of Violence*, 1995.

Willie Bosket began committing crimes at age five. By age 15, he had killed two passengers on a New York City subway. This crime led to the passage of the first law in America to try teenagers as adults. Fox Butterfield traces

Bosket's history back through five generations to their enslavement in South Carolina. He demonstrates how Bosket was a product of neglect, cruelty, and discrimination passed down through generations.

John H. Davis, *The Guggenheims: An American Epic*, 1994.

The Guggenheim family is one of the wealthiest and most influential in America. John H. Davis traces the rise of the family's standing, its tragedies, and its prominent lives.

Alice Eichholz, ed., *Red Book:*
American State, County, and Town Resources, 1992.

This revised and updated 2004 third edition of the Ancestry.com reference provides state-by-state records of each area's county and town listings and maps. Researchers can benefit from the census records of each location included, along with information on the vital records kept in various localities.

Christopher Hibbert,
The House of Medici: Its Rise and Fall, 1975.

The Medici family of Florence had an incredible influence on Renaissance politics and art. English historian Christopher Hibbert traces the rise of this dynasty from the early 1430s with Cosimo de Medici to the eras of the Medici Popes to the end of their reign in 1737 from bankruptcy.

Whitney Smith,
Flags through the Ages and Across the World, 1975.

Whitney Smith's reference represents 157 nations using over 3,000 illustrations covering historical, national, and regional flags. Smith presents flag usage, rules, types, shapes, and devices and includes coats of arms and symbols.

930 History of Ancient World to Ca. 499

Mary Beard, *Confronting the Classics:*
Traditions, Adventures, and Innovations, 2013.

Scholar Mary Beard provides essays exploring our classical heritage through stories of Roman emperors and conquerors. But she also sketches other members of society by telling their jokes and peeking into palaces and slave quarters.

Craig Childs, *Finders Keepers:*
A Tale of Archaeological Plunder and Obsession, 2010.

Nations have often imported archaeological plunder from their countries of origin. Black-market artifact trading still occurs. NPR commentator Craig Childs exposes these crimes in archaeology.

M. I. Finley, *Atlas of Classical Archaeology*, 1977.
Classical scholar M. I. Finley provides an atlas of the classical world with maps, diagrams, and descriptions for each time and place.

Marilyn Johnson, *Lives in Ruins: Archaeologists and the Seductive Lure of Human Rubble*, 2014.
Marilyn Johnson spends time sweating and digging in the dirt alongside modern archaeologists to help us understand their work lives. It's nothing like Indiana Jones. Archeologists work hard for little recognition and reward. Johnson discovers why they do it.

932 Egypt to 640

Stacy Schiff, *Cleopatra: A Life*, 2010.
Who was Cleopatra, queen of Egypt, underneath the myths? Pulitzer Prize–winning biographer Stacy Schiff goes back to contemporary sources to reveal a woman who, before age 40, was responsible for the deaths of three siblings, two of whom she had been married to. And she gave birth to children resulting from affairs with both Julius Caesar and Mark Antony. Cleopatra finally sealed her fate when she attempted to link Rome with Egypt through her alliance with Antony.

Toby Wilkinson, *The Rise and Fall of Ancient Egypt*, 2013.
While focusing on the pharaohs and other power structures, Toby Wilkinson, an expert on ancient Egypt, covers thousands of years of Egyptian history. The world he presents is filled with propaganda, violence, and oppression.

933 Palestine to 70

Flavius Josephus and Paul L. Maier, ed., *Josephus: The Essential Writings*, 1987.
The Jewish historian Josephus lived from 37 to 100 CE. He witnessed events of the time firsthand, including the First Jewish-Roman War, in which he led the Jewish forces in Galilee. He witnessed the Siege of Jerusalem and the resulting destruction of the Second Temple. While his work, especially his writings on early Christianity, is essential, historians note that he was writing for the emperor, and therefore, some of it is propaganda. This volume is a condensation of *Jewish Antiquities* and *The Jewish War*, translated by the editor.

936 Europe North & West of Italy to Ca. 499

Dianne Ebertt Beeaff, *Spirit Stones: Unraveling the Megalithic Mysteries of Western Europe's Prehistoric Monuments*, 2011.
Stone circles, monoliths, and burial chambers throughout Western Europe are majestic, mysterious, and captivating. Using extensive research, journalist

Dianne Ebertt Beeaff looks at them through an archaeological lens and considers their spiritual implications today.

Charlotte Higgins,
Under Another Sky: Journeys in Roman Britain, 2013.
The Romans occupied Britain for roughly 400 years. Charlotte Higgins looks at this epoch through the eyes of those who followed it. How does the medieval Geoffrey of Monmouth present it? How about modern poets? Then, traveling around the island on foot and by camper van, Higgins tries to see the same landscapes through the eyes of the Romans.

Christopher B. Krebs, *A Most Dangerous Book: Tacitus's Germania from the Roman Empire to the Third Reich*, 2011.
Classics professor Christopher B. Krebs looks at *Germania*, an unflattering book about the ancient Germans written in 98 CE by the Roman historian Tacitus. Throughout history, questionable ideologies have appropriated it. For instance, the Nazis held it up as a bible of how German society should be structured.

937 Italy & Adjacent Territories to 476

Mary Beard, *SPQR: A History of Ancient Rome*, 2016.
Anyone who's ever wanted to read a history of the Roman Empire from its inception as a small Iron Age village to its collapse at the hands of the barbaric hordes would do well to read this work by renowned classicist Mary Beard. After decades of study, Beard presents a history that brings the era to life, and she corrects common misconceptions in the process.

Annelise Freisenbruch, *Caesars' Wives: Sex, Power, and Politics in the Roman Empire*, 2011.
Politics in ancient Rome was often a raucous affair. Classics researcher Annelise Freisenbruch looks at the women of the era. The wives, daughters, and siblings of Rome's elite men lacked independent power, but they nevertheless had an outsized influence on the turn of events.

Tom Holland,
Rubicon: The Last Years of the Roman Republic, 2003.
When it was just over 700 years old, the Roman Republic experienced a civil war, led by Julius Caesar, transforming the republic into an empire. English historian Tom Holland tells the story of the momentous event, which began with Caesar leading his army across the Rubicon and into Rome.

D. G. Kousoulas, *The Life and Times of Constantine the Great: The First Christian Emperor*, 1997.
D. G. Kousoulas tells the story of Emperor Constantine, one of the pivotal figures of history. In some ways, Constantine's story is the story of world history.

938 Greece to 323

J. E. Lendon,
Song of Wrath: The Peloponnesian War Begins, 2010.
  Historian J. E. Lendon traces the events of the first decade of the
  Peloponnesian War, the ten years of war between Athens and Sparta. He
  details its causes, the strategies used, and the battles that resulted.

939 Other Parts of Ancient World

C. W. Ceram, *The Secret of the Hittites:*
The Discovery of an Ancient Empire, 1955.
  German journalist C. W. Ceram was the author of several popular works on
  archaeology, including this work on the Hittites of the Middle East. He based
  this history on a recently discovered trove of cuneiform tablets.

Nicholas Clapp,
The Road to Ubar: Finding the Atlantis of the Sands, 1998.
  For centuries, many thought the ancient Arabian city of Ubar, "the Atlantis of
  the sands," a myth. But in the 1980s, an amateur archaeologist, Nicolas Clapp,
  learned of the legend of Ubar while studying historical manuscripts. Taking
  his film crew, scientists, and geologists on two expeditions to the Arabian
  Peninsula, they uncovered the city for the world to see.

940 History of Europe

Stephen Greenblatt,
The Swerve: How the World Became Modern, 2012
  American scholar and literary critic Stephen Greenblatt relates the discovery,
  600 years ago, of the one surviving copy of *On the Nature of Things*, by the
  Roman poet Lucretius that contained unthinkable ideas. Two examples are
  that religion harms humanity and that matter is made up of tiny particles
  continuously in motion. The work influenced artists, scientists, and thinkers
  from Galileo to Thomas Jefferson and changed the world forever.

Adam Hochschild, *To End All Wars:*
A Story of Loyalty and Rebellion, 1914–1918, 2011.
  Adam Hochschild focuses on the controversy surrounding the First World
  War, deemed a truly senseless case of horrific carnage. Hochschild looks at
  why and how it happened. By examining the resisters brutally punished for
  their objections to the war and families split apart due to differing opinions,
  he reveals a similar time to today.

Tony Judt, *Postwar: A History of Europe Since 1945*, 2006.
  Tony Judt narrates the history of Eastern and Western Europe from the end

of World War II through the early 21st century. The events and developments encompass 34 nations to help you understand more recent events in Europe.

Graham Robb, *The Discovery of Middle Earth: Mapping the Lost World of the Celts*, 2013.

Graham Robb was planning a bicycling trip along the Heraklean Way, an ancient route from Portugal to the Alps, when he realized that the placement of towns and holy places aligned with astronomical and geometrical measurements. The path dated back to the time of the Celts, a culture that once covered Europe from Ireland to the Black Sea. Robb considers what his findings reveal about their world.

Jay Rubenstein, *Armies of Heaven: The First Crusade and the Quest for Apocalypse*, 2011.

Medieval historian Jay Rubenstein relates the chilling history of the First Crusade, a holy war that resulted in unimaginable brutality and horror. In telling the story from the vantage point those who witnessed it, he unveils the apocalyptic thought that motivated unthinkable atrocities.

Timothy Snyder, *Black Earth: The Holocaust as History and Warning*, 2015.

Historian Timothy Snyder outlines how Hitler leveraged existing anti-Semitism to scapegoat an entire people and its chilling parallels with recent events. The Holocaust, the largest genocide in history, is a warning of what could come. Snyder says we must plan for the upheavals looming ahead due to political, social, and ecological disasters like climate change.

BIOGRAPHY

Laura Hillenbrand, *Unbroken: A World War II Story of Survival, Resilience, and Redemption*, 2010.

Louis Zamperini, a young World War II bombardier whose plane crashed into the Pacific Ocean in 1943, is the subject of this narrative by Laura Hillenbrand. She shows how his unbreakable will helped him survive, at first alone on a raft and then through the events that followed.

Géraldine Schwarz, *Those Who Forget: My Family's Story in Nazi Europe—a Memoir, a History, a Warning*, 2020.

Journalist Géraldine Schwarz sheds light on a sadly common phenomenon. While her German grandparents were not instrumental in furthering the Third Reich, neither did they oppose it. Instead, they were *Mitläufer* or ones who followed the current. She discovered documents indicating that her grandfather Karl had bought a business from a Jewish family for a rock bottom price. When a surviving member of that family demanded reparations, her grandfather refused responsibility. She also explores her family's French side, and together they raise questions about guilt and accountability.

George Takei, et al., *They Called Us Enemy*, 2019.

In this graphic memoir, George Takei, the actor who portrayed Hikaru Sulu in the 1960s television series *Star Trek*, recounts his imprisonment in the U.S. Japanese internment camps during World War II. Takei was only a child when, in 1942, Japanese Americans were incarcerated. The impacts on his life were immense. There are three books in this series.

Edgar Vincent, *Nelson: Love and Fame*, 2004.

Vice admiral Horatio Nelson was a British war hero who was famed for equal success in love. In this biography, Edgar Vincent gives attention to both, from his affair with Emily Hamilton to his tragic death at Trafalgar while fighting Napoleon.

941 British Isles

Geoffrey Moorhouse, *Sun Dancing: A Vision of Medieval Ireland*, 1997.

English journalist Geoffrey Moorhouse looks at the monastic community that lived for 600 years on the isolated, barren Skellig Islands off the coast of Ireland. Placing the community within the context of medieval monasticism, he imagines what life must have been like for these monks in unbelievably harsh circumstances. In addition, he examines how Celtic mythology influenced their beliefs and uncovers surprising ties to India, Egypt, and Byzantium.

Paul Thomas Murphy, *Shooting Victoria: Madness, Mayhem, and the Rebirth of the British Monarchy*, 2012.

As European monarchies toppled, Queen Victoria of England stayed in power for 64 years. Paul Thomas Murphy examines the motivations of the nine would-be assassins who made serious attempts on the queen's life. He shows how the attacks served to strengthen Victoria's popularity and hold on power.

Graham Robb, *The Debatable Land: The Lost World Between Scotland and England*, 2019.

Graham Robb looks at the history of the border of Scotland and England from Roman Britain through today. He examines the myths and bloody disputes that were once a part of this hotly contested stretch of land.

BIOGRAPHY

Arthur Cash, *John Wilkes: The Scandalous Father of Civil Liberty*, 2006.

Eighteenth-century English politician John Wilkes lived a colorful life. As a libertarian and father of the free press, his defense of civil liberties made him a hero to the American colonists. Unfortunately, his political spats led to bloodshed and imprisonments. His private life included membership in the Hellfire Club and the composition of the dirtiest poem in the English language at that time.

David Cecil, *Melbourne*, 1939.
Originally published as two volumes, *The Young Melbourne* and *Lord M*, the author intended they be combined into one as they are here. William Lamb, the Second Viscount Melbourne, is known today as Queen Victoria's first prime minister. In addition, he was a master of conversation and had previously been married to Lady Caroline Lamb.

Antonia Fraser, *Cromwell: The Lord Protector*, 1972.
Oliver Cromwell, leader of the rebellion that resulted in the beheading of England's King Charles I, has frequently been portrayed as a puritanical zealot. But celebrated British biographer Antonia Fraser says this is a misunderstanding. Instead, she demonstrates that he genuinely sought to improve Britain and that prosperity grew under his leadership.

Antonia Fraser, *Mary, Queen of Scots*, 1969.
Antonia Fraser tells the story of Mary, Queen of Scots, a woman who seemed to have it all. But instead of following a politically prudent course, she followed her heart and lost everything, including her head.

Antonia Fraser,
Royal Charles: Charles II and the Restoration, 1979.
After Oliver Cromwell, King Charles II of England gained the throne. While he is sometimes described as a feckless, clueless womanizer, the Charles portrayed by Antonia Fraser is sensible and competent.

William Manchester, *The Last Lion: Winston Spencer Churchill: Visions of Glory*, 1874–1932, 1984.
William Manchester narrates the first 58 years of Sir Winston Churchill's life. From his birth in 1874 in Blenheim Palace to the end of World War II, Churchill experienced a combination of adventure, wealth, military prowess, and national leadership unparalleled in Britain's history.

Charles Moore, *Margaret Thatcher: Herself Alone: The Authorized Biography*, 2019.
Charles Moore's three-part biography tells the story of Britain's first female Prime Minister. Margaret Thatcher was pugnacious in pursuing her aims, which included her push for the fall of the Berlin Wall. Moore outlines her opposition to the European Union, her humiliating forced retirement, and the legacy she left behind.

942 England & Wales

David Day, *The Search for King Arthur*, 1995.
Canadian author David Day looks at the legends of King Arthur and traces
their origins. Starting with the historic Artorius from Roman Britain to today,
he examines the evolving portrait of the once and future king. Illustrations of
the Arthurian stories through the ages complement the work.

Garrett Mattingly, *The Armada*, 1959.
In 1588, the entire world's future hung in the balance as the Spanish Armada
approached the British shoreline. Acclaimed historian Garrett Mattingly
recounts and assesses the impact of the event. If the British had not won, all
of North America would likely be Spanish-speaking today.

John Stubbs,
Reprobates: The Cavaliers of the English Civil War, 2011.
Those dashing curly-haired young men dressed in long jackets and carrying swords have long been the stuff of romantic fancy. Scholar John Stubbs
sketches the cavaliers using poems, diaries, letters, and biographies describing them before, during, and after the English Civil War.

Henri and Barbara Van Der Zee, *William and Mary*, 1973.
The Van Der Zees tell how the acession of Dutch William of Orange and
Mary Stuart to the English monarchy in 1688 ushered in an era of power for
England unrivaled by any other European nation save France.

BIOGRAPHY

Anna Beer, *Patriot or Traitor:*
The Life and Death of Sir Walter Raleigh, 2018.
Sir Walter Raleigh was a star in the court of Queen Elizabeth I. His rise in
rank from the fifth son of a Devonshire gentleman resulted in careers as politician, courtier, and spy and made his forays into the military and exploration
possible. But, after Elizabeth's death, his fall was swift.

Elizabeth Jenkins, *Elizabeth the Great: A Biography*, 1958.
Novelist Elizabeth Jenkins details the daily life of Queen Elizabeth I. Rather
than focusing on policy and intrigue, Jenkins looks at topics of conversation,
meals, and living conditions to provide a glimpse into the private world of
"Good Queen Bess."

J. J. Scarisbrick, *Henry VIII*, 1968.
Tudor England historian J. J. Scarisbrick shines a spotlight on Henry VIII's

outsized personality and its effect on his life, policies, religion, and the lives of
his people.

943 Germany & Central Europe

Gordon A. Craig, *Germany 1866–1945*, 1980.

Gordon A. Craig covers the history of Germany from Prussia's defeat of
Austria in 1866 to the fall of the Third Reich in 1945, focusing on Bismarck
and Hitler. In addition, he looks at how the treatment of German women and
the role of education and religion influenced events.

Peter Hetherington, *Unvanquished: Joseph Pilsudski, Resurrected Poland, and the Struggle for Eastern Europe*, 2011.

The story of Józef Pilsudski, the father of Polish independence, contains true
tales of both world wars, train robberies, Siberian exile, prison escapes, and
assassination plots. Peter Hetherington reveals the colossal impact Pilsudski
had on the history of Poland, the Soviet Union, and Europe as a whole.

Erik Larson, *In the Garden of Beasts: Love, Terror, and an American Family in Hitler's Berlin*, 2011.

American author Erik Larson relates the year following the 1933 arrival in
Berlin of the American ambassador to Germany, William E. Dodd. At first,
Dodd, his wife, son, and daughter Martha were entranced by the parties,
romance, and impressive men they met there. Martha embarks on a series of
affairs with one man after another. But as the sinister laws and mistreatment
of Jews mount, the family comes to understand the true nature of Hitler's
intentions and the Nazi agenda.

Richard Reeves, *Daring Young Men: The Heroism and Triumph of the Berlin Airlift, June 1948–May 1949*, 2010.

The fate of West Berlin was in the hands of airmen from America, Germany,
and Great Britain in June 1948, when Joseph Stalin ordered a blockade of the
city, determined to gain control, even at the risk of a third world war. Using
the records of these servicemen, Richard Reeves tells of the creation of West
Berlin, West Germany, and NATO.

William L. Shirer, *The Rise and Fall of the Third Reich: A History of Nazi Germany*, 1960.

This worldwide bestseller by contemporary foreign correspondent William L.
Shirer traces the Nazi rise to power from 1925 onward. Using the testimony
of Nazi leaders, concentration camp inmates, diaries, transcripts, and letters,
in addition to the ample paperwork the Nazis left behind, Shirer crafted this
narrative of the most destructive and powerful empire in history.

BIOGRAPHY

Victor Klemperer, *I Will Bear Witness: A Diary of the Nazi Years 1933–1941*, 1999.

Jewish World War I veteran Victor Klemperer recognized the danger Hitler posed by 1933. Klemperer writes of everything around him in his diary, focusing mainly on average German citizens, such as the local baker and the dentist. He tells how his life's supports, from his job to his cat, are stripped away one by one.

Peter Longerich, *Hitler: A Biography*, 2019.

Rather than focus on Hitler's childhood and World War I experiences, German historian Peter Longerich focuses on Nazism's effect on him. He traces Hitler's single-minded and ruthless pursuit of power and his political giftedness that made his ascension possible. A combination of charisma and political maneuvering secured Hitler's regime. Longerich says Hitler, the man, did not create and control the Third Reich. Instead, Hitler was propaganda that embodied the movement.

Jonathan Steinberg, *Bismarck: A Life*, 2011.

Otto von Bismarck, who united Germany in the late 19th century, is regarded as one of its most intelligent leaders. Jonathan Steinberg reveals he was also a diabolical and brutal genius, with contempt for humanity as a whole and human beings in particular.

Elie Wiesel, *Night*, 1956.

Holocaust survivor Eliezer Wiesel writes of the night in 1944 when he and his family were taken from their home in Transylvania, first to Auschwitz and later to Buchenwald. A teenager at the time, Wiesel witnessed his family's deaths and wrote searingly of his confrontation with the evil in man. He stresses that this can never be allowed to happen again.

944 France & Monaco

Frederic L. Cheyette, *Ermengard of Narbonne and the World of the Troubadours*, 2004.

Viscountess Ermengard was a 12th-century woman warrior who ruled Occitania, which later became France. She traveled her extensive lands, receiving fealty, negotiating treaties, and settling disputes in an unstable political climate. Frederic L. Cheyette recreates her world, which the fabled troubadours shared.

Philip Hallie, *Lest Innocent Blood Be Shed:*
The Story of the Village of Le Chambon
and How Goodness Happened There, **1979.**

Philosophy professor Phillip Hallie tells of Le Chambon, a village in southern
France whose occupants worked together to spare thousands of Jews from the
concentration camps. Remarkably, the operation was carried out peacefully in
full view of the Vichy government and a nearby division of the Nazi SS.

Graham Robb,
The Discovery of France: A Historical Geography, **2006.**

Graham Robb traces the development of France from pre-Christian tribes to
today. He tells of the mapmakers, soldiers, scientists, and ordinary people in
its history. He also contemplates mysteries about France that remain.

Simon Schama,
Citizens: A Chronicle of the French Revolution, **1990.**

Scholar Simon Schama explores the 18th-century court of Louis XVI. Rather
than seeing it as a period of decadence and decay, he sees the era as one
of technological progress. Against this backdrop, Schama examines the
French Revolution.

Barbara Tuchman,
A Distant Mirror: The Calamitous 14th Century, **1978.**

Historian Barbara Tuchman presents a detailed examination of 14th-century
France. She provides an overview of greater European events of the time
alongside an intimate look at the daily lives of the rich and the poor.

BIOGRAPHY

Nancy Mitford, *The Sun King,* **1966.**

Nancy Mitford chronicles the life of King Louis XIV of France, with a focus on
his day-to-day life. The Sun King built the lavish palace of Versailles, turning it into the most dazzling court in Europe. Mitford highlights his military,
artistic, and romantic conquests.

Tom Reiss, *The Black Count: Glory, Revolution, Betrayal,*
and the Real Count of Monte Cristo, **2012.**

French writer Alexander Dumas, the author of *The Three Musketeers,* based
some of his best-loved heroes on his father, General Alex Dumas. Born in
Saint-Domingue, now known as Haiti, Dumas was the son of an enslaved
Black person and, for a time, was enslaved himself. But after entering the
army in France, he won his way into the French aristocracy.

Andrew Roberts, *Napoleon: A Life*, 2014.
Historian Andrew Roberts uses newly published private letters of Napoleon
Bonaparte to provide a more accurate one-volume account of the military
genius who rose from common roots to challenge the European order.

945 Italy, San Marino, Vatican City, Malta

Robert Hughes,
***Rome: A Cultural, Visual, and Personal History*, 2011.**
Australian art critic Robert Hughes began writing his biography of Rome
in 1959 because, as a new resident, he was captivated by the city's art and
color. He traces its beginnings, through its rise to empire, Christianity, the
Renaissance, and through to the early 21st century.

Frederic C. Lane, *Venice: A Maritime Republic*, 1973.
Historian Frederic Chapin Lane provides this history of Venice, one of the
world's most fascinating cities.

946 Spain, Andorra, Gibraltar, Portugal

Richard Fletcher, *The Quest for El Cid*, 1991.
Rodrigo Díaz was an 11th-century Castile warrior knight, a national hero in
Spain for taking the country back from the Muslim Moors and restoring it to
the Christian Spanish. Historian Richard A. Fletcher looks at the historical
record to determine which legends about him are true.

Robert Goodwin,
***Spain: The Centre of the World 1519–1682*, 2015.**
The years from 1519 to 1682 were the Golden Age of Spain. Robert Goodwin
explores the impact Spain had worldwide during this period and its lasting
impact today. He also brings to life colorful and notable Spaniards such as
Miguel de Cervantes and Diego Velázquez.

George Orwell, *Homage to Catalonia*, 1938.
George Orwell was sent as a journalist to cover the Spanish Civil War, and he
joined forces with the anti-fascists. He tells of his experiences in this memoir
written after he escaped from Spain and returned to England.

Paul Preston, *The Spanish Holocaust: Inquisition*
***and Extermination in Twentieth-Century Spain*, 2012.**
While the Nazis were seeking power throughout Europe, General Francisco
Franco was fighting for totalitarian control in Spain. By 1945, it was over, with
Franco as the dictator. Paul Preston reports how tens of thousands of Spanish

citizens were executed or killed in battle in the process, while women and children suffered horrific abuse.

BIOGRAPHY

Kirstin Downey, *Isabella: The Warrior Queen*, 2014.
Inspired by Joan of Arc, Queen Isabella of Spain was determined to save her kingdom from the Ottoman Empire. Kirsten Downey tells how, at 23, Isabella seized control of Castile and León by defying her brother and husband. While some of what she accomplished was good for Spain, like seeking its unification and sponsoring Columbus, she also established the infamous Spanish Inquisition.

947 Russia & East Europe

Svetlana Alexievich, *Secondhand Time: The Last of the Soviets*, 2016.
Exiled for her outspoken criticism of the government, Ukrainian journalist Svetlana Alexievich writes this emotional history of the Soviet Union, in which she grew up. She doesn't retell the rise and fall of communism. Instead, she aims to capture what living in the Soviet atmosphere was like, now that it is gone.

Anne Applebaum, *Iron Curtain: The Crushing of Eastern Europe, 1944–1956*, 2012.
Many Eastern European nations placed under Soviet control after World War II had no say in the matter. Joseph Stalin quickly set about using his secret police to convert the citizens of these countries to communism. Pulitzer Prize–winning journalist Anne Applebaum tells how alien the Soviet ideology was to people across widely different cultures. Through interviews and personal accounts, she depicts life in this now-vanished civilization.

Orlando Figes, *Natasha's Dance: A Cultural History of Russia*, 2003.
Historian Orlando Figes chronicles Russia's massive history, its people, its culture, and its spirit. He looks at daily life across social classes and in the arts, and he examines the rise in Western European influences and the rise and fall of communism.

Masha Gessen, *The Future is History: How Totalitarianism Reclaimed Russia*, 2017.
American journalist Masha Gessen tells the heartbreaking and terrifying story of Russia after the fall of the Soviet Union. She follows four individuals

who began the era with high hopes and dreams, only to have them dashed by the brutal autocracy and mafia-state that has taken its place.

China Miéville,
October: The Story of the Russian Revolution, 2017.

China Miéville presents only the essential facts of the Russian Revolution so that someone completely new to the subject can understand it.

Joshua Yaffa, *Between Two Fires:*
Truth, Ambition, and Compromise in Putin's Russia, 2020.

Foreign correspondent Joshua Yaffa tells how ordinary people try to succeed in Russia under Vladimir Putin. Interviewing the everyday people caught in the system, he tells stories of humanitarians forced to ignore persecutions, and others who try to work to procure privileges for themselves and their families. It's a stark look at life in a totalitarian state today.

BIOGRAPHY

Robert K. Massie,
Catherine the Great: Portrait of a Woman, 2011.

Catherine the Great was only fourteen when she went to Russia with her ambitious mother. Despite her bullying husband, Peter, she managed to transform herself into an intellectual. Upon her accession to the throne, she desired to be an enlightened ruler, as portrayed by the philosophies of the time. But she found Russian culture and life itself often stood in the way.

Robert K. Massie, *Peter the Great: His Life and World*, 1980.

At age ten, Peter the Great was crowned Russian monarch. At the time, Russia was still in a feudal system, and Peter, interested in and influenced by Western Europe, sought to reform it. Unfortunately, while he was interested in scientific and political progress, he could also be cruel. But he succeeded in moving Russia from a distant, unimportant country toward becoming a mighty nation.

Victor Sebestyen,
Lenin: The Man, the Dictator, and the Master of Terror, 2017.

Soviet Russia's first leader, Vladimir Lenin, was a despot who put thousands to death. But contrary to this political and militant side of Lenin, Victor Sebestyen presents a man who loved nature and was closest to the women in his life. Sebestyen maintains that while Lenin was ruthless, his intentions were often good.

Robert Service, *Stalin: A Biography*, 2010.

British scholar of Russian history Robert Service provides this one-volume work on Joseph Stalin's rise to power and his crucial role in World War

II and its aftermath. Throughout, Service seeks to find what motivated Stalin's actions.

William Taubman, *Gorbachev: His Life and Times*, 2018.

Mikhail Gorbachev, Soviet leader during the dissolution of the Soviet Union, rose to power from peasant roots. William Taubman reveals how he did it through interviews, transcripts, and archival documents.

Boris Yeltsin, *Midnight Diaries*, 2000.

Boris Yeltsin, the first democratically elected leader of Russia, was also the first to resign, after eight years in office. He tells how his leadership began with high hopes, but economic and political crises and corruption led to a loss of support.

948 Scandinavia & Finland

Michael Booth, *The Almost Nearly Perfect People: Behind the Myth of the Scandinavian Utopia*, 2014.

English food and travel writer Michael Booth lived for over a decade in the Scandinavia of Denmark, Finland, Iceland, Norway, and Sweden. The more time he spent there, the more unhappy he became with Western media's portrayal of them as ideal societies. In this book, he seeks to set the record straight.

949 Other Parts of Europe

Kapka Kassabova, *Border: A Journey to the Edge of Europe*, 2017.

Kapka Kassabova writes about the peculiar landscape and atmosphere of her childhood home near the borders of Turkey and Greece in Bulgaria during the Cold War. She looks at the long history of the area, penetrating myth and legend.

Claudio Magris, *Danube*, 1986.

German scholar Claudio Magris travels central Europe from the source of the Danube River in Bavaria and through Austro-Hungary to the Balkans and ending at the Black Sea. Along the way, he stops at towns, cities, and other areas of interest to share the events and people he encounters on his sentimental journey.

Orhan Pamuk, *Istanbul: Memories and the City*, 2006.

Orhan Pamuk's account of Istanbul has been compared to *Dublin* by James Joyce and *Buenos Aires* by Luis Borges. Born to glamourous, celebrity parents, Pamuk lived all his life in the same apartment they shared. He astutely observed the city throughout his life and wrote a portrait as he saw it.

Russell Shorto,
Amsterdam: A History of the World's Most Liberal City, **2013.**
> Shorto is not a native of Amsterdam, but he has made it his home. He traces the city's complex history from its earliest days to today, revealing what shaped the liberal ideas and governance it is known for today.

Katherine Verdery,
My Life as a Spy: Investigations in a Secret Police File, **2018.**
> While a student in Romania in the 1970s, Katherine Verdery came under scrutiny by the *Securitate*, or secret police, as a suspected spy, CIA agent, and Hungarian agitator. The government amassed a large surveillance file documenting evidence of her illicit activities. But all their accusations were wrong. Granted access to the files decades later, after the Cold War, Verdery discovered close friends had reported her for benign activities that, to them, seemed suspicious.

950 History of Asia

Edward W. Said, *Orientalism*, **1978.**
> Literature professor Edward W. Said searches for the differences and similarities of Eastern and Western cultures. He asserts that the West's centuries-long dominance in the Middle and Near East gave it a position of power used to define the East as *oriental*, meaning *other*. Said seeks to portray the East on its terms, providing a fresh, holistic look at the world.

Jack Weatherford,
Genghis Khan and the Making of the Modern World, **2005.**
> The Mongols conjure images of horse-borne hordes of nomads who used brutality on the battlefield to conquer large swaths of Asia. But under the leadership of Genghis Khan, a man of genius and foresight, they also improved living conditions for the conquered through superior governance, communication, and technology. Anthropologist Jack Weatherford shows us the real Genghis Khan and how he paved the way for the modern world.

951 China & Adjacent Areas

John F. Avedon, *In Exile from the Land of Snows:*
The Definitive Account of the Dalai Lama and Tibet
Since the Chinese Conquest, **1984.**
> John F. Avedon interviews the 14th Dalai Lama to determine how he was exiled from Tibet.

Iris Chang, *The Rape of Nanking:*
The Forgotten Holocaust of World War II, **1998.**
> Iris Chang tells the harrowing story of the Japanese invasion of Nanking,

China, in 1936. Over 300,000 Chinese civilians were raped, tortured, and murdered in the ordeal.

David Halberstam,
The Coldest Winter: America and the Korean War, 2007.

Basing his work on decades of research, David Halberstam explores the story of the Korean War and America's place in it. He covers the events and leaders of the era and sheds light on U.S. conflicts since.

Jang Jin-sung,
Dear Leader: My Escape from North Korea, 2014.

Jang Jin-sung was North Korea's state poet laureate, a coveted position in Kim Jong-il's regime. But when he lent a strictly forbidden magazine to a friend and the magazine went missing, he had to flee for his life. *Dear Leader* tells the story of how he escaped and his inside account of North Korean life.

Stephen R. Platt, *Imperial Twilight:*
The Opium War and the End of China's Last Golden Age, 2018.

Award-winning historian Stephen Platt tells of China's fall from power in the 19th-century Opium War. While the Chinese were coping with decline and using foreign trade for profit, they fell victim to brutal mistreatment in the wars. The first Opium War was fought with Great Britain beginning in 1839, and the second was fought with the combined forces of Great Britain and France starting in 1856. These wars set the stage for Chinese relations with the West today.

Joshua Wong, *Unfree Speech: The Threat to Global*
Democracy and Why We Must Act, Now, 2020.

At age 14, Joshua Wong began his career as an activist in Hong Kong when he led the first successful student protest against National Education. Since that time, he has been both imprisoned and nominated for a Nobel Peace Prize. Here, he calls for the global community to defend democratic values.

BIOGRAPHY

Jonathan Fenby, *Chiang Kai-Shek:*
China's Generalissimo and the Nation He Lost, 2005.

In 1928, Chiang Kai-shek was the leader of the government in Nanking, having risen to power in the Kuomintang, the Nationalist movement in China. Jonathan Fenby charts Chiang's fall through the conflicts between the Japanese and the Chinese Communists.

Alexander V. Pantsov, *Mao: The Real Story*, 2012.

Alexander V. Pantsov uses previously unavailable Russian documents to tell of Mao Zedong's life. His relationship with Stalin provided security for his brutal restructuring of Chinese society to bring the country out of crushing poverty.

But the country's culture suffered as the result. After Stalin's death, Mao distanced himself from the Soviet Union and renewed relations with the U.S.

952 Japan

Amy Chavez, *Amy's Guide to Best Behavior in Japan: Do It Right and Be Polite!*, 2018.

Tourist advisor and 25-year Japanese resident Amy Chavez advises you on expectations for everything from greetings to your tone of voice for your trip to Japan. It's good to have handy because many Japanese people are too polite to correct you themselves.

Norma Field, *In the Realm of a Dying Emperor: Japan at Century's End*, 1993.

Emperor Hirohito brought Japan to a devastating defeat at the end of World War II. When he died in 1989, journalists did not risk writing anything negative about him because they feared violent retaliation from the country's political right wing. But Norma Field tells of three citizens who dared to speak out: a flag-burning supermarket owner, an aging widow who protested the deification of fallen soldiers, and the mayor of Nagasaki.

Conrad Totman, *Japan Before Perry: A Short History*, 1982.

History professor Conrad Totman looks at past epochs of Japanese history, from its beginnings through the classical, medieval, and early modern periods. He traces how its leaders influenced the culture and set the stage for Japan as we know it today.

BIOGRAPHY

Herbert P. Bix, *Hirohito and the Making of Modern Japan*, 2001.

American historian Herbert P. Bix provides the first objective biography of the controversial 20th-century Japanese emperor Hirohito. In his early years, Hirohito aligned himself with a growing ultranationalist movement that contained a religious element of emperor worship, culminating with Japan's involvement in World War II. But after the war, he stayed in power with help from the Allies, who saw him as essential in maintaining peace in the Asian Pacific.

953 Arabian Peninsula & Adjacent Areas

Steve Coll, *The Bin Ladens: An Arabian Family in the American Century*, 2008.

It only took two generations for the Bin Laden family to move from poverty to extreme wealth and power. Steve Coll tells the story of how they accomplished it in a tale that mirrors the rise of Saudi Arabia.

Bradley Hope and Justin Scheck, *Blood and Oil: Mohammed bin Salman's Ruthless Quest for Global Power*, 2020.

Hope and Scheck, two *Wall Street Journal* reporters, look at Saudi Arabia's crown prince Mohammed bin Salman. While early on, the crown prince seemed to want expanded rights for his citizens, that image was tarnished with the news that he ordered the brutal death of journalist Jamal Khashoggi. After revelations that he held over 300 people, including family members, hostage for months, bin Salman has revealed himself as an autocratic leader.

954 India & South Asia

William Dalrymple, *The Anarchy: The East India Company, Corporate Violence, and the Pillage of an Empire*, 2019.

William Dalrymple provides a glimpse at what a corporate state looks like in the history of Britain's East India Company. The corporation took over the better part of southern India after defeating the Mughal emperor in 1765. It ran the nation for 47 years, using a private army to collect taxes from the populace.

Sam Miller, *Delhi: Adventures in a Megacity*, 2010.

British writer Sam Miller presents Delhi, one of the world's fastest-growing cities, precisely as he finds it. His snapshot takes you from the typical tourist sites to those commonly overlooked and everyday inhabitants, rich and poor.

Samanth Subramanian, *This Divided Island: Life, Death, and the Sri Lankan War*, 2014.

For nearly three decades in recent history, the idyllic island nation of Sri Lanka fought a bloody civil war that ended in 2009 when the leader of the Tamil Tigers' guerrilla forces was killed. Indian journalist Samanth Subramanian looks at the history of the war and its damage to the nation.

BIOGRAPHY

Ramachandra Guha, *Gandhi: The Years that Changed the World: 1914–1948*, 2018.

From the time he left South Africa for his native land in 1914 until his assassination in 1948, Mohandas Gandhi inspired millions of Indians under foreign rule to band together in nonviolent resistance. His methods succeeded in bringing about Indian independence where violence could not. His philosophy and tactics have been followed successfully worldwide, notably in the U.S. by Martin Luther King Jr. This is the second part of a two-part biography.

955 Iran

**Kim Ghattas, *Black Wave: Saudi Arabia, Iran,
and the Forty-Year Rivalry that Unraveled Culture,
Religion, and Collective Memory in the Middle East*, 2020.**
Many of us don't realize that before the Iranian Revolution of 1979, Saudi
Arabia and Iran were close allies who worked together with the U.S. to keep
the Soviet Union out of the region. The events that caused the rift between
Sunni Saudi Arabia and Shia Iran have been at the heart of a geopolitical battle ever since. International affairs correspondent Kim Ghattas tells how the
rupture happened, what resulted, and what may happen next.

**Ramita Navai, *City of Lies:
Love, Sex, Death, and the Search for Truth in Tehran*, 2014.**
British Iranian journalist Ramita Navai reports on the hidden side of
Tehran, in which gun running and sex are big industries. By looking at the
lives of eight people caught up in this secret world, including a porn star
and an assassin, Navai captures the underbelly of life in the repressive
Iranian regime.

**Scott Peterson, *Let the Swords Encircle Me:
Iran—A Journey Behind the Headlines*, 2010.**
Award-winning journalist Scott Peterson has taken over 30 trips to Iran. He
celebrates the nation once known as Persia, an ancient culture brimming with
poetry, art, and history. While Peterson admires the everyday people of Iran,
he also examines the fraught relationship between modern Iran and the U.S.

956 Middle East (Near East)

**Rania Abouzeid, *No Turning Back:
Life, Loss, and Hope in Wartime Syria*, 2019.**
Journalist Rania Abouzeid went into the heart of Syrian conflicts to figure
out exactly what is going on in the country. She uses the stories of four young
people whose lives are entangled in the battle to illustrate the larger picture.

**Michael Brenner,
In Search of Israel: The History of an Idea, 2018.**
The makeup of modern Israel has been controversial, even among its advo-
cates, since the days Theodor Herzl called the First Zionist Congress in 1897.
While many wanted it to contain both Jews and non-Jews, others wanted it
to be a solely Jewish nation, distinct and apart from its neighbors. Michael
Brenner traces the past 70 years of Israeli history with these contradictory
aims in view.

Bernard Lewis, *The Middle East:*
***A Brief History of the Last 2,000 Years*, 1997.**

Bernard Lewis traces the chronological history of the Middle East, from the beginnings of Christianity to the 20th century, using research from scholars and archaeologists.

Ilan Pappe, *The Biggest Prison on Earth:*
***A History of the Occupied Territories*, 2016.**

International studies professor Ilan Pappé examines how Israel has treated the inhabitants of the Occupied Territories in the West Bank. He uses archival research, records, and eyewitness accounts to document the abuses that effectively turn these citizens into prisoners.

Thomas E. Ricks,
***Fiasco: The American Military Adventure in Iraq*, 2006.**

American journalist Thomas E. Ricks follows the missteps that led to the chaos in Iraq after America invaded the country. Fundamental failures to understand the issues on the ground, such as the motives behind the insurgency, led the U.S. forces to make mistakes at crucial moments.

Joby Warrick, *Black Flags: The Rise of ISIS*, 2015.

On ascending to the throne in 1999, King Abdullah of Jordan released a group of political prisoners including Abu Musab al-Zarqawi, who would become a terrorist of unprecedented scale. When the Americans invaded Iraq in 2003, al-Zarqawi had become the head of a massive insurgency that later became the Islamic State, or ISIS, seeking to establish an enormous ultraconservative caliphate.

BIOGRAPHY

Francine Klagsbrun,
***Lioness: Golda Meir and the Nation of Israel*, 2017.**

The life of fourth Israeli prime minister, Golda Meir, begins in Russia in 1898, where she was born, then moves to America, where she grew up, and on to Palestine, where she relocated with her husband in 1921. She became the leader of Israel primarily through chance events that were aided by her political and organizational skills. She fought directly with some of the most imposing men of her era yet managed to maintain a grandmotherly mystique.

Alan Mikhail, *God's Shadow: Sultan Selim, His Ottoman*
***Empire, and the Making of the Modern World*, 2020.**

Western culture largely ignored or suppressed the events and history of the Ottoman Empire. Alan Mikhail focuses on the omnipotent ruler

Sultan Selim I (1470–1520) and reveals a world that sheds new light on many familiar historical events.

957 Siberia (Asiatic Russia)

Ian Frazier, *Travels in Siberia*, 2010.

American writer and humorist Ian Frazier travels to Siberia, one of the most mysterious places on the planet. He looks at the region's landscapes and history in terms of science, economics, and politics while recounting stories of the people he meets along the way.

958 Central Asia

Steve Coll, *Directorate S: The C.I.A. and America's Secret Wars in Afghanistan and Pakistan*, 2018.

Steve Coll looks at the relationship of the U.S. with the I.S.I.—the Pakistani intelligence agency. Directorate S was a hidden sector of the I.S.I. that was secretly arming, training, and trying to legitimize the Taliban during the war in Afghanistan. Coll picks apart their tangled web of deception.

William Dalrymple, *Return of a King: The Battle for Afghanistan, 1839–42*, 2013.

The first war in Afghanistan against Western forces was the tribal revolt against the British when, in 1839, they invaded the country and placed Shuja Shah on the throne to serve as their puppet ruler. William Dalrymple relates the story of the 1842 jihad resulting in British defeat in the mountains. Roughly 18,000 British troops died, with only one making it back to the British garrison at Jalalabad.

Anand Gopal, *No Good Men Among the Living: America, the Taliban, and the War through Afghan Eyes*, 2014.

According to Anand Gopal, the longest war in America's history, that in Afghanistan, could have ended within months were it not for a series of American mistakes, false intelligence, and a fixed mindset about the enemy. He says the Taliban were ready to surrender and accept the new government, but U.S. officials could not believe it. So instead of negotiating, they pressed the conflict, resulting in the escalating insurgency.

Cathy Scott-Clark and Adrian Levy, *The Exile: The Stunning Inside Story of Osama bin Laden and Al Qaeda in Flight*, 2017.

Osama bin Laden was forced into exile for years after the 9/11 attacks. Levy and Scott-Clark interview people who were with him there, including the wives of bin Laden and his right-hand man, Khaled Sheikh Mohammed. They trace how he slipped out of the sights of U.S. forces multiple times by traveling throughout Pakistan.

Doug Stanton, *Horse Soldiers:*
The Extraordinary Story of a Band of U.S. Soldiers
Who Rode to Victory in Afghanistan, **2009.**

Journalist Doug Stanton tells the stories of an American Special Forces
unit that entered Afghanistan on horses, a modern day cavalry, pursued
the Taliban across mountains, battled them, and finally captured the city of
Mazar-i-Sharif. While the citizens welcomed the Americans as liberators,
the POWs they were taking into custody turned and ambushed them. The
Americans fought off their prisoners in the city's fortress, Qala-i-Jangi, also
known as The House of War.

BIOGRAPHY

Mohamedou Ould Slahi,
Guantanamo Diary, **2017.**

In 2002, Mauritanian citizen Mohamedou Ould Slahi was imprisoned at
Guantanamo Bay in Cuba. Though never charged with a crime, he is still
there today. At one point, a U.S. federal judge ordered him released, but the
government fought against it. The diary of his daily life and the events that led
to his incarceration is now titled *The Mauritanian.*

959 Southeast Asia

The Pentagon Papers:
The Defense Department Secret History
of the Vietnam War, **1972.**

When the Pentagon Papers were leaked to the press in 1971, they revealed lies
the Johnson administration told the American people about the conflict in
Vietnam. More startling, they showed that even the top brass at the Pentagon
considered the war a hopeless cause.

Al Santoli, *Everything We Had:*
An Oral History of the Vietnam War by Thirty-Three
American Soldiers Who Fought It, **1985.**

Al Santoli tells the story of the Vietnam War through the voices of the soldiers
who were there.

William Shawcross, *Sideshow:*
Kissinger, Nixon, and the Destruction
of Cambodia, **1979.**

Richard Nixon and Henry Kissinger waged a secret and illegal war against
Cambodia from 1969 to 1973. They used the excuse that North Vietnamese
soldiers were attacking Americans from across the border, but rather than
helping the situation, William Shawcross says, secret war led to the rise of the
Khmer Rouge and the Killing Fields of Cambodia.

Neil Sheehan, *A Bright Shining Lie: John Paul Vann and America in Vietnam*, 1989.

American journalist Neil Sheehan tells of the reports leaked to him amid the Vietnam conflict from Lt. Col. John Paul Vann, who served as a field advisor to the army in the early days of the war. Vann, stonewalled when he reported the South Vietnamese corruption and indifference to his superiors, secretly told reporters, like Sheehan, his experiences.

BIOGRAPHY

Max Boot, *The Road Not Taken: Edward Lansdale and the American Tragedy in Vietnam*, 2018.

Edward Lansdale (1908–1987) was a CIA operative, the first to use "hearts and mind" diplomacy in Southeast Asia. That his methods were reviled and dismissed is a tragedy. Military historian Max Boot tells the story of the largely forgotten man who was called the T. E. Lawrence of Asia.

Jean Lacouture, *Ho Chi Minh: A Political Biography*, 1968.

French historian Jean Lacouture wrote this biography of Ho Chi Minh, the father of Vietnamese independence. As a left-leaning journalist, Lacouture supported the independence of Vietnam and came to know the leader personally.

Loung Ung, *First They Killed My Father: A Daughter of Cambodia Remembers*, 2006.

Until age 5, Loung Ung led an upper-class life, but in 1975, her father, a high-ranking Cambodian government official, was killed by the Khmer Rouge. While her siblings went to labor camps, Loung was trained as a child soldier in a work camp for orphans. She relates how her remaining family members came together again after the regime's fall.

960 History of Africa

Martin Meredith, *Born in Africa: The Quest for the Origins of Human Life*, 2011.

Over 20 species of extinct humans have been identified so far. And that they originated in Africa, along with *Homo sapiens*, is no longer in doubt. Meredith shows how we know this and speculates on what it means for all of us.

Martin Meredith, *The Fate of Africa: From Hopes of Freedom to the Heart of Despair: a History of Fifty Years of Independence*, 2005.

Most independent African nations in the late 20th century had high hopes for prosperity and peace. But most have failed to achieve their goals. Historian and journalist Meredith Martin examines the continent's state at the turn of the 21st century and looks at the events and factors that hindered its progress. A revised and updated version is available.

Jocelyn Murray, *Cultural Atlas of Africa*, 1981.
Jocelyn Murray's atlas of African historical civilizations, revised in 1998, covers those long past through the late 20th century.

962 Egypt, Sudan, South Sudan

Martin Mosebach,
***The 21: A Journey into the Land of Coptic Martyrs*, 2019.**
In 2015, ISIS militants released a video in which they beheaded 21 Christian men, all dressed in orange, on a beach in Libya. All but one of these men were Coptic Christians from Egypt. Martin Mosebach interviewed their families to understand how they came to be there.

965 Algeria

Alistair Horne,
***A Savage War of Peace: Algeria 1954–1962*, 1977.**
English journalist Alistair Horne provides a complete history of the war for independence fought against the French in Algeria. Few remember the struggle that resulted in the French government's collapse, returning Charles de Gaulle to power, almost causing a French civil war. Over a million Algerians died in the struggle.

BIOGRAPHY

Elsa Marston,
***The Compassionate Warrior: Abd el-Kader of Algeria*, 2013.**
American author Elsa Marston relates the story of 19th-century Algerian Muslim hero Abd el-Kader (1808–1883). Fighting against French colonization, he proved brilliant on the battlefield as a strategist and as a statesman. He was also a philosopher renowned for his kindness, even to his enemies. Today he is honored as a pioneer in interfaith dialogue.

966 West Africa & Offshore Islands

Greg Campbell, *Blood Diamonds: Tracing the Deadly Path of the World's Most Precious Stones*, 2004.
Greg Campbell tells the shocking story of how, for decades, diamonds were smuggled from Sierra Leone to international diamond houses in London, New York, and Antwerp. The diamond industry was complicit in their sale to

unsuspecting consumers worldwide. Campbell traces their paths from the mines to their use in funding a bloody conflict in Sierra Leone. The book has been revised in a second edition.

Dante Paradiso,
The Embassy: A Story of War and Diplomacy, 2016.

For years, Liberia was one of the most dangerous places on the planet, and its president, Charles Taylor, was a warlord. Then, in 2003, two rebel armies of militia and child soldiers marched on the capital, Monrovia, to overthrow his government. Dante Paradiso tells how the U.S. embassy aided the efforts to remove the president and tried, unsuccessfully, to stem the bloodshed.

BIOGRAPHY

Ishmael Beah,
A Long Way Gone: Memoirs of a Boy Soldier, 2007.

Ishmael Beah, now living in the U.S., tells of the destruction of his home in Sierra Leone when he was twelve. At thirteen, he was picked up by the government army and trained as a child soldier. Here he tells the heart-breaking story of his training, which took him from a gentle boy to a professional killer.

K. Riva Levinson, *Choosing the Hero: My Improbable Journey and the Rise of Africa's First Woman President*, 2016.

Lobbyist and international consultant K. Riva Levinson details her activities around the world fighting for justice. This book focuses on the work she is most proud of: her efforts to help elect Africa's first woman president, Ellen Johnson Sirleaf of Liberia. Levinson documents the events leading to the election and the successes Sirleaf has since had in turning her war-devastated country around.

967 Central Africa & Offshore Islands

Cheryl Bentsen, *Maasai Days*, 1991.

When Cheryl Bentsen began to spend time in Kenya, she entered a six-year relationship with the Maasai people. She presents photos of her friends and discusses their way of life, just as their culture became modernized.

Caroline Elkins, *Imperial Reckoning:*
The Untold Story of Britain's Gulag in Kenya, 2000.

Caroline Elkins investigates how, in the aftermath of World War II, Britain destroyed the records of the Kikuyu people's rebellion in the Mau Mau Uprising in Kenya in which they sought their freedom and lands. Instead, the British colonial government placed well over a million of them in camps. From 1952 to 1960, close to 100,000 died from ill treatment.

Adam Hochschild, *King Leopold's Ghost: A Story of Greed, Terror, and Heroism in Colonial Africa*, 1999.

King Leopold II of Belgium was a psychopathic leader who wreaked devastation on the Congo River's lands in Central Africa. While promoting a humanitarian image, he was looting the area of its riches and contributing to the deaths of roughly ten million people. Adam Hochschild tells how individuals from various nations brought the story to light at grave risk to themselves.

Ben Rawlence, *City of Thorns: Nine Lives in the World's Largest Refugee Camp*, 2016.

British journalist Ben Rawlence travels to the Dadaab refugee camp in Kenya, the largest of its type in the world. He follows nine people to uncover what life for them is like in the camp. While it's a dangerous environment, it's also the only option for its residents.

Jason K. Stearns, *Dancing in the Glory of Monsters: The Collapse of the Congo and the Great War of Africa*, 2011.

The nation of Congo is the size of Western Europe. American writer Jason K. Stearns spent ten years there and reported the forces that unleashed war and kept it going. In this book, he interviews and relates the tales of crucial players and ordinary people caught up in the conflicts through no fault of their own. Millions of lives have been lost in the conflict.

968 South Africa & Southern Africa

William Kamkwamba, *The Boy Who Harnessed the Wind: Creating Currents of Electricity and Hope*, 2009.

William Kamkwamba, born in Malawi, dreamed of bringing electricity and running water to his poor village. While people mocked him as crazy, he read books on how energy worked. He later used his books, scrap metal, tractor parts, and bicycle halves to build a small power plant providing running water and electricity to his parents.

Thomas Pakenham, *The Boer War*, 1992.

The Boer Wars were a series of skirmishes in South Africa between the Afrikaners and the British and the Dutch settlers of the region. The term *boer* is Dutch for farmer. This book contains over 200 illustrations and images to help explain the war's central figures, events, causes, and results.

BIOGRAPHY

Nelson Mandela, *Long Walk to Freedom: The Autobiography of Nelson Mandela*, 1995.

Nobel Peace Prize–winner Nelson Mandela spent 27 years in prison for his political activism in South Africa, fighting against apartheid. He told how he grew up in traditional tribal culture but gradually learned of the injustices of his country's political system as a law student in Johannesburg. He voiced the personal struggles he faced and his years of imprisonment, which ended in 1990.

970 History of North America

Roxanne Dunbar-Ortiz, *An Indigenous Peoples' History of the United States*, 2014.

Scholar Roxanne Dunbar-Ortiz fills the missing parts of U.S. history, covering 400 years from the vantage point of its native peoples. Lies and genocide form the core of their treatment.

Christopher Felver, *Tending the Fire: Native Voices & Portraits*, 2017.

To help you understand the voices of Native Americans today, Christopher Felver presents writers and poets from all across North America's Indigenous cultures. With a portrait of each artist, followed by their writings, he captures the unique voice of each.

Dina Gilio-Whitaker, *As Long as Grass Grows: The Indigenous Fight for Environmental Justice From Colonization to Standing Rock*, 2019.

Activist and American Indian Studies scholar Dina Gilio-Whitaker looks at today's environmental activism in light of the Indigenous peoples' experiences with the U.S. government and their long battles for environmental justice. She focuses on the leadership of Indigenous women.

Tony Horwitz, *A Voyage Long and Strange: Rediscovering the New World*, 2008.

When Tony Horwitz visited Plymouth Rock, the exhibit raised more questions than answers. He wondered what happened on the continent from the arrival of Columbus to the first settlement at Jamestown. So he traveled to critical locations to find out, starting with the Viking settlements in Newfoundland and ending up in Jamestown. The book's subtitle was later changed to *On the Trail of Vikings, Conquistadors, Lost Colonists, and Other Adventures in Early America*.

David Treuer, *The Heartbeat of Wounded Knee: Native America from 1890 to the Present*, 2019.

Many people think Native American culture is dying out with its people either assimilated or confined to reservations. Not so, says Ojibwe anthropologist and author David Treuer. On the contrary, the years since Wounded Knee have been a story of consolidating Native identity, leading to new resistance.

Carl Waldman, *Atlas of the North American Indian*, 1981.

Last updated in 2000, this atlas shows the territories of Indigenous peoples of North America from prehistory to the present. It considers events and issues with Indigenous cultures through the mid-20th century. Canada, the U.S., Mexico, Central America, and the Caribbean are covered.

Jack Weatherford, *Indian Givers: How the Indians of the Americas Transformed the World*, 1989.

Anthropologist Jack Weatherford explores the debt the rest of the world owes to America's Indigenous peoples. He demonstrates how they have influenced our government, medicine, agricultural practices, and architecture. In the process, Weatherford uncovers many forgotten facets of our history.

BIOGRAPHY

Charles Eastman (Ohiyesa), *Living in Two Worlds: The American Indian Experience*, 2009.

Charles Eastman (1858–1939) was born a traditional Woodland Sioux and raised as such by his grandmother. When he was fifteen, his father, who everyone thought was dead, showed up and insisted he gain a White man's education. So Eastman went to Dartmouth and to Boston University Medical School. He was the only doctor to attend the wounded victims of the Wounded Knee massacre in 1890. In this book, Eastman writes of the Native American experience of his time, using the unique perspective of his firsthand experience of truly living in both cultures.

William Least Heat-Moon, *Columbus in the Americas*, 2002.

American travel writer William Least Heat-Moon bases his portrait of Christopher Columbus on Columbus's logbooks and many other firsthand accounts. From his first landing on Guanahani, the island Columbus named San Salvador, to the year he spent in southern Jamaica, his exploits and abuses are covered. Least Heat-Moon argues Columbus set the example for Europeans that followed.

971 Canada

James West Davidson and John Rugge, *Great Heart: The History of a Labrador Adventure*, 1988.

Davidson and Rugge write of Leonidas Hubbard, a man who, in 1903, was hired by an outdoors magazine to travel Labrador by canoe. Hubbard began the expedition with his best friend Dillon Wallace and a Scots Cree guide named George Elson. Hubbard starved to death before completing the mission. Then two years later, his widow, Mina, and Wallace headed separate expeditions, each racing to be first to complete the expedition in a hostile competition.

Charlotte Gray,
Gold Diggers: Striking it Rich in the Klondike, **2010.**

Canadian writer Charlotte Gray reveals her research on the world's last great gold rush, in the Canadian Yukon. Using letters, memoirs, news articles, and stories, she highlights six men and women from the period, including writer Jack London, who made their way to Dawson City.

BIOGRAPHY

David Hackett Fischer, *Champlain's Dream,* **2008.**

Samuel de Champlain was an unusual European explorer. Born and raised on the coast of France, he fought in France's religious wars under Henri IV. He spent his life aboard ships, becoming an expert navigator. Champlain traveled through six Canadian provinces and five U.S. states while in America. He is chiefly responsible for the French presence in the New World and was committed to establishing peace with and among the Indigenous groups. His belief in peace and harmony among races and religions is exceptional for his time.

972 Mexico, Central America, West Indies

Jeff Biggers, *In the Sierra Madre,* **2007.**

After spending a year in the Sierra Madre with the Rarámuri (Tarahumara), award-winning journalist Jeff Biggers wrote this cultural and historical view of the Mexican mountain range. He explored the stories of the Indigenous cultures, mountaineers, explorers, deserters, commandos, and archaeologists, among others, who made their way to the region.

Laurent Dubois, *Avengers of the New World:*
The Story of the Haitian Revolution, **2005.**

In 1791, the island of Saint-Domingue was the most profitable colony in the Atlantic region. Laurent Dubois affirms that it was also the year the only successful slave revolt began. The insurgents forced the French to emancipate them, backed up by revolutionary Paris in 1794. Later, when a complicated combination of British, Spanish, and later French forces again attacked the island, the ex-slaves soundly defeated them, leading to the independence of Haiti and reshaping the world.

David McCullough, *The Path Between the Seas:*
The Creation of the Panama Canal 1870–1914, **1977.**

Few people realize how much effort was required to build the Panama Canal. When stock for the Panama Railroad, made to serve traffic heading from the East Coast to the Pacific, became the highest-priced stock on the New York Stock Exchange, investors decided it was time to build a 51-mile canal. In just over 40 years, the workers excavated enough dirt and rock to reach a mile

high. When Theodore Roosevelt took up the foundering project, he helped
foment a revolution to liberate Panama from Colombia and put it under control of the U.S.

Douglas Preston,
The Lost City of the Monkey God: A True Story, 2017.

Since the time of Cortés, Honduras harbored the legend of the White City,
also called the Lost City of the Monkey God. According to rumors, anyone
who enters the cursed city will fall ill and die. In 1940 Theodore Morde
claimed to have found it and had artifacts to back up his story, but he committed suicide before revealing the location. Douglas Preston recounts how
he joined a team of scientists that entered the jungle with modern equipment
and located a city. But many of the participants found, on returning, they had
contracted a horrifying disease.

Jim Rasenberger, *The Brilliant Disaster: JFK, Castro,*
and America's Doomed Invasion of Cuba's Bay of Pigs, 2011.

When Fidel Castro took over Cuba in 1959, America planned to invade with
American-trained Cubans to take back their island. Jim Rasenberger tells of
the failed attempt, in April 1961. Over 1,000 people were killed or imprisoned
in the effort. The CIA, President John F. Kennedy, and other top American
officials were involved. Rasenberger links the fiasco to the Cuban Missile
Crisis and possibly Kennedy's assassination.

Hugh Thomas, *Conquest:*
Montezuma, Cortés, and the Fall of Old Mexico, 1994.

British historian Hugh Thomas uses previously unavailable sources to share
the story of the battle between the Indigenous Mexican civilization, led by
Montezuma, and the Spanish forces, led by Cortés, for the land of Mexico.

BIOGRAPHY

P. J. Patterson,
My Political Journey: Jamaica's Sixth Prime Minister, 2018.

This autobiography of Jamaican prime minister P. J. Patterson relates his role
in shaping the country from its colonial days into today's modern nation. Not
only did he have a significant impact on Jamaica but he also garnered international recognition for the work he did to help other developing countries
around the world.

Tad Szulc, *Fidel: A Critical Portrait*, 1986.

Foreign correspondent Tad Szulc knew Cuban leader Fidel Castro personally. He describes Castro's childhood in Jesuit schools, his role in the Cuban
Revolution, and beyond. Castro led Cuba as its dictator for more than four
decades and brought the world to the brink of nuclear war.

973 United States

The number of books on U.S. history made it impossible to stick to my ten-or-fewer-books-per-category guidelines. So for this section, I broke from the DDC system. Instead, I divided these books into the following five categories:

- books covering more than one century
- books that cover the years before 1800
- books that cover 1801–1900
- books that cover 1901 to the present
- biographies of U.S. presidents

U.S. HISTORY ACROSS CENTURIES

Andrew Delbanco, *The War Before the War: Fugitive Slaves and the Struggle for America's Soul from the Revolution to the Civil War*, 2018.
American Studies professor Andrew H. Delbanco tells of pre-Civil War efforts by both Black and White Americans to abolish slavery. He uses politics, law, literature, and firsthand accounts of civil disobedience, which shed light on the plight of the slaves and the war that resulted from it.

W. E. B. Du Bois, *The Souls of Black Folk*, 1903.
In the late 19th century, people like Booker T. Washington advocated for Black Americans to work within the segregation endemic in the South. Critical of this approach, W. E. B. Du Bois published this book of essays to affirm the dignity of Black Americans. He stated they should accommodate themselves to no one because they are inherently equal. While this book polarized African American viewpoints, it influenced the struggle for civil rights through today.

Doris Kearns Goodwin, *Leadership: In Turbulent Times*, 2018.
To determine what makes a great leader, Doris Kearns Goodwin looks at the lives of four presidents about whom she has previously written: Abraham Lincoln, Theodore Roosevelt, Franklin D. Roosevelt, and Lyndon B. Johnson. She examines the qualities that made them great.

Ana Raquel Minian, *Undocumented Lives: The Untold Story of Mexican Migration*, 2018.
Many Mexicans began migrating to the U.S. in the 1970s when the Mexican government encouraged men to find higher-paying U.S. jobs to sustain their families back in Mexico. However, the U.S. government changed its policy toward them in the 1980s. As a result, the migrants previously traveling back and forth across the border to work and visit with family were now afraid to leave the U.S. for fear of not being allowed back across the border to work. Caught in the crossfire between the nations, they began to call the U.S. the cage of gold.

Ronald Takaki, *Strangers from a Different Shore:*
***A History of Asian Americans*, 1989.**

American historian and ethnographer Ronald Takaki looked at the history
of Asian immigrants in America from the early 19th through the late 20th
centuries. He discloses stories from his own family and interviews others to
provide this narrative account of diverse Asian Americans.

U.S. HISTORY UP TO 1800

Joseph J. Ellis,
***Founding Brothers: The Revolutionary Generation*, 2002.**

The U.S. government, even after it gained independence from Great
Britain, was cobbled together by imperfect human beings. Joseph J. Ellis
sketches these figures, such as Alexander Hamilton, George Washington,
Thomas Jefferson, John Adams, James Madison, and Benjamin Franklin.
Their complex relationships shaped America in ways largely unknown
and unappreciated.

John Ferling, *Whirlwind:*
***The American Revolution and the War that Won It*, 2015.**

John Ferling writes the entire history of the American Revolution in a narrative format, from beginning to end. He covers the causes of the war, the
tactics used to fight it, and its resolution.

David Hackett Fischer, *Washington's Crossing*, 2004.

Before George Washington led his men across the Delaware River in 1776,
the war was nearly over. The British seemed destined to prevail. But the
Christmas night attack on the Hessian garrison at Trenton, New Jersey, began
a series of skirmishes that turned the tide. David Hackett Fischer looks at the
differences in how the two sides fought. He found it crucial that British regi-
mentation and hierarchy were vulnerable to American flexibility.

Pauline Maier, *American Scripture:*
***Making the Declaration of Independence*, 1998.**

Historian Pauline Maier traces the influences on the U.S. Declaration of
Independence. She shows how Americans had forgotten the document until
Abraham Lincoln resurrected it. By dissecting what it meant to our founding
fathers, she shows that our current practice of holding it as an unchangeable,
inflexible document may be defeating its original purpose.

Nathaniel Philbrick,
***Bunker Hill: A City, a Siege, a Revolution*, 2013.**

History writer Nathaniel Philbrick exposes new facets of the Battle of Bunker
Hill, the first full-scale battle in the War for Independence. The stories of
familiar characters such as Paul Revere and George Washington intertwine

with less well known but equally important individuals like physician Joseph Warren, who led American forces and died in the battle.

Gordon S. Wood,
The Radicalism of the American Revolution, 1993.
When the American colonies declared their freedom from Great Britain, they weren't just taking their destiny into their hands. They were making a radical break with their civilization's past. Few today understand how unthinkable their actions were in the eyes of so many. Gordon S. Wood looks at the historical, political, cultural, and economic threads that went into the formation of an entirely new world.

BIOGRAPHY

H. W. Brands, *The First American:*
The Life and Times of Benjamin Franklin, 2002.
Benjamin Franklin did much more than work with electricity and publish *Poor Richard's Almanac*. H. W. Brands uses every source available for this portrait of "America's first Renaissance man." From Franklin's early days as a runaway in Philadelphia to his career as a diplomat and peer to Voltaire and Kant, Brands helps us understand the uniqueness of this American legend.

Ron Chernow, *Alexander Hamilton*, 2005.
Until the blockbuster musical named after him, Alexander Hamilton was a misunderstood founding father. After coming to America as an unknown self-taught orphan from the Caribbean, he served as George Washington's right-hand man, cowrote *The Federalist Papers*, became the first treasury secretary of the U.S., and was a leader in the Federalist Party. Ron Chernow tells about his private life and his death in the duel with Aaron Burr in 1804.

U.S. HISTORY 1801–1900

Fergus M. Bordewich, *Bound for Canaan: The Underground Railroad and the War for the Soul of America*, 2006.
The Americans, Black and White, who objected to slavery were increasingly bold and inventive as the 19th century progressed. Fergus M. Bordewich shows how social consciousness expressed itself in the civil disobedience of the Underground Railroad, used to help enslaved people escape north into freedom.

George C. Daughan, *1812: The Navy's War*, 2011.
The U.S., with only 20 naval vessels, was the underdog in the nation's conflict for the seas in 1812. The British, in contrast, had over a thousand. Historian George C. Daughan reveals how, despite this disadvantage, America won the war.

Shelby Foote, *The Civil War: A Narrative*, 3 vols., 1963.
While this three-volume set is lengthy, it is still considered the most comprehensive look at the Civil War. Shelby Foote not only recounts the events and figures of the war, but he also discusses the massive shifts in American economics and culture it brought. Though a Southerner, Foote based his work on facts and was as objective as possible.

Allen C. Guelzo, *Gettysburg: The Last Invasion*, 2013.
For three days, the Battle of Gettysburg raged on a small tract of land in southern Pennsylvania. It changed the course of the war. Civil War historian Allen C. Guelzo takes you into the conversations between officers, the sights, sounds, and smells of the battlefield, and the experience of the ordinary soldiers.

Joseph M. Marshall III, *The Day the World Ended at Little Big Horn: A Lakota History*, 2008.
Historian Joseph Marshall tells of the Battle of the Little Big Horn from Lakota oral tradition, previously unavailable to those outside its circles. He examines why the battle took place, the men who directed it, and the resulting tragedy for the Lakota peoples.

Brenda Wineapple, *The Impeachers: The Trial of Andrew Johnson and the Dream of a Just Nation*, 2019.
Brenda Wineapple looks at Andrew Johnson's entry into the Oval Office through the Lincoln assassination. With America still deeply divided, Johnson saw little reason to work with Congress or make the South an equitable society. Wineapple argues that due to his opposition to civil rights and support for White supremacy, Congress had no choice but to make him the first American president to be impeached.

BIOGRAPHY

Terry Alford, *Fortune's Fool: The Life of John Wilkes Booth*, 2015.
Before he was killed, John Wilkes Booth was the world's youngest entertainment celebrity. Terry Alford considers why a man with so much to lose threw it all away by publicly shooting the nation's president. Using all available historical records, Alford attempts to uncover Booth's motives.

David W. Blight, *Frederick Douglass: Prophet of Freedom*, 2018.
Historian David W. Blight uses new information to examine the life of Frederick Douglass. Because he learned to read before he escaped from slavery in Baltimore, Maryland, Douglass became a prominent, respected literary voice, a first for a former slave in America. He used his position to

fight for Black civil and political rights and significantly impacted perceptions of African Americans.

Catherine Clinton,
Harriet Tubman: The Road to Freedom, 2005.

Historian Catherine Clinton researched the life of Harriet Tubman, one of the most compelling and mysterious characters of the 19th century. Before the Civil War, Tubman proved herself to be incredibly brave, clever, and resilient through her work leading slaves to freedom as a conductor on the Underground Railroad.

David S. Reynolds, *John Brown, Abolitionist: The Man Who Killed Slavery, Sparked the Civil War, and Seeded Civil Rights*, 2006.

American Studies professor David S. Reynolds sees John Brown as a realist who understood that to rid America of slavery would require bloodshed. Brown was a deeply religious man who hastened the country to Civil War with his raid on Harper's Ferry in 1859.

T. J. Stiles,
Custer's Trials: A Life on the Frontier of a New America, 2015.

T. J. Stiles sees the love–hate relationship America has with George Armstrong Custer as a collision between the world of Custer's childhood and that of his adulthood, with the sweeping changes throughout civilization, a collision exacerbated by Custer's personality.

U.S. HISTORY 1901-PRESENT

Doris Kearns Goodwin, *The Bully Pulpit: Theodore Roosevelt, William Howard Taft, and the Golden Age of Journalism*, 2013.

Doris Kearns Goodwin examines the Progressive Era in the early 20th century through the relationship between Theodore Roosevelt and William Howard Taft. The two were close friends until the presidential election of 1912 when their bitter rivalry split not only their relationship but the Republican party, causing Woodrow Wilson's victory. It was a time, Goodwin asserts, quite like our own.

Greg Grandin, *The End of the Myth: From the Frontier to the Border Wall in the Mind of America*, 2019.

In America, where the rugged individual is free to conquer new frontiers and take on the world, it was about expansion. But Greg Grandin says once this individual dream became a memory, the nation turned its attention to spreading democracy to other countries. But now those doors are closing as well, causing America to experience a dangerous rise in reactionary populism and racist nationalism. He says it's time to end the myth of American exceptionalism.

Jane Mayer, *The Dark Side: The Inside Story of How the War on Terror Turned into a War on American Ideals*, 2008.

Few Americans understand sweeping the changes in American policy beginning shortly after the attacks on September 11, 2001. Jane Mayer shows how, using the panic and chaos of the time, Vice President Dick Cheney and advisor David Addington used the turmoil to make the executive branch more powerful and eliminate constitutional protections for average citizens. Mayer also examines the War on Iraq and its basis on a detainee's confession, obtained under torture and later proven false.

Bill Minutaglio and Steven L. Davis, *Dallas 1963*, 2013.

While many books traced the events leading to JFK's assassination in Dallas, November 1963, none talked about behind-the-scenes activity in the city itself. Kennedy was warned to stay away from Dallas because, according to Minutaglio and Davis, it was full of powerful and shadowy organizations opposing Kennedy's presidency. Radical, polarizing ideologies, they remind us, can do untold harm.

George Packer, *The Unwinding: An Inner History of the New America*, 2013.

Journalist George Packer gives insight into how we got to the current crisis in America. He looks at the lives of ordinary men and women in the Rust Belt and the Deep South, at Beltway insiders, Silicon Valley billionaires, and political and entertainment figures and what they all reveal about the unraveling of our nation's institutions.

Rick Perlstein, *Before the Storm: Barry Goldwater and the Unmaking of the American Consensus*, 2002.

Rick Perlstein asserts that if you want to understand the opposition to liberal America, you need to understand Barry Goldwater, the Republican Senator from Arizona. Goldwater hated both the federal government and liberals. His network with figures such as William F. Buckley and Nelson Rockefeller is crucial to understanding the rise of America's conservative movement.

Studs Turkel, *Hard Times: An Oral History of the Great Depression*, 1970.

Celebrated American historian Studs Turkel interviewed Americans who lived through the Great Depression of the 1930s. They came from all walks of life: those who lost fortunes, those who tried to guide the nation through the crisis, ordinary people, even children share their stories. The resulting portrait sheds direct light on what happened.

Lawrence Wright,
The Looming Tower: Al-Qaeda and the Road to 9/11, 2006.
The events leading up to 9/11 were global in scope and highly complex. But Pulitzer Prize–winning author Lawrence Wright explains what happened using four stories to represent four themes. They are those of al-Qaeda leaders Osama bin Laden and Ayman al-Zawahiri, FBI counterterrorism chief John O'Neill, and the former head of Saudi intelligence Prince Turki al-Faisal. Each perspective adds a crucial layer of understanding to how the attacks occurred.

THE PRESIDENTS

Jonathan Alter, *His Very Best: Jimmy Carter, A Life*, 2020.
Jimmy Carter is one of the most misunderstood presidents of the U.S. Political analyst Jonathan Alter interviewed Carter, his friends, family, and others who knew him, and spent five years searching through his archives to piece together this portrait. Carter was an outsider, fueled by integrity, with a mixed service record to the American people. Alter also explores Carter's humanitarian projects across many decades, partly as penance for his lack of action during the civil rights movement.

A. Scott Berg, *Wilson*, 2013.
A. Scott Berg spent years researching Woodrow Wilson, the 28th president of the U.S. Finding previously unavailable materials, he reveals events of Wilson's life, giving us a fuller portrait of the "scholar–president" who led us through World War I and shaped the world to come.

Robert A. Caro, *The Years of Lyndon Johnson:*
The Path to Power vol. 1; The Means of Ascent, vol. 2; Master
***of the Senate, vol. 3; and The Passage of Power*, vol. 4, 2012.**
Investigative journalist Robert A. Caro wrote this definitive four-volume biography of Lyndon B. Johnson, one of the most powerful politicians in the nation's history, first as Senate majority leader in Congress, then as vice president, and finally as president after the assassination of John F. Kennedy. In addition, he led the country during a significant portion of the civil rights movement and the Vietnam War.

Ron Chernow, *Grant*, 2017.
Ulysses S. Grant has been dismissed as a mediocre president and man. Ron Chernow presents him as a person who struggled with alcoholism throughout his life. And his career, it is true, was foundering before the Civil War began, but once involved in the war, Grant's gifts came to the forefront. By winning battles, he helped save the union. Members of his presidential cabinet involved themselves in scandals, but Grant did not. Instead, he impressed Frederick Douglass with his efforts to help Black Americans and defeat the Ku Klux Klan.

Ron Chernow, *Washington: A Life*, 2010.
Chernow's one-volume biography of George Washington, America's first president, depicts Washington's troubled boyhood in Virginia. Chernow relates Washington's rise in prominence through the French and Indian Wars, the battles he fought for U.S. independence against Britain, and his establishment and shaping of the federal government's executive branch.

Kenneth S. Davis,
FDR: A History: The New York Years 1928–1933,
and *FDR: A History: The New Deal Years 1933–1937*, 1986.
Historian Kenneth S. Davis wrote this third and fourth of a five-volume biography of Franklin Delano Roosevelt, *FDR: A History*. The third volume covers Roosevelt's second term as governor of New York to his election as president and through the early years of the depression. His efforts to help America through the Great Depression with his New Deal policies are the subject of volume four.

Joseph J. Ellis,
***American Sphinx: The Character of Thomas Jefferson*, 1998.**
History scholar Joseph J. Ellis looks at America's third president, Thomas Jefferson. From writing the Declaration of Independence through his retirement from public life, Jefferson was a complex character, both beloved and hated in his own time and today. Ellis gives us insights into his actions.

John A. Farrell, *Richard Nixon: The Life*, 2017.
How Richard Nixon went from an idealistic young man seeking a better world to a bitter, divisive president forced to resign in disgrace is the subject of John A. Farrell's biography. Nixon rapidly rose to power, which he wielded in divisive ways that haunt us still.

Doris Kearns Goodwin, *Team of Rivals:*
***The Political Genius of Abraham Lincoln*, 2006.**
Doris Kearns Goodwin captures the greatness of Abraham Lincoln, explaining how he won the election while running against three more privileged and polished rivals. Goodwin examines how Lincoln then held the White House and the nation together in the darkest hours of a civil war by relying on the advice of these same men, pulling them together to form a group of trusted counselors.

John F. Harris,
***The Survivor: Bill Clinton in the White House*, 2006.**
Bill Clinton was one of the most polarizing presidents in history. Correspondent John F. Harris covered the Clinton presidency for the first six of eight years. He provides an inside look at the Clinton White House and provides an objective, nonpartisan look at Clinton's goals, achievements, and failures.

Fred Kaplan, *John Quincy Adams: American Visionary*, 2014.

John Quincy Adams, America's sixth president, was the son of founding father and second president John Adams. His brilliant years as secretary of state propelled him to the White House, where his progressive ideas combining individual liberty with strong government shaped the country we live in today.

David McCullough, *John Adams*, 2001.

David McCullough based this biography of John Adams, America's second president, in part on thousands of letters between Adams and his beloved, intelligent wife, Abigail. McCullough's biography portrays Adams as highly intelligent and honest, yet inflexible and cranky when he felt the need for it.

David McCullough, *Truman*, 1992.

Harry S. Truman became president with the death of Franklin D. Roosevelt before the end of World War II. As a man from an ordinary background in Missouri, he had plenty of challenges to deal with. He presided over the decision to drop the atomic bombs on Japan, confronted Joseph Stalin at Potsdam, and decided to enter the war in Korea. Yet, in McCullough's skillful retelling, Truman is revealed to be a courageous and stabilizing figure.

Edmund Morris, *The Rise of Theodore Roosevelt*, 2001, and *Theodore Rex*, 2002.

Theodore "Teddy" Roosevelt has proved to be one of American history's most enduringly popular presidents. Biographer Edmund Morris relates Roosevelt's rise to the presidency in the first volume and his two terms in office in the second. Seemingly tireless, Roosevelt met every challenge at home and overseas with decisive action. He is remembered today for his defense of conservation and the creation of the national park system. A third volume, *Colonel Roosevelt*, completes the series.

Barack Obama, *A Promised Land*, 2020.

Barak Obama tells of his childhood, how he became the first Black president of the U.S., and how racism affected his years in office. He discloses what it's like to work with figures like Vladimir Putin and those who opposed him in Congress, while reflecting on the abilities and limitations of presidential power. He also discusses the death of Osama bin Laden in 2011.

Arthur M. Schlesinger Jr., *A Thousand Days: John F. Kennedy in the White House*, 1965.

Historian Arthur Schlesinger witnessed all the important events in the Kennedy White House as Kennedy's special assistant. He used photos and other documents from the John F. Kennedy Library, the LOC, and news outlets of the day to share this portrait of the president before his assassination.

Jean Edward Smith, *Eisenhower in War and Peace*, 2012.

Twentieth-century president Dwight D. Eisenhower was elected in 1952 after a brilliant career as a general in World War II. While some portray him as an ineffective president, political science professor Jean Edward Smith says that's unfair. Eisenhower, he says, kept America from many foreign entanglements and removed our forces from the hopeless war in Korea. And at home, he reduced defense spending and constructed the interstate highway system, among many other accomplishments.

Bob Spitz, *Reagan: An American Journey*, 2018.

Award-winning author Bob Spitz provides this nonpartisan look at Ronald Reagan, another polarizing president from the previous decades. Reagan, Spitz asserts, was not acting while serving as president, as some have suggested. Instead, after rising from a childhood of poverty to the height of power, he was a living embodiment of the American dream and wholeheartedly believed in it. Spitz divulges Reagan's weaknesses but also relates what made him great.

Bob Woodward, *Fear: Trump in the White House*, 2018.

While Donald J. Trump was still in the White House, journalist Bob Woodward spent hundreds of hours interviewing people who worked there, in addition to President Trump himself. He also used meeting notes, diaries, files, and official documents to piece together how the 45th president made his foreign and domestic policy decisions.

974 Northeastern United States

Tyler Anbinder, *City of Dreams:*
The 400-Year Epic History of Immigrant New York, 2016.

America, Tyler Anbinder reminds us, is a nation of immigrants. And New York City is the only city in the world built mainly on immigration. From its beginnings as a small settlement in 1626, the metropolis grew through its port of entry. Anbinder illuminates the stories of famous New York immigrants from Alexander Hamilton to Oscar de la Renta. And he tells the stories of its immigrants today.

Kerri Arsenault,
Mill Town: Reckoning with What Remains, 2020.

After growing up in the mill town of Mexico, Maine, Kerri Arsenault, a descendant of generations of mill workers, looks at the effects of the industry on the environment, the economy, and the health of the town's residents. After the mill closed down, only a depressed area called Cancer Valley remained. Arsenault documents all this through interviews, archives, and scientific reports.

George Bellerose, *Forty-Six Years of Pretty Straight Going:*
The Life of a Family Dairy Farm:
The Weyman Farm, Weybridge, Vermont, **2010.**

George Bellerose traces the history of Vermont's farming communities beginning with the state's first settlers. He then focuses on the Weyman family,
with photographs that provide a glimpse at what it's like to run a working
Vermont farm today.

Jim Dwyer and Kevin Flynn, *102 Minutes: The Untold Story*
of the Fight to Survive Inside the Twin Towers, **2006.**

On September 11, 2001, there were nearly 14,000 people inside the World
Trade Center when the first plane flew into the north tower. Dwyer and Flynn
trace the tragic event from the perspective of those inside the buildings. Many
people survived the impacts but were unable to get out. These are the stories
told by the survivors.

Sebastian Junger,
The Perfect Storm: A True Story of Men Against the Sea, **1997.**

While fishing out in the North Atlantic, the six-man ship *Andrea Gail* was
caught in a nor'easter that was considered a once-in-a-century storm. Junger
describes what he learned about the crew and their time battling the storm to
their tragic end.

James H. Merrell, *Into the American Woods:*
Negotiators on the Pennsylvania Frontier, **2000.**

From the time Quakers settled the Pennsylvania colony in the 1680s until the
1750s, Europeans and Indigenous Americans traveled back and forth between
the two cultures to serve as unofficial diplomats to help preserve the peace.
They were called the go-betweens. History professor James H. Merrell tells
how they survived in the spaces between two profoundly different cultures
until it all collapsed in war after 1750.

Michael Rawson,
Eden on the Charles: The Making of Boston, **2010.**

Boston, in the 19th century, brought clean water, transportation, and parks to
its inhabitants, beginning its modern incarnation. Michael Rawson explains
how innovations in Boston shaped other American cities and how various
classes and ethnic groups left their marks on today's city.

David Von Drehle,
Triangle: The Fire that Changed America, **2004.**

On March 25, 1911, a fire started in the Triangle Shirtwaist factory in
Greenwich Village, in New York City. Before workers could escape, the
fire spread to the upper floors. The ladders firefighters used to rescue
those trapped inside could not reach the top. As a result, many workers

jumped from the windows to die on the streets below. Of the 146 people killed, 123 were women. The tragedy changed the argument over U.S. labor practices.

BIOGRAPHY

Robert A. Caro, *The Power Broker: Robert Moses and the Fall of New York*, 1975.

Robert Moses never held public office, but he had more influence on the buildings and policies of New York City than any politician of his time. Robert A. Caro looks at how Moses created a political and economic machine from which he amassed a fortune and kept the city and the state from reaching their potential—until, in Nelson Rockefeller, he met his nemesis.

975 Southeastern United States

T. D. Allman, *Finding Florida: The True History of the Sunshine State*, 2013.

Florida has one of the most diverse state populations in the U.S. Originally, it was primarily swamp, but it's now filled with playgrounds for the rich and the retired. After spending ten years researching the state's history, journalist T. D. Allman uncovers the truth of Florida.

Edward L. Ayers, *The Promise of the New South: Life After Reconstruction*, 1993.

White Americans in the South tried to maintain a genteel image after Reconstruction, but underneath there was a current of racism and violence. Humanities professor Edward L. Ayers captures images across social class, race, and geography to present a social and political snapshot we are still reconciling with today.

John Berendt, *Midnight in the Garden of Good and Evil: A Savannah Story*, 1999.

New Yorker John Berendt visited Savannah in the early 1980s and began to probe into a sensational murder that occurred inside an old mansion in May 1981. Berendt got to know this southern cast of characters as the city's inhabitants grappled with the case. With its undercurrent of death and mayhem, the city of Savannah itself becomes a gothic character.

Carter Taylor Seaton, *Hippie Homesteaders: Arts, Crafts, Music, and Living on the Land in West Virginia*, 2014.

Carter Taylor Seaton tells of the Vietnam War protesters and draft evaders who flocked to the mountains of West Virginia to live off the land in the 1960s. Though many later left, Seaton profiles 40 who stayed and made their living from the arts, crafts, music, and farm work they performed.

Bertram Wyatt-Brown, *Southern Honor:*
Ethics and Behavior in the Old South, **1983.**

An ancient honor code guided White society in the American South before the
Civil War. Bertram Wyatt-Brown used legal documents, letters, diaries, and
newspaper articles from the time to shed light on where this system came
from and how it worked.

BIOGRAPHY

Henry Louis Gates Jr., *Colored People,* **1995.**

Henry Louis Gates is an internationally recognized scholar of African and
African American studies. In this memoir, he relates what growing up "col-
ored" was like in his experience as a child in a mill town in West Virginia.
Today that world is gone, but Gates ensures it's not forgotten.

Timothy B. Tyson, *Blood Done Sign My Name,* **2005.**

Timothy Tyson, the son of the minister of the all-White Methodist church in
Oxford, North Carolina, reflects on a civil rights story from his childhood.
When a 23-year-old Black Vietnam War veteran walked into a store after
returning to the States, he was quickly chased out by the owner and two of
his sons and then beaten and killed on the street. Tyson witnessed his father's
efforts to have his parishioners face up to the town's endemic racism. And for
his efforts, Tyson's family was forced to leave town.

976 South Central United States

James Agee and Walker Evans, *Let Us Now Praise Famous*
Men: Three Tenant Families, **1941.**

While this unforgettable portrait of Depression-era sharecroppers in the
Deep South was a commercial failure on publication in 1941, it is now con-
sidered one of the most influential books of the 20th century. Writer James
Agee and photographer Walker Evans completed the assignment from
Fortune magazine.

Sam Anderson, *Boom Town: The Fantastical Saga*
of Oklahoma City, It's Chaotic Founding, Its Apocalyptic
Weather, It's Purloined Basketball Team, and the Dream o
f Becoming a World-Class Metropolis, **2018.**

Oklahoma City began with a literal bang, starting with the 1889 Land Run.
Thousands of people lined up on the border of Oklahoma Territory and rushed
in to claim their land with a gunshot fired at noon. Sam Anderson tells this
story, then moves ahead to focus on the NBA basketball team the Oklahoma
City Thunder and its 2012–2013 season that kicked off a year of battles over
everything from urban planning to natural disasters.

Jason Berry, *City of a Million Dreams:*
A History of New Orleans at Year 300, **2018.**

Jason Berry tells of New Orleans from its warrior–founder Jean-Baptiste Le
Moyne de Bienville up through the tale of Michael While, who rebuilt after
losing everything in Hurricane Katrina. Through these stories and more,
Berry relates the messiness, the noise, and the glory that is New Orleans still.

David Grann, *Killers of the Flower Moon:*
The Osage Murders and the Birth of the FBI, **2017.**

When the Osage nation received lands in Oklahoma at the end of the 19th
century, the tribe insisted on keeping the mineral rights. They were granted
the rights because the land was considered worthless. But when someone
discovered petroleum there in the early 20th century, the Osage became some
of the wealthiest people in America. Then they mysteriously began to die, one
by one. Despite involvement by the fledgling FBI, there are still unanswered
questions about the murder spree today.

Diane McWhorter, *Carry Me Home: Birmingham, Alabama:*
The Climactic Battle of the Civil Rights Revolution, **2002.**

Journalist Diane McWhorter is a Birmingham native and the daughter of one
of its prominent families. In *Carry Me Home*, she reflects on the city's role in
a 1963 turning point in the civil rights movement. Police dogs and men with
fire hoses assaulted the nonviolent crowd, many of whom were children, that
was marching into the city. Later four young Black girls died in the 16th Street
Baptist Church in a bombing, placing the city in a national spotlight.

Gregory D. Smithers, *The Cherokee Diaspora: An Indigenous*
History of Migration, Resettlement, and Identity, **2015.**

In 1838–1839, the Cherokee people were forced west along the Trail of Tears.
Gregory D. Smithers recounts the brutal story and tells of the bonds that still
hold the scattered remnants of the Cherokee together.

BIOGRAPHY

John Mack Faragher, *Daniel Boone:*
The Life and Legend of an American Pioneer, **1993.**

Historian John Mack Faragher pieces together a picture of both Daniel Boone
and the times in which he lived, using myth, public record, contemporary
accounts, and the words of Boone himself.

David Thibodeau,
A Place Called Waco: A Survivor's Story, **1999.**

David Thibodeau was a drummer in a rock band when he met David Koresh
and joined his Branch Davidians in Waco, Texas. When the compound burned

to the ground, he was there with many members still inside. He is scathingly honest in his assessments of the cult members and the government. Thibodeau believes the tragedy was avoidable.

977 North Central United States

William Cronon,
Nature's Metropolis: Chicago and the Great West, 1992.
Environmental historian Bill Cronon looks at the 19th-century changes in ecological and economic factors that turned Chicago into a national powerhouse and made it a linchpin around which the nation's history evolved.

Peter Feldstein and Stephen G. Bloom,
The Oxford Project, 2008.
Oxford, Iowa, had a population of 676 when, in 1984, Peter Feldstein set up a photographer's studio in an abandoned storefront on Main Street. Before he finished, he had photographed the entire population of this small Midwestern town. In 2004 Feldstein went back with writer Stephen G. Bloom and sought to take another picture of each individual. While some had moved away or died, he caught the physical changes two decades had wrought for those remaining, and Bloom tells their story.

David Giffels,
Barnstorming Ohio: To Understand America, 2020.
Before the 2020 election, David Giffels spent the year visiting Ohio's people to understand their concerns. In Ohio, he finds a genuinely diverse, entertaining, and poignant mix of ordinary people. He reflects on what this state, sometimes called the nation's heart, has to tell us about the rest of the country.

Alex Kotlowitz, *The Other Side of the River:*
A Story of Two Towns, a Death, and America's Dilemma, 1998.
The St. Joseph River in southern Michigan separates two towns. On one side is St. Joseph, a prosperous town whose residents are 95 percent White. On the other is Benton Harbor, whose impoverished residents are 92 percent Black. Alex Kotlowitz records what happened after the body of a Black teenaged boy from Benton Harbor was discovered floating in the river. The investigation into his death opened up wounds and suspicions from both sides, forming a microcosm of race relations in the nation as a whole.

Tiya Miles, *The Dawn of Detroit: A Chronicle of Slavery*
and Freedom in the City of the Straits, 2017.
Most of us believe that the American South was home to enslavers and the northern states and territories were sympathetic to emancipation. But historian Tiya Miles demonstrates that, at least in the early days of the small settlement of Detroit, both Native Americans and African Americans were enslaved.

978 Western United States

Rinker Buck,
The Oregon Trail: A New American Journey, 2015.
Journalist Rinker Buck set out to bring the Oregon Trail back into the national consciousness by traveling all 2,000 miles of the trail, from Missouri to the Pacific Ocean, in a covered wagon, exactly as the settlers did it. In recording his adventures, he shows you the history of the area and what it looked like in those pre–Civil War years, in contrast to what is there today.

Peter Cozzens, *The Earth Is Weeping: The Epic Story*
of the Indian Wars for the American West, 2016.
Award-winning author Peter Cozzens examines the Indian Wars, which took place in the American West from the end of the Civil War to the turn of the 20th century. Cozzens traces the entire story of the Great Plains, both north and south, to the Rocky Mountains and the Sierra Madre. The saga pulls in stories of famous leaders and the unknown soldiers and warriors who fought.

Timothy Egan, *The Worst Hard Time: The Untold Story*
of Those Who Survived the Great American Dust Bowl, 2006.
The Dust Bowl of the 1930s combined wind, drought, and over-farming to create a scene of devastation across the Great Plains and on to the Rocky Mountains. It was the worst environmental disaster in U.S. history. Pulitzer Prize–winner Timothy Egan delivers the stories of 12 families who dealt with famine and death in the wake of the black dust storms.

S. C. Gwynne, *Empire of the Summer Moon:*
Quanah Parker and the Rise and Fall of the Comanches,
the Most Powerful Indian Tribe in American History, 2010.
S. C. Gwynne tells of the centuries-long battle the Comanche warriors fought against European expansion. They were largely successful until the last few decades of the 19th century. It is also the story of a White woman, Cynthia Ann Parker, whom the Comanches captured in 1836 when she was a nine-year-old in Texas. She loved her captors and didn't want to leave them. She later gave birth to Quanah, her mixed-blood son and the last great Comanche chief.

Jonathan Raban, *Bad Land: An American Romance, 1985.*
British travel writer Jonathan Raban tells the forgotten story of eastern Montana's Great American Desert. In 1909, Congress offered 320-acre tracts of land for free to anyone who would claim them. Unfortunately, the brochures advertising them were shamelessly misleading, as many duped homesteaders discovered when they set out to claim their tracts. What happened to them was often tragic. Raban visits the area to show us towns that are still there and all the abandoned spaces in between.

**Hampton Sides, *Blood and Thunder: The Epic Story
of Kit Carson and the Conquest of the American West*, 2006.**
Hampton Sides tells of the Navajo and their great chief Narbona, who fought
the Mexican settlers just as his ancestors had for centuries. But in 1846,
Narbona found these familiar enemies had been swept away by a new force,
the Army of the West, and using the Manifest Destiny ideology, they would
stop at nothing to take the Navajo lands.

BIOGRAPHY

Kingsley M. Bray, *Crazy Horse: A Lakota Life*, 2006.
The great warrior Crazy Horse was a quiet, reflective man devoted to Lakota
spirituality. Kingsley M. Bray balances his win against General Custer and the
U.S. forces with stories of his childhood and later relationships.

**Joe Jackson,
Black Elk: The Life of an American Visionary, 2016.**
While *Black Elk Speaks* has been a classic in Native American literature since
its publication in 1932, Black Elk's life was largely a mystery. Joe Jackson tells
Black Elk's life story—his childhood, the first man he killed at Little Big Horn,
and his time in Buffalo Bill's Wild West Show. Black Elk chose to be a healer
and holy man instead of a warrior, and he later converted to Catholicism.

979 Great Basin & Pacific Slope Region

**Philip P. Choy, *San Francisco Chinatown:
A Guide to Its History and Architecture*, 2012.**
Architect and Chinese American studies expert Philip P. Choy was born and
raised in San Francisco's Chinatown, one of America's most famous ethnic
neighborhoods. He traces the community's history from its earliest days
through its attempts to attract tourists as an "oriental" attraction. He also
offers walking tours and things to see in this guide.

**Michael P. Ghiglieri and Thomas M. Myers,
*Over the Edge: Death in Grand Canyon: Gripping Accounts
of All Known Fatal Mishaps in the Most Famous of the
World's Seven Natural Wonders*, 2001.**
This unique history of the Grand Canyon records deaths there from the first
river exploration in 1869 through the end of the 20th century. Ghiglieri and
Myers provide tips and lessons to help you avoid the same fate on your trip to
this natural wonder.

**J. S. Holliday, *The World Rushed In:
The California Gold Rush Experience*, 1981.**
J. S. Holliday's history of the California Gold Rush draws on the diary and

letters of William Swain, one of the 30,000 Forty-Niners who headed to California to strike it rich in 1849. Holliday also relates stories of over 500 other individuals who were part of the rush.

Benjamin Madley, *An American Genocide: The United States and the California Indian Catastrophe, 1846–1873*, 2016.

Four-fifths of California's Native American population disappeared between 1846 and 1873. By looking at the years before the Gold Rush, Benjamin Madley sets the stage for the genocide. He then traces its political, judicial, and societal support, which required nearly two million tax dollars. It's an appalling look at a devastating chapter in U.S. history.

Judith Nies, *Unreal City: Las Vegas, Black Mesa, and the Fate of the West*, 2014.

Using the history of the Black Mesa in Arizona as an example, Judith Nies tells the story of a global phenomenon in which giant corporations and corrupt governments take valuable lands from Indigenous peoples and strip the land and the people of their wealth. Nies spent two decades tracking the story of the Black Mesa's use for coal power in Los Angeles, water in Phoenix, and neon lights and fountains in Las Vegas. Nies tells of the unholy alliance that allowed it to happen and the damage the entire world suffers from the exploitation.

Daniel J. Sharfstein, *Thunder in the Mountains: Chief Joseph, Oliver Otis Howard, and the Nez Perce War*, 2018.

Law and history professor Daniel J. Sharfstein narrates the story of Oliver Otis Howard, a pro–civil rights activist for African Americans, and his clash with Chief Joseph, the young leader of the Nez Perce tribe, who was resisting his people's placement on a reservation. In 1877, Howard chased the 100 Nez Perce families over the Northern Rockies, determined to place them under government control.

Richard Shelton, *Going Back to Bisbee*, 1992.

Richard Shelton, stationed in the southeastern Arizona desert during the 1950s, fell in love with the landscape. He writes of his wanderings around the region and his respect for its flora and fauna. He also reflects on the ghost towns there, what they tell us about ourselves today, and what they may signal for the years to come.

BIOGRAPHY

Maxine Hong Kingston, *The Woman Warrior: Memories of a Girlhood Among Ghosts*, 1976.

Award-winning author Maxine Hong Kingston was the first child born in

America to Chinese immigrants, her mother a midwife and her father a Chinese scholar. Her memoir tells of her California childhood and the Chinese myths that shaped her life.

Margaret E. Murie, *Two in the Far North: A Conservation Champion's Story of Life, Love, and Adventure in the Wilderness,* 2020.

Margaret E. Murie moved to Fairbanks, Alaska, as a child. She and her husband, Arctic researcher Olaus J. Murie, were conservation activists. Murie describes their time in the Alaskan and Arctic wilderness and their efforts to pass the Wilderness Act and to create the Arctic National Wildlife Refuge.

980 History of South America

BIOGRAPHY

Marie Arana, *Bolívar: American Liberator,* 2013.

Peruvian-born author Marie Arana tells the story of Simon Bolívar, the Latin American hero who led six countries to freedom from Spanish rule. His life was an epic struggle against competing factions, rugged terrain, and personal tragedy. He died relatively young, never seeing the total outcome of his efforts.

981 Brazil

Sue and Patrick Cunningham, *Spirit of the Amazon: The Indigenous Tribes of the Xingu,* 2019.

Photojournalist Sue Cunningham works with writer Patrick Cunningham to provide this portrait of the Xingu peoples of the Amazon rainforest. After spending more than three decades befriending them, the Cunninghams have access to 48 of their villages. By examining their spiritual relationship with the Earth, the duo provides alternatives to the nature-deprived lives most of us live.

Joe Kane, *Running the Amazon,* 1990.

Joe Kane tells of the first expedition to travel the entire length of the Amazon, from its beginnings in the Peruvian Andes down the 4,200 miles to the Atlantic. On the way, the group of 12 encountered dangers both natural and manufactured, and only two of them, including Kane, completed the journey.

Monte Reel, *The Last of the Tribe: The Epic Quest to Save a Lone Man in the Amazon,* 2010.

In 1996, an Indigenous man, the only surviving member of his people, was spotted alone in the forests of southwest Brazil. In the following decade, a group of men attempted to save him from powerful businesses that could not seize his land until he died. So, the government employed the men who worked on his behalf. They had to fight people in business, politicians, and the man himself to save him.

Patrick Tierney, *Darkness in El Dorado: How Scientists and Journalists Devastated the Amazon*, 1990.

Patrick Tierney critically inspects the 1960s research by Napoleon Chagnon and Jacques Lizot. While the pair of preeminent scientists claimed to have discovered the Yanomamö, billed the most warlike Indigenous people in the world, Tierney closely examined their work and found instances of exploitation and colonization. The American Anthropological Association launched an investigation into these charges due to Tierney's work.

982 Argentina

Piers Paul Read, *Alive: The Story of the Andes Survivors*, 1974.

When a plane carrying a team of rugby players crashed into a snow-covered Andean mountain in 1972, 45 passengers and crew were on board. Piers Paul Read tells how sixteen of them made it off the mountain alive after ten horrific weeks with no food or heat.

BIOGRAPHY

Joseph A. Page, *Perón: A Biography*, 1983.

Joseph A. Pages narrates the biography of Juan Perón, president of Argentina under a military regime. Perón increased the wealth of the citizens while simultaneously suppressing dissent. Then, in 1955, a coup forced him to leave the country, and he settled for a time in Spain. Perón returned to Argentina and was again elected president in 1973. However, he made his unpopular wife, Eva, vice president. When Perón died in 1974, Eva became president.

985 Peru

Mark Adams, *Turn Right at Machu Picchu: Rediscovering the Lost City One Step at a Time*, 2011.

Travel Magazine editor Mark Adams decided to retrace the footsteps of maligned explorer Hiram Bingham III, who discovered Machu Picchu, in the Andes, in 1911. Adams wanted to determine whether Bingham could have done some things he was credited with. So, with the help of an antisocial Aussie and coca-chewing mule tenders, he made the journey and related what he discovered.

990 History of Other Areas

Mark R. Williams, *In Search of Lemuria: The Lost Pacific Continent in Legend, Myth and Imagination*, 2001.

Mark R. Williams traveled to India, Tonga, Easter Island, and other locations to find the lost Pacific continent of Lemuria. He provides references to the lost continent from myths, occult titles, and channeled information from Edgar Cayce and others.

994 Australia

Robert Hughes,
The Fatal Shore: The Epic of Australia's Founding, **1988.**
Robert Hughes traces the history of the British in Australia. After looking at its exploration and founding as a penal colony, he details the brutality of the convict transportation system and the early days of settlement. Finally, he considers the effects of these early events on the nation that later developed.

995 New Guinea & Melanesia

Carl Hoffman, *Savage Harvest: A Tale of Cannibals, Colonialism, and Michael Rockefeller's Tragic Quest*, **2014.**
Journalist Carl Hoffman travels to New Guinea and uncovers previously unknown evidence about the death of wealthy American Michael Rockefeller in 1961. While both the authorities and the family claimed that Rockefeller drowned, rumors for years indicated that he was the victim of headhunters, the Asmat people, that he had befriended there. Hoffman solves the mystery and speculates on what the truth tells us about colonialism and Indigenous cultures.

996 Polynesia & Pacific Ocean Islands

Caroline Alexander, *The Bounty: The True Story of the Mutiny on the* Bounty, **2004.**
After being forced from his ship and his arrival at safety, William Bligh wrote about the mutiny on the *HMS Bounty* led by Fletcher Christian. Caroline Alexander looks at the court-martial of the ten mutineers. By focusing on these ten men, she sheds new light on the entire historical episode.

Susanna Moore,
Paradise of the Pacific: Approaching Hawai'i, **2015.**
Susanna Moore shows how the 19th-century migrants to Hawai'i's shores, whether by accidental shipwreck or missionary activity, changed the island from a pagan kingdom to a modern capitalist, Christian state.

Appendix: Lists Consulted

Ambassador Book Award
American Book Award
American Library Association Notable Books
American Philosophical Association Sander's Book Prize
Andrew Carnegie Medal for Excellence
Arab American Book Awards
Arthur Ross Book Award
Axiom Business Book Awards
Baillie Gifford Prize for Non-Fiction
The Believer Book Awards
Body Mind Spirit Book Awards
Booklist Editors' Choice Adult Books
Boston Globe-Horn Book Awards
Catholic Book Awards
Chicago Tribune Heartland Prize
Christian Book Award
The Christian Science Monitor Best Books
Christianity Today Best Books of the Twentieth Century and Book Awards
Dartmouth Medal
Eric Hoffer Book Award
Extreme Classics from National Geographic Adventure Magazine
Fortune Magazine 75 Smartest Books We Know List
Gilder Lehrman Prize for Military History at the New York Historical Society
Grawemeyer Awards
The Guardian Best Books Lists
Hillman Prize
The Hindu Kamaladevi Chattopadhyay NIF Book Prize
IBPA Benjamin Franklin Award
Independent Publisher's Book Awards
Indie Book Awards
Indie Booksellers Choice Awards and Honors Books
James Beard Media Awards
Kirkus Best Nonfiction Books of the Year
Library Journal's Best Books of the Year
Los Angeles Times Book Prize
Mormon History Association Best Book Award
National Book Award
National Jewish Book Awards
National Outdoor Book Awards

Nautilus Book Awards

New York Historical Society Barbara and David Zalaznick Book Prize in
    American History

New York Times Best Books of the Year

Next Generation Indie Book Awards

Nonfiction Authors Association Gold Medal Winners

Parapsychological Association Book Awards

PEN E. O. Wilson Science Writing Award

PEN ESPN Awards for Literary Sports Writing

PEN Jacqueline Bograd Weld Award for Biography

PEN Jean Stein Book Award

PEN John Kenneth Galbraith Award

PEN Open Book Award

Pfizer Award from History of Science Society

Phi Beta Kappa Award in Science

Phi Beta Kappa Christian Gauss Award

Phi Beta Kappa Ralph Waldo Emerson Award

Publisher's Weekly Best Books of the Year

Pulitzer Prizes in History, Biography, Poetry, General Nonfiction, and Music

Reference and User Services Association (RUSA) Outstanding Reference Books

Rubery Book AwardsScience in Society Journalism Awards in Books Category

Thurber Prize for American Humor

Time Magazine Books of the Year

William James Award American Philosophical Association

Young Adult Library Services Association Outstanding Books for the College
    Bound and Lifelong Learners List

Author Index

Title Index

Want to find even more superlative nonfiction?

Check out Library Lin's Further Reading titles on the blog at **librarylin.com**.

You'll find thousands more books on every subject that there simply wasn't room for in this volume.

In addition, you will find a collection of book reviews written by Library Lin as she explores titles from her curated collection and the Further Reading section. Read the books and see if you agree with her assessments.

Coming in 2024

Library Lin will present a mega-list of superlative **biography**, **autobiography**, and **memoir** titles. If you love reading about other people and how they overcome adversity or celebrate life, you will find ample titles arranged by broad subject. Books on artists, educators, activists, scientists, spiritual adventurers, chefs, explorers, and sports heroes, just to name a few. Personalities of famous, infamous, and relatively unknown individuals from the past and present will be yours to discover and explore.

Stay up to date at librarylin.com

www.ingramcontent.com/pod-product-compliance
Lightning Source LLC
Chambersburg PA
CBHW080415030426
42335CB00020B/2459